Green Mobile Cloud Computing

Debashis De • Anwesha Mukherjee •
Rajkumar Buyya

Editors

Green Mobile Cloud Computing

 Springer

Editors
Debashis De (iD)
Department of Computer Science and
Engineering, Centre of Mobile Cloud
Computing
Maulana Abul Kalam Azad University
of Technology
West Bengal, Nadia, India

Anwesha Mukherjee
Department of Computer Science
Mahishadal Raj College
Mahishadal, Purba Medinipur
West Bengal, India

Rajkumar Buyya
Cloud Computing and Distributed Systems
(CLOUDS) Laboratory
School of Computing and Information
Systems
The University of Melbourne
Parkville, VIC, Australia

ISBN 978-3-031-08040-1   ISBN 978-3-031-08038-8   (eBook)
https://doi.org/10.1007/978-3-031-08038-8

Contents

Part I
Mobile Cloud Computing

Green Mobile Cloud Computing for Industry 5.0

Anwesha Mukherjee, Debashis De ⓘ, and Rajkumar Buyya

1 Introduction

Mobile Cloud Computing (MCC) integrates mobile computing and cloud computing, which brings the facilities of using cloud services to the mobile users [1–4]. With the rapid increase in the usage of smartphones, the demand for storage and access to various applications also increases. However, mobile devices face multiple challenges: limited storage, limited battery life, limited computing power, bandwidth, etc. [1]. In such a scenario, MCC has fulfilled the users' demands. Cloud computing provides three types of services: Software as a Service (SaaS), Platform as a Service (PaaS), and Infrastructure as a Service (IaaS). Cloud is a virtualized, shared resource or infrastructure that can compute, analyze, and warehouse large amounts of data. Cloud serves the client on an "on-demand," "pay as you use" basis. The elastic nature of the cloud helps the client to get the desired service according to the requirements. Various cloud providers such as Amazon EC2, Microsoft Azure, and Google Cloud Platform provide ubiquitous service along with elastic storage and immense processing facilities in an "on-demand" and "pay as you use" fashion.

A. Mukherjee (✉)
Department of Computer Science, Mahishadal Raj College, Mahishadal, Purba Medinipur, West Bengal, India
e-mail: anweshamukherjee@ieee.org

D. De
Department of Computer Science and Engineering, Centre of Mobile Cloud Computing, Maulana Abul Kalam Azad University of Technology, West Bengal, Nadia, India
e-mail: debashis.de@makautwb.ac.in

R. Buyya
Cloud Computing and Distributed Systems (CLOUDS) Laboratory, School of Computing and Information Systems, The University of Melbourne, Parkville, VIC, Australia
e-mail: rbuyya@unimelb.edu.au

© The Author(s), under exclusive license to Springer Nature Switzerland AG 2022
D. De et al. (eds.), *Green Mobile Cloud Computing*,
https://doi.org/10.1007/978-3-031-08038-8_1

In MCC, the mobile devices are the thin clients. In MCC, mobile users can offload their data and applications inside the cloud. We define MCC as [1, 2]:

The data is offloaded to the cloud in MCC for processing and storage. However, nowadays, cloudlet and intermediate fog devices are also used for offloading [5–7].

The advantages of MCC are listed as follows [1].

- *Extension of battery lifetime*: The large-scale data processing or exhaustive computation inside the mobile device drains the battery quickly due to high power consumption. As in MCC, the data processing and storage occurs outside the mobile device, the battery life is increased.
- *Extension of storage capacity*: MCC provides storage facilities to the user based on the requirement. Dropbox Amazon's simple storage service is an example of the storage supplied to the user. Google photos, flicker are photo-sharing applications. On Facebook also, the users can share images.
- *Extension of processing power*: Various power intensive applications like online gaming, transcoding, on-demand multimedia services, etc., require provision of high processing capacity. In this case, task offloading can be a solution.
- *Low probability of data loss*: As in MCC, the data and applications are maintained in multiple computers, the likelihood of losing data are more pessimistic.
- *On-demand service*: The cloud provides on-demand seamless service to the user from the cloud. The user does not need to install dedicated hardware or software as everything is available in the cloud on a "pay as you use" basis.

This chapter will discuss MCC's architecture, applications, and future scopes. The rest of the chapter is organized as follows: Section 2 discusses the architecture of MCC. Section 3 briefly describes various applications of MCC. Section 4 discusses about various simulators. Section 5 explores the future research scopes of MCC. Section 6 demonstrates green MCC, and finally, Sect. 7 concludes the chapter.

2 Architecture of MCC

This section discusses the service-oriented architecture, agent-client architecture, and collaborative architecture of MCC.

2.1 Service-Oriented Architecture

The service-oriented architecture consists of mobile network, Internet service, and cloud service, described as follows [1]:

- *Mobile network*: The mobile network consists of mobile devices such as mobile phones, tablets, laptops, etc., and the network operators. The mobile devices are connected to the network operators by the base station, access point, etc.

The network operators provide a wide spectrum of services like authentication, authorization, and accounting (AAA) that use the home agent (HA) and the subscribers' data stored in the database.

- *Internet service*: The Internet service links the mobile network with the cloud. The users receive the cloud services through high-speed Internet connectivity.
- *Cloud Service*: The cloud controller receives user requests, processes them, and provides service accordingly. Several servers inside the data center are connected with the high-speed network and high-power supply. The data center is responsible for delivering infrastructure and hardware facilities for the cloud. At the top of the data center layer, Infrastructure as a Service (IaaS) provides storage, network components, servers, hardware, etc., to the clients on a "pay as you use" basis, e.g. Amazon EC2 and S3. An elastic cloud service represents an infrastructure that expands and shrinks dynamically according to the demand of the user. The Platform as a Service (PaaS) provides the users an integrated environment or platform for building, testing, and deploying various applications, e.g. Microsoft Azure and Google App Engine. The Software as a Service (SaaS) provides multiple types of software solutions to the users on an "on-demand" basis without dedicated installation at the client site. The software and associated data are hosted on the cloud. The application service providers provide the SaaS.

2.2   Agent – Client Architecture

In the agent-client architecture, mobile agent like cloudlet connects the mobile devices to the cloud [5]. Figure 1 presents the agent-client architecture. The remote cloud is usually at a long distance from the mobile device; hence, the latency is a significant issue. For time-critical applications, latency is an important concern. Cloudlet is such an agent that, by containing the cache copies of data stored by the cloud, meets the user need of low latency [5]. Cloudlet is well connected to high-speed internet, and the users can offload their data and computation to the nearby cloudlet instead of the remote cloud [1, 5]. Small cell base station such as femtocell is famous for its use in the indoor region for better signal strength [8]. Therefore, the user may be connected to the cloud through the femtocell. Nowadays, femtolet and small cell cloud enhanced eNodeB (SCceNB) can also be used which can provide communication and computation facilities simultaneously [9–11].

2.3   Collaborative Architecture

Smartphones have their computing, storage, networking, and sensing abilities. Several smartphones' data and computing resources are collaborated in this architecture, and a smartphone cloud is generated [1, 12]. The mobile applications utilize

Fig. 1 Agent-client
architecture of MCC

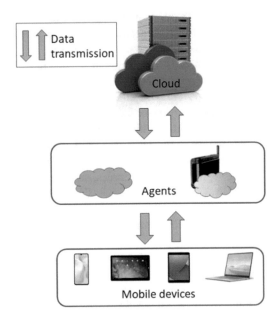

the resources of the smartphone cloud; this, in turn, overcomes the limitation of offloading to the remote cloud.

2.4 Fog-Edge Architecture

Nowadays, the intermediate devices between the mobile and cloud participate in data processing, such as access point, switch, router, etc. [7]. These intermediate devices are referred to as fog devices. In mobile edge computing architecture, edge server is used with the base station in case of cellular network, and cloudlet is used in case of WLAN (Wireless Local Area Network)/WMAN (Wireless Metropolitan Area Network) to bring the resources at the network edge for faster service provisioning [13, 14]. The edge/fog computing-based MCC architecture is presented in Fig. 2. Usually, the edge-fog-cloud architecture is famous for various types of applications [15–21], where large scale data processing is performed inside the cloud. In contrast, fog and edge devices are used for primary data processing purposes.

3 Applications of MCC

There are several applications of MCC discussed as follows.

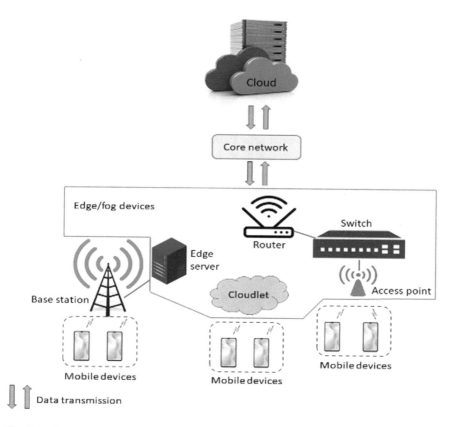

Fig. 2 Mobile Cloud-Fog-Edge computing-based architecture

3.1 *Mobile Learning*

Mobile learning is an e-learning method in which learning opportunities are provided to people who may not be at a predetermined or fixed location [1]. Here, the learning is provided through mobile technologies, and the social and content interactions occur through personal mobile devices. This is an e-learning system with mobility because the learner may move physically during the e-learning process. Therefore, portable devices such as laptops, notebooks, tablets, and mobile phones are included here to enhance portability and interactivity. However, conventional mobile learning systems have several limitations such as low data transmission rate, limited resources, high cost, etc. The use of the cloud in mobile learning has dealt with these difficulties by providing ample storage, processing power, etc. GeoSmart is a cloud-based mobile application for learning used as an online education system [1]. A cloud-based real time mobile learning strategy is discussed in [22].

3.2 Mobile Commerce

The mobile version of e-commerce is known as mobile commerce, where every utility of e-commerce is available through mobile devices [1]. Here, for computation and storage purposes cloud is used. Mobile commerce is nothing but delivering e-commerce abilities to the customer's hand, anywhere, through wireless technology [1]. There are a lot of examples of mobile commerce such as advertising, shopping, ticket purchasing, transaction, payment through mobile devices. Various mobile applications are available for online shopping, ordering food, flight booking, railway reservation, online payment, etc. However, privacy and data integrity are crucial issues because sensitive information such as the user's bank account details, credit card details, debit card details are involved. Usually, public key infrastructure (PKI) protects users' access to outsourced data.

3.3 Mobile Healthcare

Mobile health monitoring is a popular application of MCC, where e-health care is provided through mobile devices [16–21]. Low power and high precision sensor nodes are used to form a body area network to collect the health parameter values, and the health data analysis is performed inside the cloud. Based on the study, healthcare advice is provided to users through mobile devices. Intermediate fog devices can be used to process the data for faster health service provisioning. In [17, 18], small cell base stations are used for preliminary health data analysis. In [16], a route to the nearby health center is suggested based on the user's mobility information and the health data. Nowadays, various mobile applications are also available such as Samsung Health, Google Fit, etc. For epidemic trends monitoring the use of the cloud for data analysis also plays an important role [20].

3.4 Mobile Game

In mobile gaming, game execution occurs partially or fully in the cloud, and the game players interact with the screen interface of the mobile devices. In [23, 24], computation offloading strategies are discussed. Game can also be offloaded if involves exhaustive computation. The offloading can reduce the energy consumption of the mobile device while accessing various games. Cloud-based mobile gaming has been discussed in [25], in which the game rendering parameters are adjusted dynamically according to the players' demands and communication constraints.

4 Simulators of MCC

In Table 1 we have listed some simulators of cloud computing, fog computing, and networking.

5 Research Challenges of MCC

Industry 5.0 delivers a vision of the industry that intends efficiency and productivity goals. It reinforces the contribution of industry 5.0 to sustainable smart cities and societies. MCC faces various challenges towards implementing Industry 5.0, where are highlighted in this section.

5.1 Mobility Management

In MCC, the clients are mobile devices which can frequently move from one location to another, and connection interruption is significant. Hence, mobility management is a considerable challenge in MCC to maintain the Quality of Service. Here, localization is substantial and is achieved using either GPS, RFID, ultra-sound RF, etc [26, 27]. The social interaction between the users is monitored using audio signals and walking traits of individuals using phone compass and accelerometer. In this case, multiple meetings obtain various routes, and the optimal path is selected. Virtual compass is another method in which short range protocols such as Bluetooth Wi-Fi are used to form a 2D reorientation of the nearby device. Peer-to-peer message passing is used to compute the distance using signal strength and pass the information about the device's adjacent nodes and spaces. In XMPP-based peer-to-peer method GPS is used, and only the known contacts or friends' locations are visible. Mobile Collaboration Architecture (MoCA) has been proposed in [28] to support mobility management that uses component and proxy migration. Here, the users' locations are monitored, and an application proxy is switched to a more suitable place. Through researches have been performed on mobility management, novel intelligent methods are still required for optimal path finding to a destination while the user is on the move. Drone mobility is challenging for proper path planning in mobile edge networks.

5.2 Offloading Method

Usually, in offloading to the cloud, communication is performed using Remote Procedure Call (RPC), Remote Method Invocation (RMI), and sockets between

Table 1 Simulators and their inventors along with their sources

Simulator name	Source
CloudSim	https://github.com/Cloudslab/cloudsim/releases (Accessed 30th October 2021)
CloudSim Plus	https://github.com/manoelcampos/cloudsimplus (Accessed 30th October 2021)
Containernet 1.0	https://github.com/containernet/containernet (Accessed 30th October 2021)
Containernet 2.0	https://github.com/containernet/containernet/releases/tag/v2.0 (Accessed 1st November 2021)
Containernet 3.0	https://github.com/containernet/containernet/releases/tag/v3.0 (Accessed 1st November 2021)
Containernet 3.1	https://github.com/containernet/containernet/releases/tag/v3.1 (Accessed 1st November 2021)
Distrinet	https://distrinet-emu.github.io/installation.html (Accessed 2nd November 2021)
Mininet	http://mininet.org/download/ (Accessed 2nd November 2021)
Mininet CE	https://github.com/mininet/mininet/wiki/Cluster-Edition-Prototype#vision (Accessed 2nd November 2021)
Maxinet	http://maxinet.github.io/ (Accessed 2nd November 2021)
GPUCloud Sim	https://git.ce.aut.ac.ir/lpds/gpucloudsim/tree/master (Accessed 2nd November 2021)
GreenCloud	https://download.uni.lu/GreenCloud/greencloud-v2.1.2.tar.gz, https://greencloud.gforge.uni.lu/vm.html
	Online Version
	http://greencloud.uni.lu/ (Accessed 3rd November 2021)
ACE	https://bitbucket.org/manarjammal/ace-availability-aware-cloudsim-extension/wiki/Home (Accessed 3rd November 2021)
ECSNeT++	https://github.com/sedgecloud/ECSNeTpp (Accessed 3rd November 2021)
	Dependencies
	https://inet.omnetpp.org/, http://www.grinninglizard.com/tinyxml2/
RECAP Simulator	https://recap-project.eu/simulators/ (Accessed 9th November 2021)
iFogSim	https://github.com/Cloudslab/iFogSim1 (Accessed 9th November 2021)
iFogSim2	https://github.com/Cloudsla/iFogSim (Accessed 9th November 2021)
YAFS	https://github.com/acsicuib/YAFS (Accessed 12th November 2021)
DewSim	https://github.com/cmateos/mobileGridSimulator (Accessed 12th November 2021)
Network Simulator-ns-2	https://sourceforge.net/projects/nsnam/files/latest/download, https://www.isi.edu/nsnam/ns/, https://www.isi.edu/nsnam/ns/ns-build.html (Accessed 3rd November 2021)
	Dependencies
	http://www.tcl.tk/, https://sourceforge.net/projects/otcl-tclcl/files/ (Accessed 3rd November 2021)
Network Simulator-ns-3	https://www.nsnam.org/releases/ (Accessed 3rd November 2021)

the requesting device and the executing device. However, in the case of mobile devices, these services need to be pre-installed, which is a disadvantage. Hyrax is a Hadoop-based smartphone application ported on the android platform [1]. In this case, a cluster of mobile devices is used as the mobile cloud and resource provider. Hyrax Tube is an application that permits users to search multimedia files based on time, locations, and quality [1]. Hadoop distributed file system (HDFS) maintains multimedia data and threads executable on mobile devices [1]. In [29], a virtual cloud computing provider has been discussed. In [30], a framework named "Cuckoo" has been proposed based on the java stub/proxy model to improve the performance in offloading and reduce battery usage. In this case, the task is offloaded to any resource that runs a virtual machine (VM). Another critical issue in offloading is VM migration, where the memory image of a VM is transferred from one server to another server without interrupting the execution. Clone cloud is a VM migration method where a resourceful server is used to offload part of an application [31]. MobiCloud is another approach that uses mobile ad hoc networks and cloud computing [32]. Each node serves as a service broker or provider based on its available resources and computational ability. Though researches are going on offloading, mobility-aware, energy-efficient, and fast offloading is an emerging issue.

5.3   Security and Privacy

As the cloud is used for offloading data and computation, security, trust, and privacy are significant parameters in MCC [33–35]. The transmission and storage of personal data and applications to the remote cloud raise security and privacy concerns. The following issues are needed to be considered while offloading takes place to the cloud [1]:

- The cloud service providers should maintain external audits and security certifications.
- Cloud service providers should have recovery management schemes for protecting data and services in case of disaster or technical fault.
- The data are stored in a shared space inside the cloud; hence, the data of individuals should be maintained separately implementing encryption methods.
- Local privacy is also an essential factor because the exact physical location of the user's data is not transparent.
- Investigative support is also required because multiple customers are logging and maybe co-located data, and it is hard to predict any illegal or inappropriate activity.
- This is to be ensured that if the cloud company leaves the business, the users' data would also be safe and accessible.

Mobile devices may be affected by viruses and worms. Thus, installation and use of the security software is required to protect against threats. Moreover, most mobile devices use GPS-enabled location-based service that discloses the user's present location, which may be a privacy concern for a few users. Though researches are going on security, privacy, and trust. Nowadays, blockchain has become another emerging area of interest [36]. Federated learning-based MCC provides a privacy-preserving ecosystem [37]. Hashing and symmetric parameter function can be used to implement impersonation resistant biometric-based authentication [34]. The energy-efficient and secure hybrid (EESH) algorithm utilizes voltage scaling to decrease energy utilization [35]. A malicious data detection (MDD) algorithm makes EESH more secure using blockchain.

5.4   Cost and Business Model

We divide the cloud cost into ownership cost and utilization cost. The total cost of ownership determines the costs of owning and managing an IT infrastructure. In cloud computing, the ownership cost determines the commercial value of cloud investment, including service, power, cooling, facilities, software, real estate, and maintenance costs. The utilization cost denotes the cost of using dynamically elastic resources by a user. The cost and analysis of the benefit of offloading are also essential. In [3], Spectra's method has been discussed, where resources are monitored continuously, and a trade-off between application offloading and performance, quality, and energy consumption is maintained [3]. To achieve the best placement of the resource "self-tuning" is used. Here, the users' demand of available resources is carried, executed, and the profile history of the surrogates is maintained. In [3], Chroma has been discussed, which uses "tactics" and monitors resources, and performs history prediction for estimating cost. Here, a trade-off is maintained between the attributes such as speed and power consumption based on the utility function. Serialization-based cost-benefit analysis has been performed in [24], where the authors have considered the network and application's characteristics and the device's energy consumption. To take decisions regarding offloading, the relative speed, network bandwidth, utilization of surrogate, latency, task complexity, and input/output size can be considered. The comparison of energy usage between the cloud and mobile devices is performed using parametric analysis [1], where network bandwidth, mobile device and cloud speed, data amount transmission, etc., have been considered. In MCC, two types of service providers are involved: Mobile service provider (MSP) and Cloud service provider (CSP) [1]. When a mobile user is receiving service from the cloud, both the service providers are involved. Hence, an appropriate business model is required to decide how the profit will be divided between the MSP and CSP.

5.5 Deployment of Agents

In agent-client architecture, the agents such as cloudlet, femtolet, SCceNB, etc. are used to provide low latency and high bandwidth access to the network [1]. However, in agent-client architecture, the deployment of agents is a vital issue. The agent's processing power, storage, and networking capacity need to be decided. On the other hand, resource requirements based on various applications are required to be decided. The clustering of users, resource demands of individuals and groups of users, user's level of satisfaction, cost minimization, management policies, trustworthiness, etc., are also essential factors. In [5], a proxy server-based computation offloading method has been discussed where the optimum cloudlet is selected based on latency and power consumption to offload the computation. In [38] selection of cloudlets to offload has been decided based on the type of application. In the case of femtolet and SCceNB, the interference is another factor that needs attention because they are small cell base stations. In the case of the small cell network, densification is a significant concern, and interference mitigation is a challenge [39]. Hence, the allocation of femtolet/SCceNB is another research scope.

5.6 Context-Aware Service Provisioning

Various attributes such as user's location, acceleration, direction of movement etc., need to be considered while providing cloud-based service to a mobile user. This contextual information plays a vital role in delivering convenient and timely service to the user. The context element has four layers [1]. The first layer denotes a device's currently monitored context, including environmental settings, service context information, user preference settings, etc. [1]. The second layer deals with the types of functional or non-functional gaps between the contexts of two consecutive services. The third layer deals with the causes of gaps between different interfaces and implementations of a single device, which may happen due to the mismatch of service level, service component level, service interface level, and component instance level. The fourth layer contains adapters required to remove the causes. Context-aware service provisioning is a three-tier architecture [1]. The user tier includes mobile devices in which the applications are executed. The agent tier adapts service based on the context. Finally, the service tier deploys the services. The contextual information is acquired, processed, managed, and delivered by the context management architecture (CMA) [1]. The context quality enabler controls the supply of contextual information to the mobile cloud [1]. The role of contextual information for identifying resources and risk assessment is another future research scope.

5.7 Mobile Data Management

Users' data such as chat logs, photos, contacts, videos, financial documents, records, users' login credentials, etc., are sensitive information. The storage of these information in the cloud raises various questions concerning security, privacy, data interpretability, portability, trust, etc. [1]. Moreover, a tremendous amount of data transfer to the cloud faces bandwidth and network connectivity problems, especially if the user moves [1]. Data portability and interoperability are other significant concerns in MCC. A mobile database may not provide all features of a traditional database. Traffic management is another primary research scope of MCC.

5.8 Energy-Efficiency

Mobile devices have limited battery life. Hence, the execution of specific applications inside the mobile device may result in high energy consumption of the mobile device that in turn drains the device's battery life. MCC offers application offloading for saving energy. However, communication with the cloud during offloading also involves energy consumption due to data transmission. The offloading of a simple task may result in high energy consumption than executing locally. Hence, the decision-making regarding offloading is crucial. An energy-efficient software, that makes use of an energy profiling tool customized for mobile applications [40], maps the power usage to a specific code component in the application and the operating system. Another software-based approach has been proposed for energy profiling in [41]. The energy consumption incurred by computation, communication, and overall infrastructure management contributes to the cost of system energy [42]. Energy harvesting in MCC is another future scope [43, 44].

5.9 Resource Management

As mobile computing and cloud computing technologies are integrated, the resource requirements estimation, resource allocation, and resource sharing are vital issues in MCC. Nowadays, edge/fog computing and dew computing have come into the picture. In [45], the authors have used game theory in resource pricing and offloading decisions for edge computing scenario. Developing intelligent resource management strategies for edge/fog/dew computing and MCC is a significant research scope in MCC.

5.10   Integration of MCC with IoT

Internet of Things (IoT) deals with connecting identified embedded devices within an Internet infrastructure to create a computing environment [46, 47]. IoT has become a principal component in designing intelligent solutions for daily life such as smart homes, smart cities, intelligent transport, smart health, etc. While mobile users are involved, the objects' status-related data is collected by the sensors/actuators. The data processing and storage will happen inside the cloud. However, in edge-fog-cloud architecture, the edge/fog devices can also participate in data processing. However, the decision regarding which data will be forwarded to the cloud, which will be processed inside the intermediate devices, the security of the data, mobility management, and spatio-temporal data analysis, etc., need to be focused in the IoT-MCC framework.

Along with these issues, other research scopes are also there such as intelligent health care [48], use of opportunistic delay-tolerant network [49], etc.

6   Green Mobile Cloud Computing

Green Mobile Cloud Computing (GMCC) refers to energy-efficient mobile cloud computing [1]. Here, 'green' refers low energy consumption. During the execution of resource-intensive applications, the energy consumption of the mobile device may be higher, and it will drain the battery of the device. On the other hand, energy-efficient mobile network design and providing good quality service to the mobile subscribers is a challenge. For energy-efficient mobile network designing, the use of small cells has been discussed in the existing research works [50, 51]. From the mobile device's perspective, an energy-efficient strategy for application execution inside the mobile device is a vital issue. MCC provides the facility of storing data and executing applications outside the mobile device. However, the communication with the cloud incurs energy consumption of the mobile device. Hence, the implementation of an energy-efficient offloading strategy is essential. In MCC, a green data center can also play a vital role. The various components regarding GMCC are therefore summarized as follows.

Green Data Centre The number of data centers in the backhaul is increasing to fulfill the requirement of online data storage and computations of users. Green data centre is significant to achieve GMCC [52]. Storing and maintaining a vast amount of data and executing calculations at the server side also incur tremendous energy consumption. By switching on/off devices, hardware, and software depending on the user demand and traffic load, can save energy. For energy saving the inactive network links can also be switched off.

Green Cellular Network A tremendous amount of energy is consumed to operate the base stations in a conventional cellular network. Green cellular network is vital for GMCC [53, 54]. The small cells come into the picture for energy-efficient cellular network design and providing good coverage. Firstly, microcell base stations have come, later picocell base stations, and then femtocell base stations have arrived. Switching on/off the base stations depending on the traffic can save energy. User-density-based base station allocation can also be vital in developing green cellular networks. In [10, 11], the authors have discussed the small cell base stations with storage and computing capability. The users under such small cells can offload their data and applications inside these small cells.

Green Mobile Devices For energy-efficient, i.e., green mobile devices, the energy demand, user requirement, traffic pattern, and resource requirements are considered. Energy saving of mobile devices is also important in GMCC [55, 56]. User-requirement-based dynamic resource allocation can improve resource utilization and reduce energy wastage. MCC allows users to offload data and computation inside the remote cloud servers. In computation offloading, the computation-intensive tasks migrate from mobile devices to the cloud, and after execution, the result is sent to the mobile device. The motivation is to overcome the mobile device's resource limitation and save battery life by reducing energy consumption. However, communication with the cloud also requires energy consumption. In this perspective, the decision making regarding whether to offload or not and whether to offload the application fully or partially, these queries appear. For example, suppose a mobile device has to offload a computation C. The energy consumption in communication (E_{offc}) and the energy consumption in local execution (E_{locc}) are compared. If $E_{offc} < E_{locc}$, then offloading is beneficial concerning the device's energy consumption. Few applications require partial offloading concerning the energy consumption; in that case, the decision regarding which portion will be offloaded and which amount will be locally executed, is vital. Nowadays, fog/edge computing has come to the scenario that brings the facility of offloading and partial processing closer to the mobile device.

Green Mobile Application and Services The design of energy-efficient mobile applications and services is another significant aspect of GMCC. Efficient data transmission is also required for energy-efficiency [57]. The use of data compression reduces the amount of data transmission that will help to reduce the energy consumption of mobile applications and services. The data volume is reduced. Thus, the energy consumption for data processing is also reduced. Green IoT applications is also an emerging issue [58–60].

7 Summary and Conclusions

This chapter discussed the architecture, applications, and research scopes of MCC. MCC enables mobile users to use the cloud resources "on-demand" and "pay as you go" basis. Mobile users can offload their data and applications inside the cloud instead of storing data and executing applications locally inside the mobile device. The execution of resource-specific applications and storage of a vast amount of data inside the cloud overcomes the limitations of mobile devices such as resource limitation, limited battery life, limited processing power, limited storage capacity, etc. There are several applications of MCC, such as mobile commerce, mobile learning, mobile health care, mobile game, etc., which have been highlighted in this chapter. We have discussed on green MCC. Finally, future research challenges of MCC have been highlighted.

References

1. De, D.: Mobile Cloud Computing: Architectures, Algorithms, and Applications. Chapman and Hall/CRC (2019)
2. Sanaei, Z., Abolfazli, S., Gani, A., Buyya, R.: Heterogeneity in mobile cloud computing: taxonomy and open challenges. IEEE Commun. Surv. Tutor. **16**(1), 369–392 (2013)
3. Fernando, N., Loke, S.W., Rahayu, W.: Mobile cloud computing: a survey. Futur. Gener. Comput. Syst. **29**(1), 84–106 (2013)
4. Malik, S.U.R., Akram, H., Gill, S.S., Pervaiz, H., Malik, H.: EFFORT: energy efficient framework for offload communication in mobile cloud computing. Softw. Pract. Exp. **51**(9), 1896–1909 (2021)
5. Mukherjee, A., De, D., Roy, D.G.: A power and latency aware cloudlet selection strategy for multi-cloudlet environment. IEEE Trans. Cloud Comput. **7**(1), 141–154 (2019)
6. Mukherjee, A., Gupta, P., De, D.: Mobile cloud computing based energy efficient offloading strategies for femtocell network. In: 2014 Applications and Innovations in Mobile Computing (AIMoC), pp. 28–35. IEEE (2014)
7. Mukherjee, A., Deb, P., De, D., Buyya, R.: C2OF2N: a low power cooperative code offloading method for femtolet-based fog network. J. Supercomput. **74**(6), 2412–2448 (2018)
8. Mukherjee, A., Deb, P., De, D., Obaidat, M.S.: WmA-MiFN: a weighted majority and auction game based green ultra-dense micro-femtocell network system. IEEE Syst. J. **14**(1), 353–362 (2019)
9. Deb, P., Mukherjee, A., De, D.: Design of green smart room using fifth generation network device Femtolet. Wirel. Pers. Commun. **104**(3), 1037–1064 (2019)
10. Barbarossa, S., Sardellitti, S., Di Lorenzo, P.: Joint allocation of computation and communication resources in multiuser mobile cloud computing. In: 2013 IEEE 14th Workshop on Signal Processing Advances in Wireless Communications (SPAWC), pp. 26–30. IEEE (2013)
11. Mukherjee, A., De, D.: Femtolet: a novel fifth generation network device for green mobile cloud computing. Simul. Model. Pract. Theory. **62**, 68–87 (2016)
12. Yu, S., Langar, R.: Collaborative computation offloading for multi-access edge computing. In: 2019 IFIP/IEEE Symposium on Integrated Network and Service Management (IM), pp. 689–694. IEEE (2019)
13. Mukherjee, A., De, D., Ghosh, S.K., Buyya, R.: Mobile Edge Computing. Springer (2021). https://doi.org/10.1007/978-3-030-69893-5. eBook ISBN: 978-3-030-69893-5, Hardcover ISBN: 978-3-030-69892-8
14. Peng, K., Leung, V., Xiaolong, X., Zheng, L., Wang, J., Huang, Q.: A survey on mobile edge computing: focusing on service adoption and provision. Wirel. Commun. Mob. Comput. **2018** (2018)
15. Ghosh, S., Mukherjee, A., Ghosh, S.K., Buyya, R.: Mobi-iost: mobility-aware cloud-fog-edge-iot collaborative framework for time-critical applications. IEEE Trans. Netw. Sci. Eng. (2019)

16. Mukherjee, A., Ghosh, S., Behere, A., Ghosh, S.K., Buyya, R.: Internet of health things (IoHT) for personalized health care using integrated edge-fog-cloud network. J. Ambient. Intell. Humaniz. Comput., 1–17 (2020)
17. De, D., Mukherjee, A.: Femtocell based economic health monitoring scheme using mobile cloud computing. In: 2014 IEEE International Advance Computing Conference (IACC), pp. 385–390. IEEE (2014)
18. Mukherjee, A., De, D.: Femtocell based green health monitoring strategy. In: 2014 XXXIth URSI General Assembly and Scientific Symposium (URSI GASS), pp. 1–4. IEEE (2014)
19. Banerjee, P.S., Karmakar, A., Dhara, M., Ganguly, K., Sarkar, S.: A novel method for predicting bradycardia and atrial fibrillation using fuzzy logic and arduino supported IoT sensors. Med. Novel Technol. Devices. 10, 100058 (2021)
20. De, D., Mukherjee, A.: Femto-cloud based secure and economic distributed diagnosis and home health care system. J. Med. Imaging Health Inform. 5(3), 435–447 (2015)
21. Mukherjee, A., De, D., Ghosh, S.K.: FogIoHT: a weighted majority game theory based energy-efficient delay-sensitive fog network for internet of health things. Internet of Things. 11, 100181 (2020)
22. Butt, S.M.: Cloud centric real time mobile learning system for computer science. GRIN Verlag. (2014)
23. De, D., Mukherjee, A., Roy, D.G.: Power and delay efficient multilevel offloading strategies for mobile cloud computing. Wirel. Pers. Commun., 1–28 (2020)
24. Cuervo, E., Balasubramanian, A., Cho, D.-k., Wolman, A., Saroiu, S., Chandra, R., Bahl, P.: Maui: making smartphones last longer with code offload. In: Proceedings of the 8th International Conference on Mobile Systems, Applications, and Services, pp. 49–62 (2010)
25. Wang, S., Dey, S.: Rendering adaptation to address communication and computation constraints in cloud mobile gaming. In: 2010 IEEE Global Telecommunications Conference GLOBECOM 2010, pp. 1–6. IEEE (2010)
26. Constandache, I., Bao, X., Azizyan, M., Choudhury, R.R.: Did you see Bob? Human localization using mobile phones. In: Proceedings of the Sixteenth Annual International Conference on Mobile Computing and Networking, pp. 149–160 (2010)
27. Banerjee, N., Agarwal, S., Bahl, P., Chandra, R., Wolman, A., Corner, M.: Virtual compass: relative positioning to sense mobile social interactions. In: International Conference on Pervasive Computing, pp. 1–21. Springer, Berlin/Heidelberg (2010)
28. Sacramento, V., Endler, M., Rubinsztejn, H.K., Lima, L.S., Gonçalves, K., Nascimento, F.N., Bueno, G.A.: MoCA: a middleware for developing collaborative applications for mobile users. IEEE Distrib. Syst. Online. 5(10), 2–2 (2004)
29. Huerta-Canepa, G., Lee, D.: A virtual cloud computing provider for mobile devices. In: Proceedings of the 1st ACM Workshop on Mobile Cloud Computing & Services: Social Networks and Beyond, pp. 1–5 (2010)
30. Kemp, R., Palmer, N., Kielmann, T., Bal, H.: Cuckoo: a computation offloading framework for smartphones. In: International Conference on Mobile Computing, Applications, and Services, pp. 59–79. Springer, Berlin/Heidelberg (2010)
31. Qi, H., Gani, A.: Research on mobile cloud computing: review, trend and perspectives. In: 2012 Second International Conference on Digital Information and Communication Technology and It's Applications (DICTAP), pp. 195–202. IEEE (2012)
32. Huang, D., Zhang, X., Kang, M., Luo, J.: MobiCloud: building secure cloud framework for mobile computing and communication. In: 2010 Fifth IEEE International Symposium on Service Oriented System Engineering, pp. 27–34. IEEE (2010)
33. Bhowmik, A., De, D.: mTrust: call behavioral trust predictive analytics using unsupervised learning in Mobile cloud computing. Wirel. Pers. Commun. 117(2), 483–501 (2021)
34. Lu, Y., Zhao, D.: Providing impersonation resistance for biometric-based authentication scheme in mobile cloud computing service. Comput. Commun. 182, 22–30 (2022)
35. Razaque, A., Jararweh, Y., Alotaibi, B., Alotaibi, M., Hariri, S., Almiani, M.: Energy-efficient and secure mobile fog-based cloud for the Internet of Things. Futur. Gener. Comput. Syst. 127, 1–13 (2022)

36. Hati, S., De, D., Mukherjee, A.: DewBCity: blockchain network-based dew-cloud modeling for distributed and decentralized smart cities. J. Supercomput., 1–21 (2022)
37. De, D.: FedLens: federated learning-based privacy-preserving mobile crowdsensing for virtual tourism. Innov. Syst. Softw. Eng., 1–14 (2022)
38. Roy, D.G., De, D., Mukherjee, A., Buyya, R.: Application-aware cloudlet selection for computation offloading in multi-cloudlet environment. J. Supercomput. **73**(4), 1672–1690 (2017)
39. Deb, P., Mukherjee, A., De, D.: A study of densification management using energy efficient femto-cloud based 5G mobile network. Wirel. Pers. Commun. **101**(4), 2173–2191 (2018)
40. Flinn, J., Satyanarayanan, M.: Powerscope: a tool for profiling the energy usage of mobile applications. In: Proceedings WMCSA'99. Second IEEE Workshop on Mobile Computing Systems and Applications, pp. 2–10. IEEE (1999)
41. Banerjee, K.S., Agu, E.: PowerSpy: fine-grained software energy profiling for mobile devices. In: 2005 International Conference on Wireless Networks, Communications and Mobile Computing, vol. 2, pp. 1136–1141. IEEE (2005)
42. Seo, C., Malek, S., Medvidovic, N.: An energy consumption framework for distributed java-based systems. In: Proceedings of the Twenty-Second IEEE/ACM International Conference on Automated Software Engineering, pp. 421–424 (2007)
43. Zhao, Y., Leung, V.C.M., Zhu, C., Gao, H., Chen, Z., Ji, H.: Energy-efficient sub-carrier and power allocation in cloud-based cellular network with ambient RF energy harvesting. IEEE Access. **5**, 1340–1352 (2017)
44. Mao, Y., Zhang, J., Letaief, K.B.: Dynamic computation offloading for mobile-edge computing with energy harvesting devices. IEEE J. Sel. Areas Commun. **34**(12), 3590–3605 (2016)
45. Liu, Z., Jingqi, F.: Resource pricing and offloading decisions in mobile edge computing based on the Stackelberg game. J. Supercomput., 1–20 (2022)
46. Gubbi, J., Buyya, R., Marusic, S., Palaniswami, M.: Internet of Things (IoT): a vision, architectural elements, and future directions. Futur. Gener. Comput. Syst. **29**(7), 1645–1660 (2013)
47. Mukherjee, A., Deb, P., De, D., Buyya, R.: IoT-F2N: an energy-efficient architectural model for IoT using Femtolet-based fog network. J. Supercomput. **75**(11), 7125–7146 (2019)
48. Karmakar, A., Ganguly, K., Banerjee, P.S.: HeartHealth: an intelligent model for multi-attribute based heart condition monitoring using fuzzy-TOPSIS method. In: 2021 Devices for Integrated Circuit (DevIC), pp. 1–5. IEEE (2021)
49. Gupta, A.K., Bhattacharya, I., Banerjee, P.S., Mandal, J.K., Mukherjee, A.: DirMove: direction of movement based routing in DTN architecture for post-disaster scenario. Wirel. Netw. **22**(3), 723–740 (2016)
50. Mukherjee, A., Bhattacharjee, S., Pal, S., De, D.: Femtocell based green power consumption methods for mobile network. Comput. Netw. **57**(1), 162–178 (2013)
51. Sayed, S.G., Said, S.A., Salem, S.A.: Energy aware mobile cloud computing using femtocells technology. In: 2021 International Mobile, Intelligent, and Ubiquitous Computing Conference (MIUCC), pp. 90–95. IEEE (2021)
52. Heller, B., Seetharaman, S., Mahadevan, P., Yiakoumis, Y., Sharma, P., Banerjee, S., McKeown, N.: Elastictree: saving energy in data center networks. Nsdi. **10**, 249–264 (2010)
53. Marsan, M.A., Chiaraviglio, L., Ciullo, D., Meo, M.: Optimal energy savings in cellular access networks. In: 2009 IEEE International Conference on Communications Workshops, pp. 1–5. IEEE (2009)
54. Zhou, S., Gong, J., Yang, Z., Niu, Z., Yang, P.: Green mobile access network with dynamic base station energy saving. ACM MobiCom. **9**(262), 10–12 (2009)
55. Vallina-Rodriguez, N., Hui, P., Crowcroft, J., Rice, A.: Exhausting battery statistics: understanding the energy demands on mobile handsets. In: Proceedings of the Second ACM SIGCOMM Workshop on Networking, Systems, and Applications on Mobile Handhelds, pp. 9–14 (2010)
56. Dogar, F.R., Steenkiste, P., Papagiannaki, K.: Catnap: exploiting high bandwidth wireless interfaces to save energy for mobile devices. In: Proceedings of the 8th International Conference on Mobile Systems, Applications, and Services, pp. 107–122 (2010)

57. Lu, X., ElzaErkip, Y.W., Goodman, D.: Power efficient multimedia communication over wireless channels. IEEE J. Sel. Areas Commun. **21**(10), 1738–1751 (2003)
58. Nandyala, C.S., Kim, H.-K.: Green IoT agriculture and healthcare application (GAHA). Int. J. Smart Home. **10**(4), 289–300 (2016)
59. Solanki, A., Nayyar, A.: Green internet of things (G-IoT): ICT technologies, principles, applications, projects, and challenges. In: Handbook of Research on Big Data and the IoT, pp. 379–405. IGI Global (2019)
60. Arthi, B., Aruna, M., Ananda Kumar, S.: A study on energy-efficient and green IoT for healthcare applications. In: Green Computing and Predictive Analytics for Healthcare, pp. 95–114. Chapman and Hall/CRC (2020)

Optimization of Green Mobile Cloud Computing

**Amir Hossein Jafari Pozveh, Hadi Shahriar Shahhoseini,
Faezeh Arshadi Soufyani, and Morteza Taheribakhsh**

1 Introduction

In Mobile Cloud Computing (MCC), powerful computing capacity and storage resources are provided to support delivery of new digital services in a mobile environment specially in 5G network. However, energy consumption becomes as important issue in MCC when the number of active devices (e.g. IoT equipment) increase and new emerged services with high processing power and bandwidth requirements (e.g. eMBB in 5G) should be provisioned. Moreover, providing the required electrical energy for cloud nodes generated by fossil fuels leads to environmental pollution as well as global warming. In the meanwhile, Green MCC have become interested to reduce energy consumption in a friendly way to the environment [1]. In green mobile communication, mobile/IoT devices, advanced data centers and computing systems get their required electrical energy from renewable energy sources such as solar energy, which leads to carbon-free calculation and cost savings. In recent years, many practical standards and policies have been adopted by global organizations and governments, followed by leading companies in telecommunications technology, such as Apple, Google, and Intel. For

A. H. J. Pozveh (✉)
Mobile Telecommunication Company of Iran (MCI), Tehran, Iran

Iran University of Science and Technology, Tehran, Iran
e-mail: amirjafari@iust.ac.ir

H. S. Shahhoseini · F. A. Soufyani
Iran University of Science and Technology, Tehran, Iran
e-mail: shahhoseini@iust.ac.ir

M. Taheribakhsh
Mobile Telecommunication Company of Iran (MCI), Tehran, Iran
e-mail: m.taheribakhsh@mci.ir

© The Author(s), under exclusive license to Springer Nature Switzerland AG 2022
D. De et al. (eds.), *Green Mobile Cloud Computing*,
https://doi.org/10.1007/978-3-031-08038-8_2

example, the energy needed to build and design processors at Apple is provided by renewable energy sources, such as solar, wave water, and wind.

It is not costly to move towards green computing in comparison to traditional methods. In many cases, old equipment does not need to be replaced with a new one. Simple updated techniques can be used to reduce energy consumption (e.g., using low-power hardware, activating standby mode in computer systems, or using mobile phones and tablets instead of using high-power desktop computers). Given the above points, various and advanced engineering methods have been proposed to move toward green MCC. The most important approaches are:

- Recycling materials to reuse electronic components to minimize the e-waste production rate.
- Development of green data centers: Using efficient schemes to move toward effective cooling of data centers and/or making use of sustainable energy such as wind energy, water waves and solar cells as the primary sources of electricity.
- Investing on intelligent grids: applying smart architecture and techniques to utilize different sources including fossil fuel-based electric energy and green energy in peak load and according to weather conditions
- Use of energy-aware solutions: using efficient algorithms to allocate computational resources efficiently, reducing the idle time of servers in data centers and proposing new algorithms for sending and receiving data intelligently to reduce energy consumption

The book chapter highlights energy-aware algorithms in MCC and investigates the techniques that facilitate moving toward the green cloud by improving energy efficiency and reducing carbon dioxide emissions. The rest of book chapter is organized as follows: Sect. 2, energy-aware algorithms in MCC, Sect. 3, energy-aware Key Technologies, Sect. 4, Renewable energy-based MCC, Sect. 5, energy-aware algorithms for devices, Sect. 6: green AI-based algorithms in MCC, Sect. 7: challenges and future works, and conclusion.

1.1 MCC Definition

Before defining MCC, firstly, a brief review of cloud computing is presented. In cloud computing, software and hardware resources such as processing power, storage and applications are shared regarding user demand and service requirements. In the other words, cloud computing is a set composed of data storage and processing systems connected through a network. Providing services in cloud computing fall into three categories. The first category is software as a service (SaaS), which allows users to access applications in the cloud. For example, consider the processing the number of words in a file by the application installed in the cloud and the result of the program is sent back to the user. In this case, the user does not need to install the program. The second category is platform as a service (PaaS), which includes a platform (e.g. Google App Engine) for developing the applications. The third category is infrastructure a service (IaaS), which provides access to infrastructure resources such as virtual machine access or storage for data storage.

MCC is defined as the combination of cloud computing and mobile computing which uses different resources (e.g., computing, storage, and communication) for mobile users. Its infrastructure includes mobile devices, mobile networks and cloud servers, which provides processing and data storage services with the aim of extending the processing power of mobile devices close to users. By utilizing the computing servers near mobile devices, mobile applications are able to be executed on cloud servers [2]. So, new emerged service types with high computing process requirements (e.g. Augmented reality (AR), Virtual reality (VR)) can be delivered on mobile devices with limited resources like as a laptop or desktop computer.

1.2 Edge, Fog Computing and Cloudlet

Since the main goal of MCC is to bring required resources (e.g., computing, storage, and communication) for mobile applications close to mobile devices, edge layer computation topics are discussed often in this space. The implementation of the edge layer in MCC architecture, is categorized into Fog computing, Mobile Edge Computing and Cloudlet, with the aim of reducing service latency, supporting user mobility and storing and computing large-scale data. Each of these implementations can be used by operators on mobile networks according to service type and application requirements.

Fog Computing (FC)
In fog computing, the fog nodes (FN) are placed between the IoT terminals/mobile devices and the cloud node in a decentralized computing infrastructure. Fog nodes may compound of heterogeneous devices, such as routers, access points, or gateways with different communication protocols and/or different access technologies. From the end user's point of view, the heterogeneity of fog nodes is transparent such that fog layer acts as a computational and storage service layer.

Mobile Edge Computing (MEC)
In the MEC, computing servers and nodes are implemented in the radio access network or base stations to provide computing capacity and storage for offloading and caching objectives [2]. Multiple MEC hosts can be deployed on MEC servers (MES) managed by the MEC orchestrator. MEC orchestrator manages the available resources and assigns them to MEC applications according to real time information obtained from load of MEC servers as well as connected end devices information and service requirements.

Cloudlet
Cloudlet is a cluster of trusted computing nodes connected to the Internet and provide computing resources to mobile devices near the edge of the network.

Cloudlet offers high bandwidth and low latency services for applications based on a group of collocated nodes managed by a Cloudlet agent.

2 Energy-Aware Algorithms in MCC

In this section, energy-aware algorithms applied in MCC are explored in two sections that prominently affect on energy consumption including (a) content caching and (b) computational offloading.

2.1 Content Caching

This section argues with the algorithms proposed for content caching in MCC to reduce the energy consumption. In content caching, for supporting broadband traffic and reducing service delay, the users' requested contents are stored in cloud content servers for content retrievers based on storage policies and performance improvement. However, since trend is moving toward green communication, recently, many researches has focused on optimizing energy consumption of content caching as an issue along with resource utilization, privacy, mobility and QoS [3–5].

The most common area for energy efficient content sharing in MCC is finding optimized solution for energy-aware placement of caching cloud servers in MCC layers (from edge to core network). Different approaches have been proposed in this topic including machine learning-based algorithms, game theory and evolutionary solutions and heuristic and mathematical techniques. The authors in [6] have proposed a model based on multi-tier DNN for finding an optimal energy-aware solution for content caching in a multi-tier MCC architecture. In the model, a reward function has been defined to select a candidate among small access points as content caching server with minimal energy consumption. Deep RNNs have been used to accelerate the convergence of the solution. Evaluations showed that the proposed algorithm significantly improved energy efficiency in distributed content caching in an innovative and dynamic way.

Another area that energy efficient approaches for caching becomes important is the 5G V2X and intelligent Connected Vehicles (ICV). In [7] Optimal Energy Efficiency Cache node Selection (OEECS) algorithm has been proposed for ICV services' content caching. The algorithm exploited an *optimal stopping theory* to improve latency and energy efficiency of content caching in ICV services. The *optimal stopping theory* works based on rewards sequences and utilizes random variables for achieving maximum reward based on optimal edge nodes selection for improvement of energy efficiency.

Cooperation for content caching in MCC between Small Base Stations (SBS) is another area that can lead to green mobile communication. In this way, SBSs connected by back-haul infrastructure, interact with each other in a distributed manner. When a user requests a content, its neighbor SBSs which have access to the content, responds to the user such that the content transmission energy consumption in MCC network (including base stations, transport equipment) becomes minimum. Regarding SBS cooperation, in [8], energy-aware content caching has been proposed that it considers SBSs connection quality, QoS requirements and network capabilities. Zipf's law was used for estimating content popularity of each user and making the content popularity list distributed in SBSs. The neighbor SBSs of each user maintain this list and respond to the user requests by considering low latency and minimum energy consumption. The authors showed by evaluating average delay, energy available, cache collaboration, and energy consumption metrics with MATLAB simulator; this method had better performance than other methods. Moreover, authors in [9] proposed a Deep Deterministic Policy Gradient (DDPG) method for energy efficient content caching in MCC on a 5G network. The model considered energy optimization of SBSs while providing the requested cached contents. The SBSs work as a group in DDPG and the user's requests have been received to this group. The method works based on capacity of SBSs and SINR in Multi Base Stations (MBS) and terminals. The SBS selection process improves latency and energy efficiency of content forwarding toward users. Better performance in comparing with other methods, was the evaluation result.

2.2 Computational Offloading

Although smartphones have acceptable computational power, they still suffer from the limitation of processing power and power supply to handle a large amount of the traffic generated by new services (e.g. AR, VR, online gaming, and smart city-based applications). The following list is some limitations that a mobile device suffers for computing heavy tasks:

- **Processing capability**: limitation in heavy processing power
- **Limited battery power**: Lack of high-power supply for computation and data transmission
- **Memory capacity**: lack of enough memory resources for massive data analysis

To overcome above limitations, offloading techniques in MCC have been presented. So, terminals can use communication interfaces that to allow to connect to nearby computation cloud for workload offloading to save energy and reduces execution time. In the other words, MCC provides a platform for mobile cloud-based services by utilizing powerful computing nodes to increase the capabilities of small mobile devices, reduce the time and delay constraints in use cases and improve the quality of experience (QoE) of mobile users. In offloading, some of the processes are transferred to remote servers with high processing power at the edge of the network close to users. The result of the processing is sent back to the user application. Generally, offloading has been studied in two aspects and schemes [10].

Cloud level

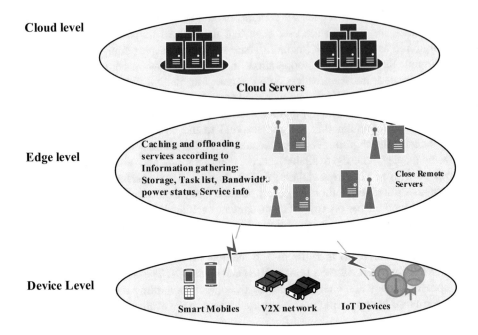

Edge level

Device Level

Fig. 1 Offloading in the cloud computing ecosystem

- Full offloading: the whole program is offloaded from the application of a mobile device on the remote server. It is suitable for programs that are not large.
- Partial offloading: Some tasks or modules of a program are offloaded from a mobile device on a remote server. The transmission overhead of each offloaded component to remote server and its run-time period must be well-handled.

Offloading is performed based on a typical computation architecture as shown in Fig. 1. The main levels are

- Device level: Depending on the available resources on the devices in terms of storage, CPU and communication interfaces, they can compute tasks and communicate with other devices and close cloud servers in coverage. The decision to offload to remote servers is made in the device layer.
- Edge level: remote servers at this level are more powerful and located close to the devices at the edge of the network (e.g. MEC, fog, cloudlet). They are implemented in a distributed architecture such that the devices are connected to them through closest access points.
- Cloud level: cloud servers at this level have unlimited computing resources and are used if edge servers do not have sufficient resources. In this case, computing requests are forwarded to cloud servers. The offloading decision at this level is made in device/edge level devices.

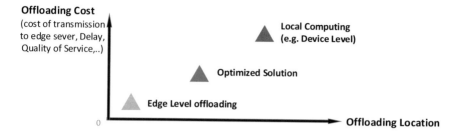

Fig. 2 Offloading cost vs. computing place (local computing or remote computing)

The most critical issues in offloading are task scheduling and resource computation to make decisions about where, when, and how much application code should be offloaded. To address these issues, different mathematical methods have been studied and various algorithms such as machine learning, game theory, alignment theory, linear and nonlinear programming, and other types of mathematical-based approaches have been discussed in different practical and academic projects [11, 12].

2.2.1 Energy-Aware Offloading Modeling

It is assumed that the scheduler on the mobile device can make a decision for when and how triggers the offloading procedure. If the conditions are favorable and the amount of battery and CPU required to process the task being enough, the task is executed locally on mobile device. Otherwise, the task to be executed will offload on the cloud nodes. In this case, offloading process is executed based on the output of the relation to optimize the reward function by considering application type, mobile device limitations such as battery status, storage and CPU capacity and energy consumption as seen on Fig. 2.

To find optimal solution for energy efficient offloading mathematically based on maximizing energy-aware reward function, it is required to study energy model consumption in offloading process. So, in this section a general model for energy consumption in *mobile devices* and *remote offloading servers* have been discussed.

Energy Consumption in Mobile Devices

When a mobile application (e.g. VR) runs on a mobile device, it runs a large number of tasks that take up a lot of computational resources and thus heavily consume battery power of the mobile device. So, it is necessary to know the energy consumption model of mobile devices when running Tasks for examining task scheduling on mobile devices and management of offloading in an energy-aware scheme.

Assume that each Task is represented by a T that has the following properties:

- Deadline: *TD*
- Task size: *Tsz*
- Instruction number: *In*

If a Task k (T_k) is executed on mobile devices, the power consumption depends on the CPU architecture and processing capacity of that device. The power consumption model for T_k that has an instruction number *In* is:

$$PDv_{jk} = \frac{In_{jk}}{CDv_j} * EC^i_{Dv} \tag{1}$$

Which PDv_{jk} is consumed energy in device j for execution of task T_k. CDv_j, In_k and EC^j_{Dv} are computing capacity of device j, number of instructions of task T_k and energy consumption per each task T_k in device j, respectively.

Energy Consumption in Remote Offloading

When task T_k is offloaded to the cloud server, the processing and execution time are calculated according sending and receiving time of from mobile device to cloud server and the total processing time in the cloud server as below:

$$D_{ik} = DTr_{ik} + DP_{ki} \tag{2}$$

DTr_{ik} is total transmission time (sending task and receiving result) of task T_k to/from cloud server i that it is calculated as:

$$DTr_{ik} = \frac{Tsz_k}{r_{ji}} + \frac{Tsz_k}{r_{ji}} \tag{3}$$

Where r_{ji} is transfer rate from mobile device j to server i for task T_k with length Tsz_k.

Also, DP_{ki} is process time Task T_k on server i and it is formulated as

$$DP_{ki} = \frac{In_k}{CR_i} \tag{4}$$

Where, CR_i is processing capacity of could server i.

Finally, Total energy consumption for offloading of task T_k from device j in server i is calculated as

$$PR_{jk} = DP_{ki} * EC^i_R + DTr_{ki} * Etr_{kj} \tag{5}$$

Where EC^i_R is energy consumption in time unit on server i and Etr_{kj} is average consumed energy by mobile device j for offloading transmission of Task T_k.

2.2.2   Green Offloading Algorithms

Various algorithms, systems and strategies have been studied in offloading for bringing down energy consumption. The main solutions have been focused on how offload the workloads to the nearby device in the mobile cloud along with different highlighted criteria such as performance, energy and utilization. The common metrics that used in energy efficient algorithms in MCC are discussed in the following.

Metrics in Energy-Aware MCC Algorithms

Delay: Delay of task computing in offloading process is result of the task execution delay on the mobile device, delay in the remote server for execution, and the delay of sending and receiving offloading request to/from remote server. In [13], delay for offloading has been formulated in offloading algorithms, it is common to consider the offloading delay as cost as well as consumed energy.

Quality of Experience (QoE): QoE presents how much the delivered service to the user is according to users' need and preferences. There are various methods proposed for calculating and evaluating QoE such as mean score (MOS), standard deviation of score scores (SOS) and net promoter score (NPS) [14]. QoE is an important metric in offloading schemes because offloading is an effective way to optimize service and resource utilization. Therefore, in Multi-objective offloading algorithms, QoE along with energy efficiency have been studied during scheduling and resource access in executing programs on nearby remote servers.

Response time: In computational offloading, response time is defined as the total time of commanding on device, execution on edge server and receiving the answer on device. In other words, the total time spent to offload a task from a mobile device to a remote server and receive a response on the mobile device. Response time should not be confused with delay. Delay includes the delay in execution and transfer of request and response between mobile device and remote server. In [15], detailed description and formulation are reviewed for response time. According to the service requirements, this criterion is considered along with energy efficiency has been evaluated in different optimization algorithms presented for offloading.

Task deadline: Tasks are parts of application program that should be offloaded and so task deadline as an important criterion may affect the entire application performance. So in offloading, task execution within a certain deadline and its dependency with other program modules have been considered in related works.

Security: although offloading helps in executing the computation-intensive tasks on remote servers at the edge of the network, however there are some security issues. Since, user data is executed outside of the mobile device/IoT device, they are vulnerable to malicious attacks and eavesdropping. Therefore, in the recent years, security has been considered as one of the criteria in offloading. A general case is presented in the article [16] with along energy consumption. Authors presented a Green MEC method that consider offloading process according to security issues. The method presented an optimizing energy consumption scheme without violating the delay requirements as well as security concerns.

In this section, the discussion about energy-efficient offloading algorithms in MCC is emphasized on two perspectives:

(a) *Single-objective and multi-objective algorithms*
(b) *Stochastic and non-stochastic algorithms*

(a) Single-objective/Multi-objective algorithms

Single-objective algorithms focus on improvement of energy consumption in offloading process. In [17], a heuristic algorithm has been proposed to reduce the power consumed in mobile devices focuses on task scheduling and offloading in the mobile cloud architecture. Authors defined a controller which is responsible for decision-making. Decision making is proposed based on computational process volume, offloaded task information, mobile device battery level and storage. These parameters are checked in an optimization function and if the mobile device cannot handle them, the tasks are uploaded to the mobile edge cloud. The proposed algorithm has been evaluated in a *Methane* simulation environment on *Cloud-Sim* and *Cloud Analyst*. The paper [18] presents an energy estimation algorithm based on task clustering to make decision on offloading the tasks in a remote server or execution locally on the mobile device. An energy estimation model has been presented for the energy consumption of task processing used in optimization algorithm which is defined based on task partitioning and parallel execution concepts in MCC.

Pan et al. [19] presented an dynamic offloading method to reduce energy consumption. The scheme was designed to reduce energy consumption during three steps including scheduling, adjusting CPU clock frequency based on dynamic voltage and frequency scaling (DVFS) technique and managing the transmission power for mobile devices. The proposed algorithm has an operational effect on computation offloading power consumption. In the article [20], energy consumption as the main object as well as processing capability has been discussed to be improved by considering task priority and load balancing based on Dynamic Voltage and Frequency Scaling (DVFS) model. Tasks were prioritized according to the urgency and the possibility of offloading in nearby remote servers placed in different areas. The optimization of energy consumption and problem has been solved by a heuristic algorithm in the case that the system load is below average.

Multi-objective algorithms in MCC deployment have been explored to address the offloading problem by a set of tradeoff solutions via jointly multiple criteria such as user and edge-node energy consumption, latency and quality of service (QoS). By modeling the problem with multi-objective solutions, the schemed introduced for energy-efficiency in MCC can consider the related parameters and their effects to user satisfaction. In this case, based on network conditions, history of service requests, service type and user satisfaction would be predicted and proper decision to improve users' requirements is made. In this regard, different articles have addressed user satisfaction issue over the years along with energy efficiency [21–24].

The solutions in multi-objective algorithms is converted to (1) single-objective optimization problem based on a cost function with weighted coefficients and multiple joint criteria (2) heuristic solutions or pareto optimal based solution such as nonlinear program and convex optimization. In the first one, i.e. cost fun*ction-based modeling*, the problem is formulated as a weighted sum that makes little sense to a decision-maker. Since, determining the weights for each criterion is a hard work and the solution depends on weighted parameters and scalarization method, only some feasible optimal answers may be obtained. On the other hand, in the second one i.e. *heuristic solution*, different approaches are utilized to achieve the solution considering tradeoff between all criteria. In [25], the offloading problem has been modeled as a nonlinear multi-objective problem to achieve the best tradeoff between task response delay, energy consumption and the deployment cost of cloudlets and edge servers. The Population Archive Multi-Objective Whale Optimization Algorithm (GPAWOA) has been used to solve the problem. The performance of the proposed algorithm was verified through simulation. Authors in [26], have modeled resource allocation for offloading in a MEC-based IoT ecosystem as a multi-objective problem called MRAM. Pareto archived evolution strategy (PAES) has been applied to find optimal policy for workload offloading to meet the service requirements (i.e. the shortest time to complete IoT applications) as well as reduce energy consumption. Minimum task execution time, load balancing and optimal energy consumption among MEC server have been taken as criteria.

(b) Stocastic/None-Stocastic Algorithms

There are many uncertainties in modeling of offloading problem in MCC due to system inputs that are not necessarily deterministic. Accordingly, proposed algorithms in this area with the aim of reducing energy consumption can be listed into two categories: non-stochastic and stochastic.

In non-stochastic solutions, the problem parameters are known and the next states of the system are deterministic. Deterministic linear/non-linear programming methods fall into the category of non-stochastic algorithms. Some works have been done in this field for energy-aware offloading.

On the other hand, in stochastic solutions, mathematical optimizations are used considering probability distributions with random variables. Markov-based modeling solutions and queuing theory fall in the stochastic methods. Different explores have been performed on offloading using stochastic based models considering uncertainty in the service request, CPU/storage status and task arrival rate. A general case has been presented in article [11]. Authors in the article proposed a resource allocation algorithm to offload an application from mobile device on remote nodes in fog layer while the energy consumption becomes minimum. The model is based on the Hidden Markov model (HMM) and the output has been defined to select an optimal edge node. The results of the authors' evaluation show that energy consumption, execution cost and resource utilization are better than local execution on mobile devices. Moreover, in [27], another new idea for offloading in a dynamic mobile cloud environment has been presented, which considers the dependency between application modules during offloading. In the proposed solution, allocation of tasks on remote server has been performed based on Markov Decision Process (MDP) framework. The decision metrics are mobile power consumption during task computing of the application and the amount of overhead in offloading the application modules. The optimal strategy in minimizing energy has been found by using the genetic algorithm to adjust the MDP parameters and so maximize the system reward.

3   Energy-Aware Key Technologies in MCC

SDN (software defined network) and NFV (Network function virtualization) as two key technologies in MCC, empower the operators to optimally increase dynamic resource utilization and provide on-demand and fast service deployment in MCC. So, optimization the energy consumption in NFV and SDN solutions helps us to move faster toward green MCC. Different algorithms have been proposed in this area that not only consider energy consumption metric but also dealing with some other criteria in a multi-objective problem. The most common metrics used along with energy efficiency are explored as the following aspects:

- Service Quality (Latency)
- Security (Trust-aware, Availability, Privacy)
- Execution Time
- Deployment Costs

In this section, common energy-aware algorithms in SDN and NFV technologies deployed in MCC architecture are investigated in two following parts:

- Energy-aware NFV deployment
- Energy-aware SDN-enabled MCC

3.1   Energy-Aware NFV Deployment

By deployment of NFV in cloud nodes in MCC architecture, mobile service provisioning is accelerated and network management is simplified. On the other hand, in MCC architecture, an important part of the energy is consumed in cloud nodes. So, by selection of proper design and deployment strategies in NFV-enabled cloud nodes, an optimization in energy consumption can be obtained in MCC. Various methods have been proposed for management and adjustment of energy consumption along with VNF consolidation, optimizing workload scheduling and edge node placement, computational offloading and avoiding SLA (service level agreement) violation. Generally, the most solutions have focused on VM and edge server placement. It is modeled as a multi-objective optimization problem by considering tradeoff between energy consumption and latency requirements [12, 28, 29]. Heuristic methods such as PSO, GA, convex solutions and ML have been used to obtain the optimal solution.

In addition, there are some research works that they have modeled the energy-aware placement and migration problem in NFV-based MCC either stochastic or non-stochastic schemes. In stochastic schemes, there is uncertainty in system modeling and mathematical optimizations in such that energy consumption improvement is modelled as a probability distribution function. The common modelling tools are Markov based models, game theory and queuing theory which used in recent works. Authors in [16] presented an energy, completion time, load balance efficient resource allocation method based on Pareto Evolution Archived Strategy (PEAS). In [21], game theory has been used for the VM allocation for maximizing the number of users and minimizing the deployment cost. In non-stochastic schemes, the problem parameters are known and the next states of the system are deterministic. Not many works such as Deterministic linear/non-linear programming have been studied in this field for energy efficient solution in NFV resource allocation problem in MCC. In [22] authors proposed a VM allocation scheme based on ILP for latency and energy efficiency. Moreover, a latency and energy efficient resource allocation method based on dynamic programming for NVF management in MCC has been proposed in [6].

3.2   Energy-Aware SDN-Enabled MCC

Software defined network (SDN) is an approach to networking to provide a customizable network infrastructure and direct traffic on the network by segmentation and sharing the underlying physical infrastructure [30].

SDN provides a flexible and controllable back-haul for MCC to handle new emerged 5G services. By applying SDN technology in MCC architecture, different challenges related to delay, load balancing and energy consumption that traditional cloud networks suffer them, can be addressed. SDN network dynamically manages the MCC network connectivity through a programmable central controller.

Figure 3 presents the general architecture of using SDN in MCC architecture that it includes three layers: node layer, control layer and application layer. In application layer, SDN applications as programs are used for presenting required functions such as networking management, analytics, or business applications. SDN controller in control layer receives instructions from SDN applications and relays them to the cloud/edge nodes in node layer. Cloud/Edge nodes in node layer are close to the users and connected to each through data plane.

SDN, as an enabler for the MCC network, highlights edge computing potentials. The main questions are

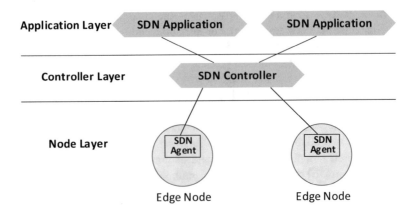

Fig. 3 SDN based MCC architecture

– How SDN can improve energy efficiency in MCC network?
– When a request for offloading or using cached contents arrives from mobile
  devices, how the SDN controller analysis different energy-aware strategies for
  resource allocation between cloud/edge nodes (forwarding the offload request to
  proper cloud/edge node) in the MCC network?

Recent proposed methods deal with selecting a strategy to contemplate energy efficiency optimization of whole system (includes all edge node energy consumption)
while load balancing status of MCC network and user satisfaction are considered
[31, 32]. In addition, by applying optimal resource allocation schemes via SDN
technology, the energy waste due idle cloud nodes can be reduced. Authors in [18]
presented a method for energy-aware SDN based MEC. In the proposed framework,
the cloud/edge nodes are initially partitioned into different zones. Then resources
have been shared among cloud nodes in each partition by making use of a multi-
objective optimization model with the aim of energy reduction, load balancing and
meeting service requirements (i.e. delay and performance).

4   Renewable Energy Based MCC

In the recent years, the interest in usage of renewable energy sources such as solar,
wind or water waves has been gradually increased in order to reducing pollution
to the environment and avoiding carbon emission by governments and regulators.
Nowadays, renewable energy sources have been vastly used in data center as source
of required electrical energy.

Even, in some cases, renewable energy source is only available solution for
mobile network sites in impassable areas with no electric power infrastructure (e.g.
some remote areas, offshore islands). Various heuristic and distributed analytical
and computational methods have been studied for investigating power electronic

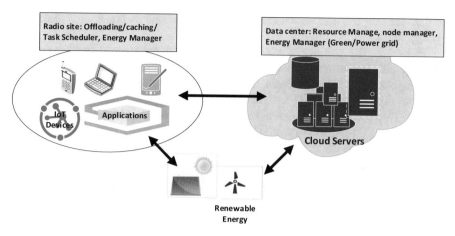

Fig. 4 Green-aware MCC network

systems and their use for MCC networks. In [33], authors have presented a survey on the optimal methods of generating renewable distribution and integration in the electricity distribution network [34].

Figure 4 shows a schematic view of the MCC green based general architecture. It consists of two parts: Data center (cloud nodes in core) and access radio sites (computational edge nodes in of network e.g. edge, fog/cloudlet nodes). Each part is feed by different energy sources including brown energy produced by fossil fuels and green energy produced by solar panels and storage batteries.

This section investigates the algorithms in which MCC network uses renewable energies in the architecture with the aim of optimizing resource sharing and service provisioning in 5G ecosystem.

4.1 Renewable Energy-Based MCC Risk Issues

Required energy for MCC components such as edge cloud and fog nodes can be supplied through integrated energy flow from renewable and non-renewable (brown) sources. However, one the one hand, the time and volume of network traffic, requested content and demand for computing service in data offloading on cloud nodes is not predictable and on the other hand the availability of renewable resources isn't available all day (It depends on weather conditions and geographical location). Moreover, the process of converting renewable energy into electrical energy is a complex task. Therefore, there may be a risk of the power shortage and so smart planning for usage of green energy supplies along with brown energy is mandatory to continuously meet required electrical energy of network equipment [35]. Article [36] examines the challenges associated with using renewable energy in data centers, and deal with unexpected energy demand and integrated renewable energy supply.

To explore the stability of power supply-based renewable sources, the power shortage risk in the micro grid-enabled MCC network can be modeled as a risk-sensitive energy template problem. One of the general models in the risk evaluation of electricity supply in MCC, in term of availability of renewable energy and brown energy (fossil fuels based sources) sources in the micro-grid network, has been presented in [37]. Authors assumed that there is uncertainty in renewable energy supplement and so the required value of electricity should be predicted, correctly. They used a deep reinforced learning method to find the best strategy for buying extra electrical energy or store a extra percentage of green unused electrical energy in batteries. The problem has been modeled as a multi-agent system. In the solution, each access point as an edge cloud node is modeled as an agent. The objective function has been defined according to system reward including the possibility of supplying electrical energy sources (green, brown) and uncertainty of computational service demand with the aim of optimization of the percentage of brown or green energy consumption in the MCC network.

4.2 Renewable Energy and MCC Functionalities

This section presents the recent proposed algorithms in green MCC network that uses renewable energy sources. It deals with the algorithms for two the MCC functionalities as computing (Task Scheduling and Offloading) and content caching.

4.2.1 Computing (Task Scheduling and Offloading)

Computing functionality in MCC discusses about sharing of computational resources for task scheduling, offloading and data Analysis to overcome the analysis and process aggregated service requests and users' data. Its advantages include but not limit to reducing the radio resource consumption (i.e., 12%), shortening the reaction time for real-time services (i.e., 10%), reducing the system latency (i.e., 14%), and diminishing the overall energy consumption (i.e., 12.35%). In this sub-section recent renewable energy-efficient algorithms for offline processing and task scheduling in MCC have been studied [38].

To reduce usage of brown energy in MCC, renewable energy sources can be used. However, for stable task scheduling and offloading, stability of electrical energy must be considered. This topic has been studied in the academic works from various point of view. One of the general methods is to provide a solution for workload distribution between the computing nodes based on the price of dynamic electricity and the status of renewable energy sources. An online algorithm for load balancing between computing data centers according to the geographical distribution pattern, called GreenGLB, has been presented in [39]. It is based on the greedy algorithm according to the current offered prices of electricity and the renewable energy levels. Authors have shown a significant reduction in electricity costs along with stable condition in electrical energy.

In the article [40], a framework of the edge computing (EC)-based smart grid networks has been presented, in which edge servers are located between data centers and IoT devices. The data collected by metering devices is offloaded on EC servers and the amount of generated renewable energy is predicted. Depending on the demand and generated energy in the grid network, an efficient cooperative task offloading and resource allocation scheme is performed. The proposed framework considers jointly transmission powers, wireless channel status, and the amount of data being offloaded.

In the paper [41] authors investigated a joint task scheduling and energy management for data analysis and computing in a MEC architecture supported by renewable hybrid power supply sources and brown electricity. The problem under study has been defined as a multi-objective function, which maximizes the utility of the whole MEC system by optimizing the load balancing between edge servers according to the dynamic task arrival rate, wireless channel condition, and energy price and the limitation of renewable energy and budget required to purchase electricity.

4.2.2 Content Caching

Caching the content locally in cloud nodes (e.g. edge nodes) is an effective solution (e.g. eMBB services), that results in increasing the costumer QoE (quality of experience) and addresses need for high capacity in the network backhaul. However, supporting these new emerged services (e.g. Ultra-HD video, massive IoT devices) and handling explosive growth of traffic on cloud nodes needs excessive electricity that it imposes a high cost to operators. In this regard, various frameworks and algorithms have been explored for investigation of utilizing renewable energy along with brown energy in the MCC network in case of content caching [42]. For more discussion a general algorithm presented in the article [43] is examined. As shown in Fig. 5, there are three layers including device, edge and data center layer. Nodes in edge level caching popular and specific contents requested by users in device layer. If the requested content is not in the edge nodes, it is provided directly from the data center. In this case, renewable energy during content prediction for caching in edge nodes is produced by a micro grid platform including green energy sources in a distributed architecture (e.g. in solar panels on rooftops). So, the edge nodes can cache the users' contents at times when solar energy has a pick. At times of the day that green energy is not available, stored energy in batteries simultaneously with brown electrical energy could be used.

The use of renewable energy in caching for the V2X network in MCC has also been interested in recent years. In [44], authors provided a scheme for roadside caching and traffic steering according to vehicle traffic status as well as

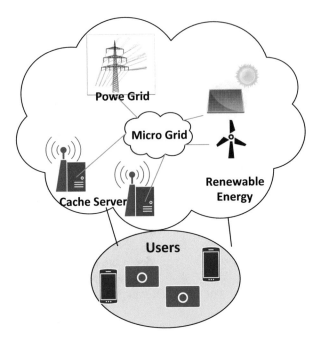

Fig. 5 Green proactive caching

renewable energy resource availability (e.g. maximum rate for solar energy in the afternoon). Moreover, the authors [45] have studied the tradeoff between hybrid energy consumption and service delay and presented a plan for utilizing green energy in HetNet with limited backhaul capacity for load balancing and caching.

A joint optimization scheme has been discussed in [46] which uses idle-active scheduling based on energy availability and caching data in the edge node. Content caching has been optimized based on time criteria in [43]. The evaluations show that the amount of energy cost is reduced by using solar energy at appropriate times to produce electrical energy for the edge nodes due to reducing energy consumption in the peak time. In [47], based on the content requested by mobile users and solar energy availability, the optimal scheduling strategy has been introduced, which has greatly reduced energy consumption while meeting the user QoE.

5   Energy-Aware Algorithms for Devices

Reducing the energy consumption in terminals as the final recipients of the service is one of the important areas for moving toward green MCC network. In this regard, the energy consumption management techniques are categorized based on deployment schemes in two levels

- Access to the network
- Software and hardware

In the first level, i.e. *access to the network*, energy consumption reduction and/or battery life incensement are performed based on parameter adjustment in network access techniques in IoT devices and terminals. Various methods have been proposed in this regard, which have focused on duty cycle, collision rate, preamble adjustment and radio access algorithms [48]. Authors in [49] designed a super frame that could increase energy efficiency in M2M communication by optimizing the duty cycle. The choice of super frame is based on the weight function of energy and delay. The solution has been founded on multiple agent RL model and the optimization procedure has been performed by the interaction of agents with the environment. Evaluation results confirm the improvement of energy consumption. Also, energy consumption can be optimized by adjusting sampling parameters such as sample rate and exponential back-off in channel access in IoT devices as studied in [50]. Another way to reduce energy consumption in end devices and terminals is reducing the collision probability. An effective method for this objective is node clustering. In this way, a send/receive plan is schedule dynamically based on two parameters including the number of nodes in each cluster and priority of data to be sent. So, in the random access and simultaneous transmissions environment, the collision rate during packet transmission is decreased and so energy consumption is reduced.

The second level, i.e. *Software and hardware level*, deals with mobile terminal software and hardware architecture to save battery level and reduce energy consumption. By development new technologies in designing mobile devices, there are many limitations in battery lifetime of mobile devices that influence the quality of receiving services specially by emerging new applications in 5G. In the ecosystem, many energy-aware methods for mobile devices have been proposed. Dynamic Voltage and Frequency Scaling (DVFS) for energy management based on computing resources, energy bug detection, energy consumption of hardware and software applications monitoring, etc. are some efficient proposed techniques in this field.

6   Green AI-Based Algorithms

Energy efficiency, resource allocation, and security challenges are the most important topics of communication networks that Artificial Intelligence (AI) -based proposed solutions have had good results in addressing them. AI is one of the best solutions for improving the energy efficiency of communication industry. AI methods are based on Machine Learning (ML), Deep Learning (DL), and heuristic algorithms. In the methods, problems with mathematical techniques are modeled and the decisions are made according to predicted system's output. The classification of AI techniques in communication area for relaxing the energy consumption divided to three groups as listed in the following [51, 52]:

- **Traditional ML and heuristic algorithms**: traditional ML algorithms including SVM, K-means, linear regression. In addition, heuristic algorithms i.e. ant colony optimization, genetic algorithm, particle swarm optimization.
- **DL based algorithms**
- **Advanced ML algorithms**

In the following sub-sections, according to mention categories, AI based solutions that have been applied for energy efficiency in MCC area has been presented. The most of them use multi-objective models with different criteria specially energy efficiency, resource allocation and service performance.

6.1   Traditional ML and Heuristic Algorithms

Traditional ML algorithms such as SVM, K-means, linear regression and heuristic algorithms i.e. ant colony optimization, genetic algorithm, particle swarm optimization are listed in this category. Many works have been investigated on computing aspects of MCC while reducing energy consumption by using ML and heuristic schemes[53, 54]. To understand how these algorithms can be used for efficient energy consumption in MCC, some general researches are reviewed in this section.

Authors in [55] introduced a model for code offloading in MCC environment. The energy consumption as well as QoS has been optimized by considering the workload and performance of mobile devices. In this method, a task allocation framework has been deployed in two parts: mobile application and server application. Mobile application consists of a library for offloading and services i.e. face recognition and optical character recognition. Offloading library uses a decision component for scheduling the computational tasks based on two ML-based classifiers for prediction of resource consumption, and an energy consumption estimator. To improve the offloading procedure as well as reduce energy consumption, the server application is modeled as a FIFO queue problem to optimize the execution of computational tasks and give back the storing results. In [56] a framework was presented for optimizing latency and energy efficiency of resource allocation and computing offloading in MEC network based on unsupervised deep learning model. The evaluation process consisted of three scenarios: Minimum Computation Offloading Scheme (MCOS), Partial Computation Offloading Scheme (PCOS), and Binary Computation Offloading Scheme (BCOS). The model consists of a trainer network for training process and a agent network for predicting process in MEC environment. Improving energy efficiency of mobile devices was the simulation result. Moreover, In [57], a new ML schemes was proposed for task scheduling with optimizing energy efficiency of mobile devices in MCC era. It has been designed as an adaptive service selection method with two parts: learning agent and context. The learning agent predicts a model based on ML classifier and processes the requests according to predicted model. The information for learning procedure comes from context such as battery usage (CPU, network card, etc.), and network connection status. In [58] authors presented a task scheduling system with optimizing energy efficiency of mobile devices in edge cloud while focusing on energy consumption. In addition, the method considers security requirements of device, tasks, and resources. The result of implemented method on AIOLOS and Cuckoo, Lenovo tablet and Samsung mobile, presented that the proposed decision module has become more efficient in securely task assigning the energy consumption in both the mobile devices and cloud servers.

6.2 Deep Learning-Based Algorithms

The most of Deep learning (DL) based algorithms use Artificial Neural Networks (ANNs). Here, only some works have been discussed about developed models using DL techniques [59]. Authors in [60] studied a latency and energy efficiency algorithm for computing offloading between mobile devices and cloud servers in MCC. The task scheduling was defined as a shortest path graph based on JointDNN, as DNN algorithm with partitioning layers. Execution in mobile devices, execution in cloud, uploading the data, and downloading the data are the nodes of this graph for online training. The solution considered energy efficiency and access connection types such as WiFi, 3G, and 4G as the decision metrics. In the evaluation, the mobile device was NVIDIA Jetson TX2 and cloud server was NVIDIA Tesla K40C. The latency and energy consumption of the proposed method decreased according to reported results. In [61], a model for computational offloading in MEC was investigated. Energy Efficient Deep learning based Offloading Scheme (EEDOS) had been used for optimizing energy saving in offloading workloads to MEC servers. The model defines an optimal decision maker for local and remote execution by taking account energy consumption of users and MEC servers. For evaluating the performance of this method, offloading accuracy, energy consumption, and a cost function measurement are considered as main criteria. In comparison with previous methods, the accuracy and energy efficiency of EEDOS increased.

6.3 Advanced ML Algorithms

Advanced ML algorithms are applied on complex networks and computation optimization. Supervised learning, unsupervised learning, deep reinforcement learning, federated learning, and transfer learning algorithms are members of this group. Here, only some of them have been discussed to understand how the AI-based algorithms can be applied in energy-aware solutions in MCC [62, 63].In [13], a latency and energy efficient computing offloading and task allocation scheme have been presented based on supervised learning method. Simulation with Tensorflow library based on python language reports the total cost evaluated as well as energy consumption have been improved. Authors in [64] proposed a Convex optimization-based Trajectory control algorithm (CAT) for decision component and a Reinforcement learning (RL) model for training procedure applied on computing offloading process in Unmanned Aerial Vehicles (UAV) applications. Overall energy consumption has been taken as a metric for evaluation. The results show the users' energy consumption reduced. Additionally, an energy efficient computing offloading approach based on deep learning has been argued in [65] for MEC environment with RF and low power backscatter communications. The proposed framework contains network profile, training scheme, reward evaluation, and action agent to offload the computing to the MEC servers. Evaluations have shown that the optimization of offloading performance has been concluded while energy consumption has been improved.

7 Challenges and Future Works

Despite the technology development in the field of green communication, since many variables affect on energy consumption such as protocol type, architecture, service quality, terminal and mobile devices and resource management methods, there are still many challenges related to energy efficiency. The most important challenges are listed here to be addressed in the future works:

- Availability of renewable energy: Renewable energy sources are not stable and their efficiency depends on geographical location and weather conditions. Therefore, the design of renewable energy sources as the electrical energy source of MCCs should be performed by considering edge server capacity and places
- Energy efficiency management in user device side: Although the device hardware has been improved in recent years, the number of applications and the needed computation of applications increase. However, reducing energy consumption of devices affects the quality of the services and the user experience will be reduced. So, new works should be performed in this area to reduce the impact of energy efficiency on quality of services.
- Energy-aware design for cloud/edge server: By reducing the number of active servers for decreasing the energy consumption of servers, enough number of available active servers for the peak time of network traffic is a challenge.
- Energy-aware offloading scheme: optimal allocation resources and tracking mobile users while receiving service are two challenges for energy-aware offloading. In this regard, proposing an energy efficient offloading scheme is a challenge.
- Energy efficient communication protocols: Some of the communication protocols i.e. UDP consume more energy than the others. Finding the best communication protocols between users' devices and cloud/edge servers is a challenge.

8 Conclusion

In recent years, advances in network technologies and the development of computing systems as well as resource virtualization have facilitated the moving of computation to the cloud to meet the communication and computational requirements of modern mobile applications and services that emerged in 5G era. In this space, Mobile Cloud Computing (MCC) can help the new service provisioning and overcome the limited resources of mobile devices. In this chapter, different approaches proposed in energy-aware MCC have been studied. Firstly, research-works have been presented for energy-aware offloading, task scheduling and content caching functionalities in MCC by categorizing the proposed methods into multi-objective/single-objective and stochastic/non-stochastic approaches. After that, renewable energy sources as an opportunity to apply in MCC environment and reducing energy consumption and costs has been studied. Finally, after presenting AI-based algorithms which have been applied for reducing the energy consumption in mobile devices and cloud server level, the main challenges and future works have been introduced.

Acknowledgement Authors would like to express their great appreciation to Dr. Nasim Kazemifard and Mr. Mahdi Moazzami Peyro from Mobile Telecommunication Company of Iran (MCI) for their valuable and constructive suggestions during writing this book chapter.

References

1. Taheribakhsh, M., et al.: 5G implementation: major issues and challenges. In: 2020 25th International Computer Conference, Computer Society of Iran (CSICC). IEEE (2020)
2. Pozveh, A.J., Shahhoseini, H.S.: IoT integration with MEC. In: Mobile Edge Computing, pp. 111–144. Springer (2021)
3. Li, J., Dai, M., Su, Z.: Energy-aware task offloading in the Internet of Things. IEEE Wirel. Commun. 27(5), 112–117 (2020)
4. Xu, Z., et al.: Energy-aware collaborative service caching in a 5G-enabled MEC with uncertain payoffs. IEEE Trans. Commun. (2021)
5. Seo, Y.-J., et al.: A novel joint mobile cache and power management scheme for energy-efficient mobile augmented reality service in mobile edge computing. IEEE Wirel. Commun. Lett. 10(5), 1061–1065 (2021)
6. Li, W., et al.: A reinforcement learning based smart cache strategy for cache-aided ultra-dense network. IEEE Access. 7, 39390–39401 (2019)
7. Wu, H., et al.: Toward energy-aware caching for intelligent connected vehicles. IEEE Internet Things J. 7(9), 8157–8166 (2020)
8. Kabir, A., et al.: Energy-aware caching and collaboration for green communication systems. Acta Montan. Slovaca. 26(1) (2021)
9. Li, Q., et al.: A green DDPG reinforcement learning-based framework for content caching. In: 2020 12th International Conference on Communication Software and Networks (ICCSN). IEEE (2020)
10. Rahmani, A.M., et al.: Towards data and computation offloading in mobile cloud computing: taxonomy, overview, and future directions. Wirel. Pers. Commun., 1–39 (2021)

11. Jazayeri, F., Shahidinejad, A., Ghobaei-Arani, M.: A latency-aware and energy-efficient computation offloading in mobile fog computing: a hidden Markov model-based approach. J. Supercomput. **77**(5), 4887–4916 (2021)
12. Anjaria, K., Patel, N.: Attainment of green computing in cloudlet-based mobile cloud computing model using squirrel search algorithm. In: Proceedings of 6th International Conference on Recent Trends in Computing: ICRTC 2020. Springer (2020)
13. Huang, L., et al.: Deep reinforcement learning-based joint task offloading and bandwidth allocation for multi-user mobile edge computing. Digit. Commun. Netw. **5**(1), 10–17 (2019)
14. Mahmud, R., et al.: Quality of Experience (QoE)-aware placement of applications in Fog computing environments. J. Parallel Distrib. Comput. **132**, 190–203 (2019)
15. Wu, S., et al.: An efficient offloading algorithm based on support vector machine for mobile edge computing in vehicular networks. In: 2018 10th International Conference on Wireless Communications and Signal Processing (WCSP). IEEE (2018)
16. Zahed, M.I.A., et al.: Green and secure computation offloading for cache-enabled IoT networks. IEEE Access. **8**, 63840–63855 (2020)
17. Ali, A., et al.: An efficient dynamic-decision based task scheduler for task offloading optimization and energy management in mobile cloud computing. Sensors. **21**(13), 4527 (2021)
18. Xing, N., et al.: A network energy efficiency measurement method for cloud-edge communication networks. In: International Conference on Simulation Tools and Techniques. Springer (2020)
19. Pan, S., et al.: Dependency-aware computation offloading in mobile edge computing: a reinforcement learning approach. IEEE Access. **7**, 134742–134753 (2019)
20. Hao, Y., et al.: Energy-aware offloading based on priority in mobile cloud computing. Sustain. Comput. Inform. Syst. **31**, 100563 (2021)
21. Colombo-Mendoza, L.O., et al.: A knowledge-based multi-criteria collaborative filtering approach for discovering services in mobile cloud computing platforms. J. Intell. Inf. Syst. **54**(1), 179–203 (2020)
22. Aliyu, A., et al.: Mobile cloud computing: taxonomy and challenges. J. Comput. Netw. Commun. **2020** (2020)
23. Kumar, J., Rani, A., Dhurandher, S.K.: Convergence of user and service provider perspectives in mobile cloud computing environment: taxonomy and challenges. Int. J. Commun. Syst. **33**(18), e4636 (2020)
24. Nugroho, K., et al.: Mobile cloud learning based on user acceptance using DeLone and McLean model for higher education. Int. J. Adv. Comput. Sci. Appl. **11**(1) (2020)
25. Zhu, X., Zhou, M.C.: Multi-objective optimized cloudlet deployment and task offloading for Mobile edge computing. IEEE Internet Things J. (2021)
26. Liu, Q., et al.: Multi-objective resource allocation in mobile edge computing using PAES for Internet of Things. Wirel. Netw, 1–13 (2020)
27. Zalat, M.S., Darwish, S.M., Madbouly, M.M.: An effective offloading model based on genetic Markov process for cloud mobile applications. In: International Conference on Advanced Intelligent Systems and Informatics. Springer (2020)
28. Zhang, L., et al., Energy-Delay Tradeoff for Virtual Machine Placement in Virtualized Multi-Access Edge Computing: A Two-Sided Matching Approach 2021
29. Peng, K., et al.: An energy-and cost-aware computation offloading method for workflow applications in mobile edge computing. EURASIP J. Wirel. Commun. Netw. **2019**(1), 1–15 (2019)
30. Power and performance efficient SDN-enabled fog architecture. arxiv (2021)
31. Alomari, A., et al.: Resource management in SDN-based cloud and SDN-based fog computing: taxonomy study. Symmetry. **13**(5), 734 (2021)
32. Singh, A., Aujla, G.S., Bali, R.S.: Container-based load balancing for energy efficiency in software-defined edge computing environment. Sustain. Comput. Inform. Syst. **30**, 100463 (2021)

33. Ehsan, A., Yang, Q.: Optimal integration and planning of renewable distributed generation in the power distribution networks: a review of analytical techniques. Appl. Energy. **210**, 44–59 (2018)
34. Jianzhong, X., Assenova, A., Erokhin, V.: Renewable energy and sustainable development in a resource-abundant country: challenges of wind power generation in Kazakhstan. Sustainability. **10**(9), 3315 (2018)
35. Zahed, M.I.A., et al.: A review on green caching strategies for next generation communication networks. IEEE Access. **8**, 212709–212737 (2020)
36. Deng, W., et al.: Harnessing renewable energy in cloud datacenters: opportunities and challenges. IEEE Netw. **28**(1), 48–55 (2014)
37. Munir, M.S., et al.: A multi-agent system toward the green edge computing with microgrid. In: 2019 IEEE Global Communications Conference (GLOBECOM). IEEE (2019)
38. Perin, G., et al.: EASE: energy-aware job scheduling for vehicular Edge networks with renewable energy resources. arXiv preprint arXiv, 2111.02186 (2021)
39. Khalil, M.I.K., Ahmad, I., Almazroi, A.A.: Energy efficient indivisible workload distribution in geographically distributed data centers. IEEE Access. **7**, 82672–82680 (2019)
40. Yang, C., et al.: Efficient task offloading and resource allocation for edge computing-based smart grid networks. In: ICC 2019-2019 IEEE International Conference on Communications (ICC). IEEE (2019)
41. Chen, Y., et al.: Joint task scheduling and energy management for heterogeneous mobile edge computing with hybrid energy supply. IEEE Internet Things J. **7**(9), 8419–8429 (2020)
42. Vallero, G., et al.: Base Station switching and edge caching optimisation in high energy-efficiency wireless access network. Comput. Netw. **192**, 108100 (2021)
43. Zahed, M.I.A., et al.: Proactive content caching using surplus renewable energy: a win–win solution for both network service and energy providers. Futur. Gener. Comput. Syst. **105**, 210–221 (2020)
44. Zhang, S., et al.: Self-sustaining caching stations: toward cost-effective 5G-enabled vehicular networks. IEEE Commun. Mag. **55**(11), 202–208 (2017)
45. Han, T., Ansari, N.: Network utility aware traffic load balancing in backhaul-constrained cache-enabled small cell networks with hybrid power supplies. IEEE Trans. Mob. Comput. **16**(10), 2819–2832 (2017)
46. Xu, D., et al.: Joint caching and sleep-active scheduling for energy-harvesting based small cells. In: 2017 9th International Conference on Wireless Communications and Signal Processing (WCSP). IEEE (2017)
47. Zahed, M.I.A., et al.: A cooperative green content caching technique for next generation communication networks. IEEE Trans. Netw. Serv. Manag. **17**(1), 375–388 (2019)
48. Zhao, F., et al.: Dynamic offloading and resource scheduling for mobile edge computing with energy harvesting devices. IEEE Trans. Netw. Serv. Manag. (2021)
49. Xu, H., et al.: Priority-aware reinforcement-learning-based integrated design of networking and control for industrial Internet of Things. IEEE Internet Things J. **8**(6), 4668–4680 (2020)
50. Li, Y., et al.: Smart duty cycle control with reinforcement learning for machine to machine communications. In: 2015 IEEE International Conference on Communication Workshop (ICCW). IEEE (2015)
51. AI based service management for 6G green communications. arXiv (2021)
52. Jafari, A.H., Shahhoseini, H.S.: A reinforcement routing algorithm with access selection in the multi-hop multi-Interface networks. J. Electr. Eng. **66**(2), 70 (2015)
53. Suryadevara, N.K.: Energy and latency reductions at the fog gateway using a machine learning classifier. Sustain. Comput. Inform. Syst., 100582 (2021)
54. Xu, C., Zhu, G.: Intelligent manufacturing lie group machine learning: real-time and efficient inspection system based on fog computing. J. Intell. Manuf. **32**(1), 237–249 (2021)
55. Nawrocki, P., Sniezynski, B., Slojewski, H.: Adaptable mobile cloud computing environment with code transfer based on machine learning. Pervasive Mobile Comput. **57**, 49–63 (2019)
56. Chen, X., et al., Unsupervised Deep Learning for Binary Offloading in Mobile Edge Computation Network. 2021

57. Nawrocki, P., Sniezynski, B.: Adaptive context-aware energy optimization for services on mobile devices with use of machine learning. Wirel. Pers. Commun. **115**(3), 1839–1867 (2020)
58. Nawrocki, P., et al.: Adaptive context-aware energy optimization for services on mobile devices with use of machine learning considering security aspects. In: 2020 20th IEEE/ACM International Symposium on Cluster, Cloud and Internet Computing (CCGRID). IEEE (2020)
59. Kilcioglu, E., et al.: An energy-efficient fine-grained deep neural network partitioning scheme for wireless collaborative fog computing. IEEE Access. (2021)
60. Eshratifar, A.E., Abrishami, M.S., Pedram, M.: JointDNN: an efficient training and inference engine for intelligent mobile cloud computing services. IEEE Trans. Mob. Comput. (2019)
61. Ali, Z., et al.: A deep learning approach for energy efficient computational offloading in mobile edge computing. IEEE Access. **7**, 149623–149633 (2019)
62. Ale, L., et al.: Delay-aware and energy-efficient computation offloading in mobile edge computing using deep reinforcement learning. IEEE Trans. Cognit. Commun. Netw. (2021)
63. Bi, S., et al.: Lyapunov-guided deep reinforcement learning for stable online computation offloading in mobile-edge computing networks. IEEE Trans. Wirel. Commun. (2021)
64. Wang, L., et al.: Deep reinforcement learning based dynamic trajectory control for UAV-assisted mobile edge computing. IEEE Trans. Mob. Comput. (2021)
65. Gong, S., et al.: Deep reinforcement learning for backscatter-aided data offloading in mobile edge computing. IEEE Netw. **34**(5), 106–113 (2020)

Part II
Green Mobile Cloud Computing

Energy Efficient Virtualization and Consolidation in Mobile Cloud Computing

Avita Katal

1 Introduction

Mobile gadgets (smartphones, tablets, and other similar devices) have become an indispensable element of human life as a means of communication that can be utilized anywhere and at any time. Customers have been supplied with a rich experience because of the availability of such a wide range of services that run on these devices or from faraway servers via wireless networks. The rapid advancement of technology has become a major trend in IT development. However, these devices confront numerous obstacles, the most significant of which is a lack of resources such as battery, computational power, and bandwidth. There are obstacles in communication, such as mobility and security. Cloud computing is widely acknowledged as the future of computing. With the rising acceptance of mobile computing and the rise of cloud computing, a new trend known as MCC has evolved, offering new types of services and capabilities for mobile users to fully utilise CC. With the rapid adoption of mobile computing and the expansion of cloud computing, a new trend of integrating CC into the mobile environment known as MCC has emerged, bringing new services and capabilities for mobile users to fully utilise CC. This has also changed the development, running, deployment as well as using mode of mobile applications. The terminals used to connect and acquire cloud solutions are designed for mobile devices like cellphones, PDAs, Tablets, and iPads rather than stationary systems like PCs, reflecting the advantages and intended purpose of cloud computing.

The term "Mobile Cloud Computing" was created soon after the concept of "Cloud Computing." It reduces the growth and operational costs of mobile appli-

A. Katal (✉)
School of Computer Science, University of Petroleum and Energy Studies, Dehradun, Uttarakhand, India

49

cations, smartphone shareholders as a modern innovation for obtaining numerous opportunities of a range of electronic service providers at a low cost, and experts as a viable approach for green IT. The mobile cloud market was worth USD 30.71 billion in 2020, and it is anticipated to be worth USD 118.70 billion by the end of 2026, growing at a CAGR of 25.28 percent over the forecast period (2021–2026) [1], demonstrating the rising popularity of mobile cloud computing. In recent years, mobile device apps have become plentiful, with applications in a variety of areas such as entertainment, health, gaming, and business. The MCC forum defines MCC as [2]: 'Even at the most fundamental, mobile cloud computing refers to a system wherein both data storage and data computation take place outside the smartphone. Mobile cloud apps move computational power and data collecting from mobile phones to the cloud, allowing programs and MC to be offered to a far larger number of people. Aepona [3] defines MCC as a new revolution for mobile applications in which processing of data and management are moved from portable devices to sophisticated and controlled cloud computing infrastructures. These centralised apps are then wirelessly accessible on mobile devices through a thin native client or web browser.

MCC has become an intriguing research area due to the vast and heavy applications on the internet. The MCC application is getting increasingly popular. Due to the increase in popularity of MCC, apps such as Gmail, Google Maps and android based applications have been created and made available to mobile users. The primary goal of MCC is to offer services, processing, and software. Applications that move data storage and computational power from mobile phones to the cloud are known as mobile cloud processing apps. It is a new paradigm for applications in which computation of data and storage are transferred from smartphones to a central and sophisticated CC platform available through the internet. All of these centralised apps are accessed via a wireless connection that is based on a web browser, a mobile device client. These days, mobile users may access resources and apps on the web using a combination of CC and the browser. The fundamental purpose of mobile cloud computing is to give consumers with a convenient and quick way to acquire and retrieve data from the cloud; this simple and quick technique comprises effectively connecting cloud computing resources via mobile devices. The features of mobile devices and wireless connections, as well as their own constraints and regulations, pose the greatest challenge to mobile cloud computing, making software application, programming, and implementation more difficult on mobile and distributed devices than on resolved cloud devices.

The paper is divided into 6 sections: Sect. 2 discusses motivation for this work, Sect. 3 discusses the basics of mobile cloud computing; including its architecture, characteristics, advantages and applications, followed by Sects. 4 and 5 discussing the various energy efficient techniques and research challenges. Section 6 describes the future directions. Section 7 concludes the chapter.

2 Motivation

Mobile Cloud Computing (MCC) is a new and popular mobile technology that uses Cloud Computing services and capabilities However, because of user mobility and intensive computing processes, energy consumption is a big concern. Energy efficiency over MCC is required since ICT-related devices use 57% of produced energy and have other negative environmental consequences [4]. Externalization of data and apps is considered as a viable option for conserving energy in mobile devices. This, however, is dependent on the MCC design under consideration. This chapter covers the basic concepts, definitions of MCC proposed by different researchers along with the difference between the cloud computing and MCC, its architecture, characteristics and applications. The chapter provides the detailed information about the energy efficient techniques for the MCC along with the consolidation and virtualization in cloud computing. Furthermore, the chapter concludes with the research challenges in reducing the energy consumption in MCC.

Figure 1 presents the taxonomy applied for studying energy efficiency on MCC. It is subdivided into multiple subdomains. These are: energy efficiency of mobile devices, limited battery lifetime of mobile devices, resource scheduling, task offloading, load balancing and resource provisioning. Energy efficiency of mobile devices includes 3 different categories of techniques like resource efficiency, Dynamic Voltage and Frequency Scaling (DVFS) and system and process level offloading. All the mentioned techniques help in energy efficiency of mobile devices by limiting the resource usage and by decreasing the overhead. Battery lifetime of mobile devices can be overcome by static partitioning, energy efficient computational offloading framework and application layer adaptive transmission protocol. Resource scheduling can be done on the basis of the different algorithms that are based on DVS and AI which helps in minimizing the energy usage in MCC. The resource provisioning can be done in two ways: static and dynamic. The diagram in Fig. 1 depicts the whole taxonomy of energy-efficient strategies that may be utilised in MCC.

3 Basics MCC

3.1 Architecture of MCC

Cellphones being so common in most people's daily lives has prompted businesses to develop services that can be easily accessed through them. Smartphone usage is increasing as a result of the Internet, GPS, and game apps. Today's lifestyle frequently necessitates staying in touch via mobile communication devices. Data transmission and reception are getting more convenient. MCC integrates CC with mobile computing ideas. This revolutionary technique takes use of the Internet's

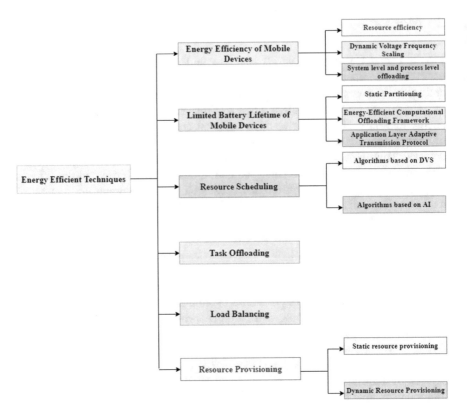

Fig. 1 Taxonomy of the energy efficient techniques for MCC

cloud computing infrastructure's capability for storage and analysis. MCC's architecture is shown in Fig. 2.

- Mobile User Layer: This tier is made up of many different mobile cloud service consumers who use mobile devices to access cloud services.
- Mobile Network Layer: This layer is made up of a number of mobile network providers who process user requests and distribute data via base stations. The home agent's mobile network services, such as Authentication, Authorization, and Accounting, manage these user requests (AAA). Mobile network carriers assist in identifying the subscribers' data held in their databases via their HA.
- Cloud Service Provider Layer: This layer is made up of numerous CC service providers who offer a variety of CC services. These CC services are elastic, meaning they may be scaled up or scaled down depending on what CC service consumers require. CC offers services to consumers, especially to those with mobile phones, who may access cloud services over the Internet.

In general, it can be concluded that this design illustrates the efficacy of CC in satisfying the expectations of MCC service consumers. The fundamental

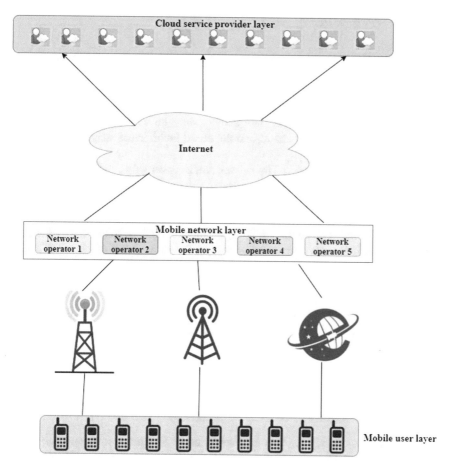

Fig. 2 Architecture of MCC

purpose for the MCC idea is to supplement the computing capacity of mobile devices. MCC has employed a variety of common designs for a variety of reasons, including enhanced execution, data management, and energy economy. The low resources of mobile devices are well-known to be a significant constraint. To carry out different storage and distribution operations, several devices have been created with CC support in view, which are frequently carried out using wireless connection technologies. Image exchange, for example, necessitates that a device be capable of processing and storing huge volumes of data. Individuals may conserve electricity by uploading photographs to the cloud soon after taking them using cloud computing. Facebook took use of this capability, and so as a response, it expanded incredibly quickly in popularity. MCC also makes data administration easier by providing synchronisation of many files and directories.

3.2   Characteristics of MCC

- Elasticity: Users can obtain rapid access to computer resources without the need for human involvement. Customer rights may be given quickly and elastically, even in certain instances automatically, allowing for easy scaling out or up.
- Infrastructure scalability: With minimal modifications to an infrastructure design and software, new nodes in data centers may be added or withdrawn from the network. Based on demand, mobile cloud architecture may rapidly expand horizontally or vertically.
- Access to a broad network: The network makes user skills and abilities accessible, and they may be retrieved via standard techniques that encourage utilisation by diverse platforms such as mobile phones, PCs, and PDAs, among others.
- Location Independence: Another feature of MCC is its independence from location. There is a distinct feeling of location independence, in which the user has no influence over or awareness of the actual location of the delivered resources. However, indicating location at different levels of abstraction beyond nation, state, or data center may be conceivable.
- Cost and Scale Effectiveness: Irrespective of installation technique, mobile cloud implementations aim to be as large as possible for the advantage of economies of scale. For cheaper costs, a large number of mobile cloud installations may be situated near inexpensive power stations and low-cost real estate.

3.3   Advantages of MCC

Smartphones may be viewed as a representation of all other resource-hungry smart mobile devices when assessing the benefits and limitations of the MCC platform. Wireless connection allows resource-hungry devices to connect to the resourceful cloud platform from anywhere. Mobile devices may offload data storage and processing to cloud platforms to save CPU time, storage space, and battery power. A cloud computing platform with more storage and processing capability can do the same task significantly faster than a mobile device. There are many advantages of MCC in different domains. Some of them are listed below:

- Extending Battery Lifetime: One of the primary problems with mobile devices is battery life. Several strategies have been presented to improve CPU performance by intelligently structuring the disc and screen to save power usage. These approaches may need structural changes to mobile devices or advanced technology, resulting in an increase in cost. These improvements, however, may not be applicable to all mobile devices. There are several computation offloading technologies available to shift big computations and complex analysis from resource-constrained devices such as mobile phones to advanced hardware such as cloud servers. MCC removes the need for lengthy program execution times on mobile devices, which can result in significant battery consumption.

- Improving Dependability: Placing information and data on the cloud is an excellent technique to boost reliability, since the data and applications are kept and backed up on several computers. Consequently, there is less chance of data and application loss on portable devices. Furthermore, MCC has the potential to be developed as a major and compact data security model for both resource operators and consumers.
- Enhancing Storage Capacity and Processing Power: MCC was designed to enable mobile users to retrieve or retain huge volumes of data in the cloud over wire-free networks. The mobile image sharing service enables mobile clients to instantly upload photos to the cloud when they are taken. Mobile users may access all photographs from any device. Facebook is today's biggest popular social network software, and it is also a wonderful example of how to use the cloud to exchange images. MCC also helps to reduce operational expenses for compute-intensive apps that take a long time and a lot of power to run on low-resource devices. CC can readily provide a number of functions for online data storage, administration, and synchronization of various works. Cloud computing may be used to convert data, play chess, and deliver multimedia services to mobile devices.
- Dynamic Provisioning: Dynamic resource provisioning is a versatile technique for service suppliers and phone devices to execute their different apps without reserving resources in advance. Data can be kept in the cloud instead of on mobile devices and accessible dynamically.
- Scalability: Because data and programs are kept and backed up on multiple computer systems, storing information or executing applications in the cloud is an effective approach to improve reliability. This one reduces the risk of data and app loss on mobile devices. Additionally, M.C.C. might be developed as an extensive data privacy paradigm for both service suppliers and mobile clients. The cloud, for example, might be utilized to prevent the unauthorized dissemination and utilization of protected intellectual assets (e.g., video clips and music). Moreover, the cloud may provide remote security services to mobile clients such as virus detection, identification, and malicious software detection.
- Multi-tenancy: Internet providers, such as network operators or data centre owners, can pool resources and prices to deliver a wide range of services to a big number of customers.
- Ease of Incorporation: To satisfy the needs of the user, several types of services from various providers may be simply connected using the cloud and the Internet.

3.4 Applications of MCC

- Image Processing: Image analysis in cloud computing is widely employed in a variety of disciplines such as science and medicine, satellite purposes, protection implementations, and so on. The authors of [5] provide a flexible cloud system that reduces hardware compatibility by integrating photogrammetry techniques for picture processing and analysis as cloud services. [6] a secure architecture comprising two clouds, one private for encryption/decryption and the other public for storage. They built the first cloud using OpenStack while adhering to the encryption as a service philosophy. They utilized paillier's homomorphic cryptosystem built particularly for pictures as an encryption technique.

- Sensor Data Applications: Almost all mobile devices now include sensors that are used to read data. GPS, accelerometer, thermometer, etc. may be time stamped and linked with the readings of another device. Various queries may be run to obtain valuable information in various situations. Patients can obtain medical services at any time and from any location with the help of mobile devices and wearable sensors. Outsourcing computation- or data-intensive operations to far away cloud centres can ease the long-standing restrictions of computing capacity and storage space on mobile devices. As a result, MCC has been identified as a viable way of providing people's everyday lives with benefits from ubiquitous healthcare services. The authors in [7] have suggested using MCC to capture, store, and analyse atmospheric data. Temperature and humidity sensors in smartphones, in particular, are utilised to capture atmospheric data in real time. The captured data is then sent to the cloud on a regular basis for storage and analysis.

- Multimedia Search: Mobile phones may hold a variety of multimedia information, including movies, pictures, and music. Shazam [8], for example, is a music recognition service for mobile phones that searches a central database for comparable songs.

- Mobile vehicular cloud: It is used in the vehicular surveillance system; it is composed of sensor nodes that act as automobiles and CC that acts as the backend system. The vehicle cloud's primary uses include urban monitoring, driving safety and digital applications. They exchange data while keeping it local due to the importance of local relevance; the sheer volume of data makes Internet uploading unappealing.

- Mobile learning: M-learning systems are made up of CC and mobile devices, and they are used to assist educational systems. The main goal of M-learning is for users to be able to read knowledge from centralised yet shared resources whenever and wherever they choose, for free. M-learning enables users to explore every topic using any resource without having to save it on the phone. The services offered by the data centres should be paid for by the client. Then individuals may use a mobile phone to learn any topic from any faraway location.

- Remote display: It is a technology that uses the cloud to perform all higher-level processing elements of an application. Users may view the results using their mobile phones' web browsers. This technology's core keywords are sink and source. The Sink is the device that displays the output, while the Source is the device that does the processing. Instead of utilising mobile devices to analyse data, remote display gives on-demand access via the cloud. In order to operate multiple services of various apps, the mobile cloud provider creates a remote screen picture. These are known as VMs. Remote Screen Images (RSIs) are gathered and sorted after obtaining the results of linked operations, and the display is captured and provided to the users' mobile.

- Health applications: Mobile devices are the key platforms for delivering, accessing, and communicating mobile patient data. Mobile devices confront a number of problems, including power supply and processing constraints. Some multimedia and security algorithms cannot be executed on mobile devices. They have minimal processing capacity and consume very little electricity. Cloud computing enables the management of information in a dispersed, omnipresent, and pervasive manner. Several concerns may be controlled if mobile devices are connected with the cloud.

- Defense sector: During the battle, the defence agency uses mobile gadgets. Many activities, including NLP, picture identification, planning of mission, and decision making, can be carried out with these devices. The precision of recognising the target and the time delay are key considerations in object recognition applications. An object recognition algorithm governs the accuracy. This technique needs a large amount of processing power, which mobile devices lack, making it impossible to detect the target item with high precision.

- Social cloud: The internet is the primary medium that links individuals from all over the world. Many of these Internet users keep in touch with one another through social networking sites. They use social networks to share information and communicate with one another. In today's world, social networking is quite essential. In social networking sites, a huge number of people are interconnected and share data, necessitating a considerable amount of memory space. This sort of storage space, termed as "social cloud," can be provided via the cloud. Storage clouds enhance the lifespan of storage-constrained devices and enable access to data at any time and from any place. Mobile Internet users have access to a wide range of social networking sites. They use such sites to contact one another and to share various sorts of vital information. A large number of people access one site at the same time; the volume of data is quite large. It is referred to as "big data," and it must be kept safe. The application server routes data from the web to the cloud server.

- Mobile multimedia storage: Mobile phone usage is rapidly increasing, and as a result, the worth of the cell databases has increased. This sort of database is known as a mobile database system, and it keeps a huge quantity of information and data in the cloud, which is accessible over the Internet. A multimedia database includes video, images, audio, and text. As a result, it needs a significant quantity of storage capacity as well as high-speed data transport. This kind of database is known as "mobile multimedia storage." MMS has a variety of uses. The necessary information from mobile multimedia storage may be accessible over the internet at any time and from any location. By inputting the required URL into the browser, the data may be quickly retrieved. These data are also well protected by the user's password as well as various other network security techniques.

4 Energy Efficient Techniques

4.1 Energy Efficiency of Mobile Devices

- Resource efficiency – To save energy, data must be offloaded from intelligent phone devices to the cloud; yet, transferring data is not always more energy efficient than local mobile phone computations. As a result, techniques have been developed to determine whether or not to offload the data. One of these methods focuses primarily on energy efficiency (EE) and spectrum efficiency (SE). To decrease energy usage and decrease the time of completion, the authors in [9] use an energy-efficient dynamic offloading and resource scheduling (eDors) strategy.
- Dynamic Voltage Frequency Scaling (DVFS) – The authors in [10] explores using the concurrent wireless information and power transfer (SWIPT) approach to solve a multi-user computational offloading problem for mobile-edge cloud computing, in which energy-limited mobile devices (MDs) collect energy from the ambient radio-frequency (RF) signal.
- System level and process level offloading – Boukerche et al. [11] defined two forms of offloading: system level and process level offloading. MCC design is evaluated in such a way that energy overhead can be decreased and execution efficiency can be increased. Overhead is obvious owing to the allotted nature of MCC since the cloud may do computations comparable to the cellular customer requests and handles a request packet, most likely concurrently.

4.2 Limited Battery Lifetime of Mobile Devices

Battery capacity is one of the most difficult and challenging aspects of mobile devices. There are several options available, two of which considered in this chapter are: static partitioning and an energy-efficient computational offloading framework (EECOF).

- Static Partitioning: Mobile phones are not as strong as personal computers in MCC because personal computers execute or run more customizable programs, which mobile devices cannot do owing to their restricted battery life. Offloading information to the server is critical for extending the battery capacity of smart phones, which is sometimes inconvenient due to communication overhead and consumption of a lot of energy.

MCC conserves energy by outsourcing the infrastructure to the cloud, however due to cloud power limitations, it is unable to offload the whole data set to the cloud at once. The cloudlet idea is utilised to boost MCC's performance. It takes into account the network type and the distance among cloud server and mobile devices, both of which have an influence on the consumption of power of offloading of applications. Cloud-based services that make use of virtual computers near to the

Cloudlets to enhance management of applications, and process a large quantity of applications compared to the application that was previously processed. The factors that impact mobile device energy consumption are classified as workload, mobile device and communication network.

- Energy-Efficient Computational Offloading Framework (EECOF): Vinh et al. [4] proposed the idea of MCC energy conservation, which leads to lower power consumption of mobile devices, when compute resources in mobile devices are restricted, as well as the need to transfer the software to a more resource-rich environment, such as the cloud, and then run the cloud applications and transmit the results back to the mobile gadgets to minimise utilization of energy and improve battery life. They suggested an EECOF for MCC that is distributed. This system transfers the processing intensive application to the cloud during runtime. As a result, when the application is offloaded to the cloud, the data transfer rate and battery efficiency of mobile devices are lowered.

To offload data to the cloud, a dynamic resource provisioning scheduler is utilised, decreasing energy consumption in processing and transfer. For adaptive resource management, scheduling may be performed using internet-based virtual data. When smart mobile devices attempt to use a face finder and take into account the data transfer delay, energy consumption increases.

- Application Layer Adaptive Transmission Protocol: Liu et al. [12] introduced AppATP with the objective of enabling energy-efficient communication among mobile sources and the network. The following two examples demonstrate the importance of AppATP: Firstly, the electricity demand in transmitting is impacted by the unpredictable nature of the wifi network; this is connected to wireless instability. Scaling in mobile devices demonstrates that a lot of energy is wasted during poor connectivity and a portion of the energy is used during good connectivity. Second, many mobile apps, such as YouTube and Netflix, are delay tolerant. AppATP makes advantage of the cloud to regulate distribution by supplying cloud services. In order to plan mobile app data delivery, it delays applications files in the database before transmitting it to mobile devices. This is excellent for a variety of delay-tolerant tasks. In this manner, one can address the issue of mobile device battery life.

4.3 Resource Scheduling

Resource scheduling techniques (RSA), which try to correctly allocate cloud-based offsite services to resource-intensive mobile app components, are a key component of MCC systems.

- Algorithms based on DVS: DVS is a revolutionary technique used in current smart devices to save energy usage by changing the server's input frequency and voltage. Multiple voltages are configured for the CPU using DVS, and each operation is executed using the level of voltage that uses the least resources. The schedulers are in charge of three primary duties: (a) finding the best execution order, (b) allocating the best voltage level to each job, and (c) guaranteeing that certain functions are done within the time restrictions. Relying on the DVFS approach and the whale optimization algorithm, an efficient task workflow scheduling strategy for mobile devices is suggested in [13]. The authors in [14] assume a smartphone app with many jobs, each with its own amount of effort and data input/output. Their goal is to reduce mobile costs by utilising both energy and time to do all activities. To begin, they use voltage scaling to reduce the cost of mobile compute. Then, to decrease wireless transmission, they utilise data compression to lower the quantity of data to communicate.

- Algorithms based on AI: Approaches based on artificial intelligence (AI) emulate nature in order to arrange work among resources. Genetic Algorithm (GA), Fuzzy Logic, and Hybrid algorithms are among the most often used AI-based approaches in scheduling tasks and energy saving in MCC. The authors of [15] proposed a neuro-fuzzy machine learning approach be used to forecast HELLP syndrome, the most difficult hypertensive illness in pregnancy. This classifier serves as an inference engine for cloud-based mobile apps, enabling for quick evaluation of symptoms reported by pregnant women. Authors in [15] introduce FUGE, a novel approach that combines fuzzy logic concepts with GAs while accounting for implementation cost and time. They boost the effectiveness of the standard GA by inventing a fuzzy-based steady-state GA.

4.4 Task Offloading

Since mobile devices have limited storage and computing capacity, offloading workloads appears to be a potential option. The concept is based on offloading heavy compute work from mobile devices to cloud servers or peer mobile devices in order to overcome the issue of mobile device limits. This method is mostly used to save energy on mobile devices when the application can turn to sleep mode.

The authors in [16] offer a framework for real-time resource allocation. To resolve the problem of allocation of resources in real time and task failure, a task movement record-based particle swarm optimization (MRPSO) technique is presented. Experiments demonstrate that the suggested technique can give an effective solution. The authors of [17] present a unique MCC architecture called Rule Generation based Energy Estimation Paradigm (RG-EEM). To calculate the energy needed for execution of tasks in the local smartphone and cloud, an energy estimation method is utilised. The authors of [18] present an energy-efficient and time-constrained task offloading system based on route restriction, with the objective of reducing smartphone energy consumption while meeting the time limitations of mobile cloud operations. The authors in [19] presents a new Energy-Efficient Cooperative Offloading Model (E2COM) for energy-traffic tradeoff, that can guarantee the equality of mobile phone energy usage, reduce

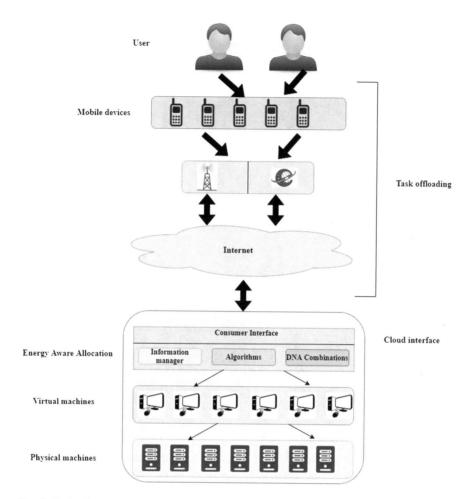

Fig. 3 Task offloading in MCC

computation repetition, and remove Web internet usage duplication via cooperative implementation and information processing results sharing.

Figure 3 shows the task offloading mechanism in MCC.

4.5 Load Balancing

The authors in [20] proposed a new offline load balancing method for managing resources in MCC. K. Singh et al. [21] suggested a novel approach to load balancing for mobile clouds. According to the findings, load balancing through-out the placement of tasks has a significant impact on the CC environment's

Fig. 4 Load balancing in
MCC

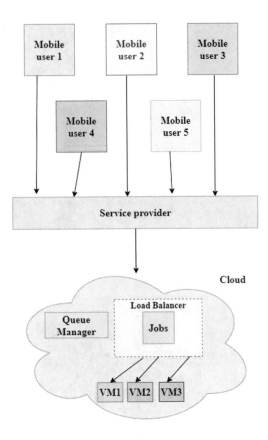

energy consumption. Authors in [22] proposed a unique architecture that needed
a sophisticated load balancer to assign resources effectively in order to increase
application system performance for information and demand response of storage
held by smart phones in a safe way. Authors of [23] suggested adaptive mobile
resource offloading (AMRO) as a method for huge tasks that can be processed
utilising mobile capabilities instead of a cloud server. AMRO is utilised in a MCC
system based on collaborative architecture. Because mobile device resources may
not be constantly accessible in this context, a load balancing solution with efficient
task partition and appropriate job assignment is necessary. Authors of [24] proposed
a multiple contextual managed service planning method to handle a high amount of
device queries, better define customer experiences, and decrease system overheads.
The suggested solution includes a sub problem for optimising mobile user quality
of service and a sub problem for optimising cloud resource allocation. Algorithm
schedules the resources according to the context information.

Figure 4 shows the load balancing mechanism in MCC.

4.6 Resource Provisioning

The notion of MCC enriches and develops mobile phone apps and computation by offering cloud-based infrastructure and utilising resources efficiently. Because cloud computing is a service-oriented computing model, resource provisioning is critical. Resource provisioning refers to the efficient method of scheduling, setting, and supplying resources to users, as well as the method of selecting, developing, deploying, and managing software and hardware resources in order to ensure application performance. One of the key problems in MCC is the effective use of resources; mobile device limits include battery lifetime, processing power, and data storage is overcome by MCC.

- Static resource provisioning: The task or job that has a predicted demand for resources and workloads and typically does not vary in demand for resources or workloads is considered to be static, thus it must employ "static provisioning resources" efficiently. The workloads are given the resources in advance, with no changes. The resources are usually under provisioned as a result of static resource provisioning or it may over-provision.
- Dynamic Resource Provisioning: In dynamic resource provisioning, resources are given on-demand by applications, which may vary or differ depending on their resource or workload demands. With dynamic provisioning, the provider provides more resources as they are required and removes them when they are no longer required. With the cloud's idea of elasticity, dynamic resource provisioning must be able to manage resources in both cloud providers and cloud consumers.

The authors of [25] solves this combined optimization issue. To tackle the problem, an approximation algorithm is presented. [26] provides an adaptive technique for effective resource allocation in mobile clouds that entails anticipating and tracking energy utilizations in a two-dimensional matrix referred to as the resource providing matrix. An impartial authority then uses these resource provisioning matrices to anticipate future resource requirements using an artificial neural network. The authors of [27] suggested an architecture for flexible hybrid mobile cloud service allocation that optimizes to enhance mobile user experience while keeping available resources and user QoS requirements in mind. The authors of [28] offer a resource allocation strategy that is demand state aware and allocates resources depending mostly on the cellular client's current contextual information, such as battery and network reliability. Various stages were used to track the client's condition, including approved, received and processing, filed and paused, restarted, accomplished, denied, and leave.

Figure 5 shows the resource provisioning in MCC.

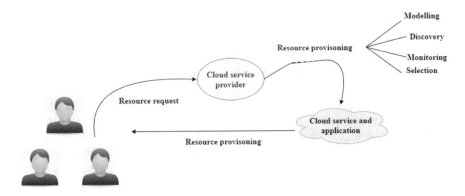

Fig. 5 Provisioning of resources in MCC

5   Research Challenges

(i) The bulk of resource scheduling approaches (RSAs) in MCC are designed to maximise one or two results (parameters), whereas the other specifications are disregarded. When assigning computing resources to heavy activities in MCC, the complexity associated with mobility, wireless connectivity, and heterogeneity necessitates multi-objective optimization.

(ii) MCC is a client-server design, which implies that applications execute on parts on the smartphone and in part on distant cloud-based services. When allocating resources, such designs necessitated end-to-end enhancement rather than targeting system throughput on one endpoint. The majority of resource scheduling approaches (RSA) solutions, on the other hand, handle optimization of time and power or other aspects solely on the device, suggesting that enhancement is ignored on the side of the cloud provider. Cloud negative effects impact resource scheduling in such as data centres, transferred VMs, cloud storage managements, and workload redistribution.

(iii) In most current algorithms that are based on DVS, the voltage switching overhead for increasing or decreasing voltage is disregarded, which imposes extra overhead on scheduling of resources and reduces its adequacy and efficiency. Furthermore, little consideration is given to the sorts of accessible resources. The bulk of solutions focus solely on cloud datacenters, ignoring the resource availability from local cloudlets or mobile devices.

(iv) The variety and complexity of smartphone OS and architectures is one of the problems in the existing compute offloading framework. It is envisaged that Smart Mobile Devices (SMDs) would have constant access to cloud services. A common offloading mechanism for various smartphone platforms remains a difficult challenge in the MCC sector.

(v) Use of cloud infrastructure services entails monetary costs on end customers, who should pay in accordance with the SLA agreed upon with the cloud service provider. In general, content dumping and data transmission across cloud providers impose additional expenses on end users. As a result, economic issues should be considered when making the offloading decisions.

(vi) The existing compute offloading frameworks must still be automated. This will allow the offloading process to be completed in a smooth manner while learning about the surrounding environment. It is not a simple task to achieve such automation.

(vii) Mobility is one of the most significant characteristics of Smart Mobile Devices (SMDs) in MCC. This is due to the fact that mobility and communication autonomy are critical requirements for user satisfaction when using mobile cloud services. However, there are several limitations that impede smooth connectivity and continuous access to cloud services when on the move. When mobile phone users move, the rate in exchange of data and bandwidth of the network may fluctuate. Furthermore, customers may break their link when transferring or receiving data; hence, offloading solutions should include sufficient fault-tolerant mechanisms to resend missing components, minimise response time, and decrease smartphone energy usage. It should be emphasised that for mobile users, the assurance of effective execution of offloaded programs is critical.

Effective approaches for MCC environments are required to: first, meet the demands of mobile CSPs; and second, accessing users to fully utilise MCC benefits such as longer battery life and enhanced storage, flexibility, and consistency.

6 Future Research

Engineering for MCC: MCC engineering studies must focus on how to use very well cost-effective modelling, simulation, verification, and evaluation methods, methodologies, and tools to allow the creation of mobile clouds and customer service. Priority should be given to mobile cloud adaptability, multi-tenanted mobile SaaS, energy-efficient mobile computing, cloud portability, and vulnerability scanning.

Mobile networking for MCC: In mobile clouds, mobile networking comprises a range of wireless networks as well as the Internet. New and revolutionary network protocols, as well as modern telecommunication, should be the primary research priority in the organization of networking to address attractive requirements in energy-efficient links, extensibility in network facilities, and intelligent connectivity among networks, gadgets, and computers.

Mobile foundation and associated innovations: Academic and commercial research have focused on developing effective and user-friendly mobile platforms on mobile devices. As mobile applications get more complex, they may outperform their desktop equivalents in terms of functionality while also being quicker and simpler to use. Two major computer manufacturers (Apple and HP) recognise the potential for huge disruption from a delicate blend of traditional desktop computing with portable devices. Furthermore, several research have been performed in the past to build virtual mobile platforms on clouds to fulfil the various demands of low-end mobile users.

Mobile cyber security in MCC: This domain tackles security challenges and expectations in mobile cloud architectures, communications, systems, and service applications at several levels. Typical areas of attention include mobile information and data security, end-to-end mobile transactions, secure mobile cloud connections, and information assurance and certification on mobile clouds.

Mobile SaaS: According to a recent Forrester research, the mobile SaaS industry will be worth more than $92 billion by 2016. Apple's Mobile Me, Funambol, and Microsoft's LiveMesh are some existing mobile SaaS examples. Exciting research topics on mobile SaaS reference infrastructures and topologies, mobile SaaS platforms and frameworks, applications, and development will arise for large-scale mobile SaaS applications.

Green computing in MCC: In mobile and cloud computing, green computing has been a significant area for research. As stated in [29], energy-efficient computing will be a prominent research subject on mobile clouds in order to handle numerous concerns and difficulties in three areas: (a) green cloud architectures and processors, (b) energy-efficient networking, and (c) energy-saving compute on devices and mobile clients' technologies. MCC is meant to solve the problem of energy efficiency as well as augment the hardware limits in portable devices [30]. According to [31], the component of Smartphones that consumes the most energy is the CPU, with an estimated energy consumption of 500–2000 mW. This suggests that there are extra hidden expenses for mobile users, which may have an impact on the future adoption of MCC. As a result, there is a considerable demand for effective solutions to improve energy efficiency, allowing mobile users to gain the full benefits of MCC [32].

Bandwidth and data transfer: MCC provides a number of advantages, including increased storage capacity and life of battery for mobile devices, which can be achieved by centralised storage and processing at data center. However, as bandwidth use and data transfers have grown, this strategy may result in greater communication overhead [33]. Unfortunately, rising transmission costs may result in extra hidden costs for mobile users and operate as a hurdle among MCC clients and MCC service providers. There is not much attention given to the bandwidth and data transfer in the domain of MCC. As a result, we contend that innovative techniques to optimal bandwidth usage are required to enable MCC customers to fully adopt it cost-effectively.

Data management and Synchronization: Due to the sheer hardware constraints of mobile devices, MCC enables compute off-loading, in which certain calculation duties are shifted to a cloud datacenter. The usage of a suitable data administration system is required for this technique. In addition, cloud datacenters can integrate mobile device apps and data to offer access to data from multiple devices or to recover data after a missed event. In other words, with frequent synchronisation periods, the same trade-off occurs. Furthermore, increasing the frequency of synchronisation intervals results in the restoration of the most recent lost data. Increased bandwidth use, on the other hand, indicates that fewer jobs can be supported and that obsolete data must be restored. As a result, it is critical to understand when to offload compute-intensive jobs and how often synchronisation periods occur. In other words, effective data management and flexible data synchronisation strategies are required in the MCC environment. In the future, further study in these areas of MCC should be conducted.

7 Conclusion

One of the major challenges in mobile computing is energy efficiency, and MCC is intended to address this issue as well as supplement the hardware limitations in mobile devices. MCC has evolved to meet the hardware restrictions of smartphones. MCC helps to inspire mobile users by providing smooth and comprehensive performance that is independent of mobile device resource constraints. MCC has the potential to become the dominant approach for mobile apps in the future. MCC aims to empower mobile users by delivering ubiquitous and robust functionality, independent of mobile device resource restrictions. This chapter provides details about the introduction and architecture of MCC. It covered the applications and characteristics of MCC in different domains. The chapter provides in-depth details about the different energy saving techniques that can be applied at MCC to reduce the energy utilization and concludes with the various research challenges in this domain of MCC.

References

1. Global Mobile Cloud Market | 2021 – 26 | Industry Share, Size, Growth – Mordor Intelligence. https://www.mordorintelligence.com/industry-reports/global-mobile-cloud-market-industry
2. Mobile Cloud Computing Forum. https://www.socialmediaportal.com/Landscape/Mobile-Cloud-Computing-Forum.aspx
3. Raju, D.N., Saritha, V.: A survey on communication issues in mobile cloud computing. Walailak J. Sci. Technol. (WJST). **15**, 1–17 (2016)
4. le Vinh, T., Pallavali, R., Houacine, F., Bouzefrane, S.: Energy efficiency in mobile cloud computing architectures. In: Proceedings – 2016 4th International Conference on Future Internet of Things and Cloud Workshops, W-FiCloud 2016, vol. 2016, pp. 326–331. https://doi.org/10.1109/W-FICLOUD.2016.72
5. Samoylov, A., Borodyansky, Y., Kostyuk, A., Polovko, I.: Mobile-cloud data processing system on digital images. IEEE Int. Conf. Ind. Inf. (INDIN). **2019**, 1674–1678 (2019)
6. Ibtihal, M., Driss, E.O., Hassan, N.: Homomorphic encryption as a service for outsourced images in mobile cloud computing environment. Int. J. Cloud Appl. Comput. **7**, 27–40 (2017)
7. Dubey, G., Verma, A.: Capturing sensor data using mobile cloud computing. Int. J. Comput. Sci. Inf. Technol. **7**, 2385–2389 (2016)
8. Wang, A.: An industrial strength audio search algorithm. In: 4th International Conference on Music Information Retrieval, pp. 27–30 (2003)

9. Guo, S., Liu, J., Yang, Y., Xiao, B., Li, Z.: Energy-efficient dynamic computation offloading and cooperative task scheduling in mobile cloud computing. IEEE Trans. Mob. Comput. **18**, 319–333 (2019)
10. Arroba, P., Moya, J.M., Ayala, J.L., Buyya, R.: DVFS-aware consolidation for energy-efficient clouds. In: Parallel Architectures and Compilation Techniques – Conference Proceedings, PACT, pp. 494–495 (2015). https://doi.org/10.1109/PACT.2015.59
11. Boukerche, A., Guan, S., de Grande, R.E.: A task-centric Mobile cloud-based system to enable energy-aware efficient offloading. IEEE Trans. Sustain. Comput. **3**, 248–261 (2018)
12. Liu, F., Shu, P., Lui, J.C.S.: AppATP: an energy conserving adaptive Mobile-cloud transmission protocol. IEEE Trans. Comput. **64**, 3051–3063 (2015)
13. Peng, H., Wen, W.S., Tseng, M.L., Li, L.L.: Joint optimization method for task scheduling time and energy consumption in mobile cloud computing environment. Appl. Soft Comput. **80**, 534–545 (2019)
14. Zhang, W., Wen, Y., Zhang, Y.J., Liu, F., Fan, R.: Mobile cloud computing with voltage scaling and data compression. In: IEEE Workshop on Signal Processing Advances in Wireless Communications, SPAWC 2017-July, pp. 1–5 (2017)
15. Shojafar, M., Javanmardi, S., Abolfazli, S., Cordeschi, N.: FUGE: a joint meta-heuristic approach to cloud job scheduling algorithm using fuzzy theory and a genetic method. Clust. Comput. **18**, 829–844 (2015)
16. Gu, Z., Takahashi, R., Fukazawa, Y.: Real-time resources allocation framework for multi-task offloading in mobile cloud computing. In: CITS 2019 – Proceeding of the 2019 International Conference on Computer, Information and Telecommunication Systems (2019). https://doi.org/10.1109/CITS.2019.8862120
17. Erana Veerappa Dinesh, S., Valarmathi, K.: A novel energy estimation model for constraint based task offloading in mobile cloud computing. J. Ambient. Intell. Humaniz. Comput. **11**, 5477–5486 (2020)
18. Wang, Y., Wu, L., Yuan, X., Liu, X., Li, X.: An energy-efficient and deadline-aware task offloading strategy based on channel constraint for Mobile cloud workflows. IEEE Access. **7**, 69858–69872 (2019)
19. Song, J., Cui, Y., Li, M., Qiu, J., Buyya, R.: Energy-traffic tradeoff cooperative offloading for mobile cloud computing. In: IEEE International Workshop on Quality of Service, IWQoS, pp. 284–289 (2014). https://doi.org/10.1109/IWQOS.2014.6914329
20. Herbert Raj, P., Ravi Kumar, P., Jelciana, P.: Load balancing in mobile cloud computing using bin packing's first fit decreasing method. Adv. Intell. Syst. Comput. **888**, 97–106 (2019)
21. Singh, K.: Energy efficient load balancing strategy for mobile cloud computing. Int. J. Comput. Appl. **132**, 6–12 (2015)
22. Cushman, I.J., Al Sadi, M.B., Chen, L., Haddad, R.J.: A framework and the design of secure mobile cloud with smart load balancing. In: Proceedings – 5th IEEE International Conference on Mobile Cloud Computing, Services, and Engineering, MobileCloud 2017, pp. 205–210 (2017). https://doi.org/10.1109/MOBILECLOUD.2017.41
23. Kim, B., Byun, H., Heo, Y.A., Jeong, Y.S.: Adaptive job load balancing scheme on mobile cloud computing with collaborative architecture. Symmetry. **9**, 65 (2017)
24. Chunlin, L., Xin, Y., Yang, Z., Youlong, L.: Multiple context based service scheduling for balancing cost and benefits of mobile users and cloud datacenter supplier in mobile cloud. Comput. Netw. **122**, 138–152 (2017)
25. Yao, J., Ansari, N.: QoS-aware fog resource provisioning and Mobile device power control in IoT networks. IEEE Trans. Netw. Serv. Manag. **16**, 167–175 (2019)
26. Sood, S.K., Sandhu, R.: Matrix based proactive resource provisioning in mobile cloud environment. Simul. Model. Pract. Theory. **50**, 83–95 (2015)
27. Chunlin, L., Min, Z., Youlong, L.: Elastic resource provisioning in hybrid mobile cloud for computationally intensive mobile applications. J. Supercomput. **73**, 3683–3714 (2017)
28. Durga, S., Daniel, E., Leelipushpam, P.G.J.: A novel request state aware resource provisioning and intelligent resource capacity prediction in hybrid mobile cloud. J. Ambient. Intell. Humaniz. Comput. **2021**, 1–14 (2021). https://doi.org/10.1007/S12652-021-03093-0

29. Chandrasekar, A., Chandrasekar, K., Ramasatagopan, H., Rahim, R.A.: Energy conservative mobile cloud infrastructure. Lect. Notes Comput. Sci. (Including Subseries Lecture Notes in Artificial Intelligence and Lecture Notes in Bioinformatics). **7296**, 152–161 (2012)
30. Cui, Y., Ma, X., Wang, H., Stojmenovic, I., Liu, J.: A survey of energy efficient wireless transmission and modeling in mobile cloud computing. Mob. Netw. Appl. **18**, 148–155 (2012)
31. Smartphone Energy Consumption. Pete Warden's blog. https://petewarden.com/2015/10/08/smartphone-energy-consumption/
32. Zeadally, S., Khan, S.U., Chilamkurti, N.: Energy-efficient networking: past, present, and future. J. Supercomput. **62**(3), 1093–1118 (2011)
33. Fernando, N., Loke, S.W., Rahayu, W.: Mobile cloud computing: a survey. Futur. Gener. Comput. Syst. **29**, 84–106 (2013)

Multi-criterial Offloading Decision Making in Green Mobile Cloud Computing

Avishek Chakraborty, Anwesha Mukherjee, Soumya Bhattacharyya, Sumit Kumar Singh, and Debashis De (ID)

1 Introduction

The rapid growth and advancement in mobile communication and computing has increased the number of mobile users as well as their demand. The users' demands are not only limited to the voice call, message service and surfing Internet, but also access several applications. Many of these applications require high resource configuration of the device as well the execution of exhaustive applications drains the battery life of the handheld mobile devices. Usually, the mobile devices suffer from resource constraints in terms of computation, storage capacity, battery life etc. In such a circumstance, execution of resource-intensive and sophisticated applications such as recognition of speech/face/object, augmented reality, natural language processing etc., inside the mobile device is quite difficult. To resolve this problem as well as to meet the user demand, the concept of Mobile Cloud

A. Chakraborty (✉)
Department of Engineering Science, Academy of Technology, Adisaptagram, West Bengal, India

A. Mukherjee
Department of Computer Science, Mahishadal Raj College, Mahishadal, Purba Medinipur, West Bengal, India
e-mail: anweshamukherjee@ieee.org

S. Bhattacharyya
Narula Institute of Technology, Agarpara, West Bengal, India
e-mail: soumya.bhattacharyya@nit.ac.in

S. K. Singh
University of Essex, Colchester, UK
e-mail: ss20727@essex.ac.uk

D. De
Department of Computer Science and Engineering, Centre of Mobile Cloud Computing, Maulana Abul Kalam Azad University of Technology, West Bengal, Nadia, India

© The Author(s), under exclusive license to Springer Nature Switzerland AG 2022
D. De et al. (eds.), *Green Mobile Cloud Computing*,
https://doi.org/10.1007/978-3-031-08038-8_4

71

Computing comes, which offers offloading facilities to the users [1–3]. In mobile cloud offloading (MCO) the user is able to offload data as well as computation inside the remote cloud servers [4, 5]. In computation offloading, the computation-intensive tasks are migrated from mobile device to the cloud, and after execution the result is sent to the mobile device. The motivation of MCO is to overcome the resource limitation of the mobile device and saves its battery life by reducing the energy consumption. However, the communication with the cloud also requires energy consumption. In this perspective, the decision making regarding whether to offload or not, and if offload then whether to fully or partially offload the application, these queries appear. Suppose, a mobile device has to offload a computation C, the energy consumption to offload C including the energy consumption in communication is E_{offc} and the energy consumption to locally execute E_{locc}, then it has to predict whether $E_{offc} < E_{locc}$. If $E_{offc} < E_{locc}$, then offloading is beneficial with respect to energy consumption of the device. Similarly, latency is another important parameter especially for time critical applications. The communication with cloud also induces some latency. Therefore, the total latency in offloading a computation C (including communication) is if denoted by L_{offc} and the latency in locally executing C is L_{locc}, then it has to predict whether $L_{offc} < L_{locc}$. If $L_{offc} < L_{locc}$, then offloading is beneficial with respect to the latency. Similarly, few applications require partial offloading with respect to the latency or energy consumption, in that case which portion will be offloaded and which portion will be locally executed, the decision is significant. Moreover, connection interruption is another major issue while communicating with remote cloud and the device is a mobile device. Mobile network environment also plays an important role on the performance of offloading as mobile users because of their movement come under dynamically changing network situations. Nowadays, fog/edge computing has come to the scenario which brings the facility of offloading, partial processing closer to the mobile device [6–8].

The conventional cloud applications such as iCloud, Siri are successful, for mobile devices there are several difficulties because of the response time of communication at the network edge. If the network connectivity is not good, offloading cannot be beneficial [4]. As the communication overhead is involved, the energy consumption and latency can be higher in case of offloading in few circumstances. Hence, several issues arise while making decision, for example, whether to fully or partially offload, if partially then which portion to offload, where to offload. Thus, the decision-making regarding offloading is a difficult at runtime unless there is a clear conception about the current and near-future network conditions. In [9, 10] the authors have used thematic taxonomy and analysed the critical aspects and implications of offloading methods while employing in MCC. The heterogeneity in mobile and cloud computing and wired and wireless networking have been studied in [11] along with its impact on decision making regarding offloading. To bring the cloud resources closer to the user the concept of cloudlet has come [12]. Cloudlet is a computer or a set of computers which store the cache copies of the data already available in the cloud. The cloudlet acts as an agent between the mobile device and cloud. The users can offload their computation to the nearby cloudlet. In [13] a power and latency-aware offloading strategy has been proposed where an optimum cloudlet is selected among multiple nearby cloudlets to provide offloading at optimal latency and power consumption of the mobile device. The concept of fog computing has been introduced for performing the data processing inside the intermediate devices between the end node and cloud instead of performing entire processing inside the cloud [14, 15]. In [16] the use of fog device for computation offloading has been discussed. Edge computing has brought the resources at the network edge to make the system faster [17, 18]. The authors in [19] have provided a comparison between MCC and MEC to demonstrate that MEC reduces the latency, however, it has comparatively less computational and storage resources than MCC. In [20] the authors have discussed on MEC architectures as well as computation offloading. From the discussion regarding various existing offloading approaches, it is observed that the research is majorly focused on resource heterogeneity, communication overhead and offloading decisions. For latency and energy-efficient offloading decision making has to consider various factors such as resource heterogeneity, network connectivity, network capacity, and amount of computation and communication. In this chapter we discuss on these factors for multi-objective decision making regarding offloading.

2 Aspects of Decision-Making Regarding Offloading

An overview of the offloading framework is presented in Fig. 1. When a request of offloading arises, the profiling module is used to accumulate the network characteristics and resource information about the mobile device [4]. The network profiler collects information regarding whether the mobile device is connected to the internet or not, and the network bandwidth. The program profiler collects the application characteristics such as the size of data, memory usage and network bandwidth. The energy profiler collects the characteristics regarding the energy consumption of the mobile device through hardware and software monitors [4, 21]. The decision regarding offloading depends on the selected cost criteria such as monetary cost, energy, latency or storage which need to be minimized, or the security, performance, robustness which are required to be maximized [4, 22]. Based on the accumulated information, the decision-making module takes the decision regarding offloading with respect to the metrics which need to be minimized or maximized. After that the partitioning module divides the application into local and remote parts. This partitioning process can be static or dynamic. The local part is executed inside the mobile device, and the remote part is offloaded [4, 23]. The cloud discovery module is used to select the cloud service for offloading [4]. When the network connectivity is good, network bandwidth is good and the computation is resource-intensive, then the offloading can be beneficial from the perspective of latency and energy consumption of the mobile device [4, 24]. The remotely executed classes can interact with the locally executed classes. After completion of remote execution, the results are sent to the mobile device. Selection of the appropriate offloading target i.e., cloud/cloudlet/edge/fog device is also an important challenge with respect to latency, energy consumption etc.

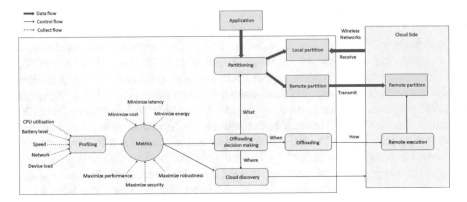

Fig. 1 Offloading service system framework

Offloading provides the facility of migrating exhaustive computation from the mobile devices to the remote cloud servers or nearby cloudlets. Nevertheless, several issues are there, which we discuss as follows [4].

- **Resource heterogeneity:** A number of mobile devices are there with various types of resources. Similarly, different cloud service providers are also there who offer various services, infrastructures, platforms, different communication technologies [4]. Hence, there exists resource heterogeneity in terms of mobile devices as well as cloud service providers. Various types of mobile devices are there like mobile phone, tablet, laptop etc. The mobile phones also differ in terms of their operating system, memory capacity, processing speed etc. The mobile devices are connected with the Internet either through the cellular network or through Wi-Fi. In edge computing scenario, the edge server is attached with the cellular base station and for WLAN the cloudlet can be used [17]. Various cloud service providers exist. Moreover, the cloud resources also vary [4], the user can offload to the remote cloud to a nearby cloudlet/edge server/fog device. If the mobile device does not have enough resources to locally execute an application, then offloading can provide a solution.
- **Complexity of applications:** A resource-exhaustive mobile application may contain a number of tasks some of which are locally executable and rests are to be offloaded [4]. In such a case, instead of offloading the entire application, it needs to be decided which tasks will be locally executed and which tasks to be offloaded, depending on the minimum response time, minimum energy consumption etc. Moreover, there exists various types of mobile applications like delay-tolerant or delay-sensitive applications may have different amounts of communication and computation costs.
- **Network connectivity:** Network connectivity is another issue that has a significant effect on offloading decision [4]. Due to the heterogeneous wireless interfaces with different bandwidth and latency, mobility of the device and availability of cloud resources, the unstable and intermittent connectivity may

exist. In such a scenario, offloading may result in high latency and high energy consumption. Moreover, the offloading process may be interrupted if the device moves beyond the network coverage. Therefore, in such cases if possible local execution of the application may be beneficial. Therefore, in case of good network connectivity and high data rate, offloading may be advantageous whereas in case of intermittent and unstable network connectivity with low data rate local execution may be fruitful.

- **Data transmission:** In offloading the data is divided into three parts: (a) input data amount during the task offloading, (b) communication data amount between the requesting node and the executing node (cloud/cloudlet/fog/edge device), and (c) the output data obtained after execution of the task [4]. Transmission of large amount of data e.g., large database of audio, video file, will result in high communication cost. In such a case, offloading may not be advantageous. Therefore, amount of data to be transmitted is another significant parameter while making decision regarding offloading. Hence, offloading decision should consider when the offloading will be performed and how effectively the data will be transmitted, with respect to minimum latency, minimum energy consumption etc.

Thus, optimal decision regarding remote and local executions of the tasks should be made considering the energy consumption, response time and network status. To minimize energy consumption, enhancing application performance, offloading decisions may consider when, what and where to offload. Fruitful offloading decisions should consider: whether fully offload or partially offload an application, if partially then which tasks to be locally executed and which tasks will be offloaded, how much data to offload, where to offload i.e., cloudlet, cloud, edge device or fog device, when to offload etc.

The main objectives of offloading are summarized as [4]:

- *Reduce Response Time:* The response time is determined as the difference between the time stamps of sending the application for offloading and receiving the result after execution. For mobile applications especially hard deadline applications the response time is highly significant. Reduction in response time is a major objective in offloading. If large amount of computation is required, the mobile device's limited resource may not be enough to execute, or if able then also the time consumption may be high due to limited resource and processing ability of the mobile device. In such a scenario, offloading to the cloud/cloudlet/edge/fog device may reduce the time consumption and improves the performance.
- *Reducing Energy Consumption:* The mobile device's energy consumption during offloading is another important aspect. The comparison between the energy consumption of the mobile device during local execution of an application and during offloading of the same application are required to estimate and evaluate the trade-off between them to optimize the energy consumption of the mobile device. In this case offloading will be considered if energy consumption of the mobile device is less compared to local execution of the application.

Battery life of a mobile device is limited and saving battery life is another important aspect. Minimization of energy consumption will save the battery life of the device.

- **Reducing response time as well as energy consumption:** Reducing the response time as well as energy consumption is a crucial objective of offloading. Sometimes reduction in energy consumption may affect the response time or vice versa. But to achieve both at the same time is a vital aspect. The trade-off between the mean response time and mean energy consumption is studied and this is a non-trivial multi-objective optimization problem.

3 Decision Making Regarding Offloading: When, What, Where and How to Offload

To make fruitful decision regarding offloading four factors have to consider: When, What, Where and How to offload.

3.1 When to Offload

To make decision regarding when to offload three following issues will be considered.

- **Communication vs. Computation:** The offloading can reduce the energy consumption and response time. The offloading is beneficial only if the local execution cost is higher than offloading, and this decision depends on time and/or energy saving. The time in offloading is calculated as the sum of the computation time on the cloud and data transmission time. If this time is less than the local execution time, the decision of offloading is beneficial with respect to time saving. Mathematically, we can represent it as follows:

$$T_{mob} > \frac{T_{mob}}{F} + \frac{D_t}{B} \tag{1}$$

where T_{mob} is the local computation execution time, F is the speedup factor that denotes how much higher the execution speed of the offloading node is compared to that of the mobile device, B is the network bandwidth, and D_t is the amount of data transmission during offloading. From Eq. (1) we can say that if D_t is low i.e., small amount of data transmission takes place, the network bandwidth B is high, and F is large i.e., the execution speed of the offloading node is much higher than the mobile device.

The offloading will be beneficial with respect to energy saving if the energy consumption of the mobile device during offloading is less than the energy consumption of the mobile device to locally execute the application. This is mathematically represented as follows:

$$P_{mob}T_{mob} > P_{id}\frac{T_{mob}}{F} + P_t\frac{D_t}{B} \tag{2}$$

where P_{mob} is the power consumption of the mobile device per unit time while executing computation, P_{id} is the power consumption of the mobile device per unit time in idle mode, P_t is the power consumption of the mobile device per unit time in data transmission/reception mode, T_{mob} is the local computation execution time, F is the speedup factor that denotes how much higher the execution speed of the offloading node is compared to that of the mobile device, B is the network bandwidth, and D_t is the amount of data transmission during offloading. Usually, offloading of exhaustive application saves energy consumption but for all applications offloading may not provide energy-efficiency. This depends on the computation and communication costs. The decisions will be taken depending on the ratio of communication and computation required for the application, distributing into three sections: never offload, trade-off and offload. When computation required is small with respect to the communication, then it is better not to offload. When computation required is large with respect to the communication, then it is better to always offload.

- *Interrupted vs. Uninterrupted Service:* Due to intermittent and unstable network connectivity, the offloading process may failure. Due to the user mobility and heterogeneous wireless network environment, the network connectivity is a major issue. When a device gets disconnected due to its movement beyond network's coverage area or if the connection is dropped due to poor status of the network, then offloading will result in performance degradation and the request may be dropped. On the other hand, the cloud servers may be unreachable due to data centre downtime, in such a case the cloud servers will be unable to provide the service.
- *On-the-Spot vs. Delayed Offloading:* When a network connection is present, all traffic is offloaded, regardless of the quality of the network. This is referred as on-the-spot offloading. In delayed offloading, when a high-quality network is available, then the offloading process will start. If no suitable network is available, then the offloading process may be delayed up to a given deadline. For delay-tolerant applications, response time may be less critical, whereas for delay-sensitive applications, response time is a critical factor.

3.2 What to Offload

Mobile applications are usually divided into fine-grained and coarse-grained tasks, which contains sequential and parallel components. In such a scenario, offloading a whole application may not be beneficial, rather partial offloading may be fruitful. In case of partial offloading, which tasks will be locally executed and which tasks will be offloaded, this decision making is crucial. The tasks are classified into two types based on the place of execution [4]:

- *Locally executable tasks:* There are some tasks for which transmission of data consumes much time and energy, and local resources will also be required for their execution. Sometimes, security is another important aspect which requires local execution rather than offloading to another node. For such kind of tasks local execution is preferable. In case of local execution, no communication cost is involved as data transmission to the cloud/cloudlet/edge/fog node is not required. However, for local execution the battery power of the device is consumed.
- *Offloadable tasks:* Few tasks are there which can be locally processed or can be offloaded. For these tasks it is quite difficult to decide whether offloading or local execution is beneficial. In such cases, the communication costs between the requesting device and offloading node (cloud/cloudlet/edge/fog device) will be considered to make decision regarding whether to locally execute or offload. The offloading decisions will depend on response time, energy consumption, network availability etc. According to the results of the dynamic optimization problem, the decision regarding offloading is to be taken.

To minimize the total execution cost, the execution of the application has to be divided between the local and remote sides. Application partitioning is a method that decides which part of the computations will be offloaded and which part will be locally executed. The more accurate and lightweight profiling information helps to take more accurate decision with lower overhead. Application partitioning can be done statistically as well as dynamically discussed as follows:

- *Static partitioning:* In this case, it has to determine earlier which parts of an application will be offloaded and which parts will be locally executed, based on the contextual parameters such as size of the data, battery level, channel state, computational intensity of each part, latency related constraints etc. The communication and computation costs are estimated earlier and based on the information the optimal portioning of offloading is decided. The communication cost depends on the transmitted amount of data and network bandwidth. The computation cost depends on the computation time. The benefit of static partitioning is that the overhead during execution is very low and applicable to a static number of partitions. Nevertheless, it performs well only if the offloading decision related parameters are predicted or known earlier.
- *Dynamic partitioning:* The resource requirement for a task may change in the user-defined objectives such as battery consumption, response time etc. The resource availability also may change at the service nodes such as memory, CPU power, file cache etc. and at the wireless network such as latency, bandwidth etc. Hence, optimal decisions regarding partitioning are to be taken dynamically during runtime to adjust with varying network conditions, delay related constraints, server state etc. In case of variability in wireless channel,

the dynamic partitioning method is more applicable. However, this scheme has higher signalling overhead, that has to be controlled.

While optimizing the energy usage and execution time for an intended communication and communication environment, Clone Cloud uses dynamic profiling and static analysis together to automatically divide applications at a fine granularity [25]. However, in offline pre-processing this method considers only limited input and requires to be bootstrapped for every new application built. For applications executing on various types of devices in diversified environments, dynamic partitioning of applications has been discussed in [26, 27]. In Think Air smart phone virtualization in the cloud has been discussed and method-level computation is provided [28]. In Think Air multiple virtual machine (VM) images are used for executing methods parallelly [28]. In [29] calculations are illustrated as graphs. In this case, the vertices can denote computational costs and edges can denote communication costs. The vertices of the graph are divided to divide the calculation among the processors of mobile nodes and cloud servers. Conventional graph partitioning algorithms consider only the weights on the edges of the graph ignoring the weight of each node, hence, cannot be directly applied to the mobile offloading systems. The partitioning methods can be used to identify the offloaded parts to save energy. Each task's energy cost is profiled and based on the results a cost graph is generated. In this graph each node denotes a task and each edge denotes the transmitted data amount between the mobile node and cloud. Lastly, for reducing the energy consumption remote parts are executed inside the cloud. To make appropriate decision of offloading it is required to estimate the energy consumption of the mobile device for offloading tasks to the cloud [30]. MAUI decides at runtime which methods will be remotely executed and achieves best energy saving possible according to the current connectivity status of the mobile device, thus, enables energy-efficient offloading of the mobile code [31]. In [32] the authors have shown that partial offloading can be advantageous than offloading the full application. In [33] the authors found the offloading and integrating points in a call sequence using depth-first search scheme and a linear time searching method, that reduces the partitioning computation on the cloud as well as able to attain low user-perceived latency.

3.3   Where to Offload

With the introduction of edge/fog computing, to select the optimal location to offload has become a crucial issue. Here, we will discuss on multi-criterial decision making, cloudlet-based decision making and hybrid offloading decision making, as follows.

- *Multi-criteria decision making:* For data storage and processing various types of cloud service providers are there, such as Google Cloud Platform, Apple iCloud, Amazon EC2 etc. For offering variety of services, they use proprietary cloud platforms. The offloading of same computation to different clouds may result in different amount of computation within a particular duration due to variation in speed of cloud servers, and variation in communication time due to the availability of cloud resources and the network. Hence, optimal cloud service selection is significant. There are three basic steps in cloud service selection discussed as follows.

- *Matching:* This method finds a list of cloud services which are available as well as functionally match with the service request of the mobile user.
- *Ranking:* This method evaluates and ranks the cloud services based on the Quality of Service (QoS) values and the results of criteria and sub-criteria determination. The criteria can be qualitative or quantitative. The qualitative criteria cannot be measured but inferred usually depending on the user's experience, e.g., security. The quantitative criteria can be estimated using hardware and software monitoring tools, e.g., speed, VM cost, bandwidth etc.
- *Selecting:* Based on the ranked list of cloud services, the optimal cloud service is selected by invoking the decision maker module. The offloading invoker module is triggered to divide the application into remotely and locally executable parts. The former part is offloaded to the selected cloud.

The decision hierarchy contains three layers. The objective of the first layer is to find the optimal one among the available cloud services satisfying the important requirements of the mobile device. In the middle layer various criteria such as cost, availability, bandwidth, security, performance etc. are considered for selecting cloud service. The criteria can be subjective (defined in qualitative/linguistic term) or objective (defined in a quantitative/monetary fashion). In the bottom layer based on the analysis of criteria hierarchy, final decision is made regarding the selection of one of the alternative clouds. For multi-criteria decision making few existing approaches have integrated the analytic hierarchy process and fuzzy method for order preference by similarity to ideal solution (TOPSIS). In the decision making, analytic hierarchy process is used to obtain the weights of the criteria for each cloud service and fuzzy TOPSIS to find out the priorities of the alternative clouds. Hence, in offloading decision making it is required to find out which resource to use and offload tasks to the appropriate server based on the energy and computing need of the task.

- *Cloudlet-based decision making:* For offloading computation nearby cloudlet can also be a good option. Mobile devices can offload their applications to the nearby resource-rich devices to reduce the energy consumption and enhancing the performance. In [34] the authors have introduced VM-based cloudlet with which the mobile device can get connected over a WLAN network to get services at low latency. Cloudlets can use the mobile devices as thin-clients to access the local resources. A mobile cloud middleware has been discussed in [35] that acts as an intermediary between the cloud and the mobile device to deal with the asynchronous delegation of tasks to the cloud and to reduce the time consumed to offload tasks from the mobile device to the cloud.

A generic MCO framework is organized as a two or three-level hierarchy [4]:

- **Two-level offloading:** A mobile node offloads parts of its computation to the cloud through one or more communication networks. This method depends critically on the cloud resource availability and reliable end-to-end communication. It can suffer from low bandwidth and high latency.
- **Three-level offloading:** In this case, instead of the remote cloud, nearby resource-rich middleware such as edge server, fog device, local cloud or cloudlet is used to achieve offloading facility at lower latency and lower battery consumption. The middleware having good internet connectivity is used to offload the application, and then migrated to the remote cloud. As single-hop network is used, the latency is reduced along with battery saving of the mobile device.

The components of an application can be deployed on multiple nodes such as mobile device, cloudlet, and cloud, and there can be multiple offloading destinations. In [36] the authors have discussed on multilevel offloading, where different parts of an application are executed on different nodes to achieve lower latency. Depending on the computational requirements and constraints, it is required to take the offloading decisions.

- **Hybrid offloading decision making:** In mobile edge computing, the network resources are brought at the edge for faster service provisioning [17]. In fog computing the users can offload their computation to the nearby fog device also [16]. In hybrid schemes, it has to decide whether to offload either mobile edge or cloud. In [37] a cloud-assisted mobile edge computing framework has been proposed. In this system the cloud resources have been leased to improve the computing capacity and edge resources have been used to decrease the latency. Based on the heterogeneity of computing resources and tasks, offloading decisions have been made for optimal utilization of cloud resources and balancing the workload between the mobile edge and cloud. For adaptive decision making at runtime, an offloading inference engine [38] can be used, that divides an application dynamically and offloads application part to a nearby edge server/cloudlet/mobile cloud middleware. In few approaches Lyapunov optimization is used to propose an adaptive offloading decision-making method that determines where to execute each task of the application (locally/ cloud/ cloudlet), so that the latency and energy will be reduced.

3.4 How to Offload

The mobile devices are connected with the network through cellular base station (cellular network) or Wi-Fi access point (WLAN). The data transmission methods vary in speed and energy requirements. Hence, it is to determine how to leverage the complementary strength of the cellular networks and Wi-Fi, through the selection of wireless interfaces for offloading. The offloading can be performed statically as well as dynamically, however, the objective is to find the appropriate way to offload. Here, we will discuss on the heterogeneity in wireless environments and queuing model, as follows.

- **Heterogeneous wireless environments:** Mobile devices have multiple wireless interfaces, e.g., cellular network, Wi-Fi, which differ in delay, availability, and energy consumption for data transfer. The cellular interface has higher availability, but the data transmission rate and energy-efficiency are less usually compared to the Wi-Fi interface [4, 39]. In most of research works [40–42], it is assumed that the mobile devices are always under the coverage of a cellular network, whereas the users move in and out of the coverage of a Wi-Fi network depending on the location. In MCO, exhaustive computation is migrated from the mobile device to the resource-rich cloud using the available wireless network (either using a cellular connection or through an available WLAN hotspot). Due to the mobility, the connectivity of the wireless links may be unstable. An intermittent and weak wireless network connectivity affects the offloading and increases power consumption of the mobile device. Hence, how to optimally offload the tasks using different wireless channels is a significant issue.

- **Queuing model:** The mobile device, wireless networks and cloud are denoted as queuing nodes which capture the delay and resource contention of the systems. It is assumed that at the mobile device the job arrives following Poisson process [4]. The average arrival rate is $(l + l_0)$, where l is the rate of offloadable jobs and l_0 denotes the rate of unoffloadable jobs. Using a Poisson process jobs are either locally executed or offloaded to the cloud. The job arrival rate depends on the characteristic of the application. The jobs arriving at a rate of l_0, are unconditionally locally executed, whereas, for the offloadable jobs with arrival rate l, the mobile device selects to offload each job with probability $0 \leq l \leq 1$. If $l = 0$, then all the offloadable jobs are locally executed, and if $l = 1$ all the jobs are remotely executed inside the cloud. There are two dispatchers [4]: one allocates offloadable jobs either to the mobile device or to the cloud, and the other one offloads the jobs either through a WLAN network or cellular network to the cloud. The total cost (response time or energy consumption) consists of local costs (processing some jobs locally) and remote costs (sending rest of the jobs to the cloud and waiting to receive result from the cloud after completion) [4, 43]. The dynamic offloading schemes consider the rise in each queue and modification in metric, whereas the static offloading schemes do not consider the dynamic increase. In [40] the authors have proposed a stochastic model for dynamic offloading using various performance metrics. The non-intermittent offloading schemes use Wi-Fi whenever available, however, switches to cellular interface if no Wi-Fi connection is available [4, 44]. Here, the data transmission takes place continuously while switching between different channels. In intermittent offloading schemes, based on the arrival jobs are assigned to one of the two parallel queues that denote the cellular or Wi-Fi transmission [4]. Data transmission of the Wi-Fi queue may interrupt due to connection loss [45].

4 Multi Criteria Decision Making (MCDM)

Decision making problem plays a necessary role to draw various realistic problems and natural phenomena in distinct zone of modern science, engineering and technology. Decision making problems have been widely studied in the branch of mathematical science, medical science, social science, socio-economic policy setting and engineering for a long time and several theoretical, structural development has been completed and still going on with respect to different characteristics and features.

MCDM/MCGDM qualitative approaches mainly focus on measuring the best choice from a set of finite alternatives depending on finite number of attributes. The preferences across the active attributes and predilection among the instances of a factor is required by MCDM for getting information. The decision maker may characterize the ranking for the attributes on the basis of its priority. For all of the appropriate attributes with maximum degree of acceptance is considered to be most favourable alternative to obtain the main target of the MCDM/MCGDM. Decision makers habitually require ranking of the alternatives which are linked with no adequate and conflicting attributes in MCDM/MCGDM problems. The assessment of a single principle to be guided as optimum choice is used for judging realistic decision making problems, which are normally too much composite and ill-structured. Moreover, unique approaches like that is a generalization of the actual nature of the problem at hand that can be guided to impractical decisions. The instantaneous consideration of all relevant factors which are associated to the problem would be more attractive approach. Enlargement and execution of decision support tools and techniques are dedicated by a modern area of operational research that the MCDM constitutes to deal with complex decision problems linking multiple criteria, aim or objectives of incompatible nature. The decision maker calculates a finite set of alternatives for certain problems, which are identified as discrete MCDM problems, to select the most suitable one and ordering them from the best to the worst choice. Continuous MCDM problems are those in which there are an infinite number of alternatives. Multi-attribute decision making (MADM) skill helps to point out Discrete MCDM problems whereas multi-objective decision making (MODM) techniques are used to identify continuous MCDM problems.

In this current era, utilization of theory of fuzzy set [46] has been incorporated within our research world to study decision making problems when vague information is characterized by "Fuzzy" terms. Fuzzy decision making is employed where solution is achieved by imperfect data. Nowadays, one of the most significant skills to tackle by the researchers in this uncertainty field of research is fuzzy multicriteria decision making model. Here, a survey is created on the latest standing of fuzzy decision-making methods, and these methods are categorized by dividing into few parts based on various techniques. MADM problem is one of the essential research topics nowadays and the decision makers' predilection information is frequently used to rank the most desirable one in fuzzy environment. However, the decision makers' choices fluctuate in form, skills and intensity. A decision maker may state his/her first choice on attributes or alternatives in meticulous way or may not eloquent at all. Decision makers may utilize numerous ways of expressing their choices different from others' views [47]. During analysis of the decision, MADM-based approaches assist the decision maker to decide which significant decisions to commence. The attributes are in general features, qualities, issues, performance indices etc. All of these are assessable features of alternative choices and indicate the decision objective assessment. Also, the attributes should be evidently and unambiguously defined. MADM is broadly employed in the areas of management, military affairs, society, economy, and engineering technology, a diversity of different investment problems, project assessment, work force service etc.

The uncertainty-based MCDM models are utilized to measure alternatives with reference to prearranged criteria through a group of decision makers (MCGDM) or single decision maker (MCDM). Here, appropriateness of criteria vs. alternatives, and the linguistic values which are characterized by fuzzy numbers, is used to calculate weights of each criterion [48]. Assessment of a language of natural or artificial language is performed through a variable, which is known as Linguistic value [49]. Several techniques and methods have been suggested to resolve MCDM problems based on uncertainty [50–54] in different environments playing a key role in mathematical research. Abdullah [55] has represented a summarized report about category in fuzzy MCDM and portrayed some of its original applications. Further, there is an extension of fuzzy set theory and its incorporated new types of uncertain parameters like intuitionistic fuzzy sets [56], neutrosophic fuzzy set [57], Pythagorean fuzzy set [58], type-2 fuzzy set [59], cylindrical neutrosophic set [60] etc. Our main goal is to encapsulate the current research area of fuzzy MCDM and classify the fuzzy MCDM methods, make divisions of publications based on their subject zones, classify the fuzzy MCGDM methods, linguistic terms related MCGDM works and a concrete literature survey of various techniques of decision making models from the page of history. Also, we will like to focus on the recent articles based on different uncertain numbers in engineering fields. Figure 2 presents the different categories of decision making models, and Fig. 3 presents the uncertain parameters.

Different decision making models are discussed as follows.

4.1 Analytical Hieratical Process (AHP)

It was developed in 1971; the Analytic-Hierarchy-Process (AHP) is a MCDM method that assists the decision maker to resolve composite problems containing multiple incompatible and subjective criterions. The main advantage of AHP is its unique hierarchical construction of criteria. It also provides users with a superior focus on specific criteria and sub-criteria to allocate the weights [61]. This hierarchy construction allows AHP to systemize a complex set of queries and separates them into decision making aspects. Estimation of relative significance and integrations

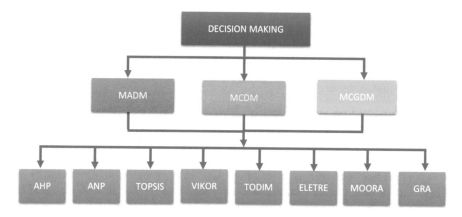

Fig. 2 Categories of decision making models

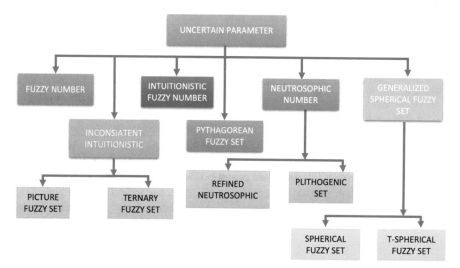

Fig. 3 Uncertain parameters in decision making models

to select the best option are used by AHP methods. The psychological and mathematical ground works employ AHP as a very common theory of measurement scale. Researchers often used this method to compute the ranking of alternatives in fuzzy environment. Liang et al. [62] have used AHP skill in cloud computing fields. Afshari et al. [63] have incorporated it in personal selection problems. The decision making in complex problems are solved by structured approach as proposed by Saaty [64]. Kahraman [65] has manifested AHP in energy evolution. Triangular fuzzy membership functions have been employed along with fuzzy AHP as the first algorithm on its kind by Laarhoven and Pedrycz [66]. Trapezoidal fuzzy numbers along with AHP as majors have been focused by Buckley [67].

Chang [68] has established extent analysis method by employing triangular fuzzy numbers. Arithmetic averaging method has been introduced by Zeng et al. [69] with various scales trapezoidal, triangular, and crisp numbers. Rezaei et al. [70] have manifested supplier selection AHP model in airline retail industry. Ozgen and Gulsun [71] have established multi-facility location problem using fuzzy AHP to modify two objective functions. Jalao et al. [72] has incorporated stochastic AHP method to solve bounded rationality. Deng et al. [73] have developed supplier selection problem using AHP method. Leisure travel industry has used fuzzy AHP in Wang et al. [74] proposal. Computation of five hydrogen storage systems has been incorporated by fuzzy AHP by Gim and Kim [75]. Impact of intellectual capital components has been measured by fuzzy AHP in the proposal of Calabrese et al. [76]. Supply chain performance has been introduced by Jakhar and Barua [77]. Factors affecting commercialization have been covered under the review of Cho and Lee [78]. Hybrid decision making model in the field of public transportation has been developed by Kaya et al. [79]. Fuzzy AHP has been extended into interval type-2 fuzzy sets by Kahraman et al. [80]. Selection problem using Type-2 fuzzy AHP strategy has been introduced by Onar et al. [81]. In order to grip as signing preference problems fuzzy AHP has been expanded into the intuitionistic fuzzy by Xu and Liao [82]. New fuzzy AHP method employing interval type-2 fuzzy set has been incorporated by Abdullah and Najib [83]. The interval-valued intuitionistic relations based MCDM has been focused by Wu et al. [84]. Intuitionistic fuzzy sets along with AHP has been recommended by Abdullah and Najib [85]. Serhat et al. [86] have proposed neutrosophic-based AHP work on safe city selection problem. Basset et al. [87] have introduced trapezoidal neutrosophic-based AHP model. Vafadarnikjoo and Scherz [88] have manifested grey analysis-based AHP model. Bolturk and Kahraman [89, 90] have proposed two works on neutrosophic domain with the help of neutrosophic theory. D. Jun Yi Tey et al. [91] with the help of AHP method have developed stock exchange-based decision making model. AHP model related to learning management has been developed by Radwan et al. [92]. Golden et al. [93] have developed AHP studies and its applications in common sectors. Kwanjira et al. [94] has invented multimodal transportation systems designed by two-Stage model of fuzzy AHP. Bilandi et al. [95] have introduced AHP model in neutrosophic domain for the selection of wireless body area network etc.

4.2 Analytical Network Process (ANP)

Generalization of AHP method is ANP method, Saaty [96] developed ANP in 1996. Hierarchical relationships among decision stages are used to resolve the difficulty of feedback and dependence among the criteria using ANP. Unidirectional hierarchical connections along with dependence and feedback are described by ANP by the inter-relationships between the decision stages and attributes. In general attribute factors of ANP method are dependent on each other. Fuzzy ANP has been incorporated by Büyüközkan et al. [97], in customers' need-based design requirements; Onut et al.

[98] have proposed a fuzzy ANP method in fuzzy TOPSIS to evaluate suppliers. Kahraman et al. [99] have manifested Fuzzy-QFD and a fuzzy optimization model based on integrated framework. To evaluate manufacturing performance, Pourjavad and Shirouyehzad [100] have introduced fuzzy ANP method. Fuzzy ANP has been used for strategic evaluating techniques as proposed by Li et al. [101]. Oztaysi et al. [102] have considered fuzzy ANP as alternative for green energy. The evaluation of supply chain performance has been incorporated by Senvar et al. [103], where a fuzzy DEMATEL and fuzzy ANP approach has been manifested. Tadic et al. [104] have proposed a hybrid model merging fuzzy DEMATEL, fuzzy ANP and fuzzy VIKOR methods for city logistics concept selection. Abdel et al. [105] have introduced neutrosophic based ANP methods in supplier selection problem. Awang et al. [106] have focused on ANP-based work in neutrosophic domain for Investigating Factors. Otayand Kahraman [107] have proposed a new ANP work on neutrosophic domain to tackle decision making. Basset et al. [108] have manifested a useful sustainable supplier selection work on neutrosophic theory.

4.3   Technique for Order of Preferences by Similarity to Ideal Solution (TOPSIS)

Hwang and Yoon [109] introduced TOPSIS in 1981. In TOPSIS technique, vector standardization is used to standardize the decision. Thereafter, within the standardized decision matrix solutions for the ideal and non-ideal are recognized. The results are being identified from a fixed set of alternatives by this method. Here, the longest from the minimal desirable solution and the minimum distance from the positive ideal solution are considered as optimal solution. Possibility theory utilizes TOPSIS method, this has been developed by Ye and Li [110]. Kahraman et al. [111] have manifested fuzzy hierarchical fuzzy TOPSIS method in industrial robotic systems. Chen and Wei [112] have enlarged and described the ranking of each alternative by linguistic terms. The ranking of green suppliers has been done by fuzzy TOPSIS method as proposed by Kannan et al. [113]. Fuzzy TOPSIS has been used by Wang [114] to calculate financial performance of shipping companies. Facility location selection problem has been described by Chu [115] using fuzzy TOPSIS model. Mandic et al. [116] have proposed integrated fuzzy model for crafting financial performance of banks. Fuzziness of the decision-makers has been manifested by Zhang and Lu [117] by integrating fuzzy TOPSIS method. Tsaura et al. [118] have developed a hybrid approach to monitor airline service quality and evaluated it; On hesitant fuzzy set, Liu and Rodriguez [119] have proposed TOPSIS method. Kahraman et al. [120] have dealt with supplier selection problems by comparative study with fuzzy TOPSIS.TOPSIS method has been used by Xu and Zhang [121] as evaluating alternatives. Satisfaction level on transportation has been defined by Celik et al. [122] using a hybrid model. Yue [123] has focused on extended fuzzy TOPSIS related MCDM in intuitionistic fuzzy area. Intuitionistic fuzzy TOPSIS method has been introduced by Joshi and Kumar [124] for portfolio selection problem. Inter valued fuzzy TOPSIS based experimental analysis problem was described by Chen and Tsao [125]. Bottani and Rizzi [126] have developed TOPSIS technique in supply chain management logistic systems. Fuzzy TOPSIS has been incorporated by Bragila et al. [127] to solve criticality analysis problems. Chakravarthi and Shyamala [128] have proposed TOPSIS skill for cloud computing based MCDM problems. Biswas et al. [129] have incorporated neutrosophic based MCDM problems on single- valued set; Ye [130] developed linguistic based MCDM work in neutrosophic area. MCDM problem based on soft neutrosophic set has been implemented by Pramanik et al. [131] using TOPSIS. Biswas et al. [132] have highlighted trapezoidal neutrosophic zone using TOPSIS technique. Giri et al. [133] have developed TOPSIS method by using interval valued trapezoidal neutrosophic area. Elhassouny and Smarandache [134] have solved MCDM problem using combined Simplified-TOPSIS method. Giri et al. [135] have focused on MADM problem in neutrosophic domain. Zeng et al. [136] have computed correlation-based MADM model in neutrosophic theory. Imtiaz et al. [137] have focused on MCDM model in octagonal intuitionistic fuzzy environment. Fahmi et al. [138] have incorporated TOPSIS model in multicellular organism based on trapezoidal neutrosophic cubic set.

4.4 VIekriterijumsko KOmpromisno Rangiranje (VIKOR)

VIKOR method-based decision making article was portrayed in 2002 [139]. Further, VIKOR has been introduced by Opricovic [140] to find a fuzzy compromise solution. The hospital service quality has been evaluated by fuzzy VIKOR method, developed by Chang [141]. Mousavi et al. [142] have focused on a new fuzzy grey analysis MCGDM with uncertain information. Alabool and Mahmood [143] has proposed fuzzy VIKOR method for service quality performance ratings in Taiwan. Risk ranking of mega projects has been focused by Ebrahimnejad et al. [144]. Aydin and Kahraman [145] have manifested fuzzy VIKOR in bus selection in public transportation problem. The performance of supply chains has been measured by utilizing fuzzy AHP and fuzzy VIKOR by Oztaysi and Surer [146]. Tadic et al. [147] have introduced city logistics concept selection. Whaiduzzaman et al. [148] have proposed an extension of VIKOR. Supply chain management problem using VIKOR has been generated by Liu et al. [149]. MCDM problems for decision makers in cloud environment using VIKOR in intuitionistic domain was proposed by Delaram et al. [150]. Suh et al. [151] introduced the concept of evaluation of mobile services using VIKOR. Zavadskas et al. [152] make a survey on MCDM/MADM for economic development. Martin-Utrillas et al. [153] have incorporated the concept of optimal infrastructure selection using VIKOR for sustainable economy. Optimal renewable energy based VIKOR in MCDM problem has been introduced by Yazdani-Chamzini et al. [154]. Evaluation of life cycle sustainability has been performed by encapsulating the VIKOR and AHP by

Ren et al. [155]. Civic and Vucijak [156] have proposed VIKOR for insulation options; Kim and Chung [157] have estimated vulnerability of the water supply. Opricovic [158] has used VIKOR for optimization in civil engineering. Interval-valued intuitionistic fuzzy environment along with extended and described VIKOR method has been explained by Zhao et al. [159]. Intuitionistic fuzzy sets along with VIKOR method have been suggested by Devi [160]. Buyukozkan et al. [161] have developed VIKOR to recognize the most suitable knowledge management tool. Park et al. [162] have incorporated dynamic intuitionistic fuzzy in MADM problems. Hasan and Şahin [163] have focused on MCDM model using Distance Measure. Iltaf Hussain et al. [164] have incorporated a MCDM model in interval valued neutrosophic domain. Huang et al. [165] have introduced MADM neutro-sophic model using VIKOR method. Bausys and Zavadskas [166] have proposed new MCDM model under interval neutrosophic set. Wang and Wang [167] have developed an extended MADM VIKOR method on interval neutrosophic set. Riaz and Tehrim [168] have introduced modified VIKOR method in bipolar neutrosophic area. Pramanik et al. [169] have incorporated VIKOR related MAGDM Strategy using Trapezoidal Neutrosophic number. Supplier selection using entropy measure has been manifested by Shemshadi et al. [170] using fuzzy VIKOR.

4.5   *Tomada de decisaointerativa e multicritévio (TODIM)*

Iterative multicriteria decision making is an abbreviation in Portuguese for TODIM method, which was proposed by Seixas et al. [171]. TODIM is based on prospect theory and it is a MCDM method. Calculation of the dominance degree of each alter-native is the prime idea of the TODIM method by the assistance of the prospect value function to calculate over the remaining ones by Wei et al. [172]. The value function of TODIM of the prospect theory is shaped identical to gain and loss function, this theory has been proposed by Mahmoodi and Jahromi [173]. Dominance degrees for both partial and overall of each alternative have been introduced by Ramooshjan et al. [174] using TODIM to calculate over the other alternatives and henceforth to rank the alternatives. Costa et al. [175] have integrated TODIM method with planning methodology of information system which assigns according to priority. TODIM method has been used by Rangel [176] for determining a reference value and evaluation of residential properties for their rents. Gomes et al. [177] have proposed a TODIM-based method for selecting optimum result for the destination of reservers of the natural gas in Brazil. Gomes et al. [178] have used TODIM and THOR methods for selection of the superior natural gas destination. Gomes and González [179] have discussed the selection of a reference point and simplification of cumulative prospect theory of TODIM method for behavioural decision theory. Uncertainty of MCDM problems has been solved by TODIM method with a fuzzy extension, as discussed by Krohling and Souza [180]. Fuzzy-based TODIM method has been used by Krohling and Souza [181] for residential properties to evaluate rents of properties in Brazil. Fuzzy-based TODIM method has been further extended by Krohling et al. [182] for intuitionistic fuzzy information that is consisted by MCDM problems. Lourenzutti and Krohling [183] have proposed a fuzzy TODIM method that contemplates underlying random vectors and intuitionistic fuzzy information that affects the outcome of alternatives. Enterprise resource planning (ERP) software has been developed by Kazancoglu and Burmaoglu [184] using TODIM method. The criteria interaction is quantified by Choquet integral in TODIM method by Gomes et al. [185]. An extended version of TODIM has been presented by Gomes et al. [186], this method has been applied in a Brazilian city to forecast property values for lease based on Choquet integral. DEMATEL and TODIM methods have been consolidated by Mahmoodi and Gelayol [173] for knowledge management in supply chain networks by deciding the criteria of weights. For interval-valued intuitionistic fuzzy environments, the TODIM method has been outstretched by Krohling and Pacheco [187]. Two-dimensional uncertain semantic information has been handled by Liu and Teng [188] in the decision process by putting forward an extension of TODIM method. The subjective and objective factors are pondered by Uysal and Tosun [189] in TODIM method for solving problem of choosing residential location. Tseng et al. [190] have evaluated green supply chain practices with TODIM method under uncertainty. Passos et al. [191, 192] have used TODIM to decide suitable contingency plans for oil spill situations to significantly help potential users. Hellinger distance in TOPSIS and TODIM methods has been used by Lourenzutti and Krohling [193] for probabilistic distributions of data to help the models for dealing with it without any manipulation. MCDM problems have been used to solve under hesitant fuzzy environment by Zhang and Xu [194]. Salomon and Rangel [195] have presented a comparative study between a fuzzy expert system and TODIM method that has fetched better solutions for TODIM method over fuzzy sets. Sen et al. [196] have introduced TODIM method for grey numbers which was further employed by robot selection problem. Li et al. [197] have presented Intuitionistic Fuzzy TODIM (IF-TODIM) to solve the problem uncertainty of distributer selection. To estimate service innovation in the hotel industry, Tseng et al. [198] have discovered an amalgamated approach based on non-addictive Choquet integral, TODIM method, and fuzzy set theory. An outstretched TODIM method for Pythagorean fuzzy information along with MCDM problems has been proposed by Ren et al. [199], moreover the proposed method has been applied for the governor selection.

4.6   Multi Objective Optimization on the Basis of Ratio Analysis (MOORA)

With the advent of the present decade, researchers across the globe are more interested in MADM, MCDM, MCGDM models in different domains using MUL-TIMOORA technique. In MULTIMOORA methods specific and distinct types of categorizations are developed and applied extensively in various fields. Presently in the decision making problem, Neutro-logic-based MULTIMOORA skill plays a significant role. Brauers and Zavadskas [200] have developed MULTIMOORA technique to assess bank loan optimization. Even in goal programming problem the method has been applied by Deliktas and Ustun [201]. The transition problem of economy has been ignited by Brauers and Zavadskas [202] using MULTIMOORA technique. Based on this technique Datta et al. [203] have proposed robot selection. Based on fuzzy and MULTIMOORA method, Farzamnia and Babolghani [204] have incorporated the supplier selection problem. In health selection problem Liu et al. [205] have manifested MULTIMOORA skill. The MULTIMOORA strategy has been extended with interval numbers in material selection problem by Hafezalkotob et al. [206]. MULTIMOORA technique has been conceptualized by Balezentis et al. [207] based on intuitionistic fuzzy number in an application of performance management concern. Application of several approaches has been proposed by Balezentis and Zeng [208] along with crisp and extended methods, encapsulated by Balezentis and Balezentis [209]. Using MOORA method the risk of failure modes has been proposed by Liu et al. [210]. Using MOORA MCDM method in fuzzy and interval 2-tuple linguistic domain, Liu et al. [211, 212] have described the evaluation of healthcare waste treatment. With hesitant fuzzy numbers, MULTIMOORA has been extended by Li [213], where the author has explained membership degree of elements over a range of various unique values.

4.7   ELimination Et Choix Traduisant la REalit´e (ELECTRE)

Roy & colleagues at SEMA Consultancy Company [214] developed ELECTRE in 1991.ELECTRE is a multifaceted decision making approach that permits decision makers to choose the premium option with imperative priority being the least amount of clash in the function of distinctive criteria. The method of ELECTRE was used while selecting a superior action from a fixed range of actions and later assigned the designation of ELECTRE I. ELECTRE I, II, III, IV and TRI are different deployed version of ELECTRE. According to the category of the decision problem, the methods vary functionally though they are established on the same fundamental concepts [215]. Precisely for selection problems, ELECTRE is used, whereas for assignment problems ELECTRE TRI is employed, and for ranking based problems ELECTRE II, III and IV are applied. The main aim of the method is the apt employment of "outranking relations". Concordance and discordance (C&D) matrices of coordination indices are used to model a decision process enabled by ELECTRE. The finest alternative is selected by the use of latest processed information by the decision maker to analyze outranking relations among various alternatives by C&D indices [216]. ELECTRE III has been developed by Roy [217], and this technique uses fuzzy binary outranking relations. A growth of ELECTRE III multicriteria outranking process has been published by Leyva-López and Fernández-González [218] to assist a set of decision makers with numerous value methods to gain consistence on a group of certain options. Belacel [219] has explained a modern method of fuzzy multicriteria classification, named PRO AFTN, for allocating prebuilt sets by various substitutes. Hatami-Marbini and Tavana [220] have addressed the gap in the literature of ELECTRE for problems consisting of conflict methods of category, variability and indistinctive details, and expanded the method of ELECTRE I to consider the unpredictable, imprecise and semantic assessments. Montazar et al. [221] have thrown light on the construction of a fuzzy logic including both modules and availing fuzzy logic for tackling the unpredictability of the issue. Comparative study between fuzzy ELECTRE and crisp ELECTRE concepts for determination of supplier choosing problem has been defined by Sevkli [222]. After determination of the standard that affected the decision model for selection of supplier, the results of crisp and fuzzy ELECTRE types are explored. Vahdani and Hadipour [223] have stated interval-valued fuzzy ELECTRE method that states objectifies at finding solution for MCDM problems are the weights of norms are unequal (meaning not clear). Split truth/falseness linguistic has been introduced by Bisdorff [224], who has instigated for a several-valued logical proceeding for modelling of fuzzy preferencing. Tolga [225] has established the selection process for projects for the software development industry in multicriteria thinking. Verification of application for academic staff selection has been presented by Rouyendegh and Erkan [226] that uses fuzzy ELECTRE for selection using a model of group decision based on the opinion from the experts. Kaya and Kahraman [227] have proposed an integrated fuzzy AHP-ELECTRE approach for quality assessment methodology for e-banking website. Intuitionistic fuzzy ELECTRE concept proposed by Wu and Chen [228], helps to solve multicriteria decision making problems. Intuitionistic fuzzy ELECTRE for selection of valid location of plant has been manifested by Devi and Yadav [229] under group decision making environment to overcome suddenness of the details provided by decision makers. Chen [230] has invented an ELECTRE-based methodology for outranking the environment of interval of type-2 fuzzy sets within multicriteria group decision making. Chen et al. [231] has developed MCDM problem under hesitant fuzzy within a hesitant fuzzy ELECTRE I (HF-ELECTRE I) method that further has employed it to estimate the environment.

4.8   Grey Relational Analysis (GRA)

The permissible information is unpredictable and inconsistent in many conditions for various criteria, so to select the premium alternative based on grey numbers, a grey possibility degree is explored. For solving the group decision-making problem, this technique is favorable in variable environment [232]. The relational grade for distinct pattern is to scrutinize in the GRA method. GRA employs information to automatically and quantitatively compare each factor from the grey system. The major path of the grey system theory among the present applications is the GRA. Incomplete and uncertain information which are often of poor grade are manifested by GRA. The degree of indistinguishable comparison between the reference sequence and comparability sequence has been signified by the grey relational grade [233]. Deng [234, 235] has set a GRA to treat vagueness issues. Later Rao and Singh [236] have manifested and modified GRA method for decision making procedure and fuzzy supplier selection basis issues. Chen [237] has focused on MADM based grey analysis computation. Olson and Wu [238] have captured GRA model in fuzzy environment. Wu [239] has incorporated supplier selection based grey analysis model. GRA-based MCGDM technique has been proposed by Pramanik and Mukhopadhayaya [240] in intuitionistic fuzzy set circumstances for faculty recruitment. Wei [241] has put forth a GRA mechanism for intuitionistic fuzzy MCDM based problem. Recently, Pramanik and Mondal [242] has come up with GRA for MADM technique in interval in neutrosophic set arena.

Apart from these literature surveys several useful and high impact works [52, 243–249] are also established in decision making domain based on various new techniques in the field of science and engineering.

5   Use of MCDM in Offloading

Several decision making approaches can be utilized to resolve the offloading problem in different scenarios. From the literature survey, we have observed that researchers from different fields have introduced various MCGDM techniques like AHP, ANP, TOPSIS, VIKOR, ELETRE etc. to detect the best alternative in this offloading decision making problems. Now, mainly AHP and ANP models are utilized widely to identify the best alternative of the offloading problem properly in any situation; although other models can also provide fruitful results in different conditions.

6   Conclusion

In this chapter we have discussed about offloading and multicriteria decision making processes. Offloading in mobile cloud computing is a significant aspect as the mobile users may prefer to offload exhaustive computation due to poor battery life and resource limitation of the handheld devices. There are various issues such as resource heterogeneity, communication overhead, intermittent connectivity, user mobility, amount of computation, bandwidth etc. Low latency and low energy consumption of the user device during offloading are major challenge. In this chapter we discuss on various factors for multi-objective decision making regarding offloading, and various MCDM models, which can be applied in offloading.

References

1. De, D.: Mobile Cloud Computing: Architectures, Algorithms and Applications. Chapman and Hall/CRC (2019), Taylor & Francis eBooks
2. Fernando, N., Loke, S.W., Rahayu, W.: Mobile cloud computing: a survey. Futur. Gener. Comput. Syst. **29**(1), 84–106 (2013)
3. Dinh, H.T., Lee, C., Niyato, D., Wang, P.: A survey of mobile cloud computing: architecture, applications, and approaches. Wirel. Commun. Mob. Comput. **13**(18), 1587–1611 (2013)
4. Wu, H.: Multi-objective decision-making for mobile cloud offloading: a survey. IEEE Access. **6**, 3962–3976 (2018)
5. Mukherjee, A., De, D.: Low power offloading strategy for femto-cloud mobile network. Eng. Sci. Technol. Int. J. **19**(1), 260–270 (2016)
6. Aazam, M., Zeadally, S., Harras, K.A.: Offloading in fog computing for IoT: review, enabling technologies, and research opportunities. Futur. Gener. Comput. Syst. **87**, 278–289 (2018)
7. Peng, K., Leung, V., Xu, X., Zheng, L., Wang, J., Huang, Q.: A survey on mobile edge computing: focusing on service adoption and provision. Wirel. Commun. Mob. Comput. **2018**, 1–16 (2018)
8. Ghosh, S., Mukherjee, A., Ghosh, S.K., Buyya, R.: Mobi-iost: mobility-aware cloud-fog-edge-iot collaborative framework for time-critical applications. IEEE Trans. Netw. Sci. Eng. **7**(4), 2271–2285 (2019)
9. Shiraz, M., Gani, A., Khokhar, R.H., Buyya, R.: A review on distributed application processing frameworks in smart mobile devices for mobile cloud computing. IEEE Commun. Surv. Tutorials. **15**(3), 1294–1313 (2012)
10. Abolfazli, S., Sanaei, Z., Ahmed, E., Gani, A., Buyya, R.: Cloud-based augmentation for mobile devices: motivation, taxonomies, and open challenges. IEEE Commun. Surv. Tutorials. **16**(1), 337–368 (2013)
11. Sanaei, Z., Abolfazli, S., Gani, A., Buyya, R.: Heterogeneity in mobile cloud computing: taxonomy and open challenges. IEEE Commun. Surv. Tutorials. **16**(1), 369–392 (2013)
12. Jia, M., Cao, J., Liang, W.: Optimal cloudlet placement and user to cloudlet allocation in wireless metropolitan area networks. IEEE Trans. Cloud Comput. **5**(4), 725–737 (2015)
13. Mukherjee, A., De, D., Roy, D.G.: A power and latency aware cloudlet selection strategy for multi-cloudlet environment. IEEE Trans. Cloud Comput. **7**(1), 141–154 (2016)
14. Mahmud, R., Kotagiri, R., Buyya, R.: Fog computing: a taxonomy, survey and future directions. In: Internet of Everything, pp. 103–130. Springer, Singapore (2018)
15. Yi, S., Cheng, L., Li, Q.: A survey of fog computing: concepts, applications and issues. In: Proceedings of the 2015 Workshop on Mobile Big Data, pp. 37–42 (2015)
16. Mukherjee, A., Deb, P., De, D., Buyya, R.: C2OF2N: a low power cooperative code offloading method for femtolet-based fog network. J. Supercomput. **74**(6), 2412–2448 (2018)
17. Mukherjee, A., De, D., Ghosh, SK., Buyya, R.: Mobile Edge Computing. Springer International Publishing, eBook ISBN: 978-3-030-69893-5, https://doi.org/10.1007/978-3-030-69893-5, Hardcover ISBN: 978-3-030-69892-8 (2021)
18. Abbas, N., Zhang, Y., Taherkordi, A., Skeie, T.: Mobile edge computing: a survey. IEEE Internet Things J. **5**(1), 450–465 (2017)
19. Mach, P., Becvar, Z.: Mobile edge computing: a survey on architecture and computation offloading. IEEE Commun. Surv. Tutorials. **19**(3), 1628–1656 (2017)
20. Mao, Y., You, C., Zhang, J., Huang, K., Letaief, K.B.: A survey on mobile edge computing: the communication perspective. IEEE Commun. Surv. Tutorials. **19**(4), 2322–2358 (2017)
21. Segata, M., Bloessl, B., Sommer, C., Dressler, F.: Towards energy efficient smart phone applications: energy models for offloading tasks into the cloud. In: 2014 IEEE International Conference on Communications (ICC), IEEE, pp. 2394–2399 (2014)
22. Wu, H., Wang, Q., Wolter, K.: Tradeoff between performance improvement and energy saving in mobile cloud offloading systems. In: 2013 IEEE International Conference on Communications Workshops (ICC), IEEE, pp. 728–732 (2013)

23. Wu, H.: Analysis of offloading decision making in mobile cloud computing. PhD dissertation (2015)
24. Flores, H., Hui, P., Tarkoma, S., Li, Y., Srirama, S., Buyya, R.: Mobile code offloading: from concept to practice and beyond. IEEE Commun. Mag. **53**(3), 80–88 (2015)
25. Chun, B.-G., Ihm, S., Maniatis, P., Naik, M., Patti, A.: Clonecloud: elastic execution between mobile device and cloud. In: Proceedings of the Sixth Conference on Computer Systems, pp. 301–314 (2011)
26. Chun, B.-G., Maniatis, P.: Dynamically partitioning applications between weak devices and clouds. In: Proceedings of the 1st ACM Workshop on Mobile Cloud Computing & Services: Social Networks and Beyond, pp. 1–5 (2010)
27. Niu, J., Song, W., Atiquzzaman, M.: Bandwidth-adaptive partitioning for distributed execution optimization of mobile applications. J. Netw. Comput. Appl. **37**, 334–347 (2014)
28. Kosta, S., Aucinas, A., Pan, H., Mortier, R., Zhang, X.: Thinkair: Dynamic resource allocation and parallel execution in the cloud for mobile code offloading. In: 2012 Proceedings IEEE Infocom, IEEE, pp. 945–953 (2012)
29. Hendrickson, B., Kolda, T.G.: Graph partitioning models for parallel computing. Parallel Comput. **26**(12), 1519–1534 (2000)
30. Altamimi, M., Abdrabou, A., Naik, K., Nayak, A.: Energy cost models of smartphones for task offloading to the cloud. IEEE Trans. Emerg. Top. Comput. **3**(3), 384–398 (2015)
31. Cuervo, E., Balasubramanian, A., Cho, D.-k., Wolman, A., Saroiu, S., Chandra, R., Bahl, P.: Maui: making smartphones last longer with code offload. In: Proceedings of the 8th International Conference on Mobile Systems, Applications, and Services, pp. 49–62 (2010)
32. Beraldi, R., Massri, K., Abderrahmen, M., Alnuweiri, H.: Towards automating mobile cloud computing offloading decisions: an experimental approach. In: Proceedings of the 8th International Conference on System Network Communication, pp. 121–124 (2013)
33. Zhang, Y., Liu, H., Jiao, L., Xiaoming, F.: To offload or not to offload: An efficient code partition algorithm for mobile cloud computing. In: 2012 IEEE 1st International Conference on Cloud Networking (CLOUDNET), IEEE, pp. 80–86 (2012)
34. Satyanarayanan, M., Bahl, P., Caceres, R., Davies, N.: The case for VM-based cloudlets in mobile computing. IEEE Pervasive Comput. **8**(4), 14–23 (2009)
35. Flores, H., Srirama, S.N.: Mobile cloud middleware. J. Syst. Softw. **92**, 82–94 (2014)
36. De, D., Mukherjee, A., Roy, D.G.: Power and delay efficient multilevel offloading strategies for mobile cloud computing. Wirel. Pers. Commun. **112**(4), 2159–2186 (2020). https://doi.org/10.1007/s11277-020-07144-1
37. Ma, X., Zhang, S., Li, W., Zhang, P., Lin, C., Shen, X.: Cost-efficient workload scheduling in cloud assisted mobile edge computing. In: 2017 IEEE/ACM 25th International Symposium on Quality of Service (IWQoS), IEEE, pp. 1–10 (2017)
38. Gu, X., Nahrstedt, K., Messer, A., Greenberg, I., Milojicic, D.: Adaptive offloading for pervasive computing. IEEE Pervasive Comput. **3**(3), 66–73 (2004)
39. Shu, P., Liu, F., Jin, H., Chen, M., Wen, F., Qu, Y., Li, B.: eTime: Energy-efficient transmission between cloud and mobile devices. In: 2013 Proceedings IEEE INFOCOM, IEEE, pp. 195–199 (2013)
40. Hyytiä, E., Spyropoulos, T., Ott, J.: Offload (only) the right jobs: robust offloading using the Markov decision processes. In: WOWMOM, pp. 1–9 (2015)
41. Kim, Y., Lee, K., Shroff, N.B.: An analytical framework to characterize the efficiency and delay in a mobile data offloading system. In: Proceedings of the 15th ACM International Symposium on Mobile ad hoc Networking and Computing, pp. 267–276 (2014)
42. Mehmeti, F., Spyropoulos, T.: Stay or switch? Analysis and comparison of delays in cognitive radio networks with interweave and underlay spectrum access. In: Proceedings of the 14th ACM International Symposium on Mobility Management and Wireless Access, pp. 9–18 (2016)
43. Wu, H., Knottenbelt, W., Wolter, K.: Analysis of the energy-response time tradeoff for mobile cloud offloading using combined metrics. In: 2015 27th International Teletraffic Congress, IEEE, pp. 134–142 (2015)

44. Mehmeti, F., Spyropoulos, T.: Performance analysis of "on-the-spot" mobile data offloading. In: 2013 IEEE Global Communications Conference (GLOBECOM), IEEE, pp. 1577–1583 (2013)
45. Wu, H., Wolter, K.: Stochastic analysis of delayed mobile offloading in heterogeneous networks. IEEE Trans. Mob. Comput. **17**(2), 461–474 (2017)
46. Zadeh, L.A.: Fuzzy sets. Inf. Control. **8**(5), 338–353 (1965)
47. Chakraborty, A., Mondal, S.P., Alam, S., Dey, A.: Classification of trapezoidal bipolar neutrosophic numbers, de-bipolarization and implementation in cloud service based MCGDM problem. Complex Intell. Syst. **7**(1), 145–161 (2021)
48. Sohaib, O., Naderpour, M., Hussain, W., Martinez, L.: Cloud computing model selection for e-commerce enterprises using a new 2-tuple fuzzy linguistic decision-making method. Comput. Ind. Eng. **132**, 47–58 (2019)
49. Portmess, L., Tower, S.: Data barns, ambient intelligence and cloud computing: the tacit epistemology and linguistic representation of Big Data. Ethics Inf. Technol. **17**(1), 1–9 (2015)
50. Chakraborty, A., Mondal, S.P., Mahata, A., Alam, S.: Cylindrical neutrosophic single- valued number and its application in networking problem, multi criterion decision making problem and graph theory. CAAI Trans. Intell. Technol. **5**(2), 68–77 (2020). https://doi.org/10.1049/trit.2019.0083
51. Liu, L., Lu, C., Xiao, F., Liu, R., Xiong, N.: A practical, integrated multi-criteria decision-making scheme for choosing cloud services in cloud systems. IEEE Access. **9**, 1–1 (2021). https://doi.org/10.1109/ACCESS.2021.3089991
52. Sun, L., Ma, J., Zhang, Y., Dong, H., Hussain, F.K.: Cloud-FuSeR: fuzzy ontology and MCDM based cloud service selection. Futur. Gener. Comput. Syst. **57**, 42–55 (2016)
53. Haque, T.S., Chakraborty, A., Mondal, S.P., Alam, S.: A new exponential operational law for trapezoidal neutrosophic number and pollution in megacities related MCGDM problem. J. Ambient Intell. Humaniz. Comput. Springer (2021). https://doi.org/10.1007/s12652-021-03223-8
54. Youssef, A.E.: An integrated MCDM approach for cloud service selection based on TOPSIS and BWM. IEEE Access. **8**, 71851–71865 (2020)
55. Abdullah, L., Najib, L.: A new preference scale mcdm method based on interval-valued intuitionistic fuzzy sets and the analytic hierarchy process. Soft Comput. **20**(2), 511–523 (2016)
56. Atanassov, K.: Intuitionistic fuzzy sets. Fuzzy Sets Syst. **20**, 87–96 (1986)
57. Smarandache, F.: A Unifying Field in Logics Neutrosophy: Neutrosophic Probability, Set and Logic. American Research Press, Rehoboth (1998)
58. Garg, H.: Linguistic Pythagorean fuzzy sets and its applications in multiattribute decision-making process. Int. J. Intell. Syst. **33**(6), 1234–1263 (2018)
59. Castillo, O., Melin, P., Kacprzyk, J., Pedrycz, W.: Type-2 fuzzy logic: theory and applications. In: 2007 IEEE International Conference on Granular Computing (GRC 2007) IEEE, pp. 145–145 (2007)
60. Chakraborty, A.: Minimal Spanning Tree in Cylindrical Single-Valued Neutrosophic Arena. Neutrosophic Graph Theory and Algorithms, Chapter-9. ISBN13:9781799813132, (2020). https://doi.org/10.4018/978-1-7998-1313-2
61. Tseng, C.-C., Hong, C.-F., Chang, H.-L.: Multiple attributes decision-making model for medical service selection: an AHP approach. J. Qual. **15**(2), 1–350 (2008)
62. Liang, H., Xing, T., Cai, L.X., Huang, D., Peng, D., Liu, Y.: Adaptive computing resource allocation for mobile cloud computing. Int. J. Distrib. Sens. Netw. **2013**, 1–11 (2013)
63. Afshari, A., Mojahed, M., Yusuff, R.M.: Simple additive weighting approach to personnel selection problem. Int. J. Innov. Manag. Technol. **1**(5), 511–515 (2010)
64. Saaty, T.L.: Decision making with the analytic hierarchy process. Int. J. Serv. Sci. **1**(1), 83–93 (2008)
65. Kahraman, C., Kaya, I.: A fuzzy multicriteria methodology for selection among energy alternatives. Expert Syst. Appl. **37**(9), 6270–6281 (2010)

66. van Laarhoven, P.J.M., Pedrycz, W.: A fuzzy extension of Saaty's priority theory. Fuzzy Set Syst. **11**(1–3), 199–227 (1983) 127
67. Buckley, J.J.: Fuzzy hierarchical analysis. Fuzzy Set Syst. **17**(3), 233–247 (1985) 128
68. Chang, D.-Y.: Applications of the extent analysis method on fuzzy AHP. Eur. J. Oper. Res. **95**(3), 649–655 (1996) 129
69. Zeng, J., An, M., Smith, N.J.: Application of a fuzzy based decision-making methodology to construction project risk assessment. Int. J. Project Manag. **25**(6), 589–600 (2007)
70. Rezaei, J., Fahim, P.B.M., Tavasszy, L.: Supplier selection in the airline retail industry using a funnel methodology: conjunctive screening method and fuzzy AHP. Expert Syst. Appl. **41**(18), 8165–8179 (2014)
71. Ozgen, D., Gulsun, B.: Combining possibilistic linear programming and fuzzy AHP for solving the multiobjective capacitated multi-facility location problem. Inform. Sci. **268**, 185–201 (2014)
72. Jalao, E.R., Wu, T., Shunk, D.: A stochastic AHP decision making methodology for imprecise preferences. Inform. Sci. **270**, 192–203 (2014)
73. Deng, X.Y., Hu, Y., Deng, Y., Mahadevan, S.: Supplier selection using AHP methodology extended by D numbers. Expert Syst. Appl. **41**(1), 156–167 (2014)
74. Wang, Y., Jung, K.A., Yeo, G.T., Chou, C.C.: Selecting a cruise port of call location using the fuzzy AHP method: a case study in East Asia. Tour. Manag. **42**, 262–270 (2014)
75. Gim, B., Kim, J.W.: Multi-criteria evaluation of hydrogen storage systems for automobiles in Korea using the fuzzy analytic hierarchy process. Int. J. Hydrog. Energy. **39**(15), 7852–7858 (2014)
76. Calabrese, A., Costa, R., Menichini, T.: Using fuzzy AHP to manage intellectual capital assets: an application to the ICT service industry. Expert Syst. Appl. **40**(9), 3747–3755 (2013)
77. Jakhar, S.K., Barua, M.K.: An integrated model of supply chain performance evaluation and decision making using structural equation modelling and fuzzy AHP. Prod. Plan. Control. **25**(11), 938–957 (2014)
78. Cho, J., Lee, J.: Development of a new technology product evaluation model for assessing commercialization opportunities using Delphi method and fuzzy AHP approach. Expert Syst. Appl. **40**(13), 5314–5330 (2013)
79. Kaya, I., Oztaysi, B., Kahraman, C.: A two-phased fuzzy multicriteria selection among public transportation investments for policy-making and risk governance. Int. J Uncertainty Fuzziness Knowledge Based Syst. **20**, 31–48 (2012)
80. Kahraman, C., Ertay, T., Buyukozkan, G.: A fuzzy optimization model for QFD planning process using analytic network approach. Eur. J. Oper. Res. **171**(2), 390–411 (2006)
81. Onar, S.C., Oztaysi, B., Kahraman, C., Ozturk, E.: Evaluation of legal debt collection services by using Hesitant Pythagorean (Intuitionistic Type 2) fuzzy AHP. J. Intell. Fuzzy Syst. **38**(1), 883–894 (2020)
82. Xu, Z., Liao, H.: Intuitionistic fuzzy analytic hierarchy process. IEEE Trans. Fuzzy Syst. **22**(4), 749–761 (2014)
83. Abdullah, L., Najib, L.: A new type-2 fuzzy set of linguistic variables for the fuzzy analytic hierarchy process. Expert Syst. Appl. **41**(7), 3297–3305 (2014)
84. Wu, J., Huang, H.B., Cao, Q.W.: Research on AHP with interval-valued intuitionistic fuzzy sets and its application in multi-criteria decision making problems. Appl. Math. Model. **37**(24), 9898–9906 (2013)
85. Abdullah, L., Najib, L.: A new preference scale of intuitionistic fuzzy analytic hierarchy process in multicriteria decision making problems. J. Intell. Fuzzy Syst. **26**(2), 1039–1049 (2014)
86. Aydın, S., Aktas, A., Kabak, M.: Neutrosophic fuzzy analytic hierarchy process approach for safe cities evaluation criteria. Conference: 13th International Conference on Applications of Fuzzy Systems and Soft Computing, At: Warsaw- Poland (2018)
87. Abdel-Basset, M., Mohamed, M., Sangaiah, A.K.: Neutrosophic AHP-Delphi Group decision making model based on trapezoidal neutrosophic numbers. J. Ambient Intell. Humaniz. Comput. **9**, 1427–1443 (2018)

88. Vafadarnikjoo, A., Scherz, M.: A hybrid neutrosophic-grey analytic hierarchy process method: decision-making modelling in uncertain environments. Math. Probl. Eng. **2021**, 1–18 (2021). https://doi.org/10.1155/2021/1239505

89. Bolturk, E., Kahraman, C.: Interval-valued neutrosophic AHP with possibility degree method. Int. J. Anal. Hierarchy Process. **10**(3), 431–446 (2018). https://doi.org/10.13033/ijahp.v10i3.545

90. Bolturk, E., Kahraman, C.: A novel interval-valued neutrosophic AHP with cosine similarity measure. Soft Comput. Fusion Found. Methodol. Appl. **22**(15), 4941–4958 (2018). https://doi.org/10.1007/s00500-018-3140-y

91. Jun Yi Tey, D., et al.: A novel neutrosophic data analytic hierarchy process for multi-criteria decision making method: a case study in Kuala Lumpur stock exchange. IEEE Access. **7**, 53687–53697 (2019). https://doi.org/10.1109/ACCESS.2019.2912913

92. Radwan, N.M., Senousy, M.B., Riad, A.: Neutrosophic AHP multi criteria decision making method applied on the selection of learning management system (2017). viXra

93. Golden, B.L., Wasil, E.A., Harker, P.T.: 'The Analytic Hierarchy Process': Applications and Studies. Springer, Berlin/Germany (1989)

94. Kaewfak, K., Huynh, V.-N., Ammarapala, V., Ratisoontorn, N.: A risk analysis based on a two-stage model of fuzzy AHP-DEA for multimodal freight transportation systems. Access IEEE. **8**, 153756–153773 (2020)

95. Bilandi, N., Verma, H.K., Dhir, R.: AHP–neutrosophic decision model for selection of relay node in wireless body area network. CAAI Trans. Intell. Technol. **5**(3), 222–229 (2020)

96. Saaty, T.L.: Theory and applications of the analytic network process. RWS Publications (2005). Journal of Computer and Communications. **5**(14) (2017)

97. Büyüközkan, G., Ertay, T., Kahraman, C., Ruan, D.: Determining the importance weights for the design requirements in the house of quality using the fuzzy analytic network approach. Int. J. Intell. Syst. **19**(5), 443–461 (2004)

98. Onut, S., Tuzkaya, U.R., Torun, E.: Selecting container port via a fuzzy ANP-based approach: a case study in the Marmara Region, Turkey. Transp. Policy. **18**(1), 182–193 (2011)

99. Kahraman, C., Ertay, T., Büyüközkan, G.: A fuzzy optimization model for QFD planning process using analytic network approach. Eur. J. Oper. Res. **171**(2), 390–411 (2006)

100. Pourjavad, E., Shirouyehzad, H.: Evaluating manufacturing systems by fuzzy ANP': a case study. Int. J. Appl. Manag. Sci. **6**(1), 65–83 (2014)

101. Li, F., Liu, L., Xi, B.: Evaluating strategic leadership based on the method of fuzzy analytic network process. Appl. Math. Inform. Sci. **8**(3), 1461–1466 (2014)

102. Öztayşi, B., Uğurlu, S., Kahraman, C.: Assessment of green energy alternatives using fuzzy ANP. In: Assessment and Simulation Tools for Sustainable Energy Systems, pp. 55–77. Springer, London (2013)

103. Senvar, O., Tuzkaya, U.R., Kahraman, C.: Supply chain performance measurement: an integrated DEMATEL and fuzzy-ANP approach. In: Kahraman, C., Öztaysi, B. (eds.) Supply Chain Management Under Fuzziness Studies in Fuzziness and Soft Computing Series, vol. 313, pp. 143–165. Springer, Berlin/Heidelberg (2014)

104. Tadic, S., Zecevic, S., Krstic, M.: A novel hybrid MCDM model based on fuzzy DEMATEL, fuzzy ANP and fuzzy VIKOR for city logistics concept selection. Expert Syst. Appl. **41**(18), 8112–8128 (2014)

105. Zaied, A.N.H., Ismail, M., Gamal, A.: An integrated of neutrosophic-ANP technique for supplier selection. Neutrosophic Sets Syst. **27**, 237–244 (2019)

106. Awang, A., Aizam, N.A.H., Abdullah, L.: An integrated decision-making method based on neutrosophic numbers for investigating factors of coastal erosion. Symmetry. **11**, 328 (2019). https://doi.org/10.3390/sym11030328

107. Otay, I., Kahraman, C.: Analytic network process with neutrosophic sets. In: Fuzzy Multi-Criteria Decision-Making Using Neutrosophic Sets, pp. 525–542 (2018) Part of the Studies in Fuzziness and Soft Computing book series (STUDFUZZ, volume 369)

108. Abdel-Baset, M., Chang, V., Gamal, A., Smarandache, F.: An integrated neutrosophic ANP and VIKOR method for achieving sustainable supplier selection: a case study in importing field. Comput. Ind. **106**, 94–110 (2019)

109. Hwang, Yoon: Multiple attribute decision making methods and applications. Springer (1981), https://doi.org/10.1007/978-3-642-48318-9, Lecture Notes in Economics and Mathematical Systems (LNE, volume 186)
110. Ye, F., Li, Y.N.: An extended TOPSIS model based on the Possibility theory under fuzzy environment. Knowl.-Based Syst. **67**, 263–269 (2014)
111. Kahraman, C., Çevik, S., Ates, N.Y., Gülbay, M.: Fuzzy multi-criteria evaluation of industrial robotic systems. Comput. Ind. Eng. **52**(4), 414–433 (2007)
112. Chen, C.B., Wei, C.C.: An approach for solving fuzzy MADM problems. Int. J. Uncertain. Fuzziness Knowl.-Based Syst. **5**(4), 459–480 (1997)
113. Kannan, D., De Sousa Jabbour, A.B.L., Jabbour, C.J.C.: Selecting green suppliers based on GSCM practices: using fuzzy TOPSIS applied to a Brazilian electronics company. Eur. J. Oper. Res. **233**(2), 432–447 (2014)
114. Wang, Y.J.: The evaluation of financial performance for Taiwan container shipping companies by fuzzy TOPSIS. Appl. Soft Comput. J. **22**, 28–35 (2014)
115. Chu, T.C.: Facility location selection using fuzzy topsis under group decisions. Int. J. Uncertain. Fuzziness Knowl.-Based Syst. **10**(6), 687–701 (2002)
116. Mandic, K., Delibasic, B., Knezevic, S., Benkovic, S.: Analysis of the financial parameters of Serbian banks through the application of the fuzzy AHP and TOPSIS methods. Econ. Model. **43**, 30–37 (2014)
117. Zhang, G., Lu, J.: An integrated group decision making method dealing with fuzzy preferences for alternatives and individual judgments for selection criteria. Group Decis. Negot. **12**, 501–515 (2003)
118. Tsaura, S.H., Chang, T.Y., Yen, C.H.: The evaluation of airline service quality by fuzzy MCDM. Tour. Manag. **23**(2), 107–115 (2002)
119. Liu, H., Rodríguez, R.M.: A fuzzy envelope for hesitant fuzzy linguistic term set and its application to multicriteria decision making. Inform. Sci. **258**, 220–238 (2014)
120. Kahraman, C., Oztaysi, B., Cevik Onar, S.: A multicriteria supplier selection model using hesitant fuzzy linguistic term sets. Pressacademia. **4**(2), 192–200 (2014). https://doi.org/10.17261/Pressacademia.2017.449
121. Xu, Z., Zhang, X.: Hesitant fuzzy multi-attribute decision making based on TOPSIS with incomplete weight information. Knowl.-Based Syst. **52**, 53–64 (2013)
122. Celik, E., Bilisik, O.N., Erdogan, M., Gumus, A.T., Baracli, H.: An integrated novel interval type-2 fuzzy MCDM method to improve customer satisfaction in public transportation for Istanbul. Transport. Res. E-Log. **58**, 28–51 (2013)
123. Yue, Z.: TOPSIS-based group decision-making methodology in intuitionistic fuzzy setting. Inform. Sci. **277**, 141–153 (2014)
124. Joshi, D., Kumar, S.: Intuitionistic fuzzy entropy and distance measure based TOPSIS method for multi-criteria decision making. Egypt. Inform. J. **15**(2), 97–104 (2014)
125. Chen, T.-Y., Tsao, C.-Y.: The interval-valued fuzzy TOPSIS method and experimental analysis. Fuzzy Set Syst. **159**(11), 1410–1428 (2008)
126. Bottani, E., Rizzi, A.: A fuzzy TOPSIS methodology to support outsourcing of logistics services. Supply Chain Manag. Int. J. **11**(4), 294–308 (2006)
127. Braglia, M., Frosolini, M., Montanari, R.: Fuzzy TOPSIS approach for failure mode, effects and criticality analysis. Qual. Reliab. Eng. Int. **19**(5), 425–443 (2003)
128. Chakravarthi, K.K., Shyamala, L.: TOPSIS inspired budget and deadline aware multi-workflow scheduling for cloud computing. J. Syst. Arch. 114, 101916, Mar 2021
129. Biswas, P., Pramanik, S., Giri, B.C.: TOPSIS method for multi-attribute group decision-making under single-valued neutrosophic environment. Neural Comput. Appl. **27**, 727–737 (2016). https://doi.org/10.1007/s00521-015-1891-2
130. Jun, Y.: An extended TOPSIS method for multiple attribute group decision making based on single valued neutrosophic linguistic numbers. J. Intell. Fuzzy Syst. **28**, 247–255 (2015). https://doi.org/10.3233/IFS-141295. IOS Press
131. Surapati, P., Partha, P.D., Giri, B.C.: TOPSIS for single valued neutrosophic soft expert set based multi-attribute decision making problems. Neutrosophic Sets Syst. **10**, 88–95 (2015)

132. Pranab, B., Surapati, P., Giri, B.C.: TOPSIS strategy for multi-attribute decision making with trapezoidal neutrosophic numbers. Neutrosophic Sets Syst. **19**, 29–39 (2018)
133. Bibhas, C.G., Uddin, M.M., Pranab, B.: TOPSIS method for MADM based on interval trapezoida neutrosophic number. Neutrosophic Sets Syst. **22**, 151–167 (2018)
134. Elhassouny, A., Florentin, S.: Neutrosophic-simplified-TOPSIS. Multi-Criteria Decision-Making using combined Simplified-TOPSIS method and neutrosophics. In: IEEE International Conference on Fuzzy Systems (FUZZ), At: Vancouver, Canada (2016). https://doi.org/10.1109/FUZZ-IEEE.2016.7738003
135. Bibhas, C.G., Mahatab, M.U., Pranab, B.: TOPSIS method for neutrosophic hesitant fuzzy multi-attribute decision making. **31**(1), 35, 35–63, 63 (2020). https://doi.org/10.15388/20-INFOR392
136. Zeng, S., Luo, D., Zhang, C., Li, X.: A correlation-based TOPSIS method for multiple attribute decision making with single-valued neutrosophic information. Int. J. Inform. Technol. Decis. Mak. **19**(01). https://doi.org/10.1142/S0219622019500512
137. Madiha, I.M.T.I.A.Z., Muhammad, S.A.Q.L.A.I.N., Muhammad, S.A.E.E.D.: TOPSIS for multi criteria decision making in octagonal intuitionistic fuzzy environment by using accuracy function. J. New Theory. **31**, 32–40 (2020)
138. Fahmi, A., Aslam, M., Abdullah, S.: Analysis of migraine in mutlicellular organism based on trapezoidal neutrosophic cubic hesitant fuzzy TOPSIS method. Int. J. Biomath. **12**(08), 1950084 (2019)
139. Tzeng, G.H., Teng, M.H., Chen, J.J., Opricovic, S.: Multicriteria selection for a restaurant location in Taipei. Int. J. Hosp. Manag. **21**(2), 171–187 (2002)
140. Opricovic, S.: A fuzzy compromise solution for multicriteria problems. Int. J. Uncertainty Fuzz. **15**(3), 363–380 (2007)
141. Chang, T.H.: Fuzzy VIKOR method: a case study of the hospital service evaluation in Taiwan. Inform. Sci. **271**, 196–212 (2014)
142. Mousavi, S.M., Vahdani, B., Tavakkoli-Moghaddam, R., Tajik, N.: Soft computing based on a fuzzy grey group compromise solution approach with an application to the selection problem of material handling equipment. Int. J. Comput. Integr. Manuf. **27**(6), 547–569 (2014)
143. Alabool, H.M., Mahmood, A.K.: Trust-based service selection in public cloud computing using fuzzy modified VIKOR method. Aust. J. Basic Appl. Sci. **7**(9), 211–220 (2013)
144. Ebrahimnejad, S., Mousavi, S.M., TavakkoliMoghaddam, R., Heydar, M.: Risk ranking in mega projects by fuzzy compromise approach: a comparative analysis. J. Intell. Fuzzy Syst. **26**(2), 949–959 (2014)
145. Aydin, S., Kahraman, C.: Vehicle selection for public transportation using an integrated multi criteria decision making approach: a case of Ankara. J. Intell. Fuzzy Syst. **26**(5), 2467–2481 (2014)
146. Oztaysi, B., Sürer, O.: Supply chain performance measurement using a SCOR based fuzzy VIKOR approach. In: Kahraman, C., Oztaysi, B. (eds.) Supply Chain Management Under Fuzziness. Springer, Berlin/Heidelberg (2014)
147. Tadic, D., Milanovic, D.D., Misita, M., Tadic, B.: New integrated approach to the problem of ranking and supplier selection under uncertainties. Proc. Inst. Mech. Eng. B J. Eng. Manuf. **225**(B9), 1713–1724 (2011)
148. Whaiduzzaman, M., Gani, A., Anuar, N.B., Shiraz, M., Haque, M.N., Haque, I.T.: Cloud service selection using multicriteria decision analysis. Sci. World J. **2014**, 1–10 (2014)
149. Liu, S., Hu, Y., Zhang, Y.: Supply chain partner selection under cloud computing environment: an improved approach based on BWM and VIKOR. Math. Probl. Eng. **2018**, 1–11 (2018)
150. Delaram, J., FatahiValilai, O., Houshamand, M., Ashtiani, F.: A matching mechanism for public cloud manufacturing platforms using intuitionistic Fuzzy VIKOR and deferred acceptance algorithm. Int. J. Manag. Sci. Eng. Manag. **16**(2), 107–122 (2021)
151. Suh, Y., Park, Y., Kang, D.: Evaluating mobile services using integrated weighting approach and fuzzy VIKOR. Plos one. **14**(6), e0217786 (2019)
152. Zavadskas, E.K., Turskis, Z., Kildienė, S.: State of art surveys of overviews on MCDM/MADM methods. Technol. Econ. Dev. Econ. **20**(1), 165–179 (2014)

153. Martin-Utrillas, M., Juan-Garcia, F., Canto-Perello, J., Curiel-Esparza, J.: Optimal infrastructure selection to boost regional sustainable economy. Int. J. Sust. Dev. World Ecol. **22**(1), 30–38 (2015)

154. Yazdani-Chamzini, A., Fouladgar, M.M., Zavadskas, E.K., Moini, S.H.H.: Selecting the optimal renewable energy using multi criteria decision making. J. Bus. Econ. Manag. **14**(5), 957–978 (2013)

155. Ren, J., Manzardo, A., Mazzi, A., Zuliani, F., Scipioni, A.: Prioritization of bioethanol production pathways in China based on life cycle sustainability assessment and multicriteria decision-making. Int. J. Life Cycle Assess. **20**(6), 842–853 (2015)

156. Civic, A., Vucijak, B.: Multi-criteria optimization of insulation options for warmth of buildings to increase energy efficiency. Procedia Eng. **69**, 911–920 (2014)

157. Kim, Y., Chung, E.S.: Fuzzy VIKOR approach for assessing the vulnerability of the water supply to climate change and variability in South Korea. Appl. Math. Modell. **37**(22), 9419–9430 (2013)

158. Opricovic, S., Tzeng, G.H.: Compromise solution by MCDM methods: a comparative analysis of VIKOR and TOPSIS. Eur. J. Oper. Res. **156**(2), 445–455 (2004)

159. Zhao, X., Tang, S., Yang, S., Huang, K.: Extended VIKOR method based on cross-entropy for interval-valued intuitionistic fuzzy multiple criteria group decision making. J. Intell. Fuzzy Syst. **25**(4), 1053–1066 (2013)

160. Devi, K.: Extension of VIKOR method in intuitionistic fuzzy environment for robot selection. Expert Syst. Appl. **38**(11), 14163–14168 (2011)

161. Büyüközkan, G., Göçer, F., Karabulut, Y.: A new group decision making approach with IF AHP and IF VIKOR for selecting hazardous waste carriers. Measurement. **134**, 66–82 (2019)

162. Park, J.H., Cho, H.J., Kwun, Y.C.: Extension of the VIKOR method to dynamic intuitionistic fuzzy multiple attribute decision making. Comput. Math. Appl. **65**(4), 731–744 (2013)

163. Eroğlu, H., Şahin, R.: A neutrosophic VIKOR method-based decision-making with an improved distance measure and score function: case study of selection for renewable energy alternatives. Cogn. Comput. **12**, 1338–1355 (2020)

164. Hussain, I., Abou, S., Mondal, P., Sankar, M., Kumar, U.: VIKOR method for decision making problems in interval valued neutrosophic environment. In: Fuzzy Multi-Criteria Decision-Making Using Neutrosophic Sets, pp. 587–602 (2018). https://doi.org/10.1007/978-3-030-00045-5_22

165. Huang, Y.-H., Wei, G.-W., Wei, C.: VIKOR method for interval neutrosophic multiple attribute group decision-making. Information (Switzerland). **8**(4), 144 (2017). https://doi.org/10.3390/info8040144

166. Bausys, R., Zavadskas, E.K.: Multicriteria decision making approach by VIKOR under interval neutrosophic set environment. Econom. Comput. Econom. Cybernet. Stud. Res./Acad. Econom. Stud. **49**(4), 33–48 (2015)

167. Wang, X., Wang, X.: An extended VIKOR method for the multiple attribute decision making problems based on interval neutrosophic set. In: IEEE 4th Advanced Information Technology, Electronic and Automation Control Conference (IAEAC) (2019)

168. Muhammad, R., Syeda, T.T.: A robust extension of VIKOR method for bipolar fuzzy sets using connection numbers of SPA theory-based metric spaces. Artif. Intell. Rev. **54**, 561–591 (2021). https://doi.org/10.1007/s10462-020-09859-w

169. Pramanik, S., Mallick, R.: VIKOR based MAGDM strategy with trapezoidal neutrosophic numbers. Neutrosophic Sets Syst. **22**, 118–130 (2018)

170. Shemshadi, A., Shirazi, H., Toreihi, M., Torakh, M.J.: A fuzzy VIKOR method for supplier selection based on entropy measure for objective weighting. Expert Syst. Appl. **38**(10), 12160–12167 (2011)

171. Seixas, C.A.P.C., Almeida, A.T., Gomes, L.F.A.M.: Priorities assignment for information systems based on TODIM multicriteria method. Inform. Sci. 322–328 (2002) https://proceedings.informingscience.org/IS2002Proceedings/papers/Costa118Prior.pdf

172. Wei, C., Zhiliang, R., Rodríguez, R.M.: A hesitant fuzzy linguistic TODIM method based on a score function. Int. J. Comput. Intell. Syst. **8**(4), 701–712 (2015)

173. Mahmoodi, M., Jahromi, G.S.: A new fuzzy DEMATEL-TODIM hybrid method for evaluation criteria of knowledge management in supply. Eur. Sci. J. August 2016/SPECIAL/edition ISSN: 1857 – 7881 (Print) e – ISSN 1857- 7431 324 chain. Int. J. Manag. Value Supply Chains (IJMVSC) **5**(2), 29–42 (2014)
174. Ramooshjan, K., Rahmani, J., Sobhanollahi, M.A., Mirzazadeh, A.: A new method in the location problem using fuzzy TODIM. J. Hum. Soc. Sci. Res. **06**(01), 1–13 (2015)
175. Gomes, L.F.A.M., Machado, M.A.S., Costa, F.F., Rangel, L.A.D.: Behavioral multi-criteria decision analysis: the TODIM method with criteria interactions. Ann. Oper. Res. **211**, 531–548 (2013b)
176. Gomes, L.F.A.M., Machado, M.A.S., Costa, F.F., Rangel, L.A.D.: Criteria interactions in multiple criteria decision aiding: a Choquet formulation for the TODIM method. Procedia Comput. Sci. **17**, 324–331 (2013a). Eur. Sci. J. August 2016/SPECIAL/ edition ISSN: 1857 – 7881 (Print) e – ISSN 1857- 7431 323
177. Gomes, L.F.A.M., Rangel, L.A.D., Maranhão, F.J.C.: Multicriteria analysis of natural gas destination in Brazil: an application of the TODIM method. Math. Comput. Modell. **50**, 92–100
178. Gomes, C.F., Simões, L.F.A., Gomes, M., Maranhão, F.J.C.: Decision analysis for the exploration of gas reserves': merging TODIM and THOR. Pesquisa Operacional. **30**(3), 601–617 (2010)
179. Gomes, L.F.A.M., González, X.I.: Behavioral multi-criteria decision analysis: further elaborations on the TODIM method. Found. Comput. Decis. Sci. **37**(1), 3–8 (2012)
180. Krohling, R.A., Souza, T.T.M.: Combining prospect theory and fuzzy numbers to multi-criteria decision making. Expert Syst. Appl. **39**, 11487–11493 (2012)
181. Krohling, R.A., Souza, T.: T. M. F-TODIM: 'AN application of the fuzzy TODIM method to rental evaluation of residential properties'. Congreso Latino-Iberoamericano de Investigacion Operativa, SymposioBrasileiro de Pesquisa Operational, 24–28 September, Rio de Janeiro, Brazil, pp. 431–443 (2012b)
182. Krohling, R.A., Pacheco, A.G.C., Siviero, A.L.T.: IF-TODIM: an intuitionistic fuzzy TODIM to multi-criteria decision making. Knowl. Based Syst. **53**, 142–146 (2013)
183. Lourenzutti, R., Krohling, R.A.: A study of TODIM in a intuitionistic fuzzy and random environment. Expert Syst. Appl. **40**, 6459–6468 (2013)
184. Kazancoglu, Y., Burmaoglu, S.: ERP software selection with MCDM: application of TODIM method. Int. J. Bus. Inf. Syst. **13**(4), 435–452 (2013)
185. Gomes, L.F.A.M., Machado, M.A.S., Santos, D.J., Caldeira, A.M.: Ranking of suppliers for a steel industry: a comparison of the original TODIM and the Choquet-extended TODIM methods. Procedia Comput. Sci. **55**, 706–714 (2015)
186. Gomes, L.F.A.M., Rangel, L.A.D.: An application of the TODIM method to the multicriteria rental evaluation of residential properties. Eur. J. Oper. Res. **193**, 204–211 (2009)
187. Krohling, R.A., Pacheco, A.G.C.: Interval-valued intuitionistic fuzzy TODIM. Procedia Comput. Sci. **31**, 236–244 (2014)
188. Liu, P., Teng, F.: An extended TODIM method for multiple attribute group decision-making based on 2-dimension uncertain linguistic variable. Complexity, 1–11 (2014). https://doi.org/10.1002/cplx.21625
189. Uysal, F., Tosun, Ö.: Multi criteria analysis of the residential properties in Antalya using TODIM method. Procedia Soc. Behav. Sci. **109**, 322–326 (2014)
190. Tseng, M.L., Lin, Y.H., Tan, K., Chen, R.H., Chen, Y.H.: Using TODIM to evaluate green supply chain practices under uncertainty. Appl. Math. Modell. **38**, 2983–2995 (2014)
191. Passos, A.C., Teixeira, M.G., Garcia, K.C., Cardoso, A.M., Gomes, L.F.A.M.: Using the TODIM-FSE method as a decision-making support methodology for oil spill response. Comput. Oper. Res. **42**, 40–48 (2014)
192. Passos, A.C., Gomes, L.F.A.M.: TODIM-FSE: a multicriteria classification method based on prospect theory. Multiple Criteria Decis. Mak. **9**, 123–139 (2014)
193. Lourenzutti, R., Krohling, R.A.: The Hellinger distance in multicriteria decision making: an illustration to the TOPSIS and TODIM methods. Expert Syst. Appl. **41**, 4414–4421 (2014)

194. Zhang, X., Xu, Z.: The TODIM analysis approach based on novel measured functions under hesitant fuzzy environment. Knowl.-Based Syst. **61**, 48–58 (2014)
195. Salomon, V.A.P., Rangel, L.A.D.: Comparing rankings from using TODIM and a fuzzy expert system. Procedia Comput. Sci. **55**, 126–138 (2015)
196. Sen, D.K., Datta, S., Mahapatra, S.S.: Extension of TODIM combined with grey numbers: an integrated decision making module. Grey Syst. Theory Appl. **5**(3), 367–391 (2015)
197. Li, M., Wu, C., Zhang, L., You, L.N.: An intuitionistic fuzzy TODIM method to solve distributor evaluation and selection problem. Int. J. Simul. Modell. **14**(3), 511–524 (2015)
198. Tseng, M.L., Lin, Y.H., Lim, M.K., Teehankee, B.L.: Using a hybrid method to evaluate service innovation in the hotel industry. Appl. Soft Comput. **28**, 411–421 (2015)
199. Ren, P., Xu, Z., Gou, X.: Pythagorean fuzzy TODIM approach to multi-criteria decision making. Appl. Soft Comput. **42**, 246–259 (2016)
200. Brauers, W.K.M., Zavadskas, E.K.: The MOORA method and its application to privatization in a transition economy. Control Cybern. **35**(2), 445–469 (2006)
201. Deliktas, D., Ustun, O.: Student selection and assignment methodology based on fuzzy MULTIMOORA and multi choice goal programming. Int. Trans. Oper. Res. (2015). https://doi.org/10.1111/itor.12185
202. Brauers, W.K.M., Zavadskas, E.K.: MULTIMOORA optimization used to decide on a bank loan to buy property. Technol. Econ. Dev. Econ. **17**(1), 174–188 (2011)
203. Datta, S., Sahu, N., Mahapatra, S.: Robot selection based on grey-MULTIMOORA approach. Grey Syst. Theory Appl. **3**(2), 201–232 (2013)
204. Farzamnia, E., Babolghani, M.B.: Group decision-making process for supplier selection using MULTIMOORA technique under fuzzy environment. Kuwait Chapter Arab. J. Bus. Manag. Rev. **3**(11a), 203–218 (2014)
205. Liu, H.C., You, J.X., Lu, C., Shan, M.M.: Application of interval 2-tuple linguistic MULTIMOORA method for health-care waste treatment technology evaluation and selection. Waste Manag. **34**(11), 2355–2364 (2014)
206. Hafezalkotob, A., Hafezalkotob, A., Sayadi, M.K.: 'Extension of MULTIMOORA method with interval numbers': an application in materials selection. Appl. Math. Modell. **40**(2), 1372–1386 (2016)
207. Balezentis, T., Zeng, S., Balezentis, A.: MULTIMOORA-IFN: a MCDM method based on intuitionistic fuzzy number for performance management. Econom. Comput. Econom. Cybernet. Stud. Res. **48**(4), 85–102 (2014)
208. Balezentis, T., Zeng, S.: Group multi-criteria decision making based upon interval-valued fuzzy numbers: an extension of the MULTIMOORA method. Expert Syst. Appl. **40**(2), 543–550 (2013)
209. Balezentis, T., Balezentis, A.: A survey on development and applications of the multi-criteria decision making method MULTIMOORA. J. Multi-Criteria Decis. Anal. **21**(3-4), 209–222 (2014)
210. Liu, H., Fan, X., Li, P., Chen, Y.: Evaluating the risk of failure modes with extended MULTIMOORA method under fuzzy environment. Eng. Appl. Artif. Intell. **34**, 168–177 (2014)
211. Liu, H., You, J.X., Lu, C., Chen, Y.Z.: Evaluating healthcare waste treatment technologies using a hybrid multi-criteria decision making model. Renew. Sust. Energ. Rev. **41**, 932–942 (2015)
212. Liu, H., You, J.X., Lu, C., Shan, M.M.: Application of interval 2-tuple linguistic MULTIMOORA method for healthcare waste treatment technology evaluation and selection. Waste Manag. **34**(11), 2355–2364 (2014)
213. Li, Z.H.: An extension of the MULTIMOORA method for multiple criteria group decision making based upon hesitant fuzzy sets. J. Appl. Math., vol. Article ID 527836, 16 pages (2014)
214. Cristobal, J.R.S.: Multi-criteria decision-making in the selection of a renewable energy project in Spain: the Vikor method. Renew. Energy. **36**(2, 2013), 498–502 (2011)

215. Mohammadshahi, Y.: A state-of-art survey on TQM applications using MCDM techniques. Decis. Sci. Lett. **2**(3), 125–134 (2013)
216. Whaiduzzaman, M., Gani, A., BadrulAnuar, N., Shiraz, M., Haque, M.N., Haque, I.T.: Cloud service selection using multicriteria decision analysis. Sci. World J. **2014**, 1–11 (2014)
217. Roy, B.: ELECTRE III: Un algorithme de classements fonde sur une representation floue des preferences en presence de criteres multiples. Cahiers du CERO. **20**(1), 3–4 (1978)
218. Leyva-López, J.C., Fernández-González, E.: A new method for group decision support based on ELECTRE III methodology. Eur. J. Oper. Res. **148**(1), 14–27 (2003)
219. Belacel, N.: Multicriteria assignment method PROAFTN: methodology and medical application. Eur. J. Oper. Res. **125**(1), 175–183 (2000)
220. Hatami-Marbini, A., Tavana, M.: An extension of the ELECTRE I method for group decision-making under a fuzzy environment. Omega-Int. J. Manag. S. **39**(4), 373–386 (2011)
221. Montazer, G.A., Saremi, H.Q., Ramezani, M.: Design a new mixed expert decision aiding system using fuzzy ELECTRE III method for vendor selection. Expert Syst. Appl. **36**(8), 10837–10847 (2009)
222. Sevkli, M.: An application of the fuzzy ELECTRE method for supplier selection. Int. J. Prod. Res. **48**(12), 3393–3405 (2009)
223. Vahdani, B., Hadipour, H.: Extension of the ELECTRE method based on interval-valued fuzzy sets. Soft Comput. **15**(3), 569–579 (2011)
224. Bisdorff, R.: Logical foundation of fuzzy preferential systems with application to the ELECTRE decision aid methods. Comput. Oper. Res. **27**(7–8), 673–687 (2000)
225. Tolga, A.Ç.: A real options approach for software development projects using fuzzy ELECTRE. J. Mult Valued Logic Soft Comput. **18**(5–6), 541–560 (2012)
226. Rouyendegh, B.D., Erkan, T.E.: An application of the fuzzy ELECTRE method for academic staff selection. Hum. Factors Ergon. Manuf. Serv. Ind. **23**(2), 107–115 (2013)
227. Kaya, T., Kahraman, C.: A fuzzy approach to ebanking website quality assessment based on an integrated AHP-ELECTRE method. Technol. Econ. Dev. Econ. **17**(2), 313–334 (2011)
228. Wu, M.-C., Chen, T.-Y.: The ELECTRE multicriteria analysis approach based on Atanassov's intuitionistic fuzzy sets. Expert Syst. Appl. **38**(10), 12318–12327 (2011)
229. Devi, K., Yadav, S.: A multicriteria intuitionistic fuzzy group decision making for plant location selection with ELECTRE method. Int. J. Adv. Manuf. Technol. **66**(9–12), 1219–1229 (2013)
230. Chen, T.Y.: An ELECTRE-based outranking method for multiple criteria group decision making using interval type-2 fuzzy sets. Inform. Sci. **263**, 1–21 (2014)
231. Chen, N., Xu, Z., Xia, M.: The ELECTRE I multi-criteria decision-making method based on hesitant fuzzy sets. Int. J. Inf. Technol. Decis. **14**(03), 621–657 (2013). https://doi.org/10.1142/S0219622014500187
232. Li, G.-D., Yamaguchi, D., Nagai, M.: A grey-based decision-making approach to the supplier selection problem. Math. Comput. Modell. **46**(3–4), 573–581 (2007)
233. Fung, C.P.: Manufacturing process optimization for wear property of fiber-reinforced polybutylene terephthalate composites with grey relational analysis. Wear. **254**(3–4), 298–306 (2003)
234. Deng, J.L.: Introduction to grey system theory. J. Grey Syst. **1**(1), 1–24 (1989)
235. Deng, J.L.: The Primary Methods of Grey System Theory. Huazhong University of Science and Technology Press, Wuhan (2005)
236. Rao, R.V., Singh, D.: An improved grey relational analysis as a decision making method for manufacturing situations. Int. J. Decis. Sci. Risk Manag. **2**, 1–23 (2010)
237. Chen, W.H.: Distribution system restoration using the hybrid fuzzy-grey method. IEEE Trans. Power Syst. **20**(1), 199–205 (2005)
238. Olson, D.L., Wu, D.: Simulation of fuzzy multi attribute models for grey relationships. Eur. J. Oper. Res. **175**(1), 111–120 (2006)
239. Wu, D.S.: Supplier selection in a fuzzy group decision making setting: a method using grey related analysis and Dempster–Shafer theory. Expert Syst. Appl. **36**, 8892–8899 (2009)

240. Pramanik, S., Mukhopadhyaya, D.: Grey relational analysis based intuitionistic fuzzy multi criteria group decision making approach for teacher selection in higher education. Int. J. Comput. Appl. **34**(10), 21–29 (2011)
241. Wei, G.W.: Grey relational analysis method for intuitionistic fuzzy multiple attribute decision making. Expert Syst. Appl. **38**, 11671–11677 (2011)
242. Pramanik, S., Mondal, K.: Interval neutrosophic multi-attribute decision-making based on grey relational analysis. Neutrosophic Sets Syst. **9**, 13–22 (2015)
243. Regunathan, R., Murugaiyan, A., Lavanya, K.: A QoS-aware hybrid TOPSIS–plurality method for multi-criteria decision model in mobile cloud service selection. In: Proceedings of the 2nd International Conference on Data Engineering and Communication Technology, pp. 499–507. Springer, Singapore (2019)
244. Hao, F., Pei, Z., Park, D.S., Phonexay, V., Seo, H.S.: Mobile cloud services recommendation: a soft set-based approach. J. Ambient Intell. Humaniz. Comput. **9**(4), 1235–1243 (2018)
245. Singla, C., Mahajan, N., Kaushal, S., Verma, A., Sangaiah, A.K.: Modelling and analysis of multi-objective service selection scheme in IoT-cloud environment. In: Cognitive Computing for Big Data Systems Over IoT, pp. 63–77. Springer, Cham (2018)
246. Nayak, S.C., Parida, S., Tripathy, C., Pati, B., Panigrahi, C.R.: Multicriteria decision-making techniques for avoiding similar task scheduling conflict in cloud computing. Int. J. Commun. Syst. **33**(13), e4126 (2020)
247. Chakraborty, A., Banik, B., Mondal, S.P., Alam, S.: Arithmetic and geometric operators of pentagonal neutrosophic number and its application in mobile communication service based MCGDM problem. Neutrosophic Sets Syst. **32**, 61–79 (2020)
248. Nawaz, F., Asadabadi, M.R., Janjua, N.K., Hussain, O.K., Chang, E., Saberi, M.: An MCDM method for cloud service selection using a Markov chain and the best-worst method. Knowl.-Based Syst. **159**, 120–131 (2018)
249. Ouadah, A., Hadjali, A., Nader, F.: A hybrid MCDM framework for efficient web services selection based on QoS. In: International Conference on Applied Smart Systems (ICASS), IEEE, pp. 1–6 (2018)

5G Green Mobile Cloud Computing Using Game Theory

Subha Ghosh ⓘ **and Debashis De** ⓘ

1 Introduction

Green refers to an environment where located systems are able to work efficiently [1]. We have divided the significant systems in mobile cloud computing (MCC) [2] into three layers, the first layer being the mobile devices layer, which creates a task and sends it to another computing storage to compute it [3]. The second is the communication layer, where 5G transmits data from mobile devices to the cloud through a variety of wireless network technologies [4, 5]. The third is the cloud layer, where data from mobile devices is received, processed, and result transferred to a specific location after completion [6]. The most important thing to make an environment green is to increase the efficiency of all the systems located within it [7, 8]. Creating a green MCC environment is possible only when the mobile devices in it, the 5G wireless network, and the cloud are able to work efficiently, and they utilize the resources properly. Identifying the right resource is an important task. This identification requires a mathematical procedure, which enables a device to select the correct resource or path based on certain parameters [9]. The most useful method for this is game theory [10–12]. Through its various types of games, a system can easily and accurately detect the right thing at the right time and in the right way. It enhances its own utility after detection, which is very useful for all systems. The lists of acronyms used in this chapter is discussed in Table 1.

S. Ghosh (✉) · D. De
Department of Computer Science and Engineering, Centre of Mobile Cloud Computing, Maulana Abul Kalam Azad University of Technology, West Bengal, Nadia, India

© The Author(s), under exclusive license to Springer Nature Switzerland AG 2022
D. De et al. (eds.), *Green Mobile Cloud Computing*,
https://doi.org/10.1007/978-3-031-08038-8_5

Table 1 List of acronyms

Acronyms	Description
MCC	Mobile cloud computing
5G	Fifth generation
D2D	Device-to-Device
HetNet	Heterogeneous network
CRAN	Cloud radio access network
HCRAN	Heterogeneous CRAN
BBU	Base band unit
RRH	Remote radio head
DCO	Data center operator
SS	Service subscriber

The rest of the chapter is arranged in this way. The advantages and requirements of MCC are listed in Sect. 2. The use of games in the case of task offloading generated from mobile devices is discussed in Sect. 3. The method of offloading the task of the mobile devices based on the cooperative game is discussed in Sect. 4. The use of games for 5G wireless networks is described in Sect. 5. The process of allocating spectrum for mobile devices based on auction game is discussed in Sect. 6. The use of games for resource allocation in cloud computing is discussed in Sect. 7. The process of allocating resources of the cloud based on non-cooperative game is discussed in Sect. 8. Section 9 describes the mathematical equations required for MCC's data to be transmitted and completed in the cloud. The delay and power consumption of the previously published articles are calculated and compared in Sect. 10. A summary of the different types of games and their relationship with MCC is discussed in Sect. 11. The need for cloud computing in the coming days and the benefits of the game are described in Sect. 12 and finally the chapter is concluded in Sect. 13.

2 Advantages of Mobile Cloud Computing

Notable among the reasons why MCC is used are listed below, and all these we have described in Fig. 1.

1. **Reduce cost:**
   Reducing cost means reducing the cost of the system and here system means two types of systems, one is the mobile device [13] and the other is the cloud [14]. To accomplish a large task or run a large application requires a mobile device with a high capacity, where having a large amount of RAM, ROM and a very high processing unit is essential. But the more hardware or better quality mobile devices increase the price value. But, if we transfer that work from a mobile device to a cloud device, the cost is much lower and the cloud provides

Fig. 1 Advantages of mobile cloud computing

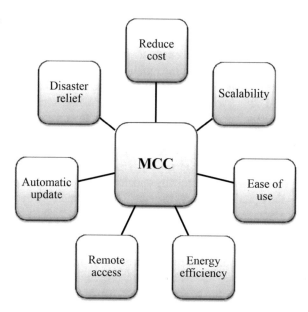

cloud service according to how much we will use and the customer sends money accordingly. This benefits both mobile devices and cloud service providers.

2. **Scalability:**
   Cloud service providers work in a scalable way [15]. Cloud service providers allocate computing storage as needed and create bills based on it [16]. As a result, users pay according to the amount of data transferred and leave the storage intact when the work is done. There is no need to acquire storage permanently or buy it permanently, which is very beneficial for any mobile user.

3. **Ease of use:**
   The cloud is easy enough to use [17], the main reason being that the cloud provides as much storage as the user needs and the user has to pay accordingly [18]. As a result when the user needs, he acquires the cloud and then leaves it, it is very easy and efficient.

4. **Energy efficiency:**
   Energy is a very valuable component for two types of systems mobile and cloud [19]. In the case of mobile system, energy refers to the capacity of the battery in it. When a large application runs in the mobile, its battery is used at that rate and it runs out quickly. In the case of the cloud, energy refers to the power consumption that is required to perform data operations in the cloud. Energy is a very important parameter in these two cases. Data generated from mobile devices and done in the cloud, increases the energy efficiency of the system, which in turn increases network performance [20]. As a result, the battery life of mobile devices increases.

5. **Remote access:**

   Remote access is an important feature of MCC [21]. This allows the user to store important data in a remote cloud storage with a specific ID and password without having to store it in the mobile, and access it from any location with the user ID and password [22]. This increases the amount of free resources on mobile devices and allows users to store as much data, applications, etc. Users are able to use the data they need in any location and at any time.

6. **Application update:**

   Because the cloud is located in a remote location, the data stored in the cloud is automatically updated [23]. Through the applications associated with that data, that data is automatically updated from anywhere, so that the user always receives the updated data and they can take the next step according to that data [24].

7. **Disaster relief:**

   Data is going to be the most important thing of the future. If this data is lost due to a disaster, it is very difficult to recover it. A lot of information is stored based on this data. From this point of view, the cloud is a very important and essential thing. Cloud makes it easy to store important data in remote locations and access that data when needed [25], so there are no signs of data loss in the event of a major disaster [26].

We have divided the process of MCC into three parts; the first part is the task offloading method of mobile devices [27, 28]. The second part is the 5G wireless network [29], through which mobile data reaches certain cloud computing very quickly and accurately. And the third part is the cloud resource allocation system. Through it the cloud service provider provides a certain amount of resources to properly process the data coming from the mobile, and after it is completed, delivers it to a specific destination or stores it [30]. Game theory plays a vital role in each of these components of MCC. Each method is done appropriately through specific game. The use of games for this is incomparable to MCC. In the next section, we discuss in detail the relationship between each of these methods with the games.

The process of offloading data from a large number of mobile devices through games, transmitting that data to the nearest cloudlet via a 5G wireless network, and then transmitting and storing it in a centralized cloud is illustrated in Fig. 2. Here, data, services, and applications generated from mobile phones are sent to the cloud through a variety of games. 5G wireless network is used for transmission through suitable games, which reduces the power consumption, interference, and delay of the network. Because the cloud is located far away, the data is transferred through the game to a nearby cloudlet device with few resources before moving to the cloud. If cloudlet fails to complete the task, it is moved to the cloud and the task is accomplished by allocating appropriate resources through games. Once done, it is stored and the feedback is sent to the specified destination. The role of games is important in each case.

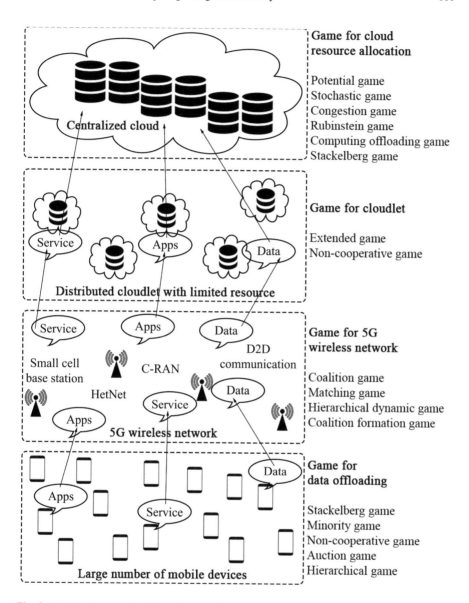

Fig. 2 Architecture of mobile cloud computing

3 The Use of Game Theory in Mobile Data Offloading

A network can only be called green when it is able to function efficiently. The battery capacity of modern mobile devices is limited. As a result, energy consumption has become a major concern for mobile applications. The method of offloading depending on the real time video application is discussed in [31]. This reduces the delay of applications and saves the battery of mobile devices.

The architecture of offloading decentralized computing in MCC based on potential game is discussed in [32]. In this article, mobile users decide to do offloading by balancing themselves, which brings a lot of benefits to complex management system.

The method of dynamic computation offloading in MCC by stochastic game is described in [10]. In this article, mobile users are dynamically active and inactive, and wireless channels vary randomly in offload calculations. Mobile users are selfish and offload data in the cloud in a self-interested way. The decision making process of this offloading is described through the game.

The process of data offloading in decentralized MCC based on congestion game is discussed in [33]. In the article, the authors try to gain expertise in data offloading through WiFi and Device-to-Device (D2D) communication through game theory approach. The purpose of the authors in this article is to maximize the revenue of mobile operators.

Now and in the days to come, the use of IoT devices is essential for any smart environment [34]. Authors of [35] have documented the association of MCC with IoT. First, each mobile device determines how much data it will send to a remote location via the rubinstein game. Depending on that application, the cloud dynamically allocates resources as needed. This process is very beneficial for time sensitive applications.

Data offloading in the cloud is a challenge for real time constraints and delay sensitive mobile applications. The process of transmitting multiple user data based on computing offloading game is discussed in [36]. In [36], the authors first consider the system model as a centralized problem, and then move it to the maximum bin packing problem. The application of this model reduces the energy consumption, time consumption and monetary cost of mobile devices, which is very useful for the system.

Mobile devices are a useful way to complete applications by working cooperatively. The process of assembling mobile devices and completing tasks based on the Stackelberg game is described in [37]. In [37], buyer of mobile computing services are used as leader and sellers are used as followers. With this method, mobile devices use their unused resources to accomplish tasks by sharing, which gives benefit both the buyer and the seller. The article proposes a cost function for buyer and a utility function for sellers, which increases the efficiency of the method.

Although cloud computing is a great way to accomplish and store the work generated by a large number of mobile device applications. The greater distance between mobile and the cloud, increases the loss of network performance. Sending data over this long distance increases the power consumption of the network, which leads the network to the opposite side of green communication. To solve this problem, a limited resource computing node near the mobile device, "cloudlet", has been proposed in [38–40]. It is located in the middle of a mobile device and a remote cloud device. It receives data from the mobile device, processes the data quickly and sends the feedback to the destination [41]. The method of offloading data by non-cooperative mobile devices based on extended game is discussed in [39]. Mobile devices selfishly try to increase their utility by sending their data to a nearby cloudlet. Depending on the game theory, the method of reducing the delay and energy consumption of mobile users by offloading data in cloudlet is described in [40]. This article uses two types of users, homogeneous mobile users and heterogeneous users.

4 Utility Function and Game Table for Mobile Task Offloading

A utility function is a mathematical equation through which players make the necessary decisions and act accordingly. An important element of game theory is the game table, where players and their data are stored. They perform necessary actions based on that data.

In this section, we have described the utility function and game table required for offloading mobile data through cooperative game.

A cooperative game [42] is a game in which a number of users come together to make a decision and follow that decision to complete their work. They work together to make a profit of all of them. The utility function for offloading mobile data through cooperative game is given as,

$$u_{CGDO} = (d_1 + d_2 + d_3 + \cdots + d_M) \tag{1}$$

The game table for offloading mobile data through cooperative game has been recorded in Table 2. Table 2 has 1 to M number of players and their data amount is D_1 to D_M. It is possible to transmit maximum TD amount of data through offloading. Here, players try to send data together in a cooperative way. Players transmit data from d_1 to d_m.

Thus, the total amount of data transmitted through players is $TDM = \sum_{i=1}^{M} d_i$ and this amount of data must always be less than or equal to the maximum TD amount of data.

The method of offloading task through cooperative game is shown in Fig. 3. Here, a number of mobile users have come together cooperatively to form some clusters (C1, C2, and C3). Within that cluster, mobile users try to offload the task to the cloud. This reduces the amount of power consumption, delay, and cost for mobile users. As they work cooperatively, the utility of all mobile users within the cluster increases.

Table 2 Cooperative game table for mobile data offloading

Players	Data	Amount of offloaded data	Total possible offloaded data	Remarks
P_1	D_1	$d_1 \leq D_1$	TD	Players collectively send data and try to reduce their energy
P_2	D_2	$d_2 \leq D_2$		
P_3	D_3	$d_3 \leq D_3$		
P_4	D_4	$d_4 \leq D_4$		
P_5	D_5	$d_5 \leq D_5$		
$\vdots$	$\vdots$	$\vdots$		
P_M	D_M	$d_M \leq D_M$		
Total data		$TDM = \sum_{i=1}^{M} d_i$	$TDM \leq TD$	

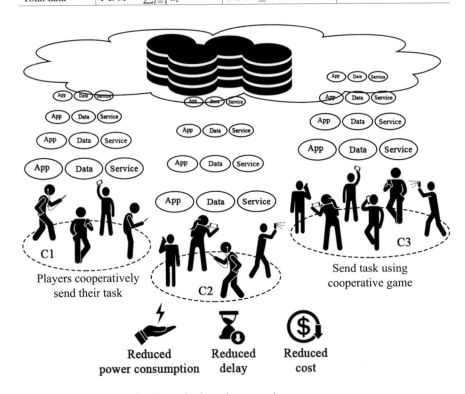

Fig. 3 Architecture of offloading tasks through cooperative game

5 The Use of Game Theory in 5G Wireless Networks

The use of 5G wireless network for green MCC is unprecedented. Mobile data is easily accessible in the cloud through a variety of 5G wireless network technologies [4, 29, 42]. The technologies of 5G wireless network are heterogeneous network (HetNet) [9, 43, 44], D2D communication [11, 34], etc. All these technologies reduce the power consumption and delay of the network. Cloud radio access network (CRAN) and D2D communication have revolutionized 5G wireless networks. In the CRAN network, a base band unit (BBU) pool is located, combines a number of resources. This BBU pool is connected to the evolved node B via the backhaul link and to the remote radio head (RRH) via the fronthaul link.

When D2D communication technology is integrated with CRAN, it becomes difficult to reduce the generated interference and allocate resources to users. The resource allocation process of the network with D2D communication and 5G heterogeneous CRAN (HCRAN) based on matching theory and coalition game is discussed in [12]. In [12], the authors study the process of allocating sub-channels with different bandwidth between D2D pairs and RRH users. This results in the reuse of pre-defined sub-channels for macrocell users, increasing the performance of the network.

Fronthaul link is a very important medium for HCRAN. Based on the matching game, the fronthaul-conscious user association process at HCRAN is discussed in [45]. The purpose of the authors in this article is to increase the wireless fronthaul link capacity to maximize the overall network throughput. The user association process is accomplished through the proposed utility functions for the user and RRH depending on the two-sided matching game.

The method of price and rate optimization of CRAN based on hierarchical dynamic game is discussed in [46]. The article uses BBU owner as leader and RRH as follower. Traffic generated by RRH users is routed based on price value for BBU acquisition.

Interference is an important factor for wireless communication, resulting in loss of network performance. The process of reducing interference in the case of CRAN based on the coalition formation game is described in [47]. In [47], the RRHs create coalitions to reduce interference and serve their customers. Through the model proposed in the article, the RRHs within the CRAN can decide on their own, whether they will provide services to the user in a cooperative manner if the throughput of the RRH improves.

6 Utility Function and Game Table for 5G Wireless Networks in Spectrum Allocation

In this section, we have described the utility function and game table required for 5G wireless networks through auction game.

The use of auction game is significant in 5G wireless networks, making it easy and accurate to allocate spectrum to the right player. The game consists of an auctioneer who acts as a spectrum operator, and a number of bidders who act as players. The utility function for capturing spectrum through auction game is given as,

Table 3 Auction game table for 5G wireless networks

Player	Price value set by the auctioneer	Price value applied by the bidder	The profit of the auctioneer	Remarks
P_1	PA	PB_1	Pro_1	The auctioneer identifies a player based on his or her maximum profit and provides him or her with the spectrum
P_2		PB_2	Pro_2	
P_3		PB_3	Pro_3	
P_4		PB_4	Pro_4	
P_5		PB_5	Pro_5	
$\vdots$		$\vdots$	$\vdots$	
P_M		PB_M	Pro_M	

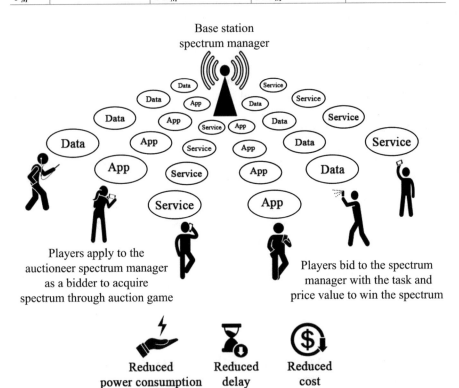

Fig. 4 Architecture of acquiring spectrum through auction game

$$u_{AFWN} = Pro_{max}(PA - PB_i) \tag{2}$$

The game table used for allocating spectrum between the auctioneer and the bidder in the auction game is discussed in Table 3. In this table, 1 to M players have participated in the auction game to acquire spectrum. The price value set by the auctioneer for the spectrum is PA. The bidders offer bids from PB_1 to PB_M at a price they can afford to acquire the spectrum. The auctioneer identifies a player based on his or her maximum profit and provides him or her with the spectrum.

The process of allocating spectrum among mobile users through auction game is illustrated in Fig. 4. Here, a number of mobile users are willing to take spectrum to send their tasks to the cloud. Mobile users apply to the auctioneer spectrum manager with a price value to acquire spectrum as a bidder. The spectrum manager identifies the mobile user on the basis of his own profit and assigns the required spectrum. This reduces the amount of power consumption, delay and cost for mobile users.

7 The Use of Game Theory in Cloud Resource Allocation

The method of allocating resources in cloud computing through the imperfect information stackelberg game is discussed in [48]. This game motivates service providers for overall utility and maximum profit through optimal strategy. The process of allocating resources based on the single cost of different types of resources is proposed in this article, which favorable benefits to the infrastructure providers.

The method of intelligent decision making among cloud providers based on minority game has been documented in [49]. The purpose of the article is to efficiently allocate resources and to exploit resources efficiently among cloud-producing partners. The minority game is designed in such a way that cloud developers can decide to use the resource properly among themselves through personal information.

The process of maximizing profits through resource allocation in the cloud environment based on a non-cooperative game is described in [50]. In [50], the resources of the cloud have been allocated based on the budget. The whole process has been completed through two rounds. Bid values arriving in the first round have been investigated and bids with insufficiently proposed budgets have been eliminated. In the second round, a number of users are identified through non-cooperative game based on user bid value, proposed budget, and deadlines and resources are allocated to these identified users.

The method of cloud resource allocation based on an online auction game is discussed in [51]. The authors suggest a lightweight mechanism to increase the use of real-world cloud applications. Here, the user's bids are sealed using the bid function through the proposed game and sent to the auctioneer. The proposed method has been used to increase the profits of providers and users.

The method of allocating dynamic resources for the highest quality of experience based on the Stackelberg game is described in [52]. In [52], the authors proposed the process of resource allocation through multi leader and multi follower two stages Stackelberg game, so that cloud resources can be allocated to the mobile terminal in the best possible way. Here, leader refers to cloud servers and follower refers to mobile terminals.

The process of allocating resources to the cloud based on the combinatorial double auction game and the services according to the user's needs is described in [53]. First, the incomplete information game of cloud resource allocation has been transformed into a complete but imperfect information game through harsanyi transformation. The authors then draw a model of infrastructure providers and service providers based on different combinations of resources, through which the use of resources between the two parties is maximized and justified.

The process of allocating resources between distributed data centers based on hierarchical game is discussed in [54]. Here, the authors discuss two types of situations between data center operators (DCOs). First, if the coordination between the DCOs is weak, then they work in a non-cooperative way, and if their coordination is sufficient, then they behave like a coalition game. In [54], DCO has acted as leader and service subscribers (SSs) as follower. The SS selects the DCO according to its required resource and assigns a price value. The DCO adjusts its price value based on feedback from SSs and other DCOs to maximize profits.

The process of allocating resources to the cloud based on dynamic Stackelberg game and long short memory model is documented in [55]. Increasing the revenue of infrastructure suppliers and improving the efficiency and quality of service of service providers is a very important task in allocating resources to the cloud. The proposed model predicts the market situation and optimizes the bidding strategy to maximize profits due to huge demand.

Properly scheduling task is a very important job for cloud computing, the main reason is the increase in the number of users. As a result of the increase in the number of users, the amount of power consumption of the network increases exponentially. The process of scheduling tasks and allocating resources to the cloud based on non-cooperative game is described in [56]. The article lists the server's utility function so that the network is power efficient.

8   Utility Function and Game Table for Non-Cooperative Game used in Cloud Resource Allocation

In this section, we have described the utility function and game table required for cloud resource allocation through non-cooperative game.

A non-cooperative game is a game where players work alone and they always try to increase their own utility. Players apply in a non-cooperative manner with price value to acquire the necessary resources from the cloud. The resource manager selects the player based on his own profit and allocates the necessary resources. The player completes his task after receiving adequate resources. The utility function for cloud resource allocation through non-cooperative game is given as,

$$u_{NCCRA} = (d_1 \vee d_2 \vee d_2 \vee d_3 \vee \cdots \vee d_M) \tag{3}$$

Table 4 Non-cooperative game table for cloud resource allocation

Players	Data	Amount of offloaded data	Price value offered by players	Available spectrum	Remarks
P_1	D_1	$d_1 \leq D_1$	PV_1	AFS	Players are non-cooperative and selfishly send data alone and try to reduce their own energy
P_2	D_2	$d_2 \leq D_2$	PV_2		
P_3	D_3	$d_3 \leq D_3$	PV_3		
P_4	D_4	$d_4 \leq D_4$	PV_4		
P_5	D_5	$d_5 \leq D_5$	PV_5		
$\vdots$	$\vdots$	$\vdots$	$\vdots$		
P_M	D_M	$d_M \leq D_M$	PV_M		
Total data		$TDM = d_1 \vee d_2 \vee d_2 \vee d_3 \vee d_4 \vee \cdots \vee d_M$		AFS	

The game table for cloud resource allocation through non-cooperative game has been recorded in Table 4. Table 4 has 1 to M number of players and their data amount is D_1 to D_M. Here, players try to send data alone in a non-cooperative and selfish way. Players transmit data from d_1 to d_m. The available spectrum is AFS.

Thus, the total amount of data transmitted through players is $TDM = d_1 \vee d_2 \vee d_2 \vee d_3 \vee \cdots \vee d_M$.

The process of allocating resources among players through non-cooperative game is illustrated in Fig. 5. Here, a total of 1 to RN resources are present and the $R6$ resource is free. Players apply to the resource manager alone with price value for the acquisition of this free resource. The resource manager identifies a user based on his or her profits and provides the resource to him or her. This reduces the amount of power consumption, delay, and cost for mobile users. Players increase their own utilities through non-cooperative game.

9 Mathematical Model

In this section, we have calculated the amount of delay and power consumption for transmitting data from mobile devices to the cloud and receiving feedback.

9.1 Delay

The uplink delay for sending D amount of data from the mobile device to the cloud is calculated as,

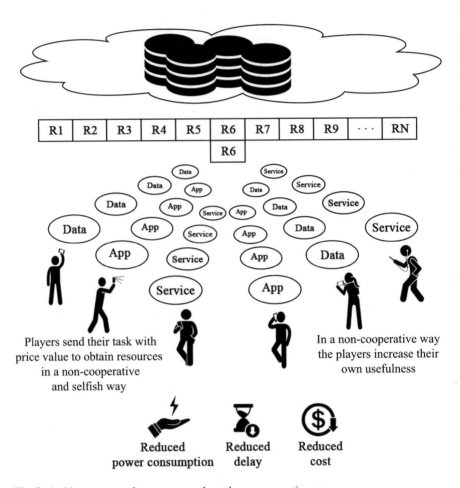

Fig. 5 Architecture to apply to resources through non-cooperative games

$$UD = (\frac{D}{UDaR})$$ (4)

where, $UDaR$ refers to uplink data rate.

The downlink delay for sending D amount of data from the cloud to the mobile device is calculated as,

$$DD = (\frac{D}{DDaR})$$ (5)

where, $DDaR$ refers to downlink data rate.

Propagation delay between mobile device and the cloud is calculated as,

$$PpD = (\frac{Dt}{SD})$$ (6)

where, Dt and SD refer to distance between mobile and cloud, and propagation speed, respectively.

The delay in processing D amount of data in the cloud is calculated as,

$$PcD = (\frac{D}{SC})$$ (7)

where, SC refers to the computing speed of cloud.

9.2 Power Consumption

The uplink power consumption for sending D amount of data from the mobile device to the cloud is calculated as,

$$UD = PCU(\frac{D}{UDaR})$$ (8)

where, PCU refers to the power consumption of sending data from a mobile to the cloud

The downlink power consumption for sending D amount of data from the cloud to the mobile device is calculated as,

$$DD = PCD(\frac{D}{DDaR})$$ (9)

where, PCD refers to the power consumption of receiving data from the cloud to the mobile device

Propagation power consumption between mobile device and the cloud is calculated as,

$$PpD = PCPp(\frac{Dt}{SD})$$ (10)

where, $PCPp$ refers to the power consumption to propagate the data

The power consumption in processing D amount of data in the cloud is calculated as,

$$PcD = PCPc(\frac{D}{SC})$$ (11)

where, $PCPc$ refers to the power consumption to compute the data in the cloud

10   Result and Discussions

In this section, we have calculated and compared the delay and power consumption for basic cloud computing, cloud computing based on game and cloud computing using cloudlet based on game.

10.1   Delay

The delay generated from basic MCC [5], game-based MCC [10], and game-based cloudlet enabled MCC [40] is illustrated in Fig. 6. Figure 6 shows that cloudlet-enabled MCC [40] using game has generated ~11%–26% and ~27%–39% less delay than game-based MCC [10] and basic MCC [5], respectively.

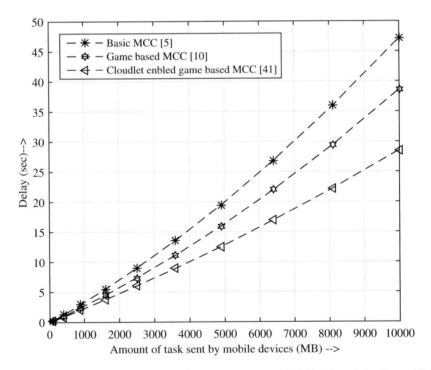

Fig. 6 Comparison of delay between basic MCC [5], game based MCC [10], and cloudlet enabled MCC using game [40]

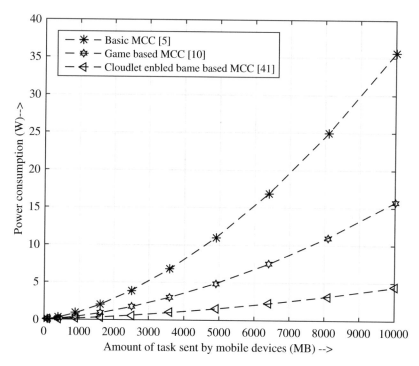

Fig. 7 Comparison of power consumption between basic MCC [5], game based MCC [10], and cloudlet enabled MCC using game [40]

10.2 Power Consumption

The power consumption generated from basic MCC [5], game-based MCC [10], and game-based cloudlet enabled MCC [40] is illustrated in Fig. 7. Figure 7 shows that cloudlet-enabled MCC using game has generated ∼31%–71% and ∼69%–87% less power consumption than game-based MCC [10] and basic MCC [5], respectively.

11 Summary of Games and Mobile Cloud Computing

This section describes the different types of games and their association with MCC.

Fig. 8 Relationship between
the task offloading of MCC
with different types of games

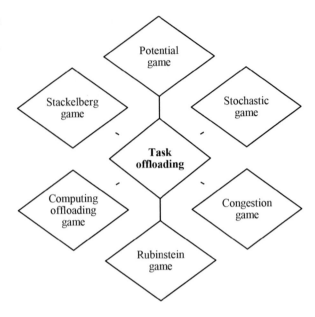

11.1 Games for Task Offloading

The relationship between the task offloading of MCC and different types of games
is illustrated in Fig. 8. In Table 5, we have discussed the features of several existing
methods of task offlanding and the games used in them.

11.2 Games for 5G Wireless Networks

The combination of offloading's through 5G wireless network with a variety of
games is illustrated in Fig. 9. In Table 6, we have discussed the features of several
existing methods of cloud related to 5G wireless networks and the games used in
them.

11.3 Games for MCC Resource Allocation

The matching of different types of games with the resource allocation of cloud is
illustrated in Fig. 10. In Table 7, we have discussed the features of several existing
methods of allocating MCC resources and the games used in them.

Table 5 Features of existing task offloading methods

Articles	Game	Features
Dynamically offload the data from mobile to cloud [32]	Potential game	As the size of the system increases, offloading performance increases and scales improves
Offloading multi-user computation for MCC under dynamic environment [10]	Stochastic Game	Increased system performance in terms of computational costs and the number of useful cloud computing users
Two decentralized data offloading methods for MCC [33]	Congestion game	Reduce payments to mobile subscribers and maximize mobile operator revenue
Effective computation offloading approach for mobile cloud and IoT [35]	Rubinstein game	The method works in distributed IoT environments while supporting timely and ubiquitous application execution
Method of distributed computation offloading in MCC of multiple mobile device users [36]	Multi-user computation offloading game	Reduces total costs, including energy costs, time costs, and financial costs for mobile device's
Cooperative application execution for MCC [37]	Stackelberg game	Encourages mobile devices to share their unused resources across MCC platforms
Cloudlet based computation offloading in MCC [39, 40]	Non-cooperative game [39] and potential game [40]	Cloudlets with limited computing resources are used, which reduces network delay and energy consumption

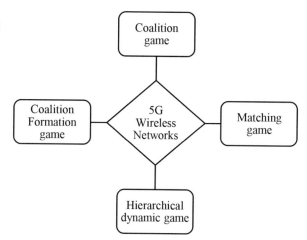

Fig. 9 Combination of mobile cloud computing's 5G wireless network with a variety of games

12   Future Scope

Cloud computing is an essential thing for completing and storing large amounts of generated data. The main sources of this data are the large number of mobile devices, the number of huge applications used in it, and the large number of IoT

Table 6 Features of offloading methods of existing 5G wireless networks

Articles	Game	Features
Allocate bandwidth sub-channels between multiple D2D pairs and RRH users included in CRAN [12]	Coalition game	Significantly improves system performance and overall throughput
Fronthaul aware user association in 5G HCRAN [45]	Matching game	Increases access rate performance along with user achievable data rates
CRAN's user traffic allocation process based on one-leader and multi-follower [46]	Hierarchical dynamic game	This method maximizes revenue and reduces traffic congestion costs
The method of cooperative intervention between RRHs in CRAN [47]	Coalition formation game	The alliance results in less intra-interference and to serve their clients collectively

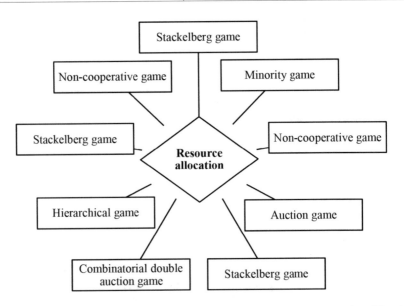

Fig. 10 Matching of different types of games with the resource allocation of mobile cloud computing

devices. Considering the rate at which the number of IoT devices is increasing, the cloud is a very necessary thing. This huge number of IoT devices sense data without any human intervention and transfer that data to the cloud for processing. The cloud processes that data and stores it as needed. Over the past few decades, fog computing, edge computing, and dew computing devices have been introduced with the cloud. These devices are located much closer to the user than the cloud and have much lower power consumption. As a result the network delay is much less. All of

Table 7 Features of existing MCC resource allocation methods

Articles	Game	Features
Dynamic resource allocation for cloud computing environment based on imperfect information with hidden markov model [48]	Stackelberg game	This approach maximizes profits for both service providers and infrastructure providers
Efficiently allocate resources and services among cloud manufacturing system partners and make exploitative decisions [49]	Minority game	This is an important process to help different types of enterprises, especially small and medium enterprises to participate and develop their business
Increasing profits in cloud computing through efficient resource allocation [50]	Non-cooperative game	The profitability of cloud providers has improved and the amount of assets sold has increased
Efficient resource allocation and asset pricing through bid function [51]	Auction game	Increases the profitability of both cloud providers and users
Dynamic resource allocation for MCC environment based on multi-leader multi-follower strategy [52]	Stackelberg game	Cloud servers and mobile terminals both selfishly try to maximize their own interests. This greatly affects the performance of the network
Resource allocation model based on bidding coordination of multiple service providers and infrastructure providers [53]	Combinatorial double auction	Successful business-related infrastructure providers and service providers are able to maximize their profits, resulting in greater social welfare
A way for multiple data center operators to simultaneously serve the asset allocation to multiple service customers [54]	Hierarchical game	Unilaterally DCOs deviate from the decision and improve their performance
Incomplete information based game theoretical method for allocating resources in the cloud [55]	Stackelberg game	Optimize bidding strategies to maximize profits while maintaining fairness for tenants with huge demand as well as profit
The efficient allocation of computing resource and task scheduling of servers located within the cloud computing system [56]	Non-cooperative game	Increases the average power efficiency of cloud computing systems

these devices can store a small amount of data, but the use of the cloud is unique in processing large amounts of data and storing it for the future.

As the number of user's increases, the data generated from them will become more difficult to transmit, complete, and store. This requires a mathematical paradigm, through which it is accomplished in a healthy way. Suitable for this is game theory. Different types of games make it possible to offloading data, transmitting it over a wireless network, and allocating resources in the right way to process that data. This is very helpful now and in the future. Accurate identification of resources through games reduces the power consumption and delay of the network, which helps to move the network towards a greener environment.

From this chapter, we can realize that green MCC is a vital necessity and games are an important component of this. It will be very helpful to process and store a lot of generated data in the near future.

13   Conclusion

This chapter discusses in detail the relationship between MCC and games. The game is a very useful medium for transmitting data and allocating the necessary resources to compute it. This increases the efficiency of the network. Data is easily and quickly transferred from mobile devices to the cloud through a variety of 5G wireless network technologies. The use of different types of games on 5G wireless networks reduces the power consumption of the network. Cloud's resource allocation is made easier through a variety of games, which is very useful for a lot of incoming data.

Acknowledgments This project is supported by Department of Science & Technology (DST), Govt. of India, a research INSPIRE Fellowship under INSPIRE Program, Ref. No.: DST/INSPIRE Fellowship/2018/IF180846.

References

1. Dash, S., Ahmad, M., Iqbal, T., et al.: Mobile cloud computing: A green perspective. In: Intelligent Systems, pp. 523–533. Springer, Berlin (2021)
2. De, D.: Mobile cloud computing: architectures, algorithms and applications. Chapman and Hall/CRC, New York (2019)
3. Malik, S.U., Akram, H., Gill, S.S., Pervaiz, H., Malik, H.: EFFORT: Energy efficient framework for offload communication in mobile cloud computing. Software: Practice and Experience **51**(9), 1896–1909 (2021)
4. Ghosh, S., De, D., Deb, P., Mukherjee, A.: 5G-zoom-game: Small cell zooming using weighted majority cooperative game for energy efficient 5G mobile network. Wirel. Netw **26**(1), 349–372 (2020)
5. Jo, B., Piran, M.J., Lee, D., Suh, D.Y.: Efficient computation offloading in mobile cloud computing for video streaming over 5G. Computers, Materials and Continua **61**(1), 439–463 (2019)

6. Chen, M.H., Liang, B., Dong, M.: Multi-user multi-task offloading and resource allocation in mobile cloud systems. IEEE Trans. Wirel. Commun. **17**(10), 6790–6805 (2018)
7. Ghosh, S., Obaidat, M.S., De, D., Hsiao, K.F.: SCHOOL: Spectrum allocation for D2D communication enabled HetNet using stackelberg and coalition formation game. In: 2021 International Conference on Computer, Information and Telecommunication Systems (CITS), pp. 1–5. IEEE, New York (2021)
8. Ghosh, S., De, D.: AGE-SVN: Auction game based 5G enabled smart vehicular network using D2D communication. In: 2021 9th International Conference on Reliability, Infocom Technologies and Optimization (Trends and Future Directions) (ICRITO), pp. 1–5. IEEE, New York (2021)
9. Ghosh, S., De, D.: E2M3: energy-efficient massive MIMO–MISO 5G HetNet using stackelberg game. J. Supercomput. **77**(11), 1–35 (2021)
10. Zheng, J., Cai, Y., Wu, Y., Shen, X.: Dynamic computation offloading for mobile cloud computing: A stochastic game-theoretic approach. IEEE Trans. Mob. Comput. **18**(4), 771–786 (2018)
11. Ghosh, S., De, D.: CG-D2D: Cooperative game theory based resource optimization for D2D communication in 5G wireless network. In: 2020 Fifth International Conference on Research in Computational Intelligence and Communication Networks (ICRCICN), pp. 171–176. IEEE, New York (2020)
12. Zhang, B., Mao, X., Yu, J.L., Han, Z.: Resource allocation for 5G heterogeneous cloud radio access networks with D2D communication: A matching and coalition approach. IEEE Trans. Veh. Technol. **67**(7), 5883–5894 (2018)
13. Mei, J., Li, K., Tong, Z., Li, Q., Li, K.: Profit maximization for cloud brokers in cloud computing. IEEE Trans. Parallel Distrib. Syst. **30**(1), 190–203 (2018)
14. Liu, G., Shen, H.: Minimum-cost cloud storage service across multiple cloud providers. IEEE/ACM Trans. Networking **25**(4), 2498–2513 (2017)
15. Lehrig, S., Sanders, R., Brataas, G., Cecowski, M., Ivanšek, S., Polutnik, J.: CloudStore—towards scalability, elasticity, and efficiency benchmarking and analysis in cloud computing. Futur. Gener. Comput. Syst. **78**, 115–126 (2018)
16. Ahmad, A.A.S., Andras, P.: Scalability analysis comparisons of cloud-based software services. Journal of Cloud Computing **8**(1), 1–17 (2019)
17. Gao, X., Zhi, S., Wang, X.: Investigating the relationship among ease-of-use, NPS, and customers' sequent spending of cloud computing products. In: International Conference on Human-Computer Interaction, pp. 417–422. Springer, Berlin (2021)
18. Madhav, N., Joseph, M.: The ease of use and intentions of use of cloud technology in higher education institutions. In: Proceedings of the 2nd International Conference on Intelligent and Innovative Computing Applications, pp. 1–6 (2020)
19. You, X., Li, Y., Zheng, M., Zhu, C., Yu, L.: A survey and taxonomy of energy efficiency relevant surveys in cloud-related environments. IEEE Access **5**, 14066–14078 (2017)
20. Bui, D.M., Yoon, Y., Huh, E.N., Jun, S., Lee, S.: Energy efficiency for cloud computing system based on predictive optimization. J. Parallel Distrib. Comput. **102**, 103–114 (2017)
21. Lin, Y., Kämäräinen, T., Di Francesco, M., Ylä-Jääski, A.: Performance evaluation of remote display access for mobile cloud computing. Comput. Commun. **72**, 17–25 (2015)
22. Tabrizchi, H., Rafsanjani, M.K.: A survey on security challenges in cloud computing: issues, threats, and solutions. J. Supercomput. **76**(12), 9493–9532 (2020)
23. Qiang, W., Chen, F., Yang, L.T., Jin, H.: MUC: Updating cloud applications dynamically via multi-version execution. Futur. Gener. Comput. Syst. **74**, 254–264 (2017)
24. Zúñiga-Prieto, M., González-Huerta, J., Insfran, E., Abrahão, S.: Dynamic reconfiguration of cloud application architectures. Software: Practice and Experience **48**(2), 327–344 (2018)
25. Apostolakis, K.C., Margetis, G., Stephanidis, C., Duquerrois, J.M., Drouglazet, L., Lallet, A., Delmas, S., Cordeiro, L., Gomes, A., Amor, M., et al.: Cloud-native 5G infrastructure and network applications (NetApps) for public protection and disaster relief: The 5G-EPICENTRE project. In: 2021 Joint European Conference on Networks and Communications & 6G Summit (EuCNC/6G Summit), pp. 235–240. IEEE, New York (2021)

26. Dubey, S., Dahiya, M., Jain, S.: Application of distributed data center in logistics as cloud collaboration for handling disaster relief. In: 2018 3rd International Conference On Internet of Things: Smart Innovation and Usages (IoT-SIU), pp. 1–11. IEEE, New York (2018)

27. Mukherjee, A., Gupta, P., De, D.: Mobile cloud computing based energy efficient offloading strategies for femtocell network. In: 2014 Applications and Innovations in Mobile Computing (AIMoC), pp. 28–35. IEEE, New York (2014)

28. De, D., Mukherjee, A., Roy, D.G.: Power and delay efficient multilevel offloading strategies for mobile cloud computing. Wirel. Pers. Commun. **112**(4), 1–28 (2020)

29. Ghosh, S., De, D., Deb, P.: Energy and spectrum optimization for 5G massive mimo cognitive femtocell based mobile network using auction game theory. Wirel. Pers. Commun. **106**(2), 555–576 (2019)

30. Mukherjee, A., De, D., Ghosh, S.K., Buyya, R.: Introduction to mobile edge computing. In: Mobile Edge Computing, pp. 3–19. Springer (2021)

31. Zhang, L., Fu, D., Liu, J., Ngai, E.C.H., Zhu, W.: On energy-efficient offloading in mobile cloud for real-time video applications. IEEE Trans. Circuits Syst. Video Technol. **27**(1), 170–181 (2016)

32. Chen, X.: Decentralized computation offloading game for mobile cloud computing. IEEE Trans. Parallel Distrib. Syst. **26**(4), 974–983 (2014)

33. Liu, D., Khoukhi, L., Hafid, A.: Decentralized data offloading for mobile cloud computing based on game theory. In: 2017 Second International Conference on Fog and Mobile Edge Computing (FMEC), pp. 20–24. IEEE, New York (2017)

34. Ghosh, S., De, D.: Power and spectrum efficient D2D communication for 5G IoT using stackelberg game theory. In: 2020 IEEE 17th India Council International Conference (INDICON), pp. 1–7. IEEE, New York (2020)

35. Kim, S.: Nested game-based computation offloading scheme for mobile cloud IoT systems. EURASIP J. Wirel. Commun. Netw. **2015**(1), 1–11 (2015)

36. Liu, Y., Wang, S., Yang, F.: A multi-user computation offloading algorithm based on game theory in mobile cloud computing. In: 2016 IEEE/ACM Symposium on Edge Computing (SEC), pp. 93–94. IEEE, New York (2016)

37. Wang, X., Chen, X., Wu, W., An, N., Wang, L.: Cooperative application execution in mobile cloud computing: A stackelberg game approach. IEEE Commun. Lett. **20**(5), 946–949 (2015)

38. Mukherjee, A., De, D., Roy, D.G.: A power and latency aware cloudlet selection strategy for multi-cloudlet environment. IEEE Transactions on Cloud Computing **7**(1), 141–154 (2016)

39. Cardellini, V., Personé, V.D.N., Di Valerio, V., Facchinei, F., Grassi, V., Presti, F.L., Piccialli, V.: A game-theoretic approach to computation offloading in mobile cloud computing. Math. Program. **157**(2), 421–449 (2016)

40. Ma, X., Lin, C., Xiang, X., Chen, C.: Game-theoretic analysis of computation offloading for cloudlet-based mobile cloud computing. In: Proceedings of the 18th ACM International Conference on Modeling, Analysis and Simulation of Wireless and Mobile Systems, pp. 271–278 (2015)

41. Roy, D.G., De, D., Mukherjee, A., Buyya, R.: Application-aware cloudlet selection for computation offloading in multi-cloudlet environment. J. Supercomput. **73**(4), 1672–1690 (2017)

42. Ghosh, S., De, D.: Weighted majority cooperative game based dynamic small cell clustering and resource allocation for 5G green mobile network. Wirel. Pers. Commun. **111**(3), 1391–1411 (2020)

43. Ghosh, S., De, D., Deb, P.: E2Beam: Energy efficient beam allocation in 5G hetnet using cooperative game. In: 2020 IEEE International Women in Engineering (WIE) Conference on Electrical and Computer Engineering (WIECON-ECE), pp. 219–222. IEEE, New York (2020)

44. Ghosh, S., De, D.: Dynamic antenna allocation in 5G MIMO HetNet using weighted majority cooperative game theory. In: 2020 IEEE 1st International Conference for Convergence in Engineering (ICCE), pp. 21–25. IEEE, New York (2020)

45. Elhattab, M., Elmesalawy, M.M., Ismail, T.: Fronthaul-aware user association in 5G hetero-geneous cloud radio access networks: A matching game perspective. In: 2018 International Symposium on Networks, Computers and Communications (ISNCC), pp. 1–6. IEEE, New York (2018)
46. Saffar, M., Kebriaei, H., Niyato, D.: Pricing and rate optimization of cloud radio access network using robust hierarchical dynamic game. IEEE Trans. Wirel. Commun. **16**(11), 7404–7418 (2017)
47. Zhan, S.C., Niyato, D.: A coalition formation game for remote radio head cooperation in cloud radio access network. IEEE Trans. Veh. Technol. **66**(2), 1723–1738 (2016)
48. Wei, W., Fan, X., Song, H., Fan, X., Yang, J.: Imperfect information dynamic stackelberg game based resource allocation using hidden markov for cloud computing. IEEE Trans. Serv. Comput. **11**(1), 78–89 (2016)
49. Carlucci, D., Renna, P., Materi, S., Schiuma, G.: Intelligent decision-making model based on minority game for resource allocation in cloud manufacturing. Manag. Decis. **58**(11). 2305–2325 (2020). Emerald Publishing Limited
50. Nezarat, A., Dastghaibyfard, G.: A game theoretical model for profit maximization resource allocation in cloud environment with budget and deadline constraints. J. Supercomput. **72**(12), 4737–4770 (2016)
51. Salehan, A., Deldari, H., Abrishami, S.: An online valuation-based sealed winner-bid auction game for resource allocation and pricing in clouds. J. Supercomput. **73**(11), 4868–4905 (2017)
52. Wang, Y., Meng, S., Chen, Y., Sun, R., Wang, X., Sun, K.: Multi-leader multi-follower stackelberg game based dynamic resource allocation for mobile cloud computing environment. Wirel. Pers. Commun. **93**(2), 461–480 (2017)
53. Li, Q., Huang, C., Bao, H., Fu, B., Jia, X.: A game-based combinatorial double auction model for cloud resource allocation. In: 2019 28th International Conference on Computer Communication and Networks (ICCCN), pp. 1–8. IEEE, New York (2019)
54. Zhang, H., Xiao, Y., Bu, S., Yu, F.R., Niyato, D., Han, Z.: Distributed resource allocation for data center networks: A hierarchical game approach. IEEE Transactions on Cloud Computing **8**(3), 778–789 (2018)
55. Liu, Y., Njilla, L.L., Wang, J., Song, H.: An lstm enabled dynamic stackelberg game theoretic method for resource allocation in the cloud. In: 2019 International Conference on Computing, Networking and Communications (ICNC), pp. 797–801. IEEE, New York (2019)
56. Zhang, L., Zhou, J.h.: Task scheduling and resource allocation algorithm in cloud computing system based on non-cooperative game. In: 2017 IEEE 2nd International Conference on Cloud Computing and Big Data Analysis (ICCCBDA), pp. 254–259. IEEE, New York (2017)

Security Frameworks for Green Mobile Cloud Computing

Tanmoy Maitra, Pinaki Sankar Chatterjee, and Debasis Giri

1 Introduction

Mobile technologies, such as smart phones and tablets, are becoming increasingly important since the most efficient computing and beneficial communication approaches are not limited by location or time [1]. Such devices are replacing laptop or desktop systems by employing the cloud computing platform or mobile cloud services. MCC is a hybrid of cloud computing and mobile computing in which data is processed and stored in the cloud while mobile devices are primarily utilized as clients to interface with apps and obtain processed results from the cloud [2]. Furthermore, the battery life-time is limited to the mobile devices; therefore, by taking the concept of green mobile network, data has been offloaded to the cloud server for processing and store. Despite such benefits, mobile cloud computing still isn't widely adopted due to the numerous aspects associated with the security of mobile cloud computing infrastructure, such as privacy, access control, service level agreements, interoperability, charging models, data protection, and even more, that must be handled.

There are numerous issues in the GMCC domain, including data duplication, continuity, instability, restricted scalability, portability (due to falling cloud provider quality), unpredictable availability of cloud resources, security, trust, and secrecy [3]. The above-mentioned difficulties have slowed the explosive growth of GMCC's customer base. According to the articles [4–6], 74% of IT executives and chief information officers are hesitant to use cloud services due to security and privacy

T. Maitra · P. S. Chatterjee
School of Computer Engineering, KIIT Deemed to be University, Bhubaneswar, India

D. Giri (✉)
Department of Information Technology, Maulana Abul Kalam Azad University of Technology, Nadia, India

© The Author(s), under exclusive license to Springer Nature Switzerland AG 2022
D. De et al. (eds.), *Green Mobile Cloud Computing*,
https://doi.org/10.1007/978-3-031-08038-8_6

133

concerns. To attract potential customers, cloud service providers must solve all security concerns in order to create a fully secure environment. To protect a cloud computing environment, research groups and academic institutions have put in massive amounts of work. Some challenges remain unanswered, like the privacy and security of users' information saved on cloud server(s), security hazards associated with many virtual machines, and intrusion detection. Because GMCC is cloud-based, all security weaknesses are carried across, with the added restriction of resource-constrained mobile devices. As there is a limitation of resources, therefore, the existing security methods for the cloud computing environment cannot be executed on a mobile device directly. On mobile devices, a portable secure architecture that delivers safeguards with little processing and communication costs is required. Security-enhanced cloud application services can be utilized to give privacy and security solutions. Secure Cloud Application Services also offers key management, user management, on-demand encryption, intrusion detection, and authentication services to mobile users in addition to privacy and security. A dependable communication link was required between cloud services and green mobile devices. To secure communication channels between mobile devices and the cloud, routing protocols with security might be used. However, while virtualization promotes the utilization of cloud resources, it can also introduce new security risks due to the absence of total segregation of virtual machines put on a single server. Virtual machine safe monitoring, mirroring, and migration can help to overcome some of the security difficulties posed by virtualization. Users must be able to audit the security level of hosted services in order to give a clear cloud environment. Cloud Service Monitor (CSM) can be used to do audits. CSM checks the running environment's security and flow. The security level must fulfill the user's security requirements, and the running environment's normal flow should be maintained. The Secure Storage Verification service can be used to verify the security of data uploaded to the cloud. The cotyledon center's physical security is critical to achieving security and privacy. Physical security refers to safeguards that prevent unauthorized employees from physically accessing cloud service provider resources. Video surveillance, security guards, security lights, sensors, and alarms can all be used to provide physical security. Many works [7–15] offer an energy-efficient high-performance computing environment. However, the GMCC environment necessitates low energy-consumption security architecture for mobile devices in order to deliver security and privacy services [16].

Generally, the security framework can be categorized into three parts: data security framework, access control framework, and communication framework. Figure 1 shows the security frameworks for GMCC. When users want to store or fetch data from cloud, at first access control will check that if the user has the access or not on that data. For this, access control framework has been taken place. Moreover, access control framework works for each service like SaaS, IaaS, and PaaS. If access control permits the user to access the data, then data security framework checks the validity of data. All the communications to get a service from cloud by the help of mobile devices will be secured by the secure communication framework.

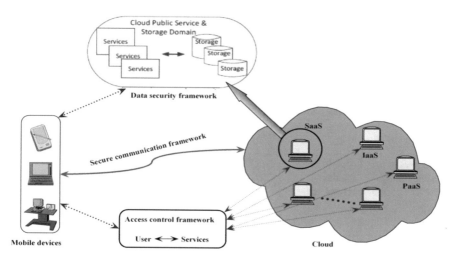

Fig. 1 Security frameworks for mobile-cloud architecture

In this chapter, the existing frameworks are discussed in Sect. 2 followed by the existing security challenges in GMCC in Sect. 3. Finally, conclusion has been given in Sect. 4.

2 Existing Frameworks

This section discusses the security frameworks for Green Mobile Cloud Computing (GMCC). The framework can be categorized by three main parts: (a) data security framework, (b) access control framework, and (c) communication framework.

2.1 Data Security Framework

There should be some systems in place to address these data security and privacy concerns. Data security frameworks that offer security, confidentiality, and reliability of users' data must be implemented or developed. This section Table 1 focuses mostly on data security approaches that reduce the computational cost of cryptographic algorithms and processes.

To avoid adversary threats, several approaches must be implemented to enhance the security of mobile users' personal data. Certain measures are required to ensure the privacy of a user's private information, ensuring that only the owner has access to his information and that no other individuals have access to the information without

Table 1 Comparison of cryptographic data security mechanism [16–18]

Mechanisms of security	Operational support	Restrictions	Assumptions	Conclusion
Coding based scheme	Multiplication of units in a matrix using a coding vector	On mobile platforms, there is an additional file management cost	Construction of Coding Vector	1. When contrast to an encryption-based system, it uses fewer resources. 2. Expensive in terms of computation
Encryption based scheme	Algorithm for symmetric cryptography	Cost in the Computing	–	1. Use up a lot of energy on Mobiles 2. Increase the level of protection
Block based sharing scheme	Strategies of action for Block Oriented Chaining	Executions of Depended Blocks. As cryptographic techniques, basic XOR procedures are utilised	The file is broken into segments logically	1. Energy-Saving 2. Use fewer resources 3. Execute at a faster rate
Sharing based scheme	X-OR operations	Accompanying activities require a lot of computing power	Arbitrary Shares are generated and uploaded	1. It takes a long time 2. A substantial amount of data storage and processing is required

the permission of the owner. Basically, in this chapter we will discuss a data security framework proposed by Patel et al. [19].

2.1.1   Data Security Framework Proposed by Patel et al. [19]

The authors in [19] improved data security and privacy using three distinct cartographic implementation strategies. (1) Counter modes of block based Encryption and Decryption; (2) MAC- Message Authentication Code, and (3) Blowfish Symmetric Cartographic Algorithm.

According to them the flow for uploading the user file on the cloud storage is as follows (Fig. 2):

The files should be exchanged with clients based on the access rights provided to certain authorized users by the data holder. There will be more opportunities

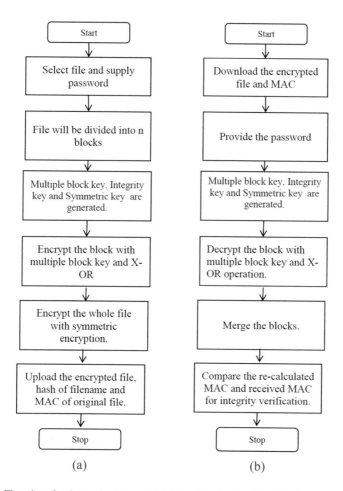

Fig. 2 (**a**) Flowchart for data uploading and (**b**) Flowchart for data downloading

to reduce the cost of cryptographic standard algorithms and to study systems that provide the similar protection with less cost than regular cryptographic algorithms.

Apart from the aforementioned data security framework [19], Jia et al. [20] introduced a secure data service for MCC. To achieve the integrity and security of mobile users' data kept in cloud server, Hsueh et al. [21] also presented a scheme which is applicable for smart phones. In addition, due to limitation of resource in mobile, Yang et al. [22] enhanced the public cloud data storage scheme which ensures the confidentiality, privacy, availability and integrity of mobile users' data. Zhou and Huang [23] introduced a secure framework for lightweight mobile devices known as Privacy Preserving Cipher Policy Attribute-Based Encryption (PP-CP-ABE). In this chapter, we also discuss the Zhou and Huang's Scheme [23].

2.1.2 Data Security Framework Proposed by Zhou and Huang [23]

In this section, this chapter briefly discusses the PP-CP-ABE [23]. In this scheme, there is five entities, (a) data owner (OW), (b) service provider for encryption (SPE), (c) service provider for decryption (SPD), (d) service provider for storage (SPS) and (e) trusted authority (TA). OW can be a mobile device or sensor that can prompt the cloud for data storage and retrieval. To increase OW's processing capabilities, a large portion of encryption and decryption operations are performed to the cloud. SPE encrypts the file for OW without knowing the security key. Similarly, SPD decrypts the file for OW without obtaining any information about the data content. The cipher data is kept on a SPS. TA generates and distributes the keys among OWs. Figure 3 depicts the architecture of the proposed scheme [23].

The steps involved in the scheme [24] are discussed as follow. However, to know details about cryptographic technique involved in this scheme, we suggest go through the article [24].

Step 1: After selecting secret parameters, TA produces a bi-liner map function. After this, TA declares the private and public keys.

Step 2: To obtain the private key each OW register themselves to TA. However, based on the owners' attributes, private key will be generated.

Step 3: Data Access Tree (DAT) should be outsourced by the OW if he/she want to enter into encryption process. DAT has two parts: (1) data access policy controlled by cloud provider SPE, namely DAT_{SPE}, and (2) data access policy controlled by OW, namely DAT_{OW}. DAT_{OW} contains only one attribute to eliminate the overhead in the owners' end. The OW randomly produces a one degree polynomial to obtain some secrets s, $s1$, $s2$. Then OW transmits DAT_{SPE} and secret $s1$ to SPE.

Step 4: Based on the obtained information, SPE produces a Temporal Cipher (TC) by using some cryptographic techniques. At the same time OW also encrypts the message M by using the remaining secrets s and $s2$ and also uses some cryptographic technique to produce TC_{OW}, C', and C. Then OW transmits $< TC_{OW}, C'$, and $C >$ to SPE.

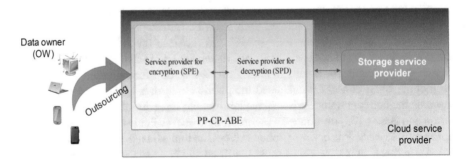

Fig. 3 System architecture for scheme [24]

Step 5: Finally, SPE produces the cipher text of M, after receiving the $< TC_{OW}, C'$, and $C >$ .and stores the data through storage cloud service.

2.2 Access Control Framework

Access control is a well-known security concern. In the literature, several access control strategies have been introduced. A list of table (see Table 2) is given as related exiting access control frameworks overview. But, among them, this chapter will discuss Li et al.'s [24] dynamic attributes based conventional access control scheme.

Table 2 Comparison of related access control frameworks

Frameworks	Static attributes	Dynamic attributes		Data confidentiality
		Spatial or temporal	Proximity	
Context aware Role Based Access Control [25]	Yes	Yes	No	No
Event driven Role Based Access Control [26]	Yes	Yes	No	No
Location aware Access Control [27]	Yes	Yes	No	No
Location based encryption [28]	Yes	Yes	No	Yes
Secure localization [29]	Yes	Yes	No	Yes
Li et al.'s Framework [24]	Yes	Yes	Yes	Yes
Attribute-based Access Control (ABAC) [30]	Yes	No	Yes	Yes
Temporal-based Access control (TBAC) [31]	Yes	Yes	Yes	Yes

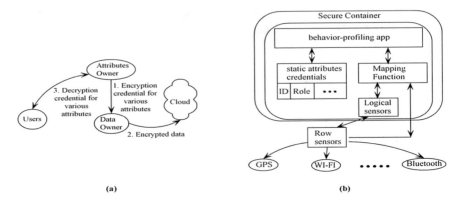

(a)   (b)

Fig. 4 (**a**) System architecture, and (**b**) application architecture for secure container

2.2.1 System Architecture of Li et al.'s Dynamic Attributes Based Conventional Access Control

This section will describe the system architecture and behavior-profiling of application of dynamic attributes based conventional access control proposed by Li et al. Figure 4a shows the system architecture, where, four components are present: (a) users (or employees), (b) data owner (or organizations), (c) cloud service provider, and (d) attribute authorities. Each user has smart device with the Internet facility and can demand data at anytime from anywhere. Data owner defines the access polices and stores the data in the cloud storage. Cloud service providers offer computing power as well as cloud storage to both data owners and customers. The attributes authority maintains the clients' static or fixed attributes.

The behaviour profiling app (See Fig. 4b) loaded on the user's smartphone could be used to validate if the customer is the rightful owner of the mobile device. As the behaviour-profiling application is stored on the user's phone, unscrupulous individuals may change it to offer fake data for dynamic features. In the technological advances in the smart device market, there are already several successful solutions for this sort of security weakness, such as KNOX [32] by Samsung and BES [33] by Blackberry. These software packages can safely install apps on the user's smartphone and evaluate the authenticity of the installed apps without interfering with the user's experience. Thus, by modifying the behaviour-profiling application to produce fake information, the data owner can be easily identified using KNOX or BES.

2.2.2 Static and Dynamic Attribute-Based Access Control Strategy for Collective Attribute Authorities

This section gives a detailed description of attributes based encryption scheme which can be applied in the framework for the access control for the GMCC. The encryption scheme has four phases: (a) setup, (b) key generation, (c) encryption, and (d) decryption.

- **Setup phase**: Attribute authority (AA) runs algorithm SP to produce bilinear parameters $G_1, G_2, G_x, p, g_1, g_2$ as $G_1, G_2, G_x, p, g_1, g_2 \leftarrow SP(1^\beta, \delta)$, where $\delta \in \{0, 1\}^\beta$ and G_1, G_2, G_x are the groups, p is the order of the group, and g_1, g_2 are the generator of the groups.

  i-th AA picks $v_i \in_R Z_q^*$ and calculates $Y_i = \hat{e}(g_1, g_2)^{v_i}$ and transmits Y_i to the another AA. After getting Y_i, each AA computes $Y = \prod Y_i = \hat{e}(g_1, g_2)^{\sum_i v_i}$. After that a shared secret $s_{kj} (= s_{jk} \in Z_q^*)$ has been transmitted to the k-th and j-th authorities randomly.

  After getting the shared secret k-th authority randomly picks x_k and computes $y_k = g_1^{x_k} \mod q$. Then k-th and j-th attribute authorities compute $y_k^{x_j/(s_{kj}+u)}$ and $y_j^{x_k/(s_{kj}+u)}$ respectively for the user u.

  i-th AA picks a confidential parameter $t_{i,k} \in Z_q^*$ randomly for k-th attributes and calculates the public key $T_{i,k} = g_2^{t_{i,k}}$ for all $k \in \{1, 2, 3, \ldots, N_k\}$ and $i \in \{1, \ldots, I\}$, where the authority k keeps track of the number of attributes N_k.

- **Key generation phase**: With individual authority k, the user u computes the following steps: (a) For $j \in \{1, \ldots, I\}$ /$\{k\}$, user obtains the D_{kj} after picking random value $R_{kj} \in Z_q^*$ as $g_1^{R_{kj}} y_k^{x_j/(s_{kj}+u)}$. (b) After calculating D_{kj}, user u computes $D_u = \prod_{(k,j)} D_{kj} = g_1^{R_u}$ where, $R_u = \sum_{(k,j)} R_{kj}$. (c) If w_k number of attributes is assured by user u, then AA chooses a w_k-degree polynomial $poly_{k,u}$ randomly with $poly_{k,u}(0) = v_i - \sum_{(k,j)} R_{kj}$. (d) Finally, k-th authority calculates $S_{k,i} = g_1^{poly_{k,u}(i)/t_{i,k}}, i \in \{1, .2, 3, .., N_k\}$ for all k.

- **Encryption phase**: Data m is encrypted by the owner of the data for attribute set $A_m = A_A^1 \cup A_A^2 \cdots \cup A_A^k \cup A_c$. Where the attribute set A_A^k kept by i-th AA: (a) Data owner chooses $S_A, S_B \in Z_q^*$ randomly and encodes the information m as $ENC^m = mY^{S_B}$. (b) Then data owner calculates $E_{do}^0 = h\left(H\left(a_{c,1}\right) \| H\left(a_{c,2}\right) \| \ldots \| H\left(a_{c,n}\right)\right) Y^{S_B+S_A}, E_{do}^1 = g_2^{S_A}, C_{k,i} = T_{k,i}^{S_A}$ for all $i \in A_A^k$. (c) Data owner then uploads $CT^m = \{ E_{do}^0, E_{do}^1, C_{k,j}, ENC^m\}$ into the cloud.

- **Decryption phase**: After getting CT^m from the cloud, user collects the necessary attributes to decode m.

  For individual authority k, the user calculates $\hat{e}\left(S_{k,i}, C_{k,i}\right) = \hat{e}(g_1, g_2)^{S_A\ poly_{k,u}(i)}$ by using $C_{k,i}$ associated with $S_{k,i}$. The user then interpolates all $\hat{e}(g_1, g_2)^{S_A\ poly_{k,u}(i)}$

and obtains $Poly_{k,u} = \hat{e}\,(g_1,g_2)^{S_A\,poly_{k,u}(0)} = \hat{e}(g_1,g_2)^{S_A\left(v_i-\sum\limits_{j\neq k}R_{kj}\right)}$. The user accumulates all $Poly_{k,u}$ together and obtains $F = \hat{e}\,(g_1,g_2)^{S_A\sum v_i-S_A\,R_u} = \dfrac{Y^{S_A}}{\hat{e}\,(g_1{}^{R_u},g_2{}^{S_A})^{P_{k,u}(i)}}$. Then user's app (that is installed in mobile devices) computes $h\left(H\left(a'_{c,1}\right)\parallel H\left(a'_{c,2}\right)\parallel \ldots \parallel H\left(a'_{c,n}\right)\right)$. If $h\left(H\left(a_{c,1}\right)\parallel H\left(a_{c,2}\right)\parallel \ldots \parallel H\left(a_{c,n}\right)\right)\ Y^{S_B+S_A} = h\left(H\left(a'_{c,1}\right)\parallel H\left(a'_{c,2}\right)\parallel \ldots \parallel H\left(a'_{c,n}\right)\right)$, then the user decrypts m as

$$ENC^m \cdot \frac{h\left(H\left(a'_{c,1}\right)\parallel H\left(a'_{c,2}\right)\parallel\ldots\parallel H\left(a'_{c,n}\right)\right)\,Q.\hat{e}\left(D_u,E^1_{do}\right)}{E^0_{do}} =$$

$$mY^{S_B}\,\frac{h\left(H\left(a'_{c,1}\right)\parallel H\left(a'_{c,2}\right)\parallel\ldots\parallel H\left(a'_{c,n}\right)\right)\,Y^{S_A}}{h\left(H\left(a'_{c,1}\right)\parallel H\left(a'_{c,2}\right)\parallel\ldots\parallel H\left(a'_{c,n}\right)\right)\,Y^{S_A+S_B}} = m.$$

In Li et al.'s Framework [24], the data owner combines smart device dynamic features with pre-defined static properties. This method provides an extra layer of security to the security provided by typical access control frameworks. However, to determine the dynamic properties by processing the sensor data, it increases the processing time or communication complexity. Therefore, this study [24] assumes that processing can be done in off-line.

2.3 Communication Framework

The communication framework and the major issues for green mobile cloud computing is presented in D. N. Raju and Saritha [34]. According to them green mobile cloud computing is a new approach in which information is recorded and computed outside of a mobile device in an energy efficient manner. The benefits of cloud computing are benefited greatly of by mobile devices, which analyze data in the cloud to preserve internal resources. The GMCC communication framework is divided in to 3 layers such as mobile environment, wireless medium and cloud environment as shown in Fig. 5. The mobile environment is comprised of mobile devices which are connected to sink nodes in order to keep the mobile devices and network interconnected.

To facilitate connection, the authentication, authorization, and accounting policies are used. The mobile users then seek services from the cloud, which the cloud handles via internet services. The mobile user's request is forwarded to cloud services by the cloud. Such architectures are not free from major QoS issues such as availability, security and reliability.

Fig. 5 Data communication framework for GMCC

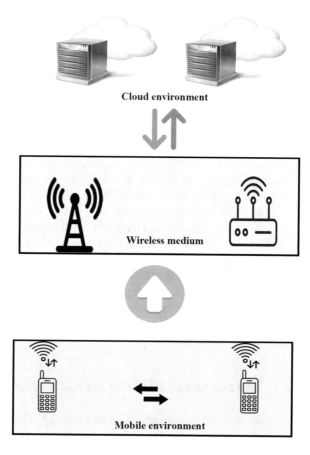

2.3.1 Benefits of GMCC Communication Framework

Such communication framework for GMCC also has some added benefits such as:

- **Extending data storage:** Clients can use GMCC's services to access cloud-based data storage. Such example of cloud storage that delivers storage as a service is Amazon S3. Facebook is one of the most popular social networking sites that use cloud services on mobile devices.
- **Improving computational capacity:** Increased computational capacity is necessary for computing-intensive applications, yet mobile devices lack the processing power needed. By synchronizing the cloud with the mobile device in terms of processing ability, GMCC aids in the reduction of application execution costs. Multimedia services, online gaming, and E-banking for mobile devices, for example, can all be provided via the cloud.
- **Enhancing battery life:** Mobile devices have a severe issue in the form of restricted battery capacity. Many proposals have been made to extend standby

time by improving CPU speed and intelligently optimizing storage and screen brightness. These solutions necessitate significant alterations to mobile devices, which necessitates the purchase of new hardware and incurs added expenses. Computational offloading is a strategy for moving difficult and big computations from mobile devices to cloud servers that can be implemented.

- **Use of better offloading strategies:** The stress on the mobile device will be reduced, and the battery's performance will improve. Using offloading strategies, various studies were carried out. Research shows that running a program remotely can save energy. In [35], for the minimization of energy in mobile devices, a mathematical model was presented. They were able to reduce their energy usage by up to 45%. For decreasing energy in MCC, Cuervo et al. [36] introduced the Mathematical Arithmetic Unit and Interface design. Their strategy was to transfer the mobile game components into cloud VMs, which resulted in a nearly 27% reduction in mobile device energy consumption.

- **Enhancing reliability:** The service becomes more trustworthy by shifting data and processing to the cloud. Data storage on servers creates a backup, which will aid in preventing data loss on mobile devices. For both consumers and providers, the GMCC has developed a complete security paradigm. The model recommended controlling unauthorized data access from the GMCC [37]. Phone users can use the cloud to get functions like identification, malware protection, and virus screening.

2.3.2 Some Issues in GMCC Communication Framework

There are some Communication issues in the GMCC communication framework:

- **QoS issues:** QoS is one of the major issues. In GMCC, mobile users are able to access resources in the cloud to reduce energy costs, but mobile users face various communication problems related to the connection to the cloud. The Fig. 6 shows different QoS issue in GMCC framework. In contrast to computers, notebooks, and other computing devices, mobile devices have limited and inadequate calculation capabilities. The services of mobile cloud computing are continually influenced by computation capacity. The interaction of GMCC is continually hampered by a lack of bandwidth.

- **Functional issues:** GMCC's functional difficulties include technical challenges like computational offloading, cost-benefit models, and connection protocols. GMCC's major function is to offload duties from mobile devices to the cloud. The basic system requires heterogeneous communication due to the distance between the mobile and cloud. The client server model is used to communicate with the network. On mobile devices, certain client and server techniques must be pre-installed. When it comes to Ad-hoc networks, this paradigm has a disadvantage. The process of exchanging source server memory images to the

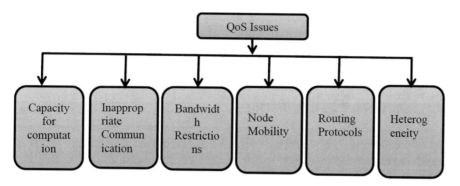

Fig. 6 QoS issues in communication framework

destination server is known as virtual machine migration. The operating system and any installed software are not involved in this operation, which replicates the memory pages. Because the VM restriction safeguards the neighboring mobile devices, this strategy ensures secure execution and no code changes are required when tasks are offloaded. To a certain extent, VM migration is tiresome, and the load on mobile devices may become enormous. In GMCC, cost is a big concern, hence shifting the task to the cloud takes into account factors such as time, energy, and cost. The authors of [38] published an assessment of the commercial cloud service provider Amazon EC2's power costs, memory use costs, and infrastructure maintenance expenses. They devised a methodology for deciding whether to purchase or rent the services. The Net Present Value (NPV) of the services is calculated using the choice model. If the NPV is zero, the service is purchased; otherwise, the service is leased. The NPV is calculated using Eq. 1. The disc controller unit cost, annual running cost, and disc lifespan salvage value are represented by C_Y, E_Y, and S, respectively. The annual lease payment is denoted by L_Y, and the annual interest rate is denoted by R_F.

$$NPV = \sum_{y=0}^{n} \frac{C_y - E_y + L_y}{(1 + R_F)^y} + \frac{S}{(1 + R_F)^n} - C \qquad (1)$$

3 Security Challenges in Green Mobile Cloud Computing (GMCC) Frameworks

The GMCC employs a variety of conventional as well as creative approaches, such as offloading, partitioning, outsourced storage, virtualization, and mobile-cloud-based apps. It combines various modern security breaches as well as existing difficulties. In this section, we provide a list of acceptable privacy and security issues inside GMCC. The problems are divided into the following categories.

3.1 Data Security Challenges

As the mobile users' information are reserved and processed at cloud ends which are located at the service providers' terminals, thus a massive data security issue arises. Data-related difficulties include data breach, data loss, data locality, data recovery, and data privacy.

The two security requirements i.e., integrity and confidentiality can be broken by data loss and data breach respectively. Data loss in this context refers to consumer data that has been damaged or lost due to any external technique during processing, transfer, or storage. In a data breach occurrence, users' data is stolen, replicated, or utilized by unauthorized people. These two can be caused by malicious insiders or external spyware.

Another issue to be concerned about is data recovery. This is the process of restoring data from a mobile user's data that has been damaged, failed, corrupted, or lost, or from a physical storage device. When data is transferred to cloud servers to increase memory space, mobile users immediately lose direct ownership of their data. As a result, in a cloud storage situation, one of the issues for mobile users is the quality of the data.

3.2 Virtualization Security Challenges

A clone of the mobile device's VM is preloaded in the cloud, and the mobile device's duties are transferred to the VM for execution. This VM is also known as a phone clone or a thin VM. The basic purpose of virtualization is to provide several virtual machines (VMs) that run on the same system or mobile device while being isolated from one another. Furthermore, when used to MCC, virtualization technologies provide a slew of security issues, including security within the VMs, unauthorized access, VM-to-VM attacks, communication security within the virtualized environment, probable threats within the Hypervisors, and information confidentiality.

3.3 Mobile Cloud Applications Security Challenges

Physical hazards to mobile devices exist. If mobiles are forgotten or stolen, data or apps may be lost, leaked, accessed, or accidentally disclosed to unauthorized users. Despite the pass code or pattern-based locking mechanisms are available, several phone users not using them Furthermore, the identification module card included within the mobile can be removed from the phone and accessed by unauthorized individuals. Furthermore, the majority of mobile devices lack a defense system against attacks. Intruders can employ several availability attack tactics, like delivering a heavy malicious traffic volume, large messages to victim mobile devices, and making them unusable or lowering their capabilities.

Because of the growing demand for mobile and apps, malware authors and hackers are focusing their efforts here. As a result, malwares pose severe potential risks to mobile users' safety, apps, and information. Furthermore, the functions of current mobile devices are very similar to those of personal computers, except with extra functionality, and these platforms for mobile devices enable a wide range of applications. As a result, in order to maintain the integrity and confidentiality of these apps, mobile platforms must also be secured. Furthermore, these mobile platforms are not immune to malware attacks.

3.4   Privacy Challenges

Privacy is one of several major issues that arise when mobile users' sensitive information or apps are processed and delivered from mobile devices to multiple scattered cloud servers when using various cloud services. These servers are housed in diverse locations owned and operated completely by the service providers. In this instance, consumers cannot individually oversee the storage of their data; hence, the security and privacy issues are handled by the service providers, and consumers are not answerable for the privacy violations. Therefore, the storage and processing of data on the cloud in many locations raises the question on privacy concerns.

There are some mobile apps accessible that may be hazardous owing to having ugly functionalities, gathering unintentionally users' private information such as preferences and whereabouts, and spreading unlawfully.

3.5   Partitioning and Offloading Security Challenges

Linkage to the cloud using wireless networks is required during the offloading process. Because mobile users have no access to or control on their offloading processes, there is a danger of unapproved access to offloaded material. Furthermore, because offloading material computations are performed on cloud or edge servers rather than mobile devices, there is the potential for offloaded material validity and confidentiality to be violated.

Hazardous material threats and availability attacks are two more problems. The accessibility of cloud services can be impacted by jamming attacks between the application and the mobile device while partitioning and between the mobile device and the cloud while offloading. Furthermore, the existence of harmful material between the partitioning and offloading stages might have an influence on data confidentiality and breach mobile users' privacy.

4 Conclusion

The most difficult part of GMCC is protecting user privacy and the security of cloud-based mobile applications. Service providers must handle IP security, data security, data location, data integrity, secure web application, data segmentation, data access, data privacy, data breaches, and other issues in order to create a secure GMCC environment. To develop a safe GMCC environment, safety issues must be identified and addressed. Typically, GMCC service claimed resources, such as processing and data storage, are transferred from service cost nodes (i.e., MD nodes) to a centralized cloud-based computing platform, which is accessed via MD-based thin local clients or mobile web browsers. Several concerns have been expressed about the framework's usefulness and efficiency [39]. To begin, the majority of the GMCC data security structures examined pay insufficient attention to MD node and communication channel vulnerabilities. Second, the scope of their warning spectrum was relatively narrow. As a result, future study can be dedicated toward mitigating the aforementioned problems in order to make GMCC more robust, efficient, and secure.

References

1. Elminaam, D.S.A., Alanezi, F.T., Hosny, K.M.: SMCACC: developing an efficient dynamic secure framework for mobile capabilities augmentation using cloud computing. In: Proceedings of the IEEE Access, vol. 7, pp. 120214–120237 (2019). https://doi.org/10.1109/ACCESS.2019.2929954
2. Gao, B., He, L., Lu, X., Chang, C., Li, K., Li, K.: Developing energy aware task allocation schemes in cloud-assisted mobile workflows. In: Proceedings of the IEEE International Conference on Computer Science and Information Technology; Ubiquitous Computing and Communication; Dependable, Autonomic Secure Computing; Pervasive Intelligence and Computing, pp. 1266–1273 (2015)
3. Zissis, D., Lekkas, D.: Addressing cloud computing security issues. In: Proceedings of the Future Generation Computer Systems, vol. 28(3), pp. 583–592 (2012)
4. Subashini, S., Kavitha, V.: A survey on security issues in service delivery models of cloud computing. In: Proceedings of the Journal of Network and Computer Applications, vol. 34(1), pp. 1–11 (2011)
5. Buyya, R., Yeo, C.S., Venugopal, S., Broberg, J., Brandic, I.: Cloud computing and emerging IT platforms: vision, hype, and reality for delivering computing as the 5th utility. In: Proceedings of the Future Generation Computer Systems, vol. 25(6), pp. 599–616 (2009)
6. Khan, A.N., Kiah, M.L.M., Khan, S.U., Madani, S.A.: Towards secure mobile cloud computing: a survey. In: Proceeding of the Future Generation Computer Systems, vol. 29(5), pp. 1278–1299 (2013). https://doi.org/10.1016/j.future.2012.08.003

7. Diaz, C.O., Guzek, M., Pecero, J.E., Bouvry, P., Khan, S.U.: Scalable and energy efficient scheduling techniques for large-scale systems. In: Proceedings of the 11th IEEE International Conference on Computer and Information Technology, CIT'11, Pafos, Cyprus, September (2011)
8. Cai, C., Wang, L., Khan, S.U., Tao, J.: Energy-aware high performance computing: a taxonomy study. In: Proceedings of the 17th IEEE International Conference on Parallel and Distributed Systems, ICPADS'11, Tainan, Taiwan, December (2011)
9. Goiri, I., Berral, J.L., Fitó, J.O., Julià, F., Nou, R., Guitart, J., Gavaldà, R., Torres, J.: Energy-efficient and multifaceted resource management for profit-driven virtualized data centers. In: Proceedings of the Future Generation Computer Systems, vol. 28(5), pp. 718–731 (2012)
10. Kliazovich, D., Bouvry, P., Khan, S.U.: DENS: data center energy-efficient network-aware scheduling. In: Proceedings of the ACM/IEEE International Conference on Green Computing and Communications, GreenCom'10, Hangzhou, China, December (2010)
11. Lindberg, P., Leingang, J., Lysaker, D., Khan, S.U., Li, J.: Comparison and analysis of eight scheduling heuristics for the optimization of energy consumption and make span in large-scale distributed systems. In: Proceedings of the Journal of Supercomputing, vol. 59(1), pp. 323–360 (2012)
12. Quan, D.M., Mezza, F., Sannenli, D., Giafreda, R.: T-alloc: a practical energy efficient resource allocation algorithm for traditional data centers. In: Proceedings of the Future Generation Computer Systems, vol. 28(5), pp. 791–800 (2012)
13. Diaz, C.O., Guzek, M., Pecero, J.E., Danoy, G., Bouvry, P., Khan, S.U.: Energy aware fast scheduling heuristics in heterogeneous computing systems. In: Proceedings of the ACM/IEEE/IFIP International Conference on High Performance Computing and Simulation, HPCS'11, Istanbul, Turkey, July (2011)
14. Khan, S.U., Ardil, C.: A weighted sum technique for the joint optimization of performance and power consumption in data centers. In: Proceeding of the International Journal of Electrical, Computer, and Systems Engineering, vol. 3(1), pp. 35–40 (2009)
15. Khan, S.U.: A self-adaptive weighted sum technique for the joint optimization of performance and power consumption in data centers. In: Proceedings of the 22nd International Conference on Parallel and Distributed Computing and Communication Systems, PDCCS'09, Louisville, KY, USA, September (2009)
16. Ren, W., Yu, L., Gao, R., Xiong, F.: Lightweight and compromise resilient storage outsourcing with distributed secure accessibility in mobile cloud computing. In: Proceedings of the Journal of Tsinghua Science and Technology, vol. 16(5), pp. 520–528 (2011)
17. Khan, A.N., Mat Kiah, M.L., Khan, S.U., Madani, S.A., Khan, A.R.: A study of incremental cryptography for security schemes in mobile cloud computing environments. In: Proceedings of the IEEE Symposium on Wireless Technology and Applications ISWTA (2013)
18. Khan, A.N., Mat Kiah, M.L., Ali, M., Madani, S.A., Khan, A.R., Shamshirband, S.: BSS: block based sharing scheme for secure data storage services in mobile cloud environment. In: Proceedings of the Journal of Supercomputing (2014)
19. Patel, C., Chauhan, S.S., Patel, B.: A data security framework for mobile cloud computing. In: Proceedings of International Journal of Advanced Research in Computer and Communication Engineering, vol. 4(2), February (2015)
20. Jia, W., Zhu, H., Cao, Z., Wei, L., Lin, X.: SDSM: a secure data service mechanism in mobile cloud computing. In: Proceedings IEEE Conference on Computer Communications Workshops, INFOCOM WKSHPS, Shanghai, China, April (2011)
21. Hsueh, S.C., Lin, J.Y., Lin, M.Y.: Secure cloud storage for conventional data archive of smart phones. In: Proceedings of the 15th IEEE International Symposium on Consumer Electronics, ISCE'11, Singapore, June (2011)
22. Yang, J., Wang, H., Wang, J., Tan, C., Yu, D.: Provable data possession of resource constrained mobile devices in cloud computing. J. Netw. 6(7), 1033–1040 (2011)
23. Zhou, Z., Huang, D.: Efficient and secure data storage operations for mobile cloud computing. IACR Cryptology ePrint Archive: 185 (2011)

24. Li, F., Rahulamathavan, Y., Conti, M., Rajarajan, M.: Robust access control framework for mobile cloud computing network. In: Proceedings of the Computer Communications, vol. 68, pp. 61–72 (2015). https://doi.org/10.1016/j.comcom.2015.07.005
25. Zhang, G., Parashar, M.: Context-aware dynamic access control for pervasive applications. In: Proceedings of the Communications Networks and Distributed Systems Modeling and Simulation Conference, pp. 21–30 (2004)
26. Bonatti, C. Galdi, D.T.: ERBAC: event driven RBAC. In: Proceedings of the 18th ACM Symposium Access Control Models and Technologies. ACM, pp. 125–136 (2013)
27. Cho, Y.S., Bao, L., Goodrich, M.T.: LAAC: a location-aware access control protocol. In: Proceedings of the IEEE 3rd Annual International Conference on Mobile and Ubiquitous Systems: Networking and Services, pp. 1–7 (2006)
28. Scott, L., Denning, D.E.: A location based encryption technique and some of its applications. In: Proceedings of the National Technical Meeting of The Institute of Navigation, Anaheim, CA, pp. 734–740 (2003)
29. Vijayalakshmi, V., Palanivelu, T.G.: Secure localization using elliptic curve cryptography in wireless sensor networks. In: Proceedings of the International Journal of Computer Science and Network Security, vol. 8(6), pp. 255–261 (2008)
30. Lv, Z., Chi, J., Zhang, M., Feng, D.: Efficiently attribute-based access control for mobile cloud storage system. In: Proceedings of the IEEE 13th International Conference on Trust, Security and Privacy in Computing and Communications, pp. 292–299 (2014). https://doi.org/10.1109/TrustCom.2014.40
31. Luo, J., Wang, H., Gong, X., Li, T.: A novel role-based access control model in cloud environments. In: Proceedings of International Journal of Computational Intelligence Systems, pp. 1–9 (2016)
32. Samsung KNOX, http://tinyurl.com/me93jcv. Accessed on 29 Oct 2021
33. BlackBerry BES12, http://tinyurl.com/ls3yxh8. Accessed on 29 Oct 2021
34. Raju, N., Saritha, V.: A survey on communication issues in mobile cloud computing. In: Proceedings of Walailak Journal of Science & Technology, vol. 15(1) (2018)
35. Rudenko, A., Reiher, P., Popek, G.J., Kuenning, G.H.: Saving portable computer battery power through remote process execution. In: Proceedings of the ACM SIGMOBILE Mobile Computing and Communications Review (1998)
36. Cuervo, A., Balasubramanian, D.K., Cho, A., Wolman, S., Saroiu, R., Chandra, P.B.: MAUI: making smartphones last longer, with code offload. In: Proceedings of the International Conference on Mobile Systems, Applications, and Services (2010)
37. Zou, C., Wang, Z., Liu, D.B.: Phosphor, "A cloud based DRM scheme with sim card". In: Proceedings of the Web Conference (2010)
38. Walker, W., Brisken, J.: Romney, "To lease or not to lease from storage clouds". In: Proceedings of the Computer (2010)
39. Ogwara, N.O., Petrova, K., Yang, M.L.: Data security frameworks for mobile cloud computing: a comprehensive review of the literature. In: Proceedings of the 29th International Telecommunication Networks and Applications Conference (ITNAC), pp. 1–4 (2019). https://doi.org/10.1109/ITNAC46935.2019.9078007

Part III
Applications and Future Research Directions of Green Mobile Cloud Computing

Sustainable Energy Management System Using Green Smart Grid in Mobile Cloud Computing Environment

Asmita Biswas, Pelle Jakovits, and Deepsubhra Guha Roy

1 Introduction

Wireless communication is trying to reach out through Mobile Cloud Computing technology to help reduce power costs to meet the growing demand [1] for environmental sustainability. Therefore, to integrate MCC technology in a Green Smart Grid data network, adopting an overlay network and the underlying electrical network has been combined. Consequently, the information network performs a vital part in exchanging real-time data. Therefore, the Smart Meters extended at the consumers' end communicate for a reliable and cost-effective power supply among the service providers, and the exponential growth in the abundance of Smart Meters raises greenhouse gas emissions [2]. Hence, building a Green Smart Grid architecture that considers environmental effects and maintains the electricity we get in the future is required.

The Smart Meters are demanded among the service providers to reach within a period interval (let us assume every 10–12 min) [3]. Thus, it means plenty of Smart Meters and real-time traffic and electricity costs. Therefore, the implementation of collaborative approaches of the Smart Meter can have a notable result in reducing the electricity expenditure in the Smart Grid. As a result, this signifies essential to offer a power-efficient technology of Mobile Cloud Computing (MCC) on the Green Smart Grid for Smart Metering. This chapter proposes a sustainable energy-

A. Biswas
School of Computational Science, Department of IT, Maulana Abul Kalam Azad University of Technology, Kolkata, India

P. Jakovits
Mobile and Cloud Lab, Institute of Computer Science, University of Tartu, Tartu, Estonia

D. G. Roy (✉)
School of Computer Science and Engineering, Vellore Institute of Technology, Vellore, India

efficient Green Smart Grid to provide effective and green energy to the environment for future betterment. In such a scenario, the MCC incorporation framework forms in Smart Meter and Green Smart Grid.

Nowadays, a growing number of Smart Mobile applications for users to use portable gadgets has attracted more people, consume more energy, and creates more traffic. The evolution of MCC and Communications intense technology places the workload fall in the cloud, and portable gadget's battery life freed from the deficit. Precisely, through a Wide Area Network, Green Smart Grid devices that use mobile application workloads are sent to the cloud. Virtual machine users to run workloads in the cloud helps offloading applications and user tools to be the sensation of the environment, including the general operation of the virtual machine and user devices, which cross a WAN (Wide Area Network), may acquire long end-to-end (E2E) delays [4], and those are significant for many MCC applications. Thus, WAN-the interaction between the user devices and the virtual machine over the long delay diminishes MCC applications. Therefore, the proposed MCC architectures are not suitable for delay-intolerant applications MCC. We have introduced Mobile Cloud Computing technology in Green Smart Grid for sustainable energy management in this chapter. Also, we have explained the advantages and the security aspects of implementing MCC in Green Smart Grid.

2 Mobile Cloud Computing and Smart Grid Overview

2.1 Mobile Cloud Computing

Mobile Cloud Computing (MCC) illustrates a foundation for information processing and information accommodation externally from mobile appliances. The Mobile-Cloud computing applications incorporate the computational power and information storage in the cloud, including bringing Mobile Cloud Computing and its applications to a more extensive reach of the subscribers and mobile users. Aepona [5] presents a new MCC model to mobile applications where data accommodation and processing are transferred to centralized and robust computing platforms from mobile devices. Those centralized appliances are located above the broadcast connection relied on a delicate primary consumer or network browser on the mobile gadgets. As an alternative, MCC represents the incorporation of cloud computing and mobile network [6, 7], which signifies the most recommended device to locate services and applications on the internet for mobile users (in Fig. 1). Concisely, in MCC, the portable device [8] does not expect a robust synopsis such as memory capability and CPU rate for the whole complicated computing module that performs the processes in clouds.

Mobile Sensing   **Cloud Analysis**

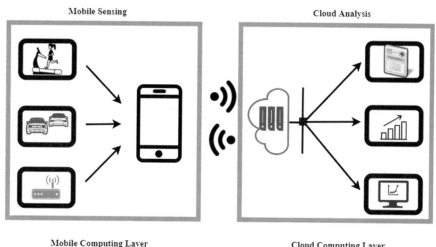

Mobile Computing Layer   **Cloud Computing Layer**

Fig. 1 System Model of Conventional MCC Architecture

2.2 Smart Grid

In the world of Internet of Things (IoT), the most popular implementation is Smart Grid. Unifying an electrical energy grid with the bidirectional interface network system is defined as Smart Grid [9]. The modern Smart Grid can provide electricity to the end-users efficiently by integrating communication and information technology. A Smart Grid design traverses fundamentally these distinct technical dominions—Transmission-side, Generation-side, and Distribution-side [10]. The Transmission-side is reliable for providing current to the Distribution-side (consumers). The Generation-side consists of conventional power-plant formation. An essential feature of the Smart grid is regulating power expenditure by the consumers' ends through ascertaining various optimization techniques [11, 12]. The essential components to be incorporated into a Smart Grid design to obtain the purpose are Micro-grids and Smart Metering.

Figure 2 interprets a Green Smart Grid outline by the Smart Metering infrastructure and Smart Distribution elements. The updated infrastructure of the Smart Grid has been effective in overall conversions based on Smart Metering and Smart Distributions. Renewable power sources for traditional Power-plants can be considered as the next generation of a Smart Grid. Using transmission lines to distribute electricity generation is conveyed to the side and enabled dynamic pricing technology. The Distribution-side is liable as distributing it and reducing the end-user's distribution losses (in Fig. 2).

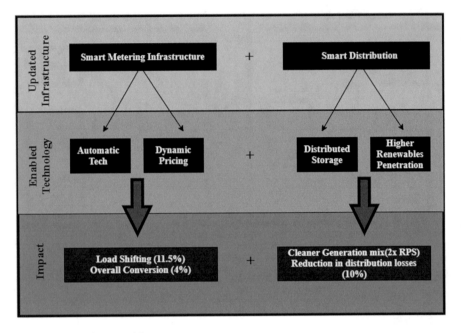

Fig. 2 Outline of smart grid

2.3 Smart Metering

Consumers to get real-time data about power use, the most emerging technology used in Smart Grid is Smart Metering. It is more proficient than the old of regulating SMI (Smart Metering Infrastructure) systems [13] (in Fig. 2). To capture real-time power consumption at the consumer's head remotely, the Smart Metering Infrastructure is established through a bidirectional transmission mechanism. Smart Meters are devices placed at the end of the distribution and fitted to take the records of electricity consumption used by consumers. As a result, utilities and consumers are served by Smart Metering Infrastructure (SMI). For instance, a consumer can determine the electricity consumption throughout the day for optimizing the cost and manage real-time monitoring for the utility supply and demand curvature.

Figure 3 shows the power management system of a Smart Grid where power distribution is monitored by real-time monitoring. The Smart Chargers interact among the base stations to switching real-time data among the service-provider. The power used through the Smart Meters for interacting among the base stations in various time slots is expressed in the form of vector as regards:

$$n_i = n_i^1, n_i^2, n_i^3, \ldots\ldots, n_i^x, \ldots\ldots n_i^X \tag{1}$$

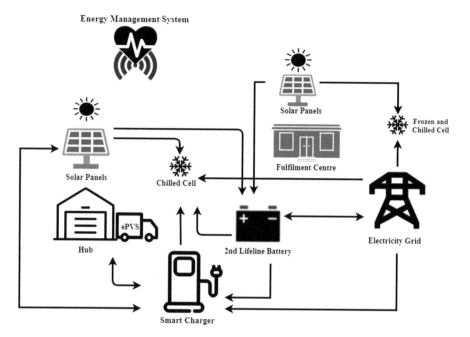

Fig. 3 Service model of smart grid

X is the entire time during the day, and the Smart meters aim to maximize utilities and reduce the power consumption price while sustaining secure data distribution. Hence, the actual Smart Meter function is shown as regards:

$$Minimize \sum_{x=1}^{X} n_x . S_x$$

about

$$S_x^{min} \leq S_x \leq S_x^{max} \tag{2}$$

$$\delta_x \leq \Delta_{max} \tag{3}$$

where S_x is the price acquired through the Smart Meters for total power consumption. Equation (2) signifies the real-time price S_x holds a maximum and a minimum value. In contrast, a data distribution delay of δ must be less than or equal to Δ_{max}, the maximum permissible delay for responsible data distribution.

2.4 Micro Grid

In this notion of Smart Grid structure, the energy distribution-side of the step-down transformer is divided into sub-groups. This sub-group, such as self-production capacity of the combined thermal power, wind, and solar manufacturing production. Additionally, control and distribution of electricity to end-users as they can. Those sub-groups are recognized as Micro-grid. A Micro-grid is a low-voltage power system, including self-production skills consolidation. A sub-group of power distribution to end-users is an autonomous control system and power supply. With the presence of the whole method, a Micro-grid mode works in islands, and in the before-mentioned cases, a Micro-grid can autonomously control the flow of electricity. Due to variations in renewable power sources, distributed energy sources to the original use of the Micro-grid shared generation is converted into operation. Below are a few of the benefits of Micro-grids [14] are listed:

1. Electrical distribution facilities are concentrated in the transition from decentralization.
2. A Micro-grid and energy management system that increases reliability.
3. Advanced real-time monitoring method can be acquired.
4. In the appearance of several interruptions, it operates in islands form and provides current to end-users safely and efficiently.
5. All Micro-grids do communicate, including different exchange power when there is a deficiency and excess.

3 Mobile Cloud Computing Key Requirements for Energy Efficiency

Mobile Cloud Computing is a key feature of a network that enables us to provide services throughout the unremitting. Solution provider of enterprise or web/mobile application developer [15], from the perspective of MCC platform objectives, are:

1. API provides access to simple, transparent portable services, and the underlying network technology does not expect any precise knowledge.
2. Under the agreement, a single industrial application across multiple carrier interfaces deployment capabilities [15].
3. Each case is assigned a specific network policy, such as the mobile subscriber [15] has chosen to opt-in or opt-out agreement unremitting handling policies and privacy control.

4 Architecture of Mobile Cloud Computing

The fundamental architecture of MCC is shown in Fig. 4. In Fig. 4, mobile devices (access points, transceiver base stations, or satellite) are connected to the network via the mobile networks and links between mobile devices (air link), and functional interfaces to set up and control. Then, tools and information are sent to mobile users (for example, ID and location), mobile network service providers connected to the server from the central processor. Here, the home agent of the mobile network operators and subscribers of mobile users is stored in databases as data-based authorization, authentication, and accounting can provide the service. Then, a cloud is provided via the Internet to consumers' requests. To provide cloud services to the cloud in order to process requests related to mobile phone users cloud controllers [16, 17]. Thus, the concept of utility computing, virtualization, and service-oriented architecture (e.g., application, web, and database servers) has evolved.

Mobile Cloud architecture features may be various in several contexts. For instance, to analyze MCC with grid computing, a four-layer design has been described in [18]. Selectively, a service-oriented design called Aneka [19] to allow

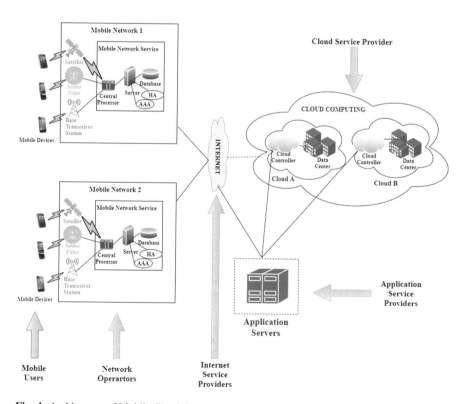

Fig. 4 Architecture of Mobile Cloud Computing

developers to design was launched. Microsoft.Net API (Applications Programming Interface) that supports multiple programming models [19].

This architecture to satisfy the MCC model user requirements is used to illustrate the effectiveness [20]. Typically, the MCC data center and server application are based on large distributed network systems. Therefore, mobile cloud services are usually categorized based on the notion of a level (Fig. 4). In the top layers of this model, IaaS (Infrastructure as a Service), PaaS (Platform as a Service), and SaaS (Software as a Service) are accumulated.

– Infrastructure as a Service (IaaS)

The data center layer is formed above the level of IaaS (Infrastructure as a Service). IaaS allows the requirement of networking elements, servers, hardware, and storage. Usually, on a per-user basis, the consumer pays. Thus, consumers can save money because they only use resources based on how many are paid. In addition, infrastructure can be dynamically shrunk or expanded as required. The examples of Infrastructure as a Service are S3 (Simple Storage Service) and Amazon Elastic Cloud Computing.

– Platform as a Service (PaaS)

Platform as a Service (PaaS) provides an improved integrated context for examining, developing, and expanding system applications. Examples of Platform as a Service are Amazon Map Simple/Reduce Storage Service, Microsoft Azure, and Google App Engine.

– Software as a Service (SaaS)

Specific conditions of delivering Software as a Service (SaaS) is to support the Software. With the level of applications and information remotely through the Internet, consumers can access and pay for just everything people can use—one of the pioneers in this service model to provide Salesforce. In addition, Microsoft Live Mesh across various devices allows sharing files and folders.

– Data Center Layer

This layer is of providing hardware facilities and infrastructure to the cloud. Data Center level, numerous servers to give services for consumers with fast networks are connected. Generally, the higher the risk of disasters, including the data center, providing security, and less populated centers are built-in.

5   MCC Advantages for Green Smart Grid

MCC is known as an assuring key for communication, dynamism, and portability [21]. Server virtualization decreases the physical server tracks through integration, which are integrated green benefits, including energy reduction, data storage improvement, reliability for Green Smart Grid. However, mobile cloud-based infrastructure, supplies, and energy to maximize productivity depend on automation. The green benefits for the Smart Grid incorporated with MCC are discussed in the following:

1. Energy Efficient Extended Battery Lifespan:
   Battery for mobile devices is a primary concern. Numerous solutions have been proposed to enhance the efficiency of the CPU [22, 23] And to wisely manage the screen and the disk [24, 25] to reduce energy expenditure. Nevertheless, those solutions need a transformation in the mobile appliance's structure or need modern hardware, which increases the value and is not reasonable for whole mobile appliances. The calculation offloading plan proposes transferring extensive calculations and complicated processing from the source-limited device such as a mobile gadget to a cloud server as the Smart machine. This mobile device takes a long moment to avoid the execution of the application, which consumes a massive amount of energy. Rudenko et al. [26] to assess the effectiveness of offloading strategies through several tests, and as per result, the remote application performance significantly can save power [26] Estimate large-scale mathematical calculations initially and show that power consumption can be decreased for symbolic matrix computations. Also, various remote processing and mobile applications take benefit of the departure task. For instance, offloading [27] algorithm reduced into the cloudlets up to one-third of the power consumption of a mobile device.

2. Processing Energy and Data Storage Capability Development:
   The storage capability is more of a barrier for mobile gadgets. Mobile users via wireless networks, a wide range of cloud information access/storage has been improved to enable the MCC. The first sample is data exchange which applies sufficient storage space into the cloud for mobile users, and another sample is amazon's simple storage service, which maintains data storage services. That mobile data-sharing service allows mobile users to observe and share to the clouds. Mobile users can obtain all data through a particular application from any device. Clouds can save storage space and a massive amount of power on mobile devices because they are transmitted and prepared into the clouds [28]. MCC-resource devices with limited execution time take a long moment, and a large volume of power for such calculation-intensive applications helps to reduce running costs—MCC multiple documents such as online data management, storage support to synchronize various functions efficiently. For instance, Cloud multimedia services on mobile gadgets can be applied for broadcasting [29] or transcoding [30]. In this case, the mobile devices calculate the energy consumption through a Smart Meter that takes a long time transcoding or recommends that all the complex estimations process on the clouds efficiently. Mobile appliances are not limited by the capacity of the data storage devices now equipped with the clouds.

3. Reliability Development:
   Improves reliability of data storage or application running on the cloud because the data and applications are stored on numerous computers and backed up. It

reduces the chance that applications on mobile devices and that missing data. Also, it can be a prototype for the design of a broad range of information protection for service providers and MCC users [31]. In addition, the cloud can securely supply mobile users with safety assistance such as malicious code detection, virus scanning, and authentication [32]. Moreover, the functionality of the cloud-based safety services to develop the user a variation of service records accumulated from the user can use efficiently.

6 Integration of MCC in Green Smart Grid

This section introduces real-time pricing for (RSM) Requirement-side Management in the Green Smart Grid. The MCC platform with Green Smart Grid integration has been shown in Fig. 5, where the different layers of MCC are interconnected with the web services and authentication and authorization process to make the grid more efficient to the users, and their utility uses. Requirement-side management (RSM) through MCC is a program executed by service firms that can play a significant function in dynamically shifting or changing power consumption to consumers [33]. RSM programs needed to improve multiple performances simultaneously can be applied to physical systems, and it is a process needed to manage utilities more efficiently, reduce costs for power consumers and reduce greenhouse gas emissions

Fig. 5 Integration of Mobile Cloud Computing and Green Smart Grid

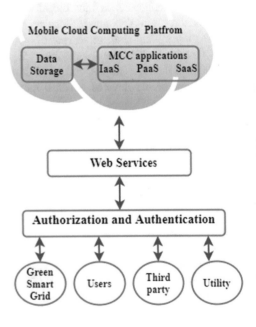

in the green grid. Moreover, users' more intelligent and efficient use of power in order to support the dynamic pricing programs as a necessary strategy RSM has attracted much attention [34].

In the dynamic models in a variety of prices, the value of the use of time-critical, real-time price is most important in Green Smart Grid [35]. At the time of use, the decision is made for the pre-determined block at the time of variable value [36]. When determining time-critical pricing, the prices are based on the requirement of time before the decision is taken. The prices are widespread retailers that offer real-time pricing for reflecting differences in the price of electricity distribution. The smart grid integrates renewable-energy sources, and often it is non-stop controlling (e.g., the volume of electrical power that fluctuates with time and weather, depending on factors such as the shuffle). Electricity grid infrastructure, renewable energy, a significant portion of the company to integrate challenging, power requirement production is needed to adjust. Also, the grid electric power storage, the additional costs are to be stored when the cost of production exceeds its limited power, and in practice, it may not be economical. Also, in addition to shutdown, ramping up a power plant can be expensive. So electric generators are to support customers to adopt more energy antagonistic prices, can be used (i.e., power consumers will be provided through the adoption). From the economic perspective, it could be justified because the prices adverse power plant to shut down and ramp-up costs for the loss-making prices could be higher than the negative. Prices may be responsive to other actors in the market to meet the terms of, for example, combined power plant and energy [37], to a heat delivery agreement, and so hostile to the cost of electricity to run the power plant was damaged.

Active mobile base stations for each of the three parts E_{BS} energy use include radiated power, signal processing, and back-hauling due to the cost of electricity, which can be identified as the following [38]:

$$E_{BS} = g E_{tx} + c E_{sb} + d E_{bh} \tag{4}$$

where E_{tx} signifies the radiated power for each base station, E_{sb} signifies the signal processing power for each base station, E_{bh} signifies the power due to back-hauling for each base station, respectively. g, c, and d refer to as measure factors associated with the type of battery backup and cooling. Each base station has radiated energy losses in the way of propagation, depending on the channel. Thus, the average radiated power per base station can be classified as follows [38]:

$$\log(E_{tx}) = \log(E_{min}) - \log k + \phi \log(r/2) \tag{5}$$

where E_{min} specifies the minimum required by the receiving power user terminal, including taking into a record for base station antenna settings of k parameter, carrier frequency, and amplification circumstances, ϕ path-loss exponent, and r represents the inter-site range.

At present, several countries pass through the liberalization of the electricity market: with state-owned power generators and controlled monopolies competing with companies from one market to another [39]. Retailers stand against all others and intend to reach most personal profits by regulating the amounts proposed to users in each country due to the liberalization of the electricity business. Green Smart Grid (GSG) is designed to distribute an efficient, flexible, universal, long-lasting, and incredibly convenient MCC platform for user devices. To provide a seamless connection between user tools and evolved NodeBs, a wide distribution of evolved NodeBs (eNBs) across LTE networks has been installed in a cloudlet GSG architectural tool connected to each eNBs to speed up the application of practical appliances as a continuous unloading speed [40, 41]. Reciprocity between an eNBs and a cloudlet can provide a dedicated link such as fast-speed fiber for end-to-end delays. Meantime, to decrease operational prices of working cloudlets and greenhouse gas trace, each cloudlet and eNBs is powered through both green energy and on-grid energy, like sustainable solar, biofuels, and wind energy. In addition, the reliability and availability of cloudlet's proposed Green Smart Grid architecture can be used to provide a public data center and communicate via the Storage Area Network (SAN) Internet. It cannot hold users' devices on networks due to the limited capacity of cloudlet. For preventing data loss in case of emergency to continue providing the user devices, the cloudlets can be transferred to the public data center [42].

The configuration of the cloudlet and evolved NodeBs can be uniform in any GSG. Green energy-powered base stations are proposed based on structure [43]. We have described a green smart grid, where the green energy resource extracting the power from the receiver green energy and transforms it into electric energy. The supervision controller manages the electrical energy from the green energy receiver and converts electrical energy by an inverter among DC and AC. The Smart Meter takes the electric power consumption records via cloudlets from Green Smart Grid.

7   Security Prospects of Green Energy Management

Green Smart Grid concept as cyber-physical systems that are physically connected to the electricity system and the consolidation of the Internet as cyber-infrastructure. This device can communicate with the customer service and integrate content and control the operations of utilities that can provide for the spine. GSG has a higher risk of cyber-attacks with online connections that could obstruct power distribution potentially [44]. One of some essential problems is energy theft by users. The attacks can be made by replacing the recorded energy usage, hacking the Smart Meter, or switching its transmission channel. Additionally, Data Manipulation is the most safety concern of Smart Grids [45]. To overcome these problems, we require to execute appropriate protection for reliable and secure GSG architectures. Security of a GSG can be applied to the customer-side, generation-side, and transmission-side.

The security prospects of the Green Smart Grid are as follows

- Increasing complexity and integration with the grid system, the interaction between the business system with safety is not easy to track.
- Smart Grid architecture is more complex than conventional power grids. Smart Sensor Networks, Wireless Communications, Smart data security issues, and systems implementation increases security complexity.
- With millions of Smart Meter, implementation of the system is delivered to the end user's network. Thus, end-users need to improve further the efficiency of protection.
- Denial-of-service (DOS) attacks affect the security of applications for Smart Grids.
- Moreover, third-party utilities can reach the user's data and private information, causing the user's privacy to be affected.

In Fig. 6, we have shown the significant security perspective of the Green Smart Grid, and those are explained as follows:

1. Data Outage: Purposely or accidentally outage data may be introduced. For example, a third party can perform the presence of cyber-physical attacks, accidental outage data. Even data breaches can occur with the user help for its convenience, which is familiar as deliberate information outage.
2. Data Control: The option within storing and deleting information is the fundamental concern. In addition, an appropriate data control system is required for real-time status monitoring. Data can be adequately handled with the integration of conventional filtering techniques.
3. Privacy Preservation: One of the largest complex problems in Smart Grid infrastructure is to preserve privacy protection. Privacy policy due to shortage

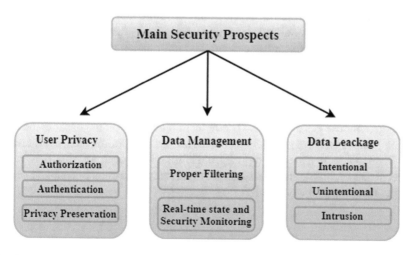

Fig. 6 Security Perspective of Green Smart Grid

of user data may be exposed to third-party utilities and vendors. Thus, an appropriate authentication and authorization method for user privacy protection needs to be applied.

8 Future Scope

In addition to the previously explained MCC applications for protection on the Green Smart Grid, several future MCC-based security opportunities also provide research challenges for future directions. First, third parties are also authorized to join in real-time monitoring operations on a smart grid, and MCC applications are supposed to provide enough protection to sustain user information privacy. Nevertheless, enabling third parties to become a part of the system, how it can be given to the security of existing technologies is not yet clear. Second, integrated fault protection systems and infrastructure support Smart Grid infrastructure with a variety of practical tools that are effective and perform efficiently. Therefore, reliable energy services for service providers to provide end users can receive adequate strategies. Third, MCC applications are required to distinguish intentional information outages on the Smart Grid. Nevertheless, unintentional information outages can also occur when incorporating MCC applications into the GSG, and research challenges to prevent unintentional data outages from the cloud or mobile device.

9 Conclusion

This chapter has introduced a Green Smart Grid architecture approach to MCC to provide efficient, safe, and reliable power distribution with green benefits. Sustainable energy control, management, and information protection are discussed in various perspectives of the Smart Grid. We have identified some significant technical problems and introduced several future research viewpoints of mobile cloud-based Smart Grids. The Green Smart Grid should be seen as an expert in cleaners, higher efficient technologies, and effective services that can significantly reduce greenhouse gas emissions. The reduction depends on the capacity of levels to install Smart Grid services and technologies that will follow later. Furthermore, there is undoubtedly a broad range of probabilities. Moreover, MCC will overcome technical and economic fragmentation that will remove barriers to cooperation will prove to be successful worldwide.

References

1. Fehske, A., Fettweis, G., Malmodin, J., Biczok, G.: The global footprint of mobile communications: The ecological and economic perspective. IEEE Commun. Mag. **49**(8), 55–62 (2011)
2. Saghezchi, F.B., Radwan, A., Rodriguez, J., Dagiuklas, T.: Coalition formation game toward green mobile terminals in heterogeneous wireless networks. IEEE Wirel. Commun. **20**(5), 85–91 (2013)
3. Li, H., Han, Z., Lai, L., Qiu, R.C., Yang, D.: Efficient and reliable multiple access for advanced metering in future smart grid. In: 2011 IEEE International Conference on Smart Grid Communications (SmartGridComm), pp. 440–444. IEEE, New York (2011)
4. Roy, D.G., Mahato, B., De, D., Buyya, R.: Application-aware end-to-end delay and message loss estimation in internet of things (IoT)—MQTT-SN protocols. Futur. Gener. Comput. Syst. **89**, 300–316 (2018)
5. Alzahrani, A., Alalwan, N., Sarrab, M.: Mobile cloud computing: advantage, disadvantage and open challenge. In: Proceedings of the 7th Euro American Conference on Telematics and Information Systems, pp. 1–4 (2014)
6. Christensen, J.H.: Using restful web-services and cloud computing to create next generation mobile applications. In: Proceedings of the 24th ACM SIGPLAN Conference Companion on Object Oriented Programming Systems Languages and Applications, pp. 627–634 (2009)
7. Liu, L., Moulic, R., Shea, D.: Cloud service portal for mobile device management. In: 2010 IEEE 7th International Conference on E-Business Engineering, pp. 474–478. IEEE, New York (2010)
8. Roy, D.G., Ghosh, A., Mahato, B., De, D.: QoS-aware task offloading using self-organized distributed cloudlet for mobile cloud computing. In: International Conference on Computational Intelligence, Communications, and Business Analytics, pp. 410–424, Springer, Berlin (2018)
9. Li, F., Qiao, W., Sun, H., Wan, H., Wang, J., Xia, Y., Xu, Z., Zhang, P.: Smart transmission grid: Vision and framework. IEEE Trans. Smart Grid **1**(2), 168–177 (2010)
10. Zou, M., Miao, Y.: Summary of smart grid technology and research on smart grid security mechanism. In: 2011 7th International Conference on Wireless Communications, Networking and Mobile Computing, pp. 1–4. IEEE, New York (2011)
11. Misra, S., Krishna, P.V., Saritha, V., Obaidat, M.S.: Learning automata as a utility for power management in smart grids. IEEE Commun. Mag. **51**(1), 98–104 (2013)
12. Vytelingum, P., Voice, T.D., Ramchurn, S.D., Rogers, A., Jennings, N.R.: Agent-Based Micro-Storage Management for the Smart Grid (2010)
13. Hart, D.G.: Using AMI to realize the smart grid. In: 2008 IEEE Power and Energy Society General Meeting-Conversion and Delivery of Electrical Energy in the 21st Century, vol. 10, sn (2008)
14. Zhang, H., Li, S.: Research on microgrid. In: 2011 International Conference on Advanced Power System Automation and Protection, vol. 1, pp. 595–598. IEEE, New York (2011)
15. Prasad, M.R., Gyani, J., Murti, P.: Mobile cloud computing: Implications and challenges. Journal of Information Engineering and Applications **2**(7), 7–15 (2012)
16. Dinh, H.T., Lee, C., Niyato, D., Wang, P.: A survey of mobile cloud computing: architecture, applications, and approaches. Wirel. Commun. Mob. Comput. **13**(18), 1587–1611 (2013)
17. Roy, D.G., De, D., Alam, M.M., Chattopadhyay, S.: Multi-cloud scenario based QoS enhancing virtual resource brokering. In: 2016 3rd International Conference on Recent Advances in Information Technology (RAIT), pp. 576–581. IEEE, New York (2016)
18. Foster, I., Zhao, Y., Raicu, I., Lu, S.: Cloud computing and grid computing 360-degree compared. In: 2008 Grid Computing Environments Workshop, pp. 1–10. IEEE, New York (2008)
19. Calheiros, R.N., Vecchiola, C., Karunamoorthy, D., Buyya, R.: The Aneka platform and QoS-driven resource provisioning for elastic applications on hybrid clouds. Futur. Gener. Comput. Syst. **28**(6), 861–870 (2012)

20. Tsai, W.-T., Sun, X., Balasooriya, J.: Service-oriented cloud computing architecture. In: 2010 Seventh International Conference on Information Technology: New Generations, pp. 684–689. IEEE, New York (2010)
21. Kumar, K., Liu, J., Lu, Y.-H., Bhargava, B.: A survey of computation offloading for mobile systems. Mobile Networks and Applications 18(1), 129–140 (2013)
22. Kakerow, R.: Low power design methodologies for mobile communication. In: Proceedings of the IEEE International Conference on Computer Design: VLSI in Computers and Processors, pp. 8–13. IEEE, New York (2002)
23. Paulson, L.D.: Low-power chips for high-powered handhelds. Computer 36(1), 21–23 (2003)
24. Davis, J.W.: Power benchmark strategy for systems employing power management. In: Proceedings of the 1993 IEEE International Symposium on Electronics and the Environment, pp. 117–119. IEEE, New York (1993)
25. Mayo, R.N., Ranganathan, P.: Energy consumption in mobile devices: why future systems need requirements–aware energy scale-down. In: International Workshop on Power-Aware Computer Systems, pp. 26–40 . Springer, Berlin (2003)
26. Rudenko, A., Reiher, P., Popek, G.J., Kuenning, G.H.: Saving portable computer battery power through remote process execution. ACM SIGMOBILE Mobile Computing and Communications Review 2(1), 19–26 (1998)
27. Guha Roy, D., Mahato, B., Ghosh, A., et al.: Service aware resource management into cloudlets for data offloading towards IoT. Microsyst Technol. 28, 517–531 (2022). https://doi.org/10.1007/s00542-019-04450-y
28. Roy, D.G., Das, M., De, D.: Cohort assembly: A load balancing grouping approach for traditional Wi-Fi infrastructure using edge cloud. In: Methodologies and Application Issues of Contemporary Computing Framework, pp. 93–108. Springer, Berlin (2018)
29. Li, L., Li, X., Youxia, S., Wen, L.: Research on mobile multimedia broadcasting service integration based on cloud computing. In: 2010 International Conference on Multimedia Technology, pp. 1–4. IEEE, New York (2010)
30. Garcia, A., Kalva, H.: Cloud transcoding for mobile video content delivery. In: 2011 IEEE International Conference on Consumer Electronics (ICCE), pp. 379–380. IEEE, New York (2011)
31. Zou, P., Wang, C., Liu, Z., Bao, D.: Phosphor: A cloud based DRM scheme with sim card. In: 2010 12th International Asia-Pacific Web Conference, pp. 459–463. IEEE, New York (2010)
32. Oberheide, J., Veeraraghavan, K., Cooke, E., Flinn, J., Jahanian, F.: Virtualized in-cloud security services for mobile devices. In: Proceedings of the First Workshop on Virtualization in Mobile Computing, pp. 31–35 (2008)
33. Masters, G.M.: Renewable and Efficient Electric Power Systems. Wiley, New York (2013)
34. Samadi, P., Mohsenian-Rad, A.-H., Schober, R., Wong, V.W., Jatskevich, J.: Optimal real-time pricing algorithm based on utility maximization for smart grid. In: 2010 First IEEE International Conference on Smart Grid Communications, pp. 415–420. IEEE, New York (2010)
35. Parvania, M., Fotuhi-Firuzabad, M.: Demand response scheduling by stochastic SCUC. IEEE Trans. Smart Grid 1(1), 89–98 (2010)
36. Shao, S., Zhang, T., Pipattanasomporn, M., Rahman, S.: Impact of TOU rates on distribution load shapes in a smart grid with PHEV penetration. In: IEEE PES T&D 2010, pp. 1–6. IEEE, New York (2010)
37. Bu, S., Yu, F.R., Cai, Y., Liu, X.P.: When the smart grid meets energy-efficient communications: Green wireless cellular networks powered by the smart grid. IEEE Trans. Wirel. Commun. 11(8), 3014–3024 (2012)
38. Fehske, A.J., Marsch, P., Fettweis, G.P.: Bit per joule efficiency of cooperating base stations in cellular networks. In: 2010 IEEE Globecom Workshops, pp. 1406–1411. IEEE, New York (2010)
39. Joskow, P.L.: Lessons learned from electricity market liberalization. Energy J. 29(Special Issue# 2), 9–42 (2008)

40. Sun, X., Ansari, N.: Green cloudlet network: a distributed green mobile cloud network. IEEE Netw. **31**(1), 64–70 (2017)
41. Roy, D.G., Mahato, B., De, D.: A competitive hedonic consumption estimation for IoT service distribution. In: 2019 URSI Asia-Pacific Radio Science Conference (AP-RASC), pp. 1–4. IEEE, New York (2019)
42. Mahato, B., Roy, D.G., De, D.: Distributed bandwidth selection approach for cooperative peer to peer multi-cloud platform. Peer-to-Peer Networking and Applications **14**(1), 177–201 (2021)
43. Han, T., Ansari, N.: Powering mobile networks with green energy. IEEE Wirel. Commun. **21**(1), 90–96 (2014)
44. Burr, M.: SMART-GRID SECURITY; intelligent power grids present vexing cyber security problems. In: Public Utilities Fortnightly, p. 43 (2008)
45. Bera, S., Misra, S., Rodrigues, J.J.: Cloud computing applications for smart grid: A survey. IEEE Trans. Parallel Distrib. Syst. **26**(5), 1477–1494 (2014)

Geospatial Green Mobile Edge Computing: Challenges, Solutions and Future Directions

Jaydeep Das and Shreya Ghosh

1   Introduction

In current century, a large number of geospatial applications of various industries are running on edge devices like mobile, smartphones, tab with the help of modern technologies like Information and Communication Technology (ICT), Wireless Sensor Network (WSN), and Internet of Things (IoT). Different computing paradigms are involved to compute a large amount of geospatial data, communicate and provide meaningful geospatial information to the user. These geospatial applications help users to analyse trajectories, weather prediction, current traffic conditions, nearby restaurants, hotels, bus-stop, railway stations, ATM searches, etc. Using the long distant cloud server can be a major challenge for latency-critical geospatial applications. For example, a user in a moving vehicle wants to know the traffic conditions of the upcoming road junctions. The traffic movement information should reach the user within a certain time period. After reaching the road junction, no use in getting the information about the traffic condition of that particular road junction to the user.

Mobile Edge Computing (MEC) is a modern technology, where idle edge nodes of the network are used for data computation and storage purposes. It reduces the latency due to its presence near the user applications which is the main drawback of the remote cloud servers. This technology is a combination of mobile computing and wireless communications. If we consider the above traffic movement application.

J. Das (✉)
School of Computer Engineering, KIIT Deemed to be University, Bhubaneswar, India
e-mail: jaydeep@iitkgp.ac.in

S. Ghosh
College of Information Sciences and Technology, The Pennsylvania State University, State College, PA, USA
e-mail: spg5897@psu.edu

MEC will help by offloading computation-intensive tasks like vehicle counting by video cameras, traffic composition, different algorithms for traffic counting to the MEC servers for cloud execution.

Edge nodes of any network are varied in battery sizes. This battery is only a source of energy. While the applications are running in the edge nodes, the battery drains of nodes. It is required to recharge the battery of the nodes from time to time. Using green energy like solar, wind leads to reducing carbon emission by minimizing the burning of coal-based brown energy. Green energy is very much dependent on the weather and geolocation of the edge nodes. A combination of green and brown energy provides a continuous power supply to the edge nodes. Saving brown energy in the MEC network can be termed as Green MEC.

Many existing methods are available in the MEC domain to provide energy-efficient solutions. In the context of geospatial applications, all of the existing solutions are may not be suitable or applicable.

Several existing energy-efficient and delay-aware solutions can be utilized for geospatial applications.

In this chapter, we are investigating:

- Existing geospatial applications used in MEC.
- Challenges in the geospatial applications while running on the MEC.
- Existing energy-efficient methods/techniques are available in MEC.
- Future scopes of Geospatial MEC.

We discuss in the chapter possible challenges in Green MEC domains for various geospatial applications. Future directions of geospatial applications with green MEC will be discussed at the end of this chapter.

2   Mobile Computing Paradigms

Mobile Computing is a technology that enables users to communicate with each other wirelessly through messages, audio, and videos. Mobile computing is supported by two computing paradigms: (i) Cloud-based, and (ii) Edge-based.

- **Mobile Cloud Computing(MCC)**: Mobile applications are running on mobile devices (like smartphones, tab) but the data storage and processing have been done in the cloud servers. It enriches user experiences by executing a plethora of mobile applications on a large number of mobile devices. Sanaei et al. [1] defined the MCC as "a rich mobile computing technology that leverages unified elastic resources of varied clouds and network technologies toward unrestricted functionality, storage, and mobility to serve a multitude of mobile devices anywhere, anytime through the channel of Ethernet or Internet regardless of heterogeneous environments and platforms based on the pay-as-you-use

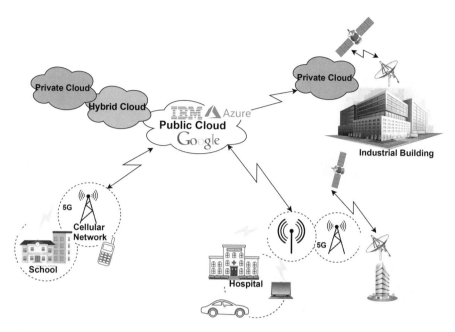

Fig. 1 Mobile Cloud Computing Architecture

principle." The detailed MEC architecture is presented in Fig. 1. Public, Private, and Hybrid Cloud can involve this MCC architecture. Public Cloud is used for a wide range of users, whereas Private Cloud is used for an organization, institutions, or government usage purpose where privacy has utmost priority. Hybrid Cloud is used for flexible, cost-effective, agile, and scalable business purposes. It allows organizations to get the best of both private and public cloud models.

- **Mobile Edge Computing(MEC)**: The cloud computing services are brought to the edge of the network by MEC. This technology is a key enabler for computation-intensive and latency-critical mobile applications [2]. Data storage and data processing are performed in the edge devices(e.g., base stations and access points) which are present in between mobile users and cloud servers. The main aim of MEC is to provide a better quality of service(QoS) to the mobile user by minimizing network congestion, and latency [3]. The detailed MEC architecture is presented in Fig. 2.

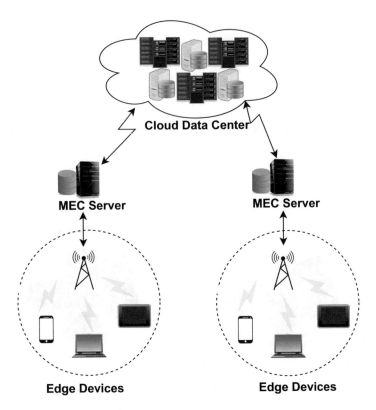

Fig. 2 Mobile Edge Computing Architecture

3 Existing Geospatial Applications on Mobile Edge Computing

A large number of geospatial applications are developed in the current decade which is running in MEC. We have categorized them into seven parts which are shown in Fig. 3.

3.1 Smart City Services

Smart city is a concept where the quality of living of people is improved with the help of information and communication technology [4, 5]. Smart cities will improve various smart things like smart economy, smart living, smart environment, smart mobility, smart governance, and smart people [6]. Green communications are made through device-to-device communications in [7]. Also, spatial parameters' effects

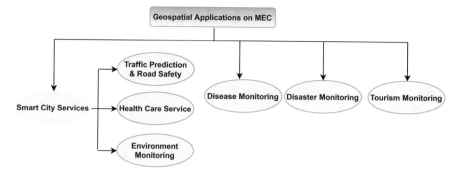

Fig. 3 Taxonomy of Geospatial Applications on MEC

on the smart city development and strategies are changed accordingly [8]. Here, we will discuss some smart city services where MEC plays an important role.

3.1.1 Traffic Prediction and Road Safety

Traffic prediction leads to an intelligent transportation system. It enhances the road safety of people. Traffic prediction can be done in several ways, i.e., traffic status prediction, traffic flow prediction, travel demand prediction [9]. Traffic predictions are done through a large number of Spatio-temporal data processing and techniques like data map-matching, data cleaning, data storage, and data compression. MEC can efficiently handle local/nearby Spatio-temporal data processing and provide local/region-specific traffic prediction.

Gillam et al. [10] proposed on-vehicle and off-vehicle data computation techniques in MEC. It increases autonomous driving efficiency by reducing end-to-end latency.

A machine learning approach was applied to Spatio-temporal data processing to get the mobility pattern of the moving agent in [11, 12]. It predicts the future locations of the moving agent in time-critical applications.

Emergency vehicles, like ambulances, can pass through quickly and safely on road through the safety corridors. A Back-Situation Awareness (BSA) application has been proposed by Halili et al. [13]. It notifies other vehicles about the presence or arrival of emergency vehicles. This helps to build a safety corridor for emergency vehicles. The nearby vehicles information is gathered through Multi-Access Edge Computing (MEC) with 5G.

Yang et al. [14] described short-term traffic prediction using the combination of vehicle velocity and traffic light prediction model. Vehicle velocity prediction has been performed with Spatio-temporal data analysis using a low-complexity semi-parametric prediction model. The model also captures traffic-light effects and driver's behavior to identify real-time traffic changes.

The distribution of MEC resources is depending on the task uploading of applications. Ale et al. [15] proposed a Spatio-temporal based learning strategy for resource management. Resource distributions using Bayesian hierarchical learning methods provided better results than equal resource distribution over all servers. Wang et al. [16] proposed unmanned aerial vehicle (UAV) for flexible MEC services. UAV provided latency-aware services after merging the geographically nearby user requests.

Ridhawi et al. [17] described a MEC collaborative reliable and secure communications among IoT devices, edge layers, and cloud-fog layers. Traffic flows are reduced by using node-to-node communications. These node communications ensure reliable and secure communications. This methodology is useful for smart city services.

3.1.2 Health Care Service

Health care service is an essential service in smart city. Geolocation-aware health care service facilitates health monitoring near to the patients [18]. Medical facilities reach quickly from nearby health care centers after determining the geolocation of the patient. MEC helps to continuous health monitoring for indoor and outdoor patients in [19]. Outdoor patient's mobility data prediction and preliminary health data analysis are done through edge devices. Any serious patient data analysis has been performed in a cloud server.

A deep learning-based heart disease identifying application, Healthfog, has been proposed by Tuli et al. [20]. Integrated IoT-Edge-Cloud platform is the backbone of the proposed architecture which made the application delay-aware and energy efficient.

A real-time healthcare service provisioning with geospatial queries in a cloud-fog-edge integrated platform has been proposed in [21]. The framework is an energy and latency-aware. It leads to a green geospatial query resolution platform.

Identifying the hotspot zone of Malaria [22, 23], Dengue [24] using geospatial map and taking immediate or preventive action accordingly are some research aspects in heathcare service.

3.1.3 Environment Monitoring

One of the environment pollutant gas is Carbon Monoxide (CO). Excessive emission of CO also increase heat of earth surface. To monitor CO level, a fog computing-based application has been proposed by Nugroho et al. [25]. Determination of the distance from the CO emitted area is calculated using Krigging method and plotted on Google map using lat/lon information.

Air quality at low concentration levels has been checked by AirSensEUR in [26]. Ganga river management using overlay analysis in MIST computing has been performed by Barik et al. [27].

3.2   Disease Monitoring

Disease identification and monitoring are necessary for contagious diseases. It controls the spreading of the disease over a geographic region. An IoT-based eHealth monitoring system has been proposed by Feriani et al. [28]. It identifies the symptoms(e.g., fever, coughing, and fatigue) of COVID-19. A learning method helps to identify the disease using MEC hierarchical framework.

3.3   Disaster Monitoring

High resolution and low latency face recognition videos have been identified the affected people in disaster prone areas [29]. A data distribution in nearby edge devices reduces the chance of data loss. Storing of disaster prediction data in nearby telephone central offices (TCOs) is proposed by Tsubaki et al. [30]. Face recognition of missing people in disaster is demonstrated by Liu et al. [31]. Facial images are transferred and stored in cloud server for saving energy and network bandwidth. Satellite image and video processed in a fog-cloud environment [32] to identify disaster-prone area.

3.4   Tourism Monitoring

Tourism helps in the economical growth of a country or a place. Monitoring of this sector is very important for business. It also has a socio-cultural impact. Behavior or movement pattern of tourists changes at a location on a seasonal or temporal basis. Tourism monitoring helps: (i) improve understanding about the effects of tourism, (ii) identify the locations where improvement is required, (iii) identify the season-specific locations, (iv) enable location-specific competitive business.

Ghazal et al. [33] captured and stored panoramic videos for a trip of tourist spots. Spatio-temporal information is also attached with videos for visualizing the videos with a location map. MEC architecture has been used for providing high-bandwidth and low-latency video experiences to end-users. Zhou et al. [34] used edge nodes for capturing Geo-tagged Flickr images. Image mining has been performed to determine the exact tourist location. Big spatial tourism data are managed through the RHadoop platform in Cloud. Van Setten et al. [35] developed a mobile-based recommendation system for tourists. A tourist guide application for Cyprus is elaborated in [36].

3.5 *Geospatial Data Collection and Query Processing*

Geospatial data are collected through edge devices. Geospatial queries are placed through geospatial applications using smart devices, i.e., mobile phone, tab, smart watch. To generate the result of the geospatial queries, huge data are needed to process along with the OGC compliant geospatial services [37] (WPS, WFS, WCS, WMS). MEC helps in processing local geospatial query processing with less delay. Also, storing, and processing geospatial data in a hierarchical manner to resolve geospatial queries has been performed in [38, 39]. This methodology not only reduces the latency of query result but also reduces the energy consumption of mobile devices as data processing is performed in edge or cloud platforms.

Essential data for services are collected from IoT devices and processed in MEC [40]. A lossy compression technique has been adopted to reduce the routing message contents. A budget and deadline constraint geospatial query processing have been done in cloud platform in [41]. Virtual Machine allocations for geospatial query processing has been performed in [42] with learning technique [43].

4 Existing Energy Efficient Methods in Mobile Edge Computing

Wu et al. [44] proposed an energy-efficient dynamic task offloading algorithm that decided where (MCC/MEC/IoT) tasks would be offloaded. Also, a blockchain-based offloading scheme has been proposed for secure task offloading. Lyapunov optimization-based dynamic secure task offloading and resource allocation algorithm described in [45]. They tried to extend the overall energy efficiency of non-orthogonal multiple access (NOMA) assisted MEC network.

Cheng et al. [46] proposed an energy-efficient algorithm for optimizing both offloading approach and the wireless resource allocation technique. It minimizes the transmission energy for computing task offloading. A greedy-based offloading algorithm [47] is described to minimize the overall energy cost for multiplayer games using MEC. Another energy-efficient task-offloading in MEC for an ultra-dense network is discussed in [48]. They reduced IoT devices' energy consumption within latency deadline optimizing devices offloading decisions.

Zhou et al. [49] discussed a reinforcement learning technique for computation offloading and resource allocation in a dynamic multi-user MEC system. The objective of this work is to reduce the long-term energy consumption of the entire MEC system. An unmanned aerial vehicle based MEC is elaborated in [50]. Objective of their work is reducing the hovering time, scheduling and resource allocation of the IoT tasks. Non-orthogonal multiple access (NOMA) based resource and energy allocation methodology in MEC has been discussed in [51, 52].

We have represented the existing energy-efficient methodologies in Table 1.

Table 1 Existing work for energy efficiency in mobile edge computing

Work	Base algorithm	Experiments	Used techniques	Working environment
Wu et al. [44]	Lyapunov Optimization	Simulation	Dynamic task offloading	IoT-Edge-Cloud Orchestrated Computing
Wang et al. [45]	Lyapunov Optimization	Simulation	Dynamic secure task offloading and resource allocation	NOMA-based MEC Network
Cheng et al. [46]	Orthogonal Frequency-Division Multiplexing Access (OFDMA)	Simulation	Joint offloading and resource allocation	Multi-MEC Server
Yang et al. [47]	Greedy algorithm	Simulation	Energy cost minimization	Multiplayer Games with cache-aided MEC
Haber et al. [48]	Successive Convex Approximation (SCA)	Numerical analysis based simulation	IoT task offloading for heterogeneous network	Ultra-dense Networks
Zhou et al. [49]	Reinforcement Learning (Q Learning)	Simulation	Computation offloading and resource allocation	Dynamic multi-user MEC system
Du et al. [50]	Block coordinate descent	Simulation	Task hovering time, scheduling and resource allocation	Unmanned aerial vehicle based MEC system
Liu et al. [51]	Non-orthogonal multiple access (NOMA)	Simulation	Resource and Power allocation	Massive IoT Networks
Fang et al. [52]	Non-orthogonal multiple access (NOMA)	Simulation	Task assignment, Power allocation and User association	Multi-user, multi-BS NOMA-MEC network
Li et al. [53]	Markov decision process	Simulation	Computing resource allocation, computing capability	Virtualized Cellular Networks with MEC

5   Challenges in Geospatial Mobile Edge Computing

There are several challenges are present in Geospatial MEC. These are-

- **Heterogeneity:** Different heterogeneous geospatial data sources are involved while resolving any user request. Also, edge devices and servers may present in heterogeneous networks. Proper synchronization and offloading policies need to develop among the geospatial data sources and computing resources to maximize utilization.
- **Seamless Connectivity:** In MEC, the mobile devices are moving around and changing the region of MEC servers. Seamless connections are very much needed while a mobile device changes one MEC server region to another MEC server region. Otherwise, mobile applications, like mobile games may get hampered and the quality of the service gets down.
- **Cost:** The amount of cost increases with the number of edge nodes involve in the edge network. Also, communication cost, coordination cost among edge nodes, geospatial data cost are taken into the cost calculation. CPU cost and IO costs are also involved for geospatial queries [41] processing in MEC. Accumulation of all these costs is needed to consider for geospatial MEC applications.
- **Data Handling:** Geospatial applications are work with a large number of data/big data. MEC servers and MEC devices need to handle this huge number of data carefully. Otherwise, data may be lost during data transmission. Also, at the time of data analysis resource constraints arise due to improper data handling.
- **Security and Privacy:** These two features are very important for critical mobile applications. Privacy of data may reveal during offloading. Also, security threats arise by masquerade attacks, passive attacks.

6   Future Directions

In this section of the chapter, we discuss the future scopes of the geospatial green mobile edge computing (GGMEC) research work. Though many explorations have been done in MEC and Green Computing, very little progress observed in the geospatial domain with energy efficiency. Still, we can think about the following aspects of Geospatial Green MEC in the future.

- **Pricing Scheme:** Investigation of pricing policies is required individually for geospatial data providers and Mobile Edge Computing service providers.
- **Data Management:** Geospatial data management in the GGMEC environment is a challenge. Storing a small amount of data within the edge nodes of a distributed manner and synchronizing them will be a challenging task.
- **Data Security:** Sensitive geospatial data or healthcare data are required proper security while data are transmitted within edge devices.

- **Data Re-usability:** Geospatial data can be reused for different applications. Storing of processed geospatial data is needed for reusing in future geospatial applications.
- **Energy Efficiency:** A very small amount of investigation has been performed for energy efficiency in the geospatial domain. Large geospatial data processing and transmission lead to huge energy consumption in MEC nodes. Proper computing resource management and geospatial data management can provide Green MEC.
- **Application Management:** Geospatial application management, MEC resource provisioning, with different kinds of machine learning techniques can be a future trend.
- **Application-aware Policy:** Every geospatial application, i.e., smart city, weather prediction, disease monitoring, crop analysis, etc. has different requirements. Application-driven policies are required for proper management in the MEC environment.
- **Web Service Orchestration:** Automation of different geospatial web service orchestration to resolve any geospatial query in MEC can also be a future scope.

7 Summary

In this chapter, we have discussed various geospatial applications in MEC. Also, we have provided a taxonomy for the applications. Different existing energy-efficient schemes in MEC are discussed and represented in a table. Thereafter, challenges in geospatial MEC are identified and discussed. At the end of the chapter, we have pointed out areas of geospatial MEC where further research can be explored.

References

1. Sanaei, Z., Abolfazli, S., Gani, A., Buyya, R.: Heterogeneity in mobile cloud computing: taxonomy and open challenges. IEEE Commun. Surv. Tutorials **16**(1), 369–392 (2013)
2. Mao, Y., You, C., Zhang, J., Huang, K., Letaief, K.B.: A survey on mobile edge computing: The communication perspective. IEEE Commun. Surv. Tutorials **19**(4), 2322–2358 (2017)
3. Mukherjee, A., De, D., Ghosh, S.K., Buyya, R.: Introduction to mobile edge computing. In: Mobile Edge Computing, pp. 3–19 (2021)
4. Batty, M., Axhausen, K.W., Giannotti, F., Pozdnoukhov, A., Bazzani, A., Wachowicz, M., Ouzounis, G., Portugali, Y.: Smart cities of the future. The European Physical Journal Special Topics **214**(1), 481–518 (2012)
5. Eremia, M., Toma, L., Sanduleac, M.: The smart city concept in the 21st century. Procedia Engineering **181**, 12–19 (2017)
6. Camero, A., Alba, E.: Smart city and information technology: A review. Cities **93**, 84–94 (2019)
7. Kai, C., Li, H., Xu, L., Li, Y., Jiang, T.: Energy-efficient device-to-device communications for green smart cities. IEEE Trans. Ind. Inf. **14**(4), 1542–1551 (2018)
8. Angelidou, M.: Smart city policies: A spatial approach. Cities **41**, S3–S11 (2014)

9. Yuan, H., Li, G.: A survey of traffic prediction: from spatio-temporal data to intelligent transportation. Data Science and Engineering **6**(1), 63–85 (2021)
10. Gillam, L., Katsaros, K., Dianati, M., Mouzakitis, A.: Exploring edges for connected and autonomous driving. In: IEEE INFOCOM 2018-IEEE Conference on Computer Communications Workshops (INFOCOM WKSHPS), pp. 148–153 . IEEE, New York (2018)
11. Ghosh, S., Mukherjee, A., Ghosh, S.K., Buyya, R.: Mobi-IoST: mobility-aware cloud-fog-edge-iot collaborative framework for time-critical applications. IEEE Transactions on Network Science and Engineering **7**(4), 2271–2285 (2019)
12. Ghosh, S., Das, J., Ghosh, S.K.: Locator: A cloud-fog-enabled framework for facilitating efficient location based services. In: 2020 International Conference on COMmunication Systems and NETworkS (COMSNETS), pp. 87–92. IEEE, New York (2020)
13. Halili, R., Yousaf, F.Z., Slamnik-Kriještorac, N., Yilma, G.M., Liebsch, M., e Silva, E.d.B., Hadiwardoyo, S.A., Berkvens, R., Weyn, M.: Leveraging MEC in a 5g system for enhanced back situation awareness. In: 2020 IEEE 45th Conference on Local Computer Networks (LCN), pp. 309–320. IEEE, New York (2020)
14. Yang, S.-R., Su, Y.-J., Chang, Y.-Y., Hung, H.-N.: Short-term traffic prediction for edge computing-enhanced autonomous and connected cars. IEEE Trans. Veh. Technol. **68**(4), 3140–3153 (2019)
15. Ale, L., Zhang, N., King, S.A., Guardiola, J.: Spatio-temporal Bayesian learning for mobile edge computing resource planning in smart cities. ACM Trans. Internet Technol. (TOIT) **21**(3), 1–21 (2021)
16. Wang, J., Liu, K., Pan, J.: Online UAV-mounted edge server dispatching for mobile-to-mobile edge computing. IEEE Internet Things J. **7**(2), 1375–1386 (2019)
17. Al Ridhawi, I., Otoum, S., Aloqaily, M., Jararweh, Y., Baker, T.: Providing secure and reliable communication for next generation networks in smart cities. Sustain. Cities Soc. **56**, 102080 (2020)
18. Das, J.: Geolocation-aware iot and cloud-fog-based solutions for healthcare. In: Machine Learning, Big Data, and IoT for Medical Informatics, pp. 37–52. Elsevier, Amsterdam (2021)
19. Mukherjee, A., Ghosh, S., Behere, A., Ghosh, S.K., Buyya, R.: Internet of health things (IoHT) for personalized health care using integrated edge-fog-cloud network. J. Ambient. Intell. Humaniz. Comput. **12**(1), 943–959 (2020)
20. Tuli, S., Basumatary, N., Gill, S.S., Kahani, M., Arya, R.C., Wander, G.S., Buyya, R.: Healthfog: an ensemble deep learning based smart healthcare system for automatic diagnosis of heart diseases in integrated iot and fog computing environments. Futur. Gener. Comput. Syst. **104**, 187–200 (2020)
21. Das, J., Ghosh, S., Mukherjee, A., Ghosh, S.K., Buyya, R.: RESCUE: Enabling green healthcare services using integrated iot-edge-fog-cloud computing environments. In: Software: Practice and Experience (2022)
22. Barik, R.K., Dubey, A.C., Tripathi, A., Pratik, T., Sasane, S., Lenka, R.K., Dubey, H., Mankodiya, K., Kumar, V.: Mist data: leveraging mist computing for secure and scalable architecture for smart and connected health. Procedia Comput. Sci. **125**, 647–653 (2018)
23. Clements, A.C., Reid, H.L., Kelly, G.C., Hay, S.I.: Further shrinking the malaria map: how can geospatial science help to achieve malaria elimination?" Lancet Infect. Dis. **13**(8), 709–718 (2013)
24. Delmelle, E.M., Zhu, H., Tang, W., Casas, I.: A web-based geospatial toolkit for the monitoring of dengue fever. Appl. Geogr. **52**, 144–152 (2014)
25. Nugroho, F.W., Suryono, S., Suseno, J.E.: Fog computing for monitoring of various area mapping pollution carbon monoxide (co) with ordinary kriging method. In: 2019 Fourth International Conference on Informatics and Computing (ICIC), pp. 1–6. IEEE, New York (2019)
26. Kotsev, A., Schade, S., Craglia, M., Gerboles, M., Spinelle, L., Signorini, M.: Next generation air quality platform: openness and interoperability for the internet of things. Sensors **16**(3), 403 (2016)

27. Barik, R.K., Lenka, R.K., Simha, N., Dubey, H., Mankodiya, K.: Fog computing based SDI framework for mineral resources information infrastructure management in India. arXiv preprint arXiv:1712.09282 (2017)
28. Feriani, A., Refaey, A., Hossain, E.: Tracking pandemics: a mec-enabled IoT ecosystem with learning capability. IEEE Internet of Things Magazine 3(3), 40–45 (2020)
29. Trinh, H., Chemodanov, D., Yao, S., Lei, Q., Zhang, B., Gao, F., Calyam, P., Palaniappan, K.: Energy-aware mobile edge computing for low-latency visual data processing. In: 2017 IEEE 5th International Conference on Future Internet of Things and Cloud (FiCloud), pp. 128–133. IEEE, New York (2017)
30. Tsubaki, T., Ishibashi, R., Kuwahara, T., Okazaki, Y.: Effective disaster recovery for edge computing against large-scale natural disasters. In: 2020 IEEE 17th Annual Consumer Communications and Networking Conference (CCNC), pp. 1–2. IEEE, New York (2020)
31. Liu, F., Guo, Y., Cai, Z., Xiao, N., Zhao, Z.: Edge-enabled disaster rescue: a case study of searching for missing people. ACM Trans. Intell. Syst. Technol. (TIST) 10(6), 1–21 (2019)
32. Chemodanov, D., Calyam, P., Palaniappan, K.: Fog computing to enable geospatial video analytics for disaster-incident situational awareness. In: Fog Computing: Theory and Practice, pp. 473–503 (2020)
33. Ghazal, M., AlKhalil, Y., Mhanna, A., Dehbozorgi, F.: Mobile panoramic video maps over mec networks. In: 2016 IEEE Wireless Communications and Networking Conference, pp. 1–6. IEEE, New York (2016)
34. Zhou, X., Xu, C., Kimmons, B.: Detecting tourism destinations using scalable geospatial analysis based on cloud computing platform. Comput. Environ. Urban. Syst. 54, 144–153 (2015)
35. Van Setten, M., Pokraev, S., Koolwaaij, J.: Context-aware recommendations in the mobile tourist application compass. In: International Conference on Adaptive Hypermedia and Adaptive Web-Based Systems, pp. 235–244. Springer, Berlin (2004)
36. Kamilaris, A., Pitsillides, A.: A web-based tourist guide mobile application. In: Proceedings of the International Conference on Sustainability, Technology and Education (STE), Kuala Lumpur, Malaysia, vol. 29 (2013)
37. Zhao, P., Yu, G., Di, L.: Geospatial web services. In: Emerging spatial information systems and applications, pp. 1–35. IGI Global, New York (2007)
38. Das, J., Mukherjee, A., Ghosh, S.K., Buyya, R.: Spatio-fog: a green and timeliness-oriented fog computing model for geospatial query resolution. Simul. Model. Pract. Theory 100, 102043 (2020)
39. Das, J., Mukherjee, A., Ghosh, S.K., Buyya, R.: Geo-cloudlet: time and power efficient geospatial query resolution using cloudlet. In: 2019 11th International Conference on Advanced Computing (ICoAC), pp. 180–187. IEEE, New York (2019)
40. Cao, X., Madria, S.: Efficient geospatial data collection in IoT networks for mobile edge computing. In: 2019 IEEE 18th International Symposium on Network Computing and Applications (NCA), pp. 1–10. IEEE, New York (2019)
41. Das, J., Ghosh, S., Ghosh, S.K., Buyya, R.: LYRIC: deadline and budget aware spatio-temporal query processing in cloud. In: IEEE Transactions on Services Computing (2021)
42. Das, J., Addya, S.K., Ghosh, S.K., Buyya, R.: Optimal geospatial query placement in cloud. In: Intelligent and Cloud Computing, pp. 335–344. Springer, Berlin (2021)
43. Das, J., Dasgupta, A., Ghosh, S.K., Buyya, R.: A learning technique for vm allocation to resolve geospatial queries. In: Recent Findings in Intelligent Computing Techniques, pp. 577–584. Springer, Berlin (2019)
44. Wu, H., Wolter, K., Jiao, P., Deng, Y., Zhao, Y., Xu, M.: EEDTO: an energy-efficient dynamic task offloading algorithm for blockchain-enabled IoT-edge-cloud orchestrated computing. IEEE Internet Things J. 8(4), 2163–2176 (2020)
45. Wang, Q., Hu, H., Hu, R.Q., et al.: Secure and energy-efficient offloading and resource allocation in a NOMA-based MEC network. In: 2020 IEEE/ACM Symposium on Edge Computing (SEC), pp. 420–424. IEEE, New York (2020)

46. Cheng, K., Teng, Y., Sun, W., Liu, A., Wang, X.: Energy-efficient joint offloading and wireless resource allocation strategy in multi-mec server systems. In: 2018 IEEE international conference on communications (ICC), pp. 1–6. IEEE, New York (2018)

47. Yang, X., Luo, H., Sun, Y., Obaidat, M.S.: Energy-efficient collaborative offloading for multiplayer games with cache-aided MEC. In ICC 2020-2020 IEEE International Conference on Communications (ICC), pp. 1–7. IEEE, New York (2020)

48. El Haber, E., Nguyen, T.M., Assi, C., Ajib, W.: An energy-efficient task offloading solution for MEC-based IoT in ultra-dense networks. In: 2019 IEEE Wireless Communications and Networking Conference (WCNC), pp. 1–7. IEEE, New York (2019)

49. Zhou, H., Jiang, K., Liu, X., Li, X., Leung, V.C.: Deep reinforcement learning for energy-efficient computation offloading in mobile edge computing. IEEE Internet Things J. **9**(2), 1517–1530 (2021)

50. Du, Y., Wang, K., Yang, K., Zhang, G.: Energy-efficient resource allocation in UAV based MEC system for IoT devices. In: 2018 IEEE Global Communications Conference (GLOBECOM), pp. 1–6. IEEE, New York (2018)

51. Liu, B., Liu, C., Peng, M.: Resource allocation for energy-efficient MEC in NOMA-enabled massive IoT networks. IEEE J. Sel. Areas Commun. **39**(4), 1015–1027 (2020)

52. Fang, F., Wang, K., Ding, Z., Leung, V.C.: Energy-efficient resource allocation for NOMA-MEC networks with imperfect CSI. IEEE Trans. Commun. **69**(5), 3436–3449 (2021)

53. Li, M., Yu, F.R., Si, P., Zhang, Y.: Energy-efficient machine-to-machine (m2m) communications in virtualized cellular networks with mobile edge computing (MEC). IEEE Trans. Mob. Comput. **18**(7), 1541–1555 (2018)

Dynamic Voltage and Frequency Scaling Approach for Processing Spatio-Temporal Queries in Mobile Environment

Shreya Ghosh and Jaydeep Das

1   Introduction

The recent decade has shown significant increase in accumulation of IoT data (including mobility, health sensory information, cellular data etc.) and adapting data-driven decision systems in every aspect of our lives. The computational and storage requirement led to the growing popularity of cloud data centers as well as edge and fog nodes. On the other hand, with the prevalence of GPS-enabled smart-devices, almost all the data-instances are associated with location and temporal dimension. These datasets are denoted as spatio-temporal data. Few examples are: trajectory information of people, climate data, taxi or bus datasets, temporal data in health context [8, 15, 16] and time-critical applications [7]. Spatio-temporal query processing is the backbone of provisioning any location-based services such as route optimization, recommendation, weather prediction or remote sensing applications. The major challenge in analysing this data-instances are the huge volume as the instances change with time-scale. Further, data-centers utilized for analysis of this data become unsustainable in terms of power consumption and growing energy costs. It has been estimated that the energy consumption of these data centers is 205 terawatt-hours of electricity which is between 1.1% and 1.5% of the worldwide electricity consumption, which led to excessive CO2 emissions. It further poses a great challenge to Cloud providers to find a trade-off between power and energy consumption and providing services satisfying strict Service Level Agreement

S. Ghosh (✉)
College of Information Sciences and Technology, The Pennsylvania State University, State College, PA, USA
e-mail: spg5897@psu.edu

J. Das
School of Computer Engineering, KIIT Deemed to be University, Bhubaneswar, India
e-mail: jaydeep@iitkgp.ac.in

© The Author(s), under exclusive license to Springer Nature Switzerland AG 2022
D. De et al. (eds.), *Green Mobile Cloud Computing*,
https://doi.org/10.1007/978-3-031-08038-8_9

185

conditions. Therefore, it is essential to trade-off between energy and power costs and performances of the systems or services. Here, Dynamic voltage and frequency scaling (DVFS) plays a critical role in understanding the correlations among power, DVFS, amount of spatio-temporal data and performance of the query processor tool.

DVFS is a key feature which we considered in this work to reduce the energy consumption while placing the geospatial queries to the virtual machines. As the processing of geospatial data is not same for the different geospatial queries, the workload is different (dynamic) for each virtual machine (resources). DVFS is used to decrease the power consumption of underutilized resources considering the fact that performance does not degrade. Dynamic Voltage and Frequency Scaling strategies modify frequency according to the variations on the utilization performed by dynamic workload. These policies help to dynamically reduce the consumption of resources as dynamic power is frequency dependent. Dynamic Voltage and Frequency Scaling has been traditionally applied to decrease the power consumption of underutilized resources as it may incur on service level agreement (SLA) violations. The major contributions of this chapter are as follows:

- We explore Dynamic Voltage and Frequency Scaling (DVFS) approach to modify frequencies according to the variation of the utilization performance of the spatio-temporal query processing.
- We propose a spatial architecture that can process the queries in an energy-efficient way.
- We present different existing works and challenges to develop an energy-efficient query scheduler algorithm proposing efficient policy
- We evaluate the architecture and the algorithms in terms of query processing performance using two datasets and present the visualization results of the spatio-temporal queries.

It may be noted that the proposed framework is energy-aware as it utilizes the dynamic voltage and frequency scaling (DVFS) for the individual geospatial query according to the user's requirement. It particularly utilizes the Dynamic Voltage and Frequency Scaling (DVFS) capability of modern CPU processors to keep the CPU operating at the minimum voltage level (and consequently minimum frequency and power consumption) that enables the application to complete before a user-defined deadline. We use the DVFS module to execute the query and return the response based on the user's priority level. DVFS can be applied at the CPU level or operating system level. Our module aims to provide maximum frequency levels to be assigned during the execution of the query. It may be noted that the query execution task is a non-preemptive, and the user-defined deadline is a soft-deadline.

While we have analysed our framework using spatio-temporal datasets, however, the framework is generic enough to consider any other data instances effectively. In future, we aim to extend the DVFS approach in MapReduce based algorithm of movement datasets of people in a country and find interesting insights in low power and low energy environments (Fig. 1).

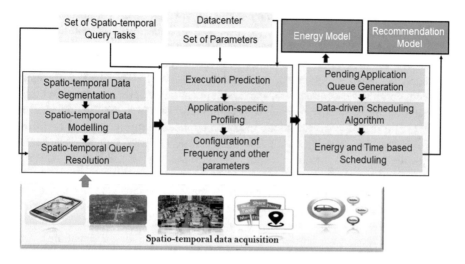

Fig. 1 Overall building blocks of the framework

2 Related Work

To combat the challenge of exponential rate of energy consumption and green house gas emissions by data centers, there are several research methods focusing on optimization and utilization of hosts via dynamic consolidation of virtual machines [1, 6]. In summary, in these researches, low utilized VMs are placed together on a single host. Then, other hosts are shut down. In DVFS technique, the frequency and voltage are reduced simultaneously of the CMOS circuit. Also, the timing constraint of processes are maintained accordingly. An algorithm is presented in [19] for energy-efficient scheduling of VMs in hosts consisting of a virtualized cluster. In these techniques, the VMs are considered as "black boxes". Therefore, these techniques are unable to satisfy the deadlines of time-critical applications within the VMs.

Garg et al. [5] proposes a novel approach for scheduling tasks in the cloud environment. The work emphasizes on the reduction of emission of carbon dioxide gas using DVFS technique. Another work is presented in [20] considering the slack time to schedule dependent tasks in homogenous clusters using DVFS scheduling algorithm. A scheduling algorithm, namely, DVFS-enabled Energy-efficient Workflow Task Scheduling (DEWTS) is proposed in [17] by mapping tasks to VMs satisfying the requirements and resulted in reduced consumption of energy. An energy-aware algorithm to schedule tasks based on heterogeneous clusters is presented in [14]. Although the approach aims to provision the services in minimal execution time, it does not consider deadline constraints for different applications. Furthermore, the method does not leverage DVFS algorithm. It considers varied power consumption statistics by heterogeneous nodes. Another study explores the features of HPC services and computes energy savings based on different types of applications [2]. Minyu et al. [3] proposes a framework for real-time task mapping under different DVFS schemes. The authors propose a novel system combining distinct reliability enhancement techniques considering different set-ups such as, task-level, processor-level and system-level DVFS. The task mapping problem optimizes task allocation, and task duplication by developing mathematical formulation using integer non-linear programming problem. Another interesting study [12] utilizes DVFS technique in health application by introducing real-time DVFS aware deep learning method for fall detection of aged people. The system is typically beneficial for home health monitoring as well as minimizing resource constraints of mobile devices.

A system named, *Ring-DVFS*, which is reliability-aware DVFS for real-life applications, is proposed in [21]. Here, the reinforcement learner takes the decision analyzing power savings and task-reliability variations and outputs the suitable voltage-frequency level considering the time criteria of the applications. The proposed methodology has the capacity to adapt in different situations without sacrificing reliability for sporadic tasks. Another energy efficient scheduling algorithm is proposed in [11] which also considers reliability factor. The work incorporates fault detection and correction and rollback recovery process. The work has achieved 30%–50% reduction in energy consumption and speed up to 97% faster than the existing approaches. The novel algorithm deploys a distribution technique of the target deadline where it is guaranteed that each task finishes before its deadline. A multi-objective evolutionary scheduling algorithm is developed using Neural network technique considering the energy consumption, execution time of the tasks and reliability of the system [13]. Another work is presented in [17] where a scheduling algorithm based on the DVFS technique is proposed. The framework is named as *DVFS-enabled Energy-efficient Workflow Task Scheduling (DEWTS)*. Here, the tasks are mapped to VMs and makespan requirement is met along with reduced consumption of energy.

Gupta et al. [10] present a dynamic workload aware DVFS for muticore system. The proposed system utilizes the workload profile information along with power constraints to provision the best-suited voltage–frequency. It is specifically used for maintaining a global power budget at chip-level. Also, it maximizes the performance and satisfies power constraints at the per-core level. The authors developed and implemented the system with the workload characterizer and application requirements to use the knowledge in order to find the next setting for the core. Another work by Umair et al. [18] proposed energy efficient mechanism on edge-devices for IoT-based healthcare system. An energy-aware static scheduler is proposed which considers tasks with conditional constraints and incorporated DVFS specifically for the IoT-based real-time and time-critical applications in healthcare. Next, a scheduling and voltage scaling approach is presented using non linear programming technique.

The rest of the book chapter is presented as follows: Sect. 3 presents different types of spatio-temporal query and their outcomes. Section 4 presents the overall framework and energy related issues to resolve spatio-temporal query, and finally in Sect. 5 summarizes and concludes the chapter.

3 Spatio-Temporal Query Processing and Experimentation on Two Dataset

Spatio-temporal query is defined as a sequence (ST_Q) of n-length ordered spatio-temporal predicates, which can be represented as:

$$ST_Q = (ST_{Q_1}, T_1), (ST_{Q_2}, T_2), \ldots (ST_{Q_n}, T_n) \tag{1}$$

where T_i presents the time-interval of the query and ST_{Q_i} is the spatial predicate of the query. For simplicity, we illustrate the types of spatial queries along with different predicates with examples as follows: Consider 4 independent repositories of a region P, namely, ROAD (R), DRAINAGE (D), VILLAGE (V) and ADMIN BLOCKS (A). Figure 2 depicts the class diagram of the use-case.[1]
Road: Polyline; Drainage: Polyline; Village: Point; Admin: Polygon

Query 1: Find the villages which are likely to be affected during flood. Flood: Areas within 1 km of a drainage network are inundated.

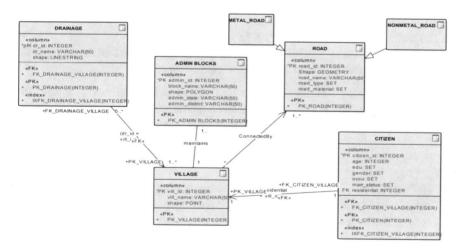

Fig. 2 Class diagram of the use-case

---

[1] Details are provided in our tutorial at https://www.orsac.gov.in/Workshop_materials/NFSD/DAY3/IITKgp-Demo-201218.pdf.

```
SELECT V.vill-id, V.vill-name FROM
VILLAGE V, DRAINAGE D WHERE
OVERLAP(V.shape,BUFFER(D.shape,1000))=1;
```

Query 2: Find the Roads likely to be affected if River R1 is flooded.

```
SELECT R.road-id, V.vill-name FROM
VILLAGE V, DRAINAGE D WHERE
OVERLAP(V.shape, BUFFER(D.shape,1000))=1 AND
D.dr-name="R1";
```

Query 3: To setup a new industry the requirement is: It should be in Admin Blocks A2 or A7, 2 km from NH, no Drainage within 1 km, within 5 km of villages with working population (20–50yrs) greater than 100.

```
  Create VIEW REG AS(
SELECT INTERSECT(V.shape,A.shape) AS REG-SHAPE
FROM ROAD R, DRAINAGE D, VILLAGE V, CITIZEN C WHERE
OVERLAP(V.shape, BUFFER(D.shape,1000))=0 AND
OVERLAP(V.shape, BUFFER(R.shape,2000))=1 AND
COUNT(C.citizen-id)>=100 WHERE
C.age>20 AND C.age<50 AND
C.residential==V.vill-id)
```

```
  SELECT INTERSECT (REG-SHAPE,A.shape) FROM
REG, ADMIN-BLOCKS A WHERE
A.block-name IN ("A2","A7") AND
OVERLAP(A.shape, BUFFER(REG-SHAPE,5000))==1
```
In the above illustration, we have used different spatial predicates such as:

- OVERLAP: This identifies whether two spatial objects intersects or not. The predicate returns 1 if a geometry instance overlaps another geometry instance, otherwise it returns zero. It has the following structure:

$$Overlaps(geometry, geometry) : boolean \qquad (2)$$

- BUFFER: It creates a new geometry by computing the defined distance value around any point, line, or polygon that encompasses all of the area within a specified distance of the feature. It has the following structure:

$$Buffer(geometry, buffer - value) : geometry \qquad (3)$$

We have carried out experiment with synthetic data to showcase basic spatio-temporal operations and real-life data of IIT Kharagpur campus, which is shown in the following example: Fig. 3 shows the visualization of synthetic dataset on map. The structure of the tables are presented as follows:

Fig. 3 Illustration of
synthetic spatio-temporal
dataset

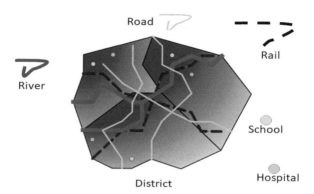

- Road [gid, road_name, road_km, road_type, geom]
- Rail [gid, track_type, track_km, geom]
- Hospital [gid, hospital_name, hospital_type, geom]
- School [gid, school_name, school_type, geom]
- District [gid, dist_name, dist_perimeter, dist_area, geom]
- River [gid, river_name, river_km, geom]

Extract data from tables

```
SELECT * FROM hospital;
```

The query extracts all data from *hospital* table, which is shown in Fig. 4.

Spatial Query: Buffer

- **Point Buffer Query**

```
SELECT hospital_n, ST_Buffer(hospital.geom, 4) FROM
hospital;
```

- **Polyline Buffer Query**

```
SELECT river_name, geom, ST_Buffer(river.geom, 0.5)
FROM river;
```

The outcome of the query is presented in Fig. 5

Cross and Touch Operation

```
SELECT road.road_name, rail.track_type FROM road, rail
WHERE ST_Crosses(road.geom, rail.geom);

SELECT b.dist_name FROM district a, district b WHERE
ST_Touches(a.geom, b.geom) AND a.dist_name = 'DIST_1';
```

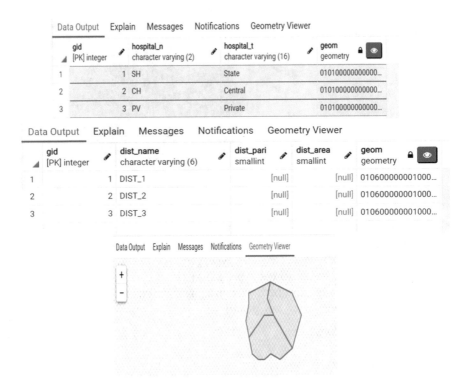

Fig. 4 Snapshot of spatio-temporal query: Extract data from table

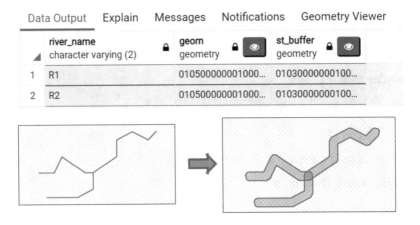

Fig. 5 Snapshot of spatio-temporal query: Buffer

Intersection Operation

```
SELECT d.dist_name, r.road_name FROM
district d, road r
WHERE ST_Intersects(d.geom, r.geom)
ORDER BY (dist_name);
```

Spatio-temporal Query: Area and Perimeter calculation of districts

```
SELECT dist_name, ST_Area(geom) AS Area,
ST_PERIMETER(district.geom) AS Perimeter
FROM district
ORDER BY ST_Area(geom) DESC;
```

Spatial Query: Nearest Neighbor

```
SELECT school.gid, school.school_name,
ST_Distance(school.geom, hospital.geom) AS distance
FROM school, hospital
WHERE hospital.hospital_n = 'SH'
ORDER BY ST_Distance(school.geom, hospital.geom) ASC;
```

Figure 6 depicts the IIT Kharagpur map on spatial database. In the spatial database the map is stored as *shape* or *geometry (geom)* field and there are three data-types: *point, polygon* and *polyline*. Figure 7 shows the attributes of *point-of-interests* and *road-network* of IIT Kharagpur.

Spatial Query: Areas of the Halls in the IIT Kharagpur campus

```
Select name,geom, st_area(geom) as area from
```

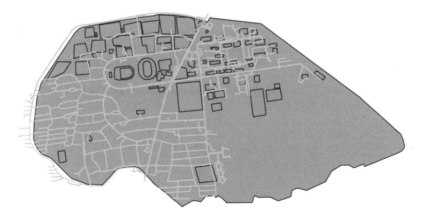

Fig. 6 Demonstration of IIT Kharagpur map in spatial database

gid		r_name		start_pnt		end_pnt		const_type		
[PK] integer		character varying (50)		character varying (50)		character varying (50)		character varying (50)		
1	110	IIT Main Road		Puri Gate		Prembazzar		Pakka		
2	226	IIT Main Road		Puri Gate		Prembazzar		Pakka		
3	375	IIT Main Road		Puri Gate		Prembazzar		Pakka		
4	383	Nursery Road		Dreamland		Super Duper		Pakka		
5	386	Nursery Road		Dreamland		Super Duper		Pakka		

no_of_lane		type		speed_lim		direction		geom		
smallint		character varying (50)		smallint		character varying (50)		geometry		
	2	[null]			30	N-S		010500000001000...		
	2	[null]			30	N-S		010500000001000...		
	2	[null]			30	N-S		010500000001000...		
	2	[null]			30	E-W		010500000001000...		
	2	[null]			30	E-W		010500000001000...		

Data Output   Explain   Messages   Notifications   Geometry Viewer

gid		osm_id		name		amenity		geom		
[PK] integer		character varying (254)		character varying (254)		character varying (254)		geometry		
1	6	[null]		Indian Institute of Technology ...		university		010600000001000...		
2	3	7255545		TSG Lake		Lake/Pool		010600000001000...		
3	7	[null]		New Wagon Shop		Shop		010600000001000...		
4	13	[null]		Police Quarters		[null]		010600000001000...		
5	14	[null]		Jubilee Park		[null]		010600000001000...		
6	22	[null]		VIKRAMSHILA SCHOOL OF M...		[null]		010600000001000...		

Fig. 7 Snapshot of spatio-temporal query result and spatial data structure in the database

```
kgp_poi where
amenity='Hall of Residence' order by area;
```
This query computes the area of the hall of residence at IIT Kharagpur campus and lists those in ascending order. Figure 8 represents the extracted results both in list-format and the geometry of the result is also presented in the figure.

Spatial Query: Find the road segments within 50meter of Takshila

```
select r.r_name,r.geom,kgp.geom from
road_NETWORK r, kgp_poi kgp where
st_intersects(r.geom, st_buffer(kgp.geom,50)) and
kgp.name='Takshila Complex';
```

This query uses *buffer* and *intersection* operations to find out road segments within 50 meter of a building. Figure 9 depicts the outcome of the query.

Spatial Query: Find the distance between computer science and engineering department and student halls

```
SELECT B.name, A.name,
st_distance(B.geom, A.geom) dis FROM
kgp_poi B, kgp_poi A WHERE
B.name='DEPT OF COMPUTER SCIENCE AND ENGINEERING' and
A.amenity='Hall of Residence'
order by dis;
```

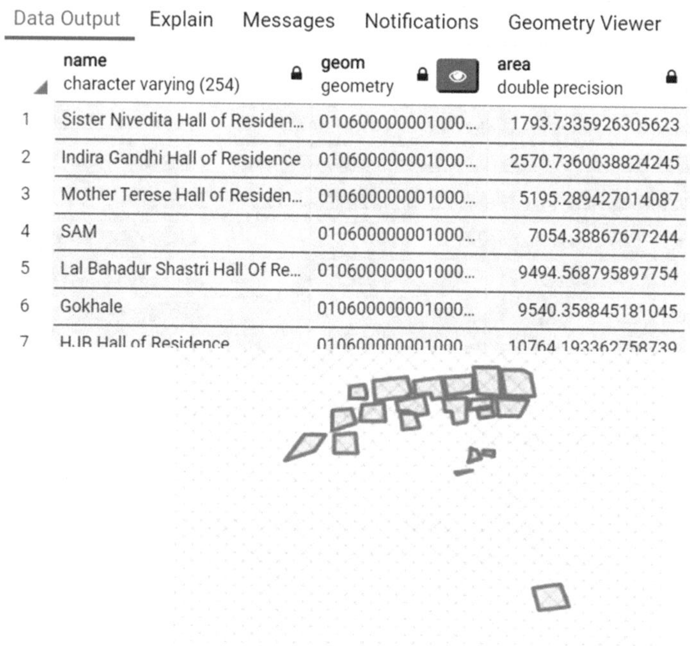

	name character varying (254)	geom geometry	area double precision
1	Sister Nivedita Hall of Residen...	010600000001000...	1793.7335926305623
2	Indira Gandhi Hall of Residence	010600000001000...	2570.7360038824245
3	Mother Terese Hall of Residen...	010600000001000...	5195.289427014087
4	SAM	010600000001000...	7054.38867677244
5	Lal Bahadur Shastri Hall Of Re...	010600000001000...	9494.568795897754
6	Gokhale	010600000001000...	9540.358845181045
7	HJB Hall of Residence	010600000001000	10764.193362758739

Fig. 8 Snapshot of spatio-temporal query: Compute Area

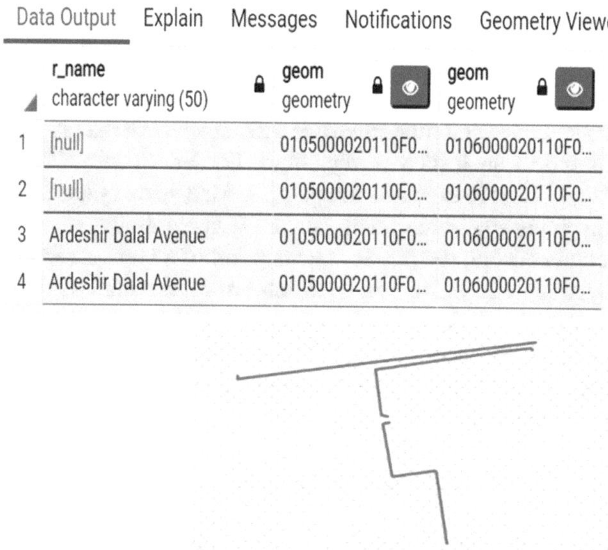

	r_name character varying (50)	geom geometry	geom geometry
1	[null]	0105000020110F0...	0106000020110F0...
2	[null]	0105000020110F0...	0106000020110F0...
3	Ardeshir Dalal Avenue	0105000020110F0...	0106000020110F0...
4	Ardeshir Dalal Avenue	0105000020110F0...	0106000020110F0...

Fig. 9 Snapshot of spatio-temporal query result: find the road segments within 50 m of Takshila

| Data Output | Explain | Messages | Notifications | Geometry Viewer |

name	name	dis
character varying (254) 🔒	character varying (254) 🔒	double precision 🔒
1 DEPT OF COMPUTER SCIENC...	Indira Gandhi Hall of Residence	167.1834011325025
2 DEPT OF COMPUTER SCIENC...	Mother Terese Hall of Residen...	244.47008446460518
3 DEPT OF COMPUTER SCIENC...	Bidhan Chandra Roy Hall of R...	255.22709207325013
4 DEPT OF COMPUTER SCIENC...	SAM	294.1172468864576
5 DEPT OF COMPUTER SCIENC...	Sister Nivedita Hall of Residen...	324.7456225175059
6 DEPT OF COMPUTER SCIENC...	Gokhale	364.56701643152473
7 DEPT OF COMPUTER SCIENC...	Rajendra Prasad Hall of Resid...	385.0800371694558

Fig. 10 Snapshot of spatio-temporal query result: Find the distance between computer science and engineering department and student halls

This query uses *distance* operation to extract spatial distance between two objects to compare the same. Figure 10 represents the query outcome.

4 Energy and Power-Aware Spatio-Temporal Query Processing

In the previous section, we have shown different types of spatio-temporal operations and query-processing tasks. We have also carried out the query-processing experiments with two different datasets. It is observed that spatio-temporal query processing is compute-intensive and time-intensive task, since such data is dynamic in nature and the volume of such data is very high. For this reason, it requires significant amount of CPU-time to execute such queries. Also, to carry out compute-intensive training on such big spatio-temporal data, GPU is required.

From the fundamental concept, the power consumption of a GPU is represented by the function of dynamic and static power which are represented as $Power_D$ and $Power_S$ respectively. The static power is computed by leakage and amount of energy consumption when the system is idle. It is monitored by varied sleep-states of the machine. The dynamic power is proportional to the run-time to complete the execution. It can be represented as:

$$Power_D \propto Voltage^2 \times Freq \tag{4}$$

where $Voltage$ is the supply voltage and $Freq$ denotes the operating frequency. Also, GPUS has different frequency domains, therefore, regulating frequency is one of the major step here.

Next, we have to predict the execution time of the spatio-temporal query. Here, we have utilized the game-theory based method from [4]. Here, a query-plan is generated based on user's task-priority and associated budget for the particular task. We consider there are m query-tasks which are denoted as vectors: $QT = Q_1, Q_2, \ldots, Q_m$. Each of this task has their own arrival and deadlines. Now, it can be observed that the power curve is non-linear with the execution time of the query-processing tasks. Our objective is to configure the frequency such that the application deadline is satisfied and the power consumption becomes the least. The energy consumption minimization problem can be represented as:

$$minimize \quad Power_{overall} = \sum_{j=1}^{m} Power_j \tag{5}$$

$$such \ that \ \forall exec_{time_j} \leq deadline_j$$

where $exec_{time_j}$ is the runtime of query-task j and deadline of the task is denoted by $deadline_j$. It is quite obvious that the optimization problem is a NP-hard problem, therefore we have used a heuristic approach to solve the same. Figure 1 shows the building blocks of the framework. The processing steps are as follows:

- Spatio-temporal data is accumulated using different mobile-nodes and GPS-enabled IoT-devices. The data-points include location, time and other contextual information (weather, health data, mobility information etc.)
- Such huge amount of data is segmented based on temporal intervals and spatial extension. Then, spatio-temporal indexing [9] is used to speed-up the information retrieval process.
- Next, execution-time prediction method is computed, which provides the predicted runtime of each spatio-temporal query processing task.
- Next, GPU frequency scaling heuristic algorithm is executed.
- According to the arrival time of the application, the available assignments are sorted in ascending order by the due deadline, priority to ensure that the assignment with the earliest due deadline is executed first. Considering that newly arrived tasks which only have default values: Clock input profile data, we found its related applications and use its detailed profile data to make predictions. In addition, for power and execution time, we have used predictive models to make predictions for all supported GPU frequency clock sets. For a given job, the clock with the lowest power consumption Cost and predicted execution time is less than its The due date has been selected. Finally, the selected application Configure the clock and execute the application.

5 Conclusion and Future Directions

In this chapter, we emphasize on energy-aware spatio-temporal query processing. The unprecedented usages of mobile terminals, such as handheld smartphones or smart devices, edge-nodes have a significant effect on wireless networks. On the other side, due to the ever-increasing growth in accumulated geospatial data, there are significant research interests in extracting meaningful insights and implicit knowledge from the voluminous geospatial data pool. Nevertheless, the major challenge lies in high computational and storage cost of this dynamic geospatial dataset along with increasing latency in provisioning real-world geospatial applications. In this aspect, DVFS is a feasible option to reduce the energy consumption, therefore, we present a spatio-temporal query processing framework which supports DVFS by scaling frequency of GPUs. In future, we would like to extend the deadline-based scheduling algorithm and aim to propose end-to-end energy-aware spatio-temporal query processing system.

References

1. Beloglazov, A., Buyya, R.: Optimal online deterministic algorithms and adaptive heuristics for energy and performance efficient dynamic consolidation of virtual machines in cloud data centers. Concurrency and Computation: Practice and Experience **24**(13), 1397–1420 (2012)
2. Chetsa, G.L.T., Lefrvre, L., Pierson, J.M., Stolf, P., Da Costa, G.: A runtime framework for energy efficient hpc systems without a priori knowledge of applications. In: Proceedings of the 2012 IEEE 18th International Conference on Parallel and Distributed Systems, pp. 660–667. IEEE, New York (2012)
3. Cui, M., Kritikakou, A., Mo, L., Casseau, E.: Fault-tolerant mapping of real-time parallel applications under multiple DVFS schemes. In: Proceedings of the 2021 IEEE 27th Real-Time and Embedded Technology and Applications Symposium (RTAS), pp. 387–399. IEEE, New York (2021)
4. Das, J., Ghosh, S., Ghosh, S.K., Buyya, R.: LYRIC: Deadline and budget aware spatio-temporal query processing in cloud. IEEE Trans. Serv. Comput. (2021)
5. Garg, S.K., Yeo, C.S., Anandasivam, A., Buyya, R.: Environment-conscious scheduling of hpc applications on distributed cloud-oriented data centers. J. Parallel Distrib. Comput. **71**(6), 732–749 (2011)
6. Geronimo, G.A., Werner, J., Westphall, C.B., Westphall, C.M., Defenti, L.: Provisioning and resource allocation for green clouds. In: Proceedings of the 12th International Conference on Networks (ICN). sn (2013)
7. Ghosh, S., Mukherjee, A., Ghosh, S.K., Buyya, R.: Mobi-iost: mobility-aware cloud-fog-edge-iot collaborative framework for time-critical applications. IEEE Transactions on Network Science and Engineering **7**(4), 2271–2285 (2019)
8. Ghosh, S., Das, J., Ghosh, S.K., Buyya, R.: CLAWER: Context-aware cloud-fog based workflow management framework for health emergency services. In: 2020 20th IEEE/ACM International Symposium on Cluster, Cloud and Internet Computing (CCGRID), pp. 810–817. IEEE, New York (2020)
9. Ghosh, S., Ghosh, S.K., Buyya, R.: Mario: A spatio-temporal data mining framework on google cloud to explore mobility dynamics from taxi trajectories. J. Netw. Comput. Appl. **164**, 102692 (2020)
10. Gupta, M., Bhargava, L., Indu, S.: Dynamic workload-aware DVFS for multicore systems using machine learning. Computing **103**(8), 1747–1769 (2021)
11. Hassan, H.A., Salem, S.A., Saad, E.M.: A smart energy and reliability aware scheduling algorithm for workflow execution in dvfs-enabled cloud environment. Futur. Gener. Comput. Syst. **112**, 431–448 (2020)

12. Hsieh, J.H., Zhang, H.L., Lin, C.H.: An intelligent fall detection design for mobile health-care applications. In: 2020 IEEE International Conference on Consumer Electronics-Taiwan (ICCE-Taiwan), pp. 1–2. IEEE, New York (2020)
13. Ismayilov, G., Topcuoglu, H.R.: Neural network based multi-objective evolutionary algorithm for dynamic workflow scheduling in cloud computing. Futur. Gener. Comput. Syst. **102**, 307–322 (2020)
14. Li, Y., Liu, Y., Qian, D.: An energy-aware heuristic scheduling algorithm for heterogeneous clusters. In: Proceedings of the 15th International Conference on Parallel and Distributed Systems (ICPADS), pp. 2888–2904 (2009)
15. Mukherjee, A., Ghosh, S., Behere, A., Ghosh, S.K., Buyya, R.: Internet of health things (IoHT) for personalized health care using integrated edge-fog-cloud network. J. Ambient. Intell. Humaniz. Comput. **12**(1), 943–959 (2021)
16. Poonia, A., Ghosh, S., Ghosh, A., Nath, S.B., Ghosh, S.K., Buyya, R.: Confront: Cloud-fog-dew based monitoring framework for covid-19 management. Internet of Things **16**, 100459 (2021)
17. Tang, Z., Qi, L., Cheng, Z., Li, K., Khan, S.U., Li, K.: An energy-efficient task scheduling algorithm in dvfs-enabled cloud environment. J. Grid Comput. **14**(1), 55–74 (2016)
18. Tariq, U.U., Ali, H., Liu, L., Hardy, J., Kazim, M., Ahmed, W.: Energy-aware scheduling of streaming applications on edge-devices in iot-based healthcare. IEEE Transactions on Green Communications and Networking **5**(2), 803–815 (2021)
19. Von Laszewski, G., Wang, L., Younge, A.J., He, X.: Power-aware scheduling of virtual machines in dvfs-enabled clusters. In: 2009 IEEE International Conference on Cluster Computing and Workshops, pp. 1–10. IEEE, New York (2009)
20. Wang, L., Von Laszewski, G., Dayal, J., Wang, F.: Towards energy aware scheduling for precedence constrained parallel tasks in a cluster with DVFS. In: 2010 10th IEEE/ACM International Conference on Cluster, Cloud and Grid Computing, pp. 368–377. IEEE, New York (2010)
21. Yeganeh-Khaksar, A., Ansari, M., Safari, S., Yari-Karin, S., Ejlali, A.: Ring-DVFS: Reliability-aware reinforcement learning-based dvfs for real-time embedded systems. IEEE Embed. Syst. Lett. **13**(3), 146–149 (2020)

Green Cloud Computing for IoT Based Smart Applications

Sangeeta Kakati, Nabajyoti Mazumdar, and Amitava Nag

1 Introduction

In the preceding two decades, reducing energy usage with green computing approaches has resulted in a considerable decrease in carbon dioxide emissions, as well as a reduction in the use of fossil fuels in power plants and transportation. Mobile cloud computing allows a large number of related mobile users who can use massive volumes of cloud computing resources, helping to compensate for the resource constraint nature of mobile devices. When the battery life of the mobile device is a big problem for the mobile user's experience, a fundamental challenge in the mobile application platform is making deployment decisions for particular jobs. There are various deployment schemes to offload expensive computing work from light mobile devices to powerful systems in the cloud, allowing us to extend battery life while providing rich user experiences for such mobile applications.

Before the days when we were not exploiting cloud resources, the technologies are submerged in server rooms that used excessive energy consumption. Besides using more energy, those systems also required large infrastructure supports. As the use of cloud computing grew, so did energy consumption. The goal now is to minimize power consumption even more with green computing and cloud computing. This rise in energy use has resulted in a significant increase in carbon

S. Kakati
Department of CSE, IIIT, Guwahati, India

N. Mazumdar
Department of IT, IIIT Allahabad, Allahabad, India
e-mail: nabajyoti@cse.ism.ac.in

A. Nag (✉)
Department of CSE, CIT Kokrajhar, Kokrajhar, India
e-mail: amitava.nag@cit.ac.in

emissions in the atmosphere. Gougeon et al. [1] discussed how the exponential growth of data servers and other infrastructure is causing a rise in energy usage. Carbon emissions can be reduced which will further result in lower energy usage. The deployment of green cloud computing results in a greener environment by reducing the emission of carbon significantly. Some of the approaches to green mobile cloud computing platforms will be presented in the next sections. In the further sections, we will be focusing more on virtualization towards cloud and fog.

1.1 Motivation

Motivated by above limitations, this study present an extensive review. Although for IoT, the use of the cloud is nearly mandatory these days, but cloud is rather used for storage and processing management. The use of related platforms such as fog and edge needs to be properly deployed along with concepts such as virtualization to reap the benefits of green cloud computing to the fullest.

1.2 Contribution

The main contribution of this study is highlighted as follows:

This study highlights going towards greener clouds with the most ever-increasing application of IoT to preserve a trade-off between the benefits of IoT and the impact on the environment.

2   Related Works

The fast expansion in big data has necessitated the use of progressively larger data centers, escalating the problem of a cloud storage system and energy usage.

Energy-aware software techniques, such as workload consolidation as discussed in Srikantaiah et al. [2], Prekas et al. [3], job or task scheduling in Tang et al. [4], data concentration in Iwata et al. [5], data replication in Farahanakian et al. [6], VM migration in Al Shayeji and Samrajesh [7], etc. are utilized to improve energy efficiency in the cloud-related environment. Usvub et al. [8] offered various energy-saving solutions for cloud computing. Han et al. [9] presented a resource-utilization-aware energy-saving server consolidation technique that can be employed to allow better resource utilization while reducing the number of virtual machine migrations. The findings of the experiments suggest that it is capable of lowering the consumption of energy and service-level agreement (SLA).

Sharma [10] discussed the aspects of sustainable green computing that looked into the construction of efficient computer programs that used all available cores of a CPU, resulting in faster execution than a single-core version, as well as energy savings. A case study is also presented to help support the research. Aside from that, the study found that with the increase in the number of computations, the multi-core technique performs better than single-core calculation.

For distributed Wireless Sensor Networks, Kumar et al. [11] presented Huffman code and an Ant Colony-based Lifetime Maximization approach (WSNs). They demonstrated the advantages of their system over state-of-the-art methods. Farooqi et al. [12] compared and contrasted various green cloud computing strategies as well as their outcomes.

Kharchenko et al. [13] described the concepts and classifications of green IT engineering, as well as the basic ideas for implementation and execution, green computing indicators, and values. More and Ingle [14] investigated several energy-efficient green cloud computing approaches, models, and algorithms with virtualization. The research focuses on virtual machine consolidation (VMs).

Disabling and restarting physical machines according to the live workload need can save power usage. The methods discussed are centered on reducing power consumption and making data centers more energy-efficient.

Shaikh et al. [15] examined the green Internet of Things by examining approaches to conduct an assessment of current IoT applications, projects, and standardization efforts, as well as the identification of a few obstacles that must be addressed shortly to achieve a green IoT. A holistic approach on green cloud computing has been discussed in [16].

3 Mobile Computing

The cloud can effectively protect data generated from various sources with various volumes. Users benefit from cloud storage since it permits them to access materials according to their needs. Another essential advantage is the low probability of data misplacement, as is sometimes the case with storage devices in data centers.

Using cloud computing and environmental sustainability, businesses may go fully digital. Green computing in the cloud can manage technology resources with improvement in productivity and a decrease in costs. Example of storage that is used today includes Google Drive, OneDrive, and so on. The aim to provide services in the hand tip with effortless usability.

4 Green Cloud Computing

Green cloud computing is the creation, manufacturing, and use of digital upliftments that have no downside impact on the environment as discussed in Saha [17].

A green cloud solution can save energy while also lowering operational costs for businesses. It allows benefiting the resources of cloud storage while reducing the negative effects on the environment and also has an impact on human well-being. It entails the following procedures:

- The cloud platform model incorporates resource assistance to huge data-producing applications and uses significantly less power.
- Green production: During recycling excursions, the cloud platform emits minimal pollution, leading to a far more ecologically responsible atmosphere.
- Green usage: When using a cloud-based product, it reduces the amount of energy produced by 27%, Radu [29].

5   Approaches for Green Computing

To ensure cloud computing infrastructures are environmentally responsible, some approaches being followed are:

- Approaches of distributing resources or virtualization: In a cloud computing system, each framework contains a range of virtual computers upon which services are executed. These virtual computers can be moved between hosts based on their requirements and available resources as discussed in Sarkar and Misra [18]. The VM migration approach focuses on migrating virtual machines with the least amount of power increase. The most energy-efficient nodes are chosen, and the VMs are moved to them. This strategy will be discussed in greater depth in further sections.
- Algorithmic methods: Several studies, for instance, Jeba et al. [27] have used algorithmic approaches to support green cloud computing. Experimentation results proved that an optimal server occupies roughly 69% of the energy used by a highly saturated server. The green scheduling techniques estimate the required dynamic workload on the servers using a neural network predictor. Then, in an attempt to reduce the count of running servers, unneeded servers are shut off, reducing energy consumption at the points of consumption and benefiting the other dependent services. Numerous servers have also been integrated to ensure hand-to-hand agreement. The final basis is to protect the environment while lowering the total cost of ownership and maintaining service quality.

6   Towards Green Fog Computing

In the context of managing a large number of resources, the cloud/fog computing domains have emerged as promising options for Green Computing. As a result, researchers are more focused on the energy efficiency and long-term viability of their resources. Green cloud and fog are employed to address concerns and obstacles in establishing energy-efficient and sustainable infrastructures, protocols, and applications. The emerging green cloud approaches can be as follows:

Virtualization: Virtualization is a computing technique that enables better virtual machine administration as well as efficiency improvements by pooling resources. Dynamic migration facilitates the pooling of real resources, enhances resource use efficiency, and boosts uptime. The hypervisor allows many operating system instances to run simultaneously. Virtual machines are instances of a physical host with their operating system and hosted test programs that run within the same physical host. It enables higher hardware utilization rates and cost savings by integrating multiple dedicated servers into a central server.

Use of cloudlets: It is a decentralized infrastructure that is preferred over traditional data centers due to its low energy use. It is built on the notion of expanding the count of micro data centers, scattered regionally and interlinked, rather than those standard storages, which are massive and less in quantity. With a 30% lower energy use, we can do this inside a fog/cloud architecture.

7 Virtualization

"Virtualization," allows cloud providers to improve their power consumption. It is the practice of showing a system as a collection of processing assets that allows them to be accessible in ways that benefit the original configuration. Companies can reduce cost in terms of space, maintenance, and energy by consolidating unused servers into several virtual components coordinating with a common deployed. If a user application wants more resources, virtual devices used for Cloud systems possess the ability to get transferred to some other host. Cloud providers keep track of estimated demand, allocating resources accordingly. Programs that demand fewer assets can be grouped on a common server.

Server Usage: At an average, the on-premise architecture uses a fairly low consumption rate, as low as 5%–10% of average. Multiple programs can be hosted and operated in isolation on the same server using virtualization technologies, resulting in utilization levels of up to 70%. As a result, the count of active servers is drastically reduced. Although higher server utilization causes higher energy costs, with the same amount of electricity, workstations with more utilization can encounter an increasing volume of work.

The performance of fog computing may be hampered by user mobility [19–21]. Because mobility changes the access points, the fog service housed in the original cloudlet may see an increase in delay. To minimize access delay, when a mobile user switches access points, their data and existing applications should ideally transfer to the cloudlet at the new access point. To do so, the user has a virtual machine (VM) or container that houses its processes and data, comparable to cloud computing services. Since most of the IoT applications require mobility because the applications are dynamic hence fog computing and the technique of migration play a major role in the efficient running of services in real-time applications.

8 Fog Serves a more Green Purpose

The Fog paradigm is highly reliant on latency by enabling cloud services at the edge of the network, as discussed in Mazumdar et al. [28]. The perceived latency by application users is a significant parameter for this type of design. Because latency is such a significant limitation, greedy algorithms are preferred for providing quick, energy-efficient allocation rules. Lowest Latency, First Green, and Most Green are the three greedy allocation algorithms used to select a host for a work submitted to a certain node. Then, to combine the Fog burden, Gougeon et al. [1] provided three greedy consolidation policies: Consolidate All, Consolidate Brown, and Consolidate Ratio.

Lowest Latency: The goal of this first method is to lower the job's end-to-end latency, from the initial node to the host nodes. A task may be submitted on the initial node, which is by definition the nearest node to the end-user. There is a host node where the current job is under execution. The algorithm searches the hierarchical architecture for the existing node which is nearer to the primary node. This method is anticipated to have the lowest latency among the other algorithms evaluated. First Green: it seeks to select a host with minimum latency while also creating green power locally.

Because traditional cloud computing architectures are centralized, they can't provide reliable service to time constraint applications such as in IoT. This significant drawback of cloud computing can be attributed to the property that the cloud paradigm works on the method of virtualization of real-time services. Virtualization allows cloud service providers to provide services to their consumers from geographically distant locations, resulting in substantial latency in service provisioning as discussed in Yannuzzi et al. [22]. As a result, to satisfy the needs of these emergency responsive IoT systems, a computationally intelligent model is necessary to supplement the standard cloud environment. Fog computing is not a competitor for cloud computing; contrary, both these infrastructures support one other. Users can discover a different generation of advanced technologies that suit the requirements of concurrent applications, reduced latency IoT systems serving at the user end, and also intricate analysis and lengthy data storage at network, owing to the integrated performance of the internet of things, cloud and fog.

The magnification of the Internet of Things (IoT) along with cloud services has accelerated the establishment of a notch technology known as Fog, which encourages data storage, processing, and analysis close to its source. It promises to provide several compelling qualities, including lower latency, high responsiveness in low time, more emergency support has proved to be a companion to the IoT platform [23].

9 IoT Use Cases in Green Computing

From surveillance to space exploration, the Internet of Things (IoT) is a major enabler to several updated software. In contrast to the limited energy storage of IoT devices, sophisticated processes (such as device connections, data transfer, and service optimization) consumes significant energy. The green design of IoT has become increasingly important to increase architectural sustainability and, as a result, lower systemic costs. A smart world is surrounded by enormous IoT data that seeks energy-efficient processing and networking technologies as shown in Fig. 1.

Smart Agriculture: The numerous sensors and devices used in smart farming, precision agriculture to gather the data for further analysis, for instance, monitoring the condition of the soil using IoT allow creators to regulate soil quality from the top layers to the roots that provide real-time visibility. Farmers may use detailed soil quality data to decrease waste and boost crop yields, as well as to examine historical patterns and make better long-term crop management decisions.

Smart Cities: To empower a sustainable society, IoT can be characterized by the use of active energy. By sensing and detecting encircling items and exchanging data with one another throughout the city, communication can be done in a smarter

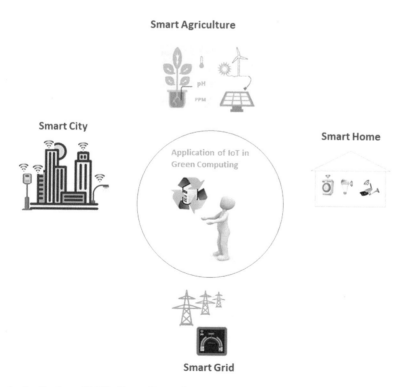

Fig. 1 Application of IoT in Green Computing

method. Smart parking, sharp lighting, top-notch air with superior AQI, smart vehicles, smart traffic execution, smart buildings, garbage collection, water sensors, smart metering, etc. are all part of the concept of a smarter city.

A smart street lighting system is one of the key applications of smart cities. Street lighting plays a significant role in the smart city for traffic and pedestrian safety. The existing streetlight system uses a manual technique that has several problems such as timing problems, high electric power consumption, manual faults (damaged, broken, stolen, etc.) detection.

Smart Home: Home automation is commonly used to minimize possible risks and ensure safety as well as to save time. We can not only control but also monitor device status globally via IoT, and we may turn on or off certain devices remotely based on users' needs and convenience.

To control devices, users can utilize an android device or a web browser. This might be useful if residents are outside of the house and want to manage a few appliances before returning home or to control appliances remotely.

Smart Grid: The Smart Grid is the network we connect with, through any gadget or appliance that uses energy.

Smart IoT technology allows for proper ventilation of heat generated by servers and data centers, resulting in energy savings. Green IoT's entire life cycle is around green planning, green creation, green use, and finally green removal/reuse.

We are more inclined towards data and its responsiveness to real-time systems which necessitates a review of tools and technologies that can be accommodated with these IoT applications as discussed in Bansal et al. [24].

The expansion of the Internet of Things (IoT) paints an unparalleled image of future collaboration between things and humans, in which each individual will be surrounded by hundreds of things on average. Furthermore, even without direct communication links, it can be predicted that every entity on the internet is interconnected. For example in a driverless car; sensors, controllers, actuators, and other components, are anticipated to create around 1 GB of data per second. The data deluge becomes out of control as the number of sensors increases, posing tremendous issues if it is all relayed and handled in a faraway cloud. High bandwidth requirements, high latency, and high cost are all common parameters.

Aside from proximity, another significant benefit of fog is that it supports heterogeneity, which is widely regarded as the most distinguishing feature of the Internet of Things. It frequently incorporates several subnetworks that use a variety of communication technologies.

Virtualization can be done at cloud or fog level and is not limited to just object virtualization. The data centers, the tasks being computed by nodes, all these are components of virtualization. Masdari and Khezri [25] proposed a virtual fog framework that was applied to a smart living case for verification, followed by a mathematical exposure to show how low latency application can be supported by the implementation of virtualization.

Furthermore, virtual objects improve the capabilities of their physical counterparts with limited resources by taking on some responsibilities such as security. Then, by detaching network functions from hardware platforms and mapping conventional networking services to virtual objects, network function virtualization flattens the interaction line among consumers and data generators while also increasing security and scalability. The cloud applications from diverse suppliers are then assembled through service virtualization to provide the beholders with a more reliable usage at a generic cost.

9.1 Green IoT Outdoor Lights

The traditional system to operate the outdoor lights causes enormous energy waste all over the world [26]. Furthermore, such systems employ high-power pulps, which are inefficient in terms of energy conservation, resulting in a massive waste of energy around the world. To tackle such challenges, a green and smart street lighting system is required, especially with the rise of smart cities. As a result, the goal is to provide an overview of a use case to build a smart and green street lighting system that saves energy while maximizing the use of renewable energy sources. The suggested system combines powerful ideas and concepts to efficiently regulate the operation of street lighting based on the availability of sunlight and motion detection by utilizing Arduino-based controllers with IR wireless connection support. It also replaces traditional high-power lights with low-power LEDs. To turn on the lights, two conditions must be met: the LDR sensor detects a lower level of light intensity and the IR motion sensor recognizes the presence of an object in the roadway (vehicle or human). The street lights will be turned off if the conditions are not satisfied. As a result of deploying this system, the electricity consumption for street lights will be lowered, while CO_2 levels can be reduced by employing renewable energy sources. The lamps brighten up before pedestrians and cars arrive and continue to be in a dim state when no one is present. The overview of the system is shown in Fig. 2. The data generated are transferred to a cloud platform namely Thinkspeak which can further be used in Fog to bring energy efficiency and green results.

IoT has supplied a new development technique that applies to all fields and replaces the old manual controlling structure with an automated system that employs maximum efficiency in utilized services. It allows real-time monitoring of all battery characteristics and outputs, including the luminance of solar panels, wind generators, and LED lamps, which will be useful for effective control, preventive maintenance, and extending the total system life.

10 Scope for Future Research

Along with the advantages of green cloud computing, there also comes the need to ensure the conservation of other parameters which leads us to future research directions.

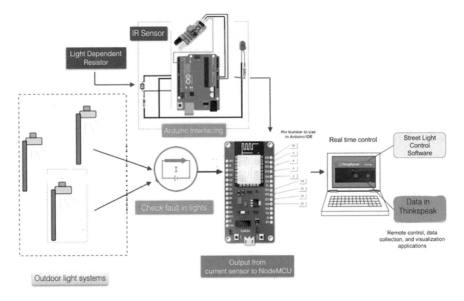

Fig. 2 IoT Use Case: Street light system

1. The cost of deploying a green cloud environment is way higher than the conventional ones hence proper infrastructure is to be built in accordance to serve a greener purpose along with affordability.
2. Since most of the IoT devices are battery-powered, hence developing adaptive IoT infrastructure becomes vital.
3. Virtualization can be leveraged according to application demands in Cloud, Fog, or edge platforms. More research needs to be performed in this area for performing specific implementations. Also reducing the number of physical servers might help further to minimize power consumption.
4. There has been a remarkable growth of the cloud, and it will continue to develop exponentially in the future. As a result, green communications should serve as a foundation for cloud computing.

11 Conclusion

This study proposes an idea for virtualization along with IoT and its data storage and processing task in response to the rapid growth of the emerging IoT spectrum. Real-time applications want it because they want to bring sophisticated data processing and output with latency as its biggest unit. Fog computing, in particular, effectively combines the unique features of IoT domains while addressing the green needs. Finally, this architecture offers an appealing idea for the increasing smart devices and their applications by combining the benefits of both the centralized cloud, decentralized fog, and cutting-edge IoT technology. Fog computing doesn't guarantee a replacement for the cloud, but in anticipation of the future generation of IoT systems and the rising need for emergency responsiveness applications, fog computing will work in companion to centralized data storage and processing models along with virtualization to provide a greener computing platform.

References

1. Gougeon, A., Camus, B., Orgerie, A.C.: Optimizing green energy consumption of fog computing architectures. In: 2020 IEEE 32nd International Symposium on Computer Architecture and High Performance Computing (SBAC-PAD), pp. 75–82. IEEE (2020)
2. Srikantaiah, S., Kansal, A., Zhao, F.: Energy aware consolidation for cloud computing. In: Proceedings of the Workshop Power Aware Computer System (HotPower), pp. 10 (2008)
3. Prekas, G., et al.: Energy proportionality and workload consolidation for latency-critical application. In: Proceedings of the SoCC, pp. 342–355 (2015)
4. Tang, Q., Gupta, S.K.S., Varsamopoulos, G.: Energy-efficient thermal-aware task scheduling for homogeneous high-performance computing data centers: a cyber-physical approach. IEEE Trans. Parallel Distrib. Syst. **19**, 1458–1472 (2008)
5. Iwata, S., Shiozawa, K.: A simulation result of replicating data with another layout for reducing media exchange of cold storage. In: Proceedings of the 8th USENIX Workshop Hot Topics Storage File System, pp. 10–21 (2016)
6. Farahanakian, F., Ashraf, A., Liljeberg, P.: Energy-aware dynamic VM consolidation in cloud data centers using ant colony system. In: Proceedings of the IEEE 7th International Conference Cloud Computing (CLOUD), pp. 104–111 (2014)
7. Al Shayeji, M.H., Samrajesh, M.D.: An energy-aware virtual machine migration algorithm. In: Proceedings of the International Conference Advances in Computing and Communication (ICACC), pp. 9–11 (2012)
8. Usvub, K., Farooqi, A.M., Afshar Alam, M.: Edge up green computing in cloud data centers. Int. J. Adv. Res. Comput. Sci. **8**, 2 (2017)
9. Han, G., et al.: Resource-utilization-aware energy efficient server consolidation algorithm for green computing in IIOT. J. Netw. Comput. Appl. **103**, 205–214 (2018)
10. Sharma, M.K.: Software level green computing with multi-core processors using fork-and-join framework (2017)
11. Kumar, S., Kaiwartya, O., Abdullah, A.H.: Green computing for wireless sensor networks: optimization and Huffman coding approach. Peer-to-Peer Netw. Appl. **10**(3), 592–609 (2017)
12. Farooqi, A.M.: Comparative analysis of green cloud computing. Int. J. Adv. Res. Comput. Sci. **8**, 2 (2017)
13. Kharchenko, V., Illiashenko, O.: Concepts of green IT engineering: taxonomy, principles and implementation. In: Green IT Engineering: Concepts, Models, Complex Systems Architectures, pp. 3–19. Springer, Cham (2017)
14. More, N.S., Ingle, R.B.: Challenges in green computing for energy saving techniques. Emerging Trends & Innovation in ICT (ICEI), 2017 International Conference on. IEEE (2017)
15. Shaikh, F.K., Zeadally, S., Exposito, E.: Enabling technologies for green internet of things. IEEE Syst. J. **11**(2), 983–994 (2017)
16. Anbuselvi, R.: Holistic approach for green cloud computing and environmental sustainability. Int. J. Comput. Sci. Eng. **5**(3), 218–225 (2015)
17. Saha, B.: Green computing: current research trends. Int. J. Comput. Sci. Eng. **6**(3), 467–469 (2018)
18. Sarkar, S., Misra, S.: Theoretical modelling of fog computing: a green computing paradigm to support IoT applications. Iet Netw. **5**(2), 23–29 (2016)

19. Toor, A., ul Islam, S., Sohail, N., Akhunzada, A., Boudjadar, J., Khattak, H.A., et al.: Energy and performance aware fog computing: a case of DVFS and green renewable energy. Futur. Gener. Comput. Syst. **101**, 1112–1121 (2019)
20. Li, J., Jin, J., Yuan, D., Zhang, H.: Virtual fog: a virtualization enabled fog computing framework for Internet of Things. IEEE Internet Things J. **5**(1), 121–131 (2017)
21. Varghese, B., Reano, C., Silla, F.: Accelerator virtualization in fog computing: moving from the cloud to the edge. IEEE Cloud Comput. **5**(6), 28–37 (2018)
22. Yannuzzi, M., van Lingen, F., Jain, A., Parellada, O.L., Flores, M.M., Carrera, D., Olive, A., et al.: A new era for cities with fog computing. IEEE Internet Comput. **21**(2), 54–67 (2017)
23. Samann, F.E.F., Zeebaree, S.R., Askar, S.: IoT provisioning QoS based on cloud and fog computing. J. Appl. Sci. Technol. Trends. **2**(01), 29–40 (2021)
24. Bansal, M., Kumar, A., Virmani, A.: Green IoT: current scenario & future prospects. J. Trends Comput. Sci. Smart Technol. (TCSST). **2**(04), 173–180 (2020)
25. Masdari, M., Khezri, H.: Efficient VM migrations using forecasting techniques in cloud computing: a comprehensive review. Clust. Comput., 1–30 (2020)
26. Ananth, A., Danush Venkatesh, S., Kanimozhi, G., MohanBabu, P., Senthil Arumugam, S.: IOT based street lighting control system. Int. J. Emerg. Trends Eng. Res. **8**(7), 3610–3616 (2020)
27. Jeba, J.A., Roy, S., Rashid, M.O., Atik, S.T., Whaiduzzaman, M.: Towards green cloud computing an algorithmic approach for energy minimization in cloud data centers. In: Research Anthology on Architectures, Frameworks, and Integration Strategies for Distributed and Cloud Computing, pp. 846–872. IGI Global, Hershey (2021)
28. Mazumdar, N., Nag, A., Singh, J.P.: Trust-based load-offloading protocol to reduce service delays in fog-computing-empowered IoT. Comput. Electr. Eng. **93**, 107223 (2021)
29. Radu, L.-D.: Green cloud computing: a literature survey. Symmetry. **9**(12), 295 (2017)

Green Internet of Things Using Mobile Cloud Computing: Architecture, Applications, and Future Directions

Anindita Raychaudhuri, Anwesha Mukherjee, Debashis De ⬤**, and Sukhpal Singh Gill**

1 Introduction

In the last few decades, the number of mobile users has increased drastically and the mobile devices have become popular medium for accessing Internet services. Various mobile applications have been introduced for learning purpose, video conferencing, chatting, health monitoring, playing games, listening music, editing photos and videos, accessing social networking sites and professional sites, etc. However, the handheld mobile devices suffer from various drawbacks such as limited storage capacity, limited processing capability, limited battery life, etc. Due to these constraints the execution of exhaustive applications and storage of high-volume data inside the mobile devices may not be possible. In such a scenario, MCC has come that permits to store data and execute applications outside the

A. Raychaudhuri (✉)
Department of Computer Science, Sarojini Naidu College for Women, Kolkata, West Bengal, India
e-mail: anindita.raychaudhuri@sncwgs.ac.in

A. Mukherjee
Department of Computer Science, Mahishadal Raj College, Mahishadal, Purba Medinipur, West Bengal, India
e-mail: anweshamukherjee@ieee.org

D. De
Department of Computer Science and Engineering, Centre of Mobile Cloud Computing, Maulana Abul Kalam Azad University of Technology, West Bengal, Nadia, India
e-mail: debashis.de@makautwb.ac.in

S. S. Gill
School of Electronic Engineering and Computer Science, Queen Mary University of London, London, UK
e-mail: s.s.gill@qmul.ac.uk

mobile device and into the cloud [1–3]. Nowadays, the use of edge/fog computing can provide the facility to perform processing in the intermediate device and can bring the resources at the network edge [4–6]. With the rapid advancement in different technological aspects, people are seeking smart solutions for their daily lives such as smart home, smart transportation, smart education, smart banking, smart retail, smart healthcare, smart agriculture, etc. To provide smart solutions IoT comes into the picture, where the uniquely identified embedded devices are connected within an Internet infrastructure to build a computing environment [6–7]. In IoT, the sensors and actuators are used, and the objects' status information collected by the sensors are transmitted to the servers for storage and processing. The use of cloud computing in IoT provides the facility of processing and storing huge volume of sensory information inside the cloud. The integration of IoT with MCC can be referred as *Internet of Things* using *Mobile Cloud Computing* (IoT-MCC). In IoT-MCC, the sensory information collected by the sensor nodes are transmitted to the cloud through the mobile device. The mobile device is connected to the network either through a cellular base station or through a Wi-Fi access point. In both the cases, the data processing and storage happen inside the cloud. After the introduction of fog computing the intermediate devices such as switch, router, gateway, etc. also participate in data processing [5–6]. The edge computing has brought the resources at the edge of the network [4–5]. In edge computing, the edge server is attached with the base station in case of the cellular network [4–5]. In case of Wireless Local Area Network (WLAN)/Wireless Metropolitan Area Network (WMAN), the cloudlet is used in case of edge computing [4–5]. The edge server/cloudlet is used for providing the facilities to offload data and computation inside the edge server/cloudlet. In case of edge-fog-cloud-based IoT framework, the intermediate fog devices or the edge server or cloudlet can participate in the processing and storage of the sensory information. An overview of the IoT-MCC architecture is presented in Fig. 1.

The mobile device can be used for data collection and accumulation purposes before forwarding to the next hop. Nowadays, various sensors are attached with mobile devices. Various mobile applications (apps) are also available to collect the number of footsteps went, acceleration, temperature, humidity, etc. Camera and GPS are also available inside the smartphones. The preliminary processing on the collected sensor data can be performed inside the mobile device itself. This in turn can reduce the unnecessary data transmission over the network. The use of edge/fog devices for data processing also reduces the amount of data transmission to the cloud. In [8–9], the edge/fog devices have been used for preliminary data processing in IoT-based healthcare. In [8–9], only if abnormal health condition has been predicted, the data transmission takes place to the cloud. This in turn provides faster health care service and reduces unnecessary data transmission over the network [8–9].

Mobile devices especially smartphones have become an important part of our life. The use of smartphones in IoT has brought several advantages to the users also, for example, using body area network and smartphone, the health parameter

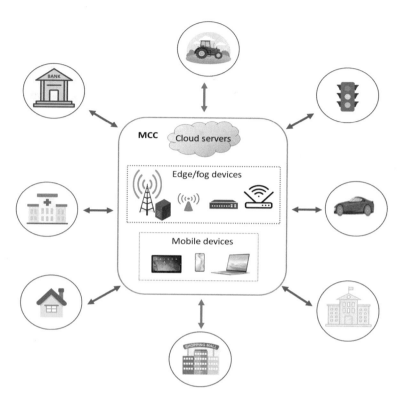

Fig. 1 Overview of IoT-MCC architecture

values, location, and movement information are collected and processed inside the smartphone/edge device/fog device/cloud to predict the current health condition of individual [8–9]. In case of abnormal health conditions, health care advice is provided to the user through the mobile phone. In the case of smart home, smart retailing, the smartphone acts as a medium of interaction. Augmented Reality (AR) provides a virtual environment to the users through which the users see the real world with virtual objects composited with the real world [10]. In IoT-MCC-based AR, a virtual reality can be provided to the user even at home to view the virtual objects superimposed with the real world. The IoT is largely used in smart agriculture. Various mobile apps related to agriculture are nowadays available.

In this chapter, we discuss on the architecture, applications, and research scopes of IoT-MCC. The rest of the chapter is organized as: Sect. 2 discusses the architecture of IoT-MCC. Section 3 illustrates the delay and power consumption in IoT-MCC, Sect. 4 briefly describes the IoT-MCC Convergence, and Sect. 5 describes various applications of IoT-MCC. Section 6 briefly illustrates enabling technologies for Green IoT-MCC, Sect. 7 summarizes different energy harvesting techniques for Green IoT, Sect. 8 investigates various research challenges of Green IoT-MCC, and finally, Sect. 9 concludes the chapter.

2 Architecture of MCC

Nowadays, due to the massive use of IoT devices in variety of application an enormous volume of data is generated. These large scales of data demand new architectures and technologies for data management both for capturing and processing. The IoT-MCC architecture serves the purpose. The IoT-MCC architecture consists of four layers as presented in Fig. 2. The principle components of IoT-MCC are:

- Sensors and actuators
- Mobile devices
- Edge/fog devices
  Cloud servers.

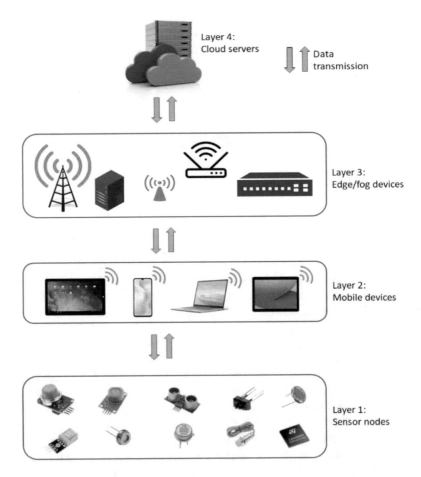

Fig. 2 Four-layer Architecture of MCC

The working model of IoT-MCC is described as follows.

- The layer 1 consists of sensor nodes and actuators. The sensor nodes are attached with the objects to collect their status. The collected sensor data is transmitted to the mobile device at layer 2.
- The mobile devices such as smartphone, tablet, laptop, etc. are present at layer 2. The mobile device receives sensor information from the sensor nodes. The mobile device performs preliminary processing on the data and then sends it to the connecting edge/fog device at layer 3. However, the mobile device can send the raw data also to the connecting edge/fog device at layer 3.
- At layer 3 the devices which connect the mobile device with the network are present. In case of cellular network, the base station, and in case of WLAN/WMAN, the Wi-Fi access point connects the mobile device with the network [4–5]. The access point is connected with the network through switch, router, etc. In cellular network, small cells exist [11–12]. In case of fog computing, the intermediate devices such as switches, routers and small cells participate in data processing before forwarding to the cloud. In case of edge computing, the edge server attached with the base station or the cloudlet participates in data processing. The data storage can happen inside the edge/fog devices after processing, or the data can be transmitted to the cloud at layer 4 according to the requirement.
- The cloud servers are present at layer 4. Usually, the data storage happens inside the cloud. The cloud can process the data, usually, for exhaustive computation cloud is used. If required the cloud can send the processed data or result after processing to the connected edge/fog device from which the user can receive the data or access the data using his/her mobile device.

3 Delay and Power Consumption of IoT-MCC Based Network

To calculate the delay, we have considered the data collection, transmission, and processing delays. The power consumption by the devices of IoT-MCC during these periods is calculated [5, 8–9] (Table 1).

The time period in data transmission from layer 1 to layer 2 is given as,

$$T_{sm} = (1 + f_{sm}) \frac{Data_{sm}}{R_{sm}} \tag{1}$$

The time period in data processing at layer 2 is given as,

$$T_m = \frac{Data_m}{S_m} \tag{2}$$

Table 1 Parameters used in delay and power consumption model

Parameter	Definition
T_s	Data collection period by sensors at layer 1
$Data_{sm}$	Amount of data transmitted from sensors at layer 1 to the connected mobile device at layer 2
R_{sm}	Data transmission rate from layer 1 to layer 2
f_{sm}	Link failure rate from layer 1 to layer 2
$Data_m$	Amount of data processed inside the mobile device at layer 2
S_m	Data processing speed of the mobile device
$Data_{me}$	Amount of data transmitted from the mobile device at layer 2 to the connected edge/fog device at layer 3
R_{me}	Data transmission rate from layer 2 to layer 3
f_{me}	Link failure rate from layer 2 to layer 3
$Data_e$	Amount of data processed by the participating edge/fog device at layer 3
S_e	Data processing speed of the edge/fog device participating in data processing
$Data_{ec}$	Amount of data transmitted from the edge/fog device at layer 3 to the cloud at layer 4
R_{ec}	Data transmission rate from layer 3 to layer 4
f_{ec}	Link failure rate from layer 3 to layer 4
$Data_c$	Amount of data processed inside the cloud at layer 4
S_c	Data processing speed of the cloud
P_s	Power consumption of a sensor node during data collection period T_s
N	Number of sensor nodes at layer 1
P_{st}	Power consumption of a sensor node per unit time during data transmission
P_{mr}	Power consumption of a mobile device per unit time during data reception
P_{mp}	Power consumption of a mobile device per unit time during data processing
P_{mt}	Power consumption of a mobile device per unit time during data transmission
P_{er}	Power consumption of an edge/fog device per unit time during data reception
P_{ep}	Power consumption of an edge/fog device per unit time during data processing
P_{et}	Power consumption of an edge/fog device per unit time during data transmission
P_{cr}	Power consumption of the cloud per unit time during data reception
P_{cp}	Power consumption of the cloud per unit time during data processing

The time period in data transmission from layer 2 to layer 3 is given as,

$$T_{me} = (1 + f_{me}) \frac{Data_{me}}{R_{me}} \tag{3}$$

The time period in data processing at layer 3 is given as,

$$T_e = \frac{Data_e}{S_e} \tag{4}$$

The time period in data transmission from layer 3 to layer 4 is given as,

$$T_{ec} = (1 + f_{ec}) \frac{Data_{ec}}{R_{ec}} \tag{5}$$

The time period in data processing at layer 4 is given as,

$$T_c = \frac{Data_c}{S_c} \tag{6}$$

Therefore, the total delay in data collection, processing, and transmission in the IoT-MCC framework is given as,

$$T_{tot} = T_s + T_{sm} + T_m + T_{me} + T_e + T_{ec} + T_c \tag{7}$$

The power consumption of the sensor nodes at layer 1 for data collection and transmission is given as,

$$P_{sct} = \sum_N P_s + \sum_N (P_{st} \bullet T_{sm}) \tag{8}$$

The power consumption of the mobile device at layer 2 for data reception, processing, and transmission is given as,

$$P_{mrpt} = (P_{mr} \bullet T_{sm}) + (P_{mp} \bullet T_m) + (P_{mt} \bullet T_{me}) \tag{9}$$

The power consumption of the edge/fog device at layer 3 for data reception, processing, and transmission is given as,

$$P_{erpt} = (P_{er} \bullet T_{me}) + (P_{ep} \bullet T_e) + (P_{et} \bullet T_{ec}) \tag{10}$$

The power consumption of the cloud at layer 4 for data reception and processing is given as,

$$P_{crp} = (P_{cr} \bullet T_{ec}) + (P_{cp} \bullet T_c) \tag{11}$$

Therefore, the total power consumption of the devices of the IoT-MCC framework is given as,

$$P_{tot} = P_{sct} + P_{mrpt} + P_{erpt} + P_{crp} \tag{12}$$

In the IoT-MCC framework, the intermediate mobile device and edge/fog device participate in data processing, therefore, the amount of data transmission from the end node to the cloud is reduced, which reduces the amount of data traffic, delay, and consequently, power consumption of the entire framework. In Table 2 and Fig. 4, we have presented the total delay and power consumption of the IoT-MCC framework for data collection, processing, and transmission.

Table 2 Delay in Edge/fog-based-IoT-MCC framework and Cloud-only IoT framework

	Delay (sec)	
Collected sensor data (MB)	Edge/fog-based IoT-MCC framework	Cloud-only IoT framework
100	3.8992	5.0717
200	7.8217	10.1867
300	11.7675	15.3450
400	15.7367	20.5467
500	19.7292	25.7917
600	23.7450	31.0800

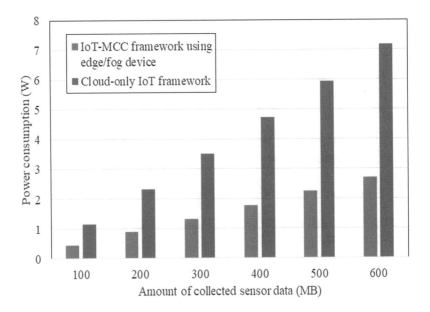

Fig. 3 Power consumption in Edge/fog-based IoT-MCC framework and Cloud-only IoT framework

We observe that the use of mobile device and edge/fog device in data processing reduces the delay and power consumption than transmission and processing of the entire collected sensor data inside the cloud. Table 2 shows that the use of edge/fog device in IoT-MCC reduces the delay ~23% than the cloud-only IoT framework. We observe from Fig. 3 that using the edge/fog device in the IoT-MCC framework the power consumption is reduced ~62% than the cloud-only IoT framework.

4 Contribution of IoT- MCC Convergence

The fruitfulness of IoT mainly depends on high performance, reliability, pervasiveness, and scalability. In recent days, it becomes possible through the integration of IoT with MCC which enables "everything as a service" model [13–15]. The integration of IoT with MCC provides several advantages mentioned as follows:

- Flexible and efficient architecture: Integration of IoT and MCC provides a flexible and efficient architecture.
- Unlimited data storage capacity: Convergence of IoT and MCC provides a solution towards the storage limitation of mobile device. It provides unlimited data storage capacity on cloud.
- Extending battery lifetime: One of the major limitations of the mobile device is its limited battery lifetime. IoT-MCC integration provides the facility of offloading. In order to reduce power consumption of mobile devices, large computation can be offloaded to the powerful cloud server.
- On-demand service: IoT-MCC integration extends various services of cloud computing to the edge of the network. Through MCC it is possible to distribute data in such a way that it will be easily accessible to the end users. Every IoT device is uniquely identifiable. Through IoT-MCC integration the request of users along with the ID and location are transmitted to the central processors of the cloud. After processing requested services are provided to the mobile users.

5 Applications of IoT- MCC

Integration of IoT and MCC technologies creates exciting opportunities in variety of real world applications [6–34] in which energy management [6, 16], environment monitoring, agriculture[17–19], healthcare [9, 12, 20–24], smart city [25–32], and Industrial automation [33–34] are worth mentioning. Table 3 presents recent IoT-MCC-based publications in various application domains. Here, we have considered the applications of sensor-mobile-cloud also.

6 Enabling Technologies for Green IoT-MCC

Green IoT means it should be environment-friendly and energy-efficient. Initially IoT devices remained switched on even when not required. In recent days, the main focus is on smart operation of devices to achieve green IoT [35–45]. It is achievable by enforcing that the devices will be only on when it is required otherwise it will remain idle or off. Green IoT-MCC is achievable through the collaboration of several enabling technologies [35] as shown in Fig. 4.

Table 3 List of recent IoT-MCC based publications in various application domains

Application domain	Papers	Journal/Conference/Book Chapter name	Author name	Year of publication	Publication type
Energy management	[6]	*The Journal of Supercomputing*	Mukherjee, A., Deb, P., De D.and Buyya, R.	2019	Journal
	[16]	*International Journal of Energy Research*	Hashmi, S.A., Ali, C.F. and Zafar, S.	2021	Journal
Agriculture	[17]	*IEEE Wireless Communications*	J. Ruan et al.	2019	Journal
	[18]	*IEEE access*	Ferrag, M.A., Shu, L., Yang, X., Derhab, A. and Maglaras, L.	2020	Journal
	[19]	*Materials Today: Proceedings.*	Kiran, S., Kanumalli, S.S., Krishna, K.V.S.S.R. and Chandra, N.	2021	Journal
Healthcare Application	[9]	*Journal of Ambient Intelligence and Humanized Computing*	Mukherjee, A., Ghosh, S., Behere, A., Ghosh, S.K. and Buyya, R.	2020	Journal
	[12]	*Journal of Medical Imaging and Health Informatics*	De, D. and Mukherjee, A.	2015	Journal
	[20]	*Journal of medical systems*	Suciu, G., Suciu, V., Martian, A., Craciunescu, R., Vulpe, A., Marcu, I., Halunga, S. and Fratu, O.	2015	Journal
	[21]	*International Journal of Smart Home*	Nandyala, C.S. and Kim, H.K.	2016	Journal
	[22]	*IEEE Access*	Islam, M.M., Razzaque, M.A., Hassan, M.M., Ismail, W.N. and Song, B.	2017	Journal
	[23]	*Sensors*	Oueida, S., Kotb, Y., Aloqaily, M., Jararweh, Y. and Baker, T.	2018	Journal

Table 3 (continued)

	[24]	*Electronics*	Ijaz, M., Li, G., Lin, L., Cheikhrouhou, O., Hamam, H. and Noor, A.	2021	Journal
Smart City	[25]	*Computer Communications.*	Jiang, D et al.	2020	Journal
	[26]	*Multimedia Tools and Applications*	Kumar, M., Raju, K.S., Kumar, D., Goyal, N., Verma, S. and Singh, A.	2021	Journal
	[27]	*IEEE Wireless Communications*	Chen, N., Qiu, T., Zhao, L., Zhou, X. and Ning, H.	2021	Journal
	[28]	*Sustainable Cities and Society*	Haseeb, K., Din, I.U., Almogren, A., Ahmed, I. and Guizani, M.	2021	Journal
	[29]	*Handbook of Green Engineering Technologies for Sustainable Smart Cities*	Kumar, K.S., Kumar, T.A., Sundaresan, S. and Kumar, V.K.	2021	Book chapter
	[30]	*Green Computing in Smart Cities: Simulation and Techniques*	Sarkar, N.I. and Gul, S.	2021	Conference paper
	[31]	*Towards Smart World*	Jokanović, V.	2020	Book chapter
	[32]	*2018 International symposium on networks, computers and communications (ISNCC)*	Rajab, H. and Cinkelr, T.	2018	Conference paper
Industrial Automation	[33]	*Materials Today: Proceedings*	Sundari, V.K., Nithyashri, J., Kuzhaloli, S., Subburaj, J., Vijayakumar, P. and Jose, P.S.H.	2021	Journal
	[34]	*Procedia Computer Science*	Xenakis, A., Karageorgos, A., Lallas, E., Chis, A.E. and González-Vélez, H.	2019	Journal

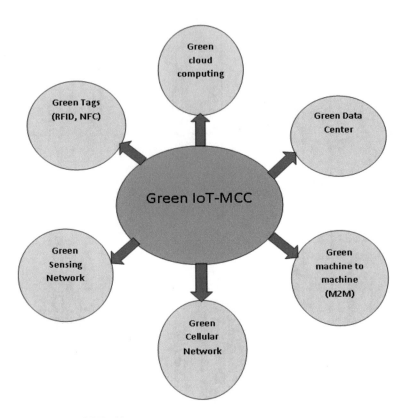

Fig. 4 Green IoT-MCC Enablers

Green tags are one of the important enabling technologies which include RFID (Radio Frequency Identification). It is a promising wireless system to enable green IoT. Near Field Communications (NFC) is one of the most recent short-range wireless system which is similar to RFID and more customer-oriented [35].Due to the tiny size, low cost, and reduced energy consumption these green tags are nowadays integrated in every device. In addition, several clustering algorithms including bio-inspired algorithms are playing important role for making green sensor network which is the main component of green IoT [39–42]. Energy-efficient cloud computing, data management, machine-to-machine communication, and green cellular network are also vital for Green IoT-MCC.

7 Energy Harvesting Techniques for Green IoT

Energy harvesting also plays a significant role in successful implementation of green IoT. Energy harvesting receives considerable research attention both from Industry

Table 4 Summary of energy efficient solutions for IoT

Papers	Contribution	Type
[44]	Energy harvesting architecture for IoT	Hardware
[45]	Energy-efficiency using virtual object reconfiguration	Software
[46]	Energy optimization using smart ant colony algorithm	Software
[47]	Energy-efficiency using fog computing model	Software
[48]	Energy-efficiency through data compression	Software
[49]	Energy-efficient system on chip (Soc) design.	Hardware
[50]	Green RFID tags and sensing network	Software
[51]	Smart location-based energy control in buildings	Hardware
[52]	Smart energy harvesting framework for IoT networks supported by femtocell access points (FAPs)	Hardware
[53]	Street illumination system and emergency e-vehicle charging	Hardware
[54]	An energy management scheme which includes reduction of data volume	Software

and Academia [44–56]. In addition, the role of other energy-efficient techniques is also important [57–60]. Table 4 summarizes various energy efficient solutions and their contribution towards green IoT [60].

8 Future Research Directions of IoT-MCC

Although IoT-MCC integration can overcome several limitations of IoT and provide several advantages, still there are a lot of research challenges need to be addressed, which we mention as follows:

- Security and privacy: Most of the real world IoT-MCC application requires communication between huge numbers of heterogeneous IoT devices which challenges the data security and privacy of individual users [36–38].
- Energy harvesting: The functioning of IoT devices mainly depends on the continuous power supply which becomes difficult in remote deployment. In this respect energy harvesting using ambient energy source can play an important role [52–56]. However, usefulness of this type of ambient energy mainly depends on the location of the devices and compromises the mobility of the device [60]. In addition, minimizing energy consumption of IoT devices, energy-efficient data aggregation and transmission from sensor nodes plays important role in implementing green IoT-MCC [57–63].
- Reusability: Due to the vast use of IoT devices, percentage of carbon foot print is also increasing rapidly. Therefore, reusability of IoT devices is becoming necessary for successful implementation of sustainable green IoT-MCC [64].
- Heterogeneity: The services offered by the IoT-MCC require communication between heterogeneous devices. Most of the IoT data which are coming from

dispersed sources are either unstructured or semi structured. Hence, the real time data processing and service provisioning are becoming major challenges [65–66].

- Interoperability: Interoperability among various heterogeneous IoT devices as well as between IoT/Cloud infrastructures is one of the main challenges of green IoT-MCC [67–70].
- Scalability: Scalability of the IoT device is one of the crucial design challenges which need to be addressed for fruitful implementation of green IoT-MCC [71–72].

9 Conclusion

IoT and MCC are two emerging areas of smart computing. In this chapter, we have illustrated the integration of IoT and MCC, and discussed the architecture and applications of IoT-MCC. We have mathematically formulated the delay and power consumption model for the IoT-MCC framework. We have discussed on the enabling technologies and applications of IoT-MCC. Green i.e. power-efficiency is a major concern for an eco-friendly system. The aspect of power-efficiency we have also highlighted in this chapter. Accordingly, the use of energy-harvesting in IoT has been also discussed. Finally, this chapter covers the future research directions of IoT-MCC.

References

1. De, D.: Mobile Cloud Computing: Architectures, Algorithms and Applications. Chapman and Hall/CRC (2019)
2. Fernando, N., Loke, S.W., Rahayu, W.: Mobile cloud computing: a survey. Futur. Gener. Comput. Syst. **29**(1), 84–106 (2013)
3. Dinh, H.T., Lee, C., Niyato, D., Wang, P.: A survey of mobile cloud computing: architecture, applications, and approaches. Wirel. Commun. Mob. Comput. **13**(18), 1587–1611 (2013)
4. Peng, K., Leung, V., Xu, X., Zheng, L., Wang, J., Huang, Q.: A survey on mobile edge computing: focusing on service adoption and provision. Wirel. Commun. Mob. Comput. **2018** (2018)
5. Mukherjee, A., De, D., Ghosh, S.K., Buyya, R.: Mobile Edge Computing. Springer (2021). https://doi.org/10.1007/978-3-030-69893-5. eBook ISBN: 978-3-030-69893-5. Hardcover ISBN: 978-3-030-69892-8
6. Mukherjee, A., Deb, P., De, D., Buyya, R.: IoT-F2N: an energy-efficient architectural model for IoT using Femtolet-based fog network. J. Supercomput. **75**(11), 7125–7146 (2019)
7. Gubbi, J., Buyya, R., Marusic, S., Palaniswami, M.: Internet of Things (IoT): a vision, architectural elements, and future directions. Futur. Gener. Comput. Syst. **29**(7), 1645–1660 (2013)
8. Ghosh, S., Mukherjee, A., Ghosh, S.K., Buyya, R.: Mobi-IoST: mobility-aware cloud-fog-edge-IOT collaborative framework for time-critical applications. IEEE Trans. Netw. Sci. Eng. (2019)

9. Mukherjee, A., Ghosh, S., Behere, A., Ghosh, S.K., Buyya, R.: Internet of health things (IoHT) for personalized health care using integrated edge-fog-cloud network. J. Ambient. Intell. Humaniz. Comput., 1–17 (2020)
10. Van Krevelen, D.W.F., Poelman, R.: A survey of augmented reality technologies, applications and limitations. Int. J. Virtual Real. **9**(2), 1–20 (2010)
11. Deb, P., Mukherjee, A., De, D.: A study of densification management using energy efficient femto-cloud based 5g mobile network. Wirel. Pers. Commun. **101**(4), 2173–2191 (2018)
12. De, D., Mukherjee, A.: Femto-cloud based secure and economic distributed diagnosis and home health care system. J. Med. Imaging Health Inform. **5**(3), 435–447 (2015)
13. Psannis, K.E., Xinogalos, S., Sifaleras, A.: Convergence of internet of things and mobile cloud computing. Syst. Sci. Cont. Eng. An Open Access J. **2**(1), 476–483 (2014)
14. Biswas, A.R., Giaffreda, R.: IoT and cloud convergence: opportunities and challenges. In: 2014 IEEE World Forum on Internet of Things (WF-IoT), pp. 375–376. IEEE (2014, March)
15. Botta, A., De Donato, W., Persico, V., Pescapé, A.: Integration of cloud computing and internet of things: a survey. Futur. Gener. Comput. Syst. **56**, 684–700 (2016)
16. Hashmi, S.A., Ali, C.F., Zafar, S.: Internet of things and cloud computing-based energy management system for demand side management in smart grid. Int. J. Energy Res. **45**(1), 1007–1022 (2021)
17. Ruan, J., et al.: Agriculture IoT: emerging trends, cooperation networks, and outlook. IEEE Wirel. Commun. **26**(6), 56–63 (December 2019). https://doi.org/10.1109/MWC.001.1900096
18. Ferrag, M.A., Shu, L., Yang, X., Derhab, A., Maglaras, L.: Security and privacy for green IoT-based agriculture: review, blockchain solutions, and challenges. IEEE Access. **8**, 32031–32053 (2020)
19. Kiran, S., Kanumalli, S.S., Krishna, K.V.S.S.R., Chandra, N.: Internet of things integrated smart agriculture for weather predictions and preventive mechanism. Mater. Today Proc. (2021)
20. Suciu, G., Suciu, V., Martian, A., Craciunescu, R., Vulpe, A., Marcu, I., Halunga, S., Fratu, O.: Big data, internet of things and cloud convergence–an architecture for secure e-health applications. J. Med. Syst. **39**(11), 1–8 (2015)
21. Nandyala, C.S., Kim, H.K.: Green IoT agriculture and healthcare application (GAHA). Int. J. Smart Home. **10**(4), 289–300 (2016)
22. Islam, M.M., Razzaque, M.A., Hassan, M.M., Ismail, W.N., Song, B.: Mobile cloud-based big healthcare data processing in smart cities. IEEE Access. **5**, 11887–11899 (2017)
23. Oueida, S., Kotb, Y., Aloqaily, M., Jararweh, Y., Baker, T.: An edge computing based smart healthcare framework for resource management. Sensors. **18**(12), 4307 (2018)
24. Ijaz, M., Li, G., Lin, L., Cheikhrouhou, O., Hamam, H., Noor, A.: Integration and applications of fog computing and cloud computing based on the internet of things for provision of healthcare services at home. Electronics. **10**(9), 1077 (2021)
25. Jiang, D.: The construction of smart city information system based on the Internet of Things and cloud computing. Comput. Commun. **150**, 158–166 (2020)
26. Kumar, M., Raju, K.S., Kumar, D., Goyal, N., Verma, S., Singh, A.: An efficient framework using visual recognition for IoT based smart city surveillance. Multimed. Tools Appl., 1–19 (2021)
27. Chen, N., Qiu, T., Zhao, L., Zhou, X., Ning, H.: Edge intelligent networking optimization for internet of things in smart city. IEEE Wirel. Commun. **28**(2), 26–31 (2021)
28. Haseeb, K., Din, I.U., Almogren, A., Ahmed, I., Guizani, M.: Intelligent and secure edge-enabled computing model for sustainable cities using green internet of things. Sustain. Cities Soc. **68**, 102779 (2021)
29. Kumar, K.S., Kumar, T.A., Sundaresan, S., Kumar, V.K.: Green IoT for 9 Sustainable Growth and Energy Management in Smart Cities, p. 155. Handbook of green engineering technologies for sustainable smart cities (2021)
30. Sarkar, N.I., Gul, S.: Green computing and internet of things for smart cities: technologies, challenges, and implementation. In: Green Computing in Smart Cities: Simulation and Techniques, pp. 35–50. Cham, Springer (2021)

31. Jokanović, V.: Smart healthcare in smart cities. In: Towards Smart World, pp. 45–72. Chapman and Hall/CRC (2020)
32. Rajab, H., Cinkelr, T.: IoT based smart cities. In: 2018 International Symposium on Networks, Computers and Communications (ISNCC), pp. 1–4. IEEE (2018, June)
33. Sundari, V.K., Nithyashri, J., Kuzhaloli, S., Subburaj, J., Vijayakumar, P., Jose, P.S.H.: Comparison analysis of IoT based industrial automation and improvement of different processes–review. Mater. Today Proc. **45**, 2595–2598 (2021)
34. Xenakis, A., Karageorgos, A., Lallas, E., Chis, A.E., González-Vélez, H.: Towards distributed IoT/cloud based fault detection and maintenance in industrial automation. Proc. Comput. Sci. **151**, 683–690 (2019)
35. Shaikh, F.K., Zeadally, S., Exposito, E.: Enabling technologies for green internet of things. IEEE Syst. J. **11**(2), 983–994 (2015)
36. Choudhury, T., Gupta, A., Pradhan, S., Kumar, P., Rathore, Y.S.: Privacy and security of cloud-based internet of things (IoT). In: 2017 3rd International Conference on Computational Intelligence and Networks (CINE), pp. 40–45 (2017). https://doi.org/10.1109/CINE.2017.28
37. Sahmim, S., Gharsellaoui, H.: Privacy and security in internet-based computing: cloud computing, internet of things, cloud of things: a review. Proc. Comput. Sci. **112**, 1516–1522 (2017)
38. Najafizadeh, A., Salajegheh, A., Rahmani, A.M., Sahafi, A.: Privacy-preserving for the internet of things in multi-objective task scheduling in cloud-fog computing using goal programming approach. Peer-to-Peer Netw. Appl., 1–26 (2021)
39. Ray, A., De, D.: An energy efficient sensor movement approach using multi-parameter reverse glowworm swarm optimization algorithm in mobile wireless sensor network. Simul. Model. Pract. Theory. **62**, 117–136 (2016)
40. Ray, A., De, D.: Energy efficient clustering protocol based on K-means (EECPK-means)-midpoint algorithm for enhanced network lifetime in wireless sensor network. IET Wirel. Sens. Syst. **6**(6), 181–191 (2016)
41. Ray, A., De, D.: Energy efficient clustering algorithm for multi-hop green wireless sensor network using gateway node. Adv. Sci. Eng. Med. **5**(11), 1199–1204 (2013)
42. Raychaudhuri, A., De, D.: Bio-inspired algorithm for multi-objective optimization in wireless sensor network. In: Nature Inspired Computing for Wireless Sensor Networks, pp. 279–301. Singapore, Springer (2020)
43. Kaur, G., Tomar, P., Singh, P.: Design of cloud-based green IoT architecture for smart cities. In: Internet of Things and Big Data Analytics Toward Next-Generation Intelligence, pp. 315–333. Cham, Springer (2018)
44. Liu, X., Ansari, N.: Toward green IoT: energy solutions and key challenges. IEEE Commun. Mag. **57**(3), 104–110 (2019)
45. Eteläperä, M., Vecchio, M., Giaffreda, R.: Improving energy efficiency in IoT with re-configurable virtual objects. In: 2014 IEEE World Forum on Internet of Things (WF-IoT), pp. 520–525. IEEE (2014, March)
46. Chen, J.I.Z., Lai, K.L.: Machine learning based energy management at Internet of Things network nodes. J. Trends Comput. Sci. Smart Technol. September. **2020**(3), 127–133 (2020)
47. Oma, R., Nakamura, S., Duolikun, D., Enokido, T., Takizawa, M.: An energy-efficient model for fog computing in the internet of things (IoT). Internet of Things. **1**, 14–26 (2018)
48. Azar, J., Makhoul, A., Barhamgi, M., Couturier, R.: An energy efficient IoT data compression approach for edge machine learning. Futur. Gener. Comput. Syst. **96**, 168–175 (2019)
49. Tcarenko, I., Huan, Y., Juhasz, D., Rahmani, A.M., Zou, Z., Westerlund, T., Liljeberg, P., Zheng, L., Tenhunen, H.: Smart energy efficient gateway for internet of mobile things. In: 2017 14th IEEE Annual Consumer Communications & Networking Conference (CCNC), pp. 1016–1017. IEEE (2017, January)
50. Albreem, M.A., El-Saleh, A.A., Isa, M., Salah, W., Jusoh, M., Azizan, M.M., Ali, A.: Green internet of things (IoT): an overview. In: 2017 IEEE 4th International Conference on Smart Instrumentation, Measurement and Application (ICSIMA), pp. 1–6. IEEE (2017, November)

51. Pan, J., Jain, R., Paul, S., Vu, T., Saifullah, A., Sha, M.: An internet of things framework for smart energy in buildings: designs, prototype, and experiments. IEEE Internet Things J. **2**(6), 527–537 (2015)
52. Sangoleye, F., Irtija, N., Tsiropoulou, E.E.: Smart energy harvesting for internet of things networks. Sensors. **21**(8), 2755 (2021)
53. Hans, M.R., Tamhane, M.A.: IoT based hybrid green energy driven street lighting system. In: 2020 Fourth International Conference on I-SMAC (IoT in Social, mobile, Analytics and Cloud)(I-SMAC), pp. 35–41. IEEE (2020)
54. Said, O., Al-Makhadmeh, Z., Tolba, A.M.R.: EMS: an energy management scheme for green IoT environments. IEEE Access. **8**, 44983–44998 (2020)
55. Yau, C.W., Kwok, T.T.O., Lei, C.U., Kwok, Y.K.: Energy harvesting in internet of things. Internet of Everything, 35–79 (2018)
56. Sanislav, T., Mois, G.D., Zeadally, S., Folea, S.C.: Energy harvesting techniques for internet of things (IoT). IEEE Access. **9**, 39530–39549 (2021)
57. Tahiliani, V., Dizalwar, M.: Green iot systems: an energy efficient perspective. In: 2018 Eleventh International Conference on Contemporary Computing (IC3), pp. 1–6. IEEE (2018, August)
58. Solanki, A., Nayyar, A.: Green internet of things (G-IoT): ICT technologies, principles, applications, projects, and challenges. In: Handbook of Research on Big Data and the IoT, pp. 379–405. IGI Global (2019)
59. De, D., Mukherjee, A., Ray, A., Roy, D.G., Mukherjee, S.: Architecture of green sensor mobile cloud computing. IET Wirel. Sens. Syst. **6**(4), 109–120 (2016)
60. Sarkar, S., Debnath, A.: Green IoT: design goals, challenges and energy solutions. In: 2021 6th International Conference on Communication and Electronics Systems (ICCES), pp. 637–642. IEEE (2021, July)
61. Arshad, R., Zahoor, S., Shah, M.A., Wahid, A., Yu, H.: Green IoT: an investigation on energy saving practices for 2020 and beyond. IEEE Access. **5**, 15667–15681 (2017)
62. Poongodi, T., Ramya, S.R., Suresh, P., Balusamy, B.: Application of IoT in green computing. In: Advances in Greener Energy Technologies, pp. 295–323. Singapore, Springer (2020)
63. Ray, A., De, D.: Performance evaluation of tree based data aggregation for real time indoor environment monitoring using wireless sensor network. Microsyst. Technol. **23**(9), 4307–4318 (2017)
64. Sharma, N., Panwar, D.: Green IoT: advancements and sustainability with environment by 2050. In: 2020 8th International Conference on Reliability, Infocom Technologies and Optimization (Trends and Future Directions) (ICRITO), pp. 1127–1132. IEEE (2020)
65. Medhi, K., Mondal, M.A., Hussain, M.I.: An approach to handle heterogeneous healthcare IoT data using deep convolutional neural network. In: Emerging Technologies for Smart Cities, pp. 25–31. Singapore, Springer (2021)
66. Booij, T.M., Chiscop, I., Meeuwissen, E., Moustafa, N., den Hartog, F.T.: ToN_IoT: The Role of Heterogeneity and the Need for Standardization of Features and Attack Types in IoT Network Intrusion Datasets. IEEE Internet of Things J (2021)
67. Noura, M., Atiquzzaman, M., Gaedke, M.: Interoperability in internet of things: taxonomies and open challenges. Mob. Netw. Appl. **24**(3), 796–809 (2019)
68. Abbasi, M.A., Memon, Z.A., Durrani, N.M., Haider, W., Laeeq, K., Mallah, G.A.: A multi-layer trust-based middleware framework for handling interoperability issues in heterogeneous IoTs. Clust. Comput., 1–28 (2021)
69. Ahmad, R., Asim, M.A., Khan, S.Z., Singh, B.: Green IOT—issues and challenges. In: Proceedings of 2nd International Conference on Advanced Computing and Software Engineering (ICACSE) (2019)
70. Raychaudhuri, A., Mukherjee, A., De, D.: SMEC: sensor mobile edge computing. In: Mobile Edge Computing, pp. 89–110. Springer, Cham (2021)
71. Tuysuz, M.F., Trestian, R.: From serendipity to sustainable green IoT: technical, industrial and political perspective. Comput. Netw. **182**, 107469 (2020)
72. Abdul-Qawy, A.S.H., Srinivasulu, T.: SEES: a scalable and energy-efficient scheme for green IoT-based heterogeneous wireless nodes. J. Ambient. Intell. Humaniz. Comput. **10**(4), 1571–1596 (2019)

Predictive Analysis of Biomass with Green Mobile Cloud Computing for Environment Sustainability

Santanu Koley, Pinaki Pratim Acharjya, Piyush Keshari, and Kunal Kumar Mandal

1 Introduction

This article seeks to help different types of users move towards a renewable source of energy called green energy. Basically, the focus is on one of the bio-energy fuels called biomass. Every year large amount of biomass is produced from various sectors such as forest land, agricultural fields and various other sources. These residues are sometimes utilized and sometimes not. As there is a growing need of energy, biomass can perform an imperative part in minimizing the need. The collection of data on biomass from various sources that are mentioned in the references, afterwards analyzed all the data with the help of python programming language. The implementation of regression and classification techniques of machine learning is used to complete the whole process and to store the model as well as data in the mobile cloud. Amazon web services (AWS) is used at this point as cloud platform. The total procedure has been mentioned into the procedure section in this article.

S. Koley (✉) · P. P. Acharjya
Department of Computer Science & Engineering, Haldia Institute of Technology, Haldia, West Bengal, India

P. Keshari
Department of Computer Science & Engineering, Budge Budge Institute of Technology, Kolkata, West Bengal, India

K. K. Mandal
Department of Computer Science, Mankar College, Mankar, Purba Bardhaman, West Bengal, India
e-mail: kunal@turiyan.com

2 Mobile Cloud

Mobile Cloud Computing (MCC) employs cloud computing to carry its functions on mobile devices. This type of mobile applications can be set up over distances using speed, flexibility and development tools. They are immediately set up or modified through cloud amenities. These can be distributed to dissimilar devices through several operating systems, computing functions then data repository. As a result, users can switch to applications that are not otherwise supported. Cloud computing refers to the concept of distribution of hardware, software, and data over the internet. Mobile cloud is basically an amalgamation of established technology, that provides various services. The Deployment model and the Service model are two distinct cloud computing models. Software as a Service (SaaS), Platform as a Service (PaaS), and Cloud Infrastructure as a Service (IaaS) are the three types of service models. They are based on the NIST (National Institute of Standards and Technology) model [1]. The cloud architecture for MCC is described here (Fig. 1):

On-demand services, broad network access, resource pooling, rapid elasticity, measured service, self-provisioned, pay per use (lower cost), scalability, ease of use, quality of service, reliability, outsourcing, simplified maintenance and upgrade, low barrier to energy are some of the key characteristics of cloud computing [2–7]. The processing task is delegated to the cloud server rather than the mobile device. In this sector, power and memory usage are also lower, and the mobile device eventually becomes incredibly quick.

Mobile cloud applications [8–12] are often operated by a third-party on a remote data centre, where data is stored and computation cycles are performed. A backend

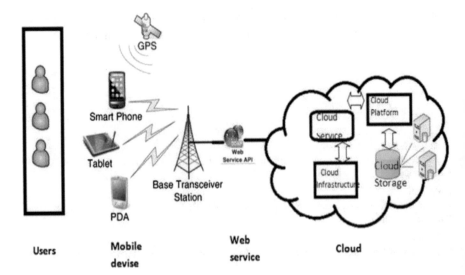

Fig. 1 Cloud architecture with mobile devices

manages the uptime, integration, and security aspects, as well as providing support for a variety of access ways. These program's work well in the online mode, but they must be updated from time to time. They are not stored permanently in the device, but they do not always take up storage space on a computer or other communication device. It also provides the same user experience as a desktop application while maintaining the portability of a web application.

3 Green Cloud Computing

The term "green cloud computing" denotes that it is environmentally benign. The goal is to reduce energy usage and garbage disposed into the environment. Cloud computing is a green technology in and of itself, as many businesses have switched from physical servers to cloud servers. Cloud computing is rethinking how to work in a more energy-efficient manner. The goal of green cloud computing is to identify and produce energy-saving digital technologies to reduce carbon emissions to the environment (Fig. 2).

Green cloud computing reimbursements have decreased power usage to the point where many server rooms have had their cooling machines removed. Because flexibility has enhanced productivity and condensed employees' daily commutes to the workplace, remote working minimizes the carbon impact on the environment. This reduction in travel has resulted in lower fuel use and emissions into the atmosphere. This has aided firms in lowering real estate expenditures as well as energy consumption in the workplace. Going paperless saves money by storing data securely and allowing access anytime, anywhere, as well as reducing the expense of hard drives for businesses, as OneDrive, SharePoint, Google Drive, and Dropbox are widely used today.

Green computing in the cloud can help manage technology resources while increasing productivity and lowering expenses while providing competent customer support. Another advantage of reducing e-waste output is that it reduces pollution.

Fig. 2 Green cloud computing model

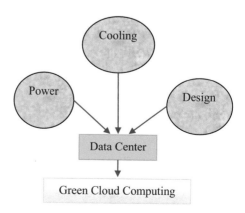

In the United States, 24 million computers are discarded on an annual basis [13]. Computers and phones, which account about 25% of e-waste, are mostly donated or repurposed by them [14]. E-waste is then imported into emerging countries, where it travels through a commerce network. Unused materials are scrapped, parts are reused, and the rest is burned. E-waste that has been burned ends up in rivers, polluting the air, water, and rivers.

4 Biomass and Their Composition

Biomass is a renewable organic matter that comes from plants and animals. It is been categorized into several types and each of them has different energy values.

4.1 Wood and Agriculture Products

Woods and agricultural products constitute the major part of the biomass about 44% of the total biomass. The entire worldwide biomass source as of agriculture and forestry is projected at around 11.9 billion tons of dehydrated stuff per annum, of which 61% is formed by farming and 39% by forestry [15–20]. Industries use this product to power up their factories. Another reason behind is, they are widely available. This sort of biomass product includes wood saw, wood dust various types of fruit wastes such as fruit peel, fruit seeds, grains, cereal, dry leaves, herbs, and shrubs [21–25]. All of them have a diverse calorific value which determines the amount of energy it can produce after some transformation process such as steaming, burning. All through the burning process, some of the energy gets wasted as it leaves some byproduct such as ash and water content. In ancient times it was the only source of producing energy from woods. Till date, our earth comprises 40% of grasslands. There are 14 different types of forests [21] in India, they can be named as:

- Wet Evergreen Forest
- Semi- Evergreen Forest
- Moist Deciduous Forest
- Dry Deciduous Forest
- Littoral Swamp Forest/Mangrove Forest
- Dry Evergreen Forest
- Thorn forest Subtropical
- Broad-leaved forest
- Subtropical Pine Forest
- Subtropical Dry Evergreen Forest
- Montane Wet Temperate Forest
- Montane Moist Temperate Forest

- Montane Dry Temperate Forest
- Sub Alpine Forest

These forests constitute the major portion of the wood fuel. The agricultural land constitutes 60.4% of the total land of India.

4.2   Solid Wastes

Solid waste [22] is defined as any garbage, refuse, sludge from a wastewater treatment plant, water supply treatment plant, or air pollution control facility, and other discarded materials, including solid, liquid, semi-solid, or contained gaseous material, according to the New York state department of environmental conservation [23]. Municipal solid wastes, hazardous wastes, industrial wastes, agricultural wastes, and bio-medical wastes are some of the several forms of solid wastes.

4.3   Landfill Gas and Biogas

Anaerobic bacteria produce biogas, which is a mixture of various gases. Agricultural waste or municipal solid wastes, for example, are commonly used as raw materials. Landfill gas is the complex mixture of different types of gases produced within a landfill with the microorganisms present in it. It is generally 40–60% methane.

4.4   Alcohol Fuels

Alcohol fuels [24] are very much cleaner than any other biomass fuel without leaving any byproduct. Basically, ethanol is made from sugar fermentation, and methanol is made from synthesis gas, however there are more modern techniques to get both fuels.

5   Procedure

The total procedure is dived into several parts. Step by step procedure is mentioned below which needs to be done before implementing. The flowchart of the given procedure is mentioned below (Fig. 3):

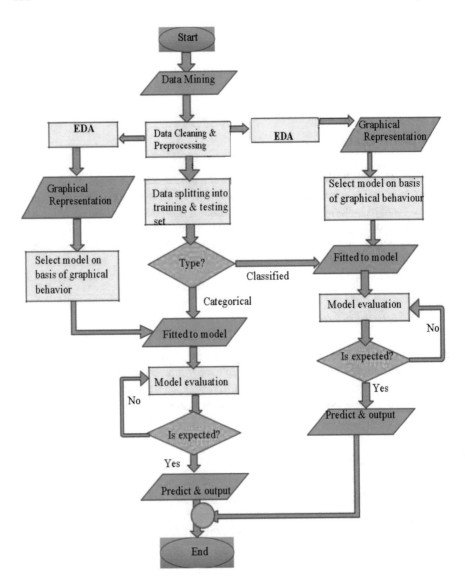

Fig. 3 The flowchart for entire workflow

5.1 Data Mining/Collecting

Data obtained from various research papers [25, 26] and websites for further data analysis and to create machine learning models and place them in the cloud. This dataset contains information on the amount of organic matter produced in a year, what class it belongs to, and how much energy it can produce. Mathematical formulas for calculating the amount of energy produced by biomass are calculated here.

5.2 Data Cleaning and Preprocessing

Some of the data were missing or miss interrupted. The data preprocessing techniques [27] applied to tackle these kinds of problems and converted the data into machine readable form, thus the high amount of accuracy for the model is obtained.

5.3 Exploratory Data Analysis (EDA)

Subsequently the data preprocessing task concludes, here and now applied exploratory data analysis to know the characteristics of the data. Thus, the proposed model has received various graphical representations for further improvement.

5.4 Data Splitting

In this context, splitting the data into training set and testing set [28]. Leaving the amount of energy produced, all the attributes are fitted into parameter set and energy produced into prediction set.

5.5 Selection & Application of Suitable Algorithm

The data has been divided into two sets: training and testing; the dataset is now ready to be fitted into the appropriate model for further evaluation and output.

5.6 Obtaining Result and Model Evaluation

Once the dataset has been attached to the model, it is time to determine the accuracy and error of the proposed model and reduce it to [29].

5.7 Model Creation and Deployment into Cloud

This is the last stage of the procedure where it is needed to load the model into a file for external use and deploy it into the cloud-based platform.

5.8 Testing the Overall Process

Once everything is done, it needs to be checked over and again with different scenarios so that appropriate changes can be done.

6 Software Required

In the software part python v3.5 and above based on anaconda navigator platform is used. Several packages such as scikit-learn, pandas, numpy, seaborn, matplotlib. pyplot, joblib, pickle is also utilized. All these packages were essential for the overall process.

7 Cloud Server

Cloud services like AWS come into picture for procuring a large amount of data. This includes storing data to secure & retrieving it. AWS is a cloud computing platform that is adaptable, dependable, scalable, simple to use, and cost-effective (Fig. 4).

Amazon provides a comprehensive, user-friendly computer platform. Infrastructure as a service (IaaS), platform as a service (PaaS), and packaged software as a service (SaaS) are all used to build the platform. Besides the use of its relational databases are pretty helpful for all types of data that was gathered.

8 Data Analysis Using Python

Python is open-source software. It provides assorted packages/modules for data analysis. Various packages such as NumPy, Seaborn, panda, matplotlib&matplotlib. Pyplot package have used for analysis of the accumulated data. PyCharm and anaconda navigatoris used as software tool for data analysis. Numpy and panda package for statistical analysis and Seaborn, matplotlib.pyplot for graphical representation of the data. Sorting of the data has been done on the basis of the scale of

Fig. 4 AWS cloud server [37]

application. The data has been categorized as small scale, medium scale and large scale. Likewise, there is a categorization of data on the basis of the required energy and types of biomasses. The first dataset (on the basis of the scale of application) is the primary dataset and the second dataset (on the basis of requirement& biomass) is the secondary dataset. The primary dataset was once again separated into three subsets: small scale, medium scale, and big scale. The secondary data set has been sorted into the appropriate biomass categories as well. The mathematical formula used to calculate as:

8.1 Gross Residue Potential

The gross residue potential [30] of a crop is determined by three factors: (i) the crop's area covered, (ii) the crop's yield, and (iii) the crop's RPR value. The gross residue potential is calculated using these parameters:

$CRg(j)$ is gross crop residue potential in tonne at jth state from n number of crops; $A(i,j)$ is area under ith crop at jth state; $Y(i,j)$ is yield of ith crop at jth state, tonne ha^{-1}; and $RPR(i,j)$ is residue production ratio of ith crop at jth state. Within a state, spatial changes in yield and RPR are ignored.

8.2 Bioenergy Potential

The following expression is used to calculate the bioenergy potential [16] of agricultural residual biomass:

Where E(j) is the bioenergy potential of n crops in the jth state, measured in MJ; CRs I j) is the excess residue potential of ith crop in the jth state, measured in tone; and HV I j) is the heating value of ith crop in the jth state, measured in MJ tonne^{-1} (Fig. 5).

The proposed model is based on a novel number system. This does not imply a new set of symbols to be utilized as the system's digits. It employs the same ten digits as the decimal system, namely 0–9, but the representation is slightly different. A number is represented by an ordered pair of two numbers in this manner. The final value of the number is calculated using these two integers and a specific formula.

Examining the following example can help to clarify the concept:

Consider the number 859 in the decimal system. The number is now calculated as (8*100 + 5*10 + 9). The value of 859 will be (8*i*i + 5*i + 9), just as it will be in any other number system, assuming base "i."

As can be seen, every number system necessitates working with the digits in order to obtain the end value. Similarly, the projected system uses digits to get the final result, but the process is different. In the system, a decimal number like 859 is written as (40, 39). For an ordered pair, the calculation is done using the formula ((Y*(Y + 1)/2) + Z). (Y, Z). ((40*41)/2) + 39 = ((20*41) + 39) = 820 + 39 = 859 is now the value of (40, 39).

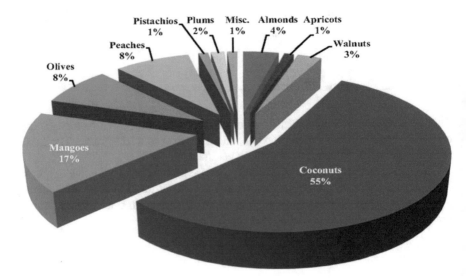

Fig. 5 Bioenergy potential [38]

Within the system, the division is done differently at this stage. Any quantity of a commodity is taken and counted as (1), (1,2), (1,2,3), (1,2,3,4), (1,2,3,4,5), (1,2,3,4,5,6), (1,2,3,4,5,6,7), (1,2,3,4,5,6,7,8)... dividing the group in such a way that the first group can contain one number, the second group can contain two numbers, and the nth group can contain 'n' numbers. As a result, when representing the number given by 5 in the seventh group as (6, 5), the method generates the value $6*7/2 + 5 = 21 + 5 = 26$. This can be verified by counting the italic 5's location as shown above. It's the 26th number form that's still available. As a result, the ordered (x, y) pair has the following definition:

X represents the number of groups that have been entirely finished, including the number that is being considered, and Y represents the number of extra elements that remain.

As a result, examining the number 7 of the seventh group and incorporating '7,' it is possible to have 7 completed groups; now the value of $x = 7$, but there is no extra element left, therefore $y = 0$. Following that, the number is given as (7, 0).

9 Algorithm

The code of the algorithm is given below:

```
step1:  import numpy as np
        import pandas as pd
        import seaborn as sns
        import matplotlib.pyplot as plt
step2:  df=pd.read_csv()
        df1=df.copy().

step3:  Fromsklearn.preprocessing import minmaxscalar,
        LabelEncoder, OnehotEncoder

#Performing exploratory data analysis for sub dataset agro and
obtaining the necessary prediction

step4:  bt=pd.read_excel("Biomass Tables.xlsx")
step5:  bt1=bt.copy()
step6:  bt1.head()
step7:  bt3=bt1[bt1['Biomass Class''] =='Forest&wasteland']
step8:  bt3
step9:  fromsklearn.preprocessing import LabelEncoder
step10: le=LabelEncoder ()
step11: bt1['Biomass']. nunique()
step12: bt1['Species label''] =le.fit_transform
        (bt1['Species'])
step13: bt1['biomass label''] =le.fit_transform
        (bt1['Biomass'])
step14: bt1['biomass_class label''] =le.fit_transform
        (bt1['Biomass Class'])
step15: bt2=bt1.dropna()
```

```
step16: bt2
step17: bt2['Biomass(kT/yr)''] =bt2.apply(lambda x
step18: x['BiomassGeneration(kT/Yr)''] +x['BiomassSurplus
        (kT/Yr)'], axis=1)
step19: bt2
step20: sns.pairplot(bt2,hue='Biomass')
step21: plt.figure(figsize=(10,8))
step22: plt.plot(bt2['BiomassGeneration(kT/Yr)'],
        bt2['PowerPotential(MWe)'],color="blue",
        lw=1, ls='', marker='o',markerfacecolor="yellow",
        markersize=10)
step23: sns. regplot(bt2['BiomassGeneration(kT/Yr)'],
        bt2['PowerPotential(MWe)'])
step24: plt.xlabel('\nBiomassGeneration(kT/Yr)',fontsize=20)
step25: plt.ylabel('\nPowerPotential(MWe)',fontsize=20)
step26: plt.style.use('bmh')
step27: bw=bt2.drop(['BiomassGeneration(kT/Yr)',
        'BiomassSurplus(kT/Yr)'], axis=1) bw
step28: plt.figure(figsize=(10,5))
step29: sns.heatmap(bt2.corr(),cmap='coolwarm',annot=True)
step30: Linear regression
step31: bt2.columns
step32: x=bt2[['Species label',
step33: 'Biomasslabel','Area(kHa)', 'CropProduction(kT/Yr)',
step34: 'BiomassGeneration(kT/Yr)', 'BiomassSurplus(kT/Yr)']]
step35: y=bt2['PowerPotential(MWe)']
step36: fromsklearn.model_selection import train_test_split
step37: xtrain,xtest,ytrain,ytest=train_test_split
        (x,y,test_size=0.2)
step38: fromsklearn.linear_model import LinearRegression
step39: dt=LinearRegression(normalize=True)
step40: dt.fit(xtest,ytest)
step41: pred=dt.predict(xtest)
step42: pred
step43: dt.score(xtest,ytest) # getting the accuracy score
        of predicted value
step44: print(dt.intercept_)
step45: plt.figure(figsize=(10,5))
step46: plt.plot(pred,ytest,color="blue", lw=0.5, ls='',
        marker='o',markerfacecolor="yellow",markersize=12)
step47: sns.regplot(pred,ytest,color='black')
step48: plt.ylabel('\nPowerPotential(MWe)',fontsize=20)
step49: plt.style.use('bmh')
step50: Errors
step51: fromsklearn.metrics import mean_squared_error,
        mean_absolute_error
step52: mse=mean_squared_error(pred,ytest)
        mse
step53: mae=mean_absolute_error(pred,ytest)
step54: mae
step55: rmse=np.sqrt(mean_squared_error(pred,ytest))
step56: rmse
```

```
#Performing exploratory data analysis for sub dataset forest &
wasteland and obtaining the necessary prediction

step57: fw=pd.read_excel("Biomass Tables.xlsx")
step58: f1=fw.copy()
step59: f1. head ()
step60: plt.figure(figsize=(10,5))
step61: sns.heatmap(f1.corr(),cmap='coolwarm',annot=True)
step62: plt. plot(f1['BiomassGeneration(kT/Yr)'],f1['Power
        Potential(MWe)'],color="blue", lw=1, ls='',
        marker='o',markerfacecolor="yellow",markersize=12)
step63: sns. regplot(f1['BiomassGeneration(kT/Yr)'],
        f1['PowerPotential(MWe)'],color='black')
step64: plt.xlabel('\nBiomassGeneration(kT/Yr)',fontsize=20)
step65: plt.ylabel('\nPowerPotential(MWe)',fontsize=20)
step66: plt.style.use('bmh')
step67:
step68: f1. columns
step69:
step70: plt.figure(figsize=(10,5))
step71: sns.violinplot(f1['Biomass'],
        f1['PowerPotential(MWe)'])
step72: plt.xlabel('\nBiomass',fontsize=20)
step73: plt.ylabel('\nPowerPotential(MWe)',fontsize=20)
step74:
step75: from mpl_toolkits. mplot3d import Axes3D
step76:
step77: fig = plt.figure( figsize=(10,5))
step78: ax = fig.add_subplot(111, projection='3d')
step79: plt.
plot(f1['Area(kHa)'],f1['BiomassGeneration(kT/Yr)'],
f1['PowerPotential(MWe)'],color ='black',alpha=0.8,marker='o',
markerfacecolor='Yellow',markersize=7)
step80: plt.xlabel('Area\n\n',fontsize=20)
step81: plt.ylabel('\nBiomass generation',fontsize=20)
step82: plt.style.use('bmh')
step83: ax.view_init(20, 180)
step84: plt.show()
step85: plt.figure(figsize=(20,10))
step86: sns.pairplot(f1,hue='Biomass')

#Prediction using linear regression model

step87: f1=f1[f1['Biomass Class']=='Forest&wasteland']
step88: f1.head()
step89: f1.sort_values(by=f1['Species'])
step90: x=f1[['Area(kHa)','BiomassGeneration(kT/Yr)',
        'BiomassSurplus(kT/Yr)']]
step91: y=f1['PowerPotential(MWe)']
step92: fromsklearn.model_selection import train_test_split
step93: xtrain,xtest,ytrain,ytest=train_test_split
        (x,y,test_size=0.2)
step94: fromsklearn.linear_model import LinearRegression
step95: lr=LinearRegression(normalize=True)
```

```
step96:   lr.fit(xtrain,ytrain)
step97:     pr=lr.predict(xtest)
step98:     pr
step99:     plt.figure(figsize=(6,5))
step100:    plt.plot(pr,ytest,color="blue", lw=0.5, ls='',
            marker='o',markerfacecolor="yellow",markersize=12)
step101:    sns.regplot(pr,ytest,color='b')
step102:    plt.ylabel('\nPowerPotential(MWe)',fontsize=20)
step103:    plt.style.use('bmh')
step104:
step105:    lr.score(x,y)
step106:    Errors
step107:
step108:    from sklearn.metrics import mean_squared_error,
            mean_absolute_error
step109:
step110:    mse=mean_squared_error(pr,ytest)
step111:    mse
step112:
step113:    mae=mean_absolute_error(pr,ytest)
step114:    mae
step115:
step116:    rmse=np.sqrt(mean_squared_error(pr,ytest))
step117:    rmse
            #Creating external file that can be accessed from anywhe
step118:    from sklearn.externals import joblib
step119:    filename = 'finalized_model.sav'
step120:    joblib.dump(lr, filename)
step121:    lm = joblib.load(filename)
step122:    result = lm.score(x,y)
step123:    print(result)
```

10   Deployment of the Model

The main motto is to provide a safeguard to protect the biomass data in cloud
server and access through mobile cloud. This topic motivates the development of an
algorithm for safeguarding data stored in cloud storage that is accurate, efficient, and
secure. The algorithm recommends encrypting the files that will be uploaded to the
cloud. The integrity and confidentiality of the data supplied by the user is double-
encrypted, and access to the data is granted only after successful authentication.
The Advanced Encryption Standard (AES) technique will be used to encrypt the
existing file on the device [31]. To improve security, the AES key will be encrypted
with a mathematical model and stored on an intern server. The authorized user can
also download and view any of the encrypted files that have been submitted to the
system (Fig. 6).

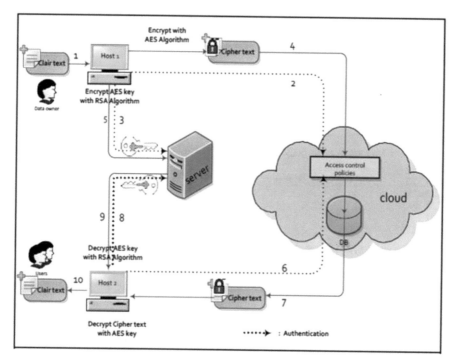

Fig. 6 Proposed model of data storage in cloud computing

10.1 File Upload Algorithm

There are two steps in this method. The algorithm encrypts the biomass data with the AES algorithm in the first stage. In the second stage, mathematical models are used to encrypt the AES key (MM).It employs a set of the following functions:

```
Biomass_Data_File (DF): It returns the block number of data
file DF.
ENCPT_AES (M, KE): Encrypts the data file into M using AES
Algorithm with key KE.
Send_to_Cloud_File (FC): Send the encrypted file M in mobile
cloud storage.
ENCPT_ MM (KE): It encrypts KE using MM.
Save_in_cloud_server (ke): It permits to save "ke" in the server.

Steps followed:
step1:    Encrypt_file (M)
step2:    {
step3:    /* Encrypting algorithm of file onto mobile
          cloud storage*/
step4:    /* to transform Biomass data in file DF into Cipher
          text in file M */
step5:    /* Phase 1: Encrypt Biomass data with AES Algorithm */
```

```
step6:    For M ← 1 to Biomass Data (DF)
step7:    do
step8:    {
step9:    M = ENCPT_AES (M, KE)
step10:   }
step11:   send_to_cloud_file (FC)
step12:   /* Phase 2: Encrypt AES key with MM*/
step13:   For ke←1 to Size Of (KE)
step14:   do
step15:   {
step16:   ke=ENCPT_MM(KE)
step17:   }
step18:   Save_in_cloud_server(ke)
step19:   }
```

10.2 File Download Algorithm

There are two steps to this method as well. The approach uses MM to decrypt the AES key in the first step. It decrypts biomass data (text data) in the second step using an AES key acquired from the server. It makes use of the functions listed below:

Biomass_Data_File (DF): It returns the Biomass Data File (DF).
DECPT_ MM (ke): It decrypts ke using MM.
DECPT_AES (M, KE): It decrypts the block M using AES Algorithm with key KE. The steps followed:

```
step1:   Decrypt_file (DF)
step2:   {
step3:   /* algorithm to decrypt file downloaded from
         mobile cloud storage*/
step4:   /* to transform Cipher text in file M
         into data text in file DF */4.
step5:   /* Phase 1: Decrypt AES Key with MM */
step6:   For ke←1 to Size Of (KE) do 8.
step7:   {
step8:            KE = DECPT_MM (ke)
step9:   }
step10:  return (KE) 12.
step11:  /* Phase 2: Decrypt Cipher text with AES Algorithm*/
step12:  For M'←1 to number Of Block (DF)do
step13:  {
step14:           DF=DEC_AES (M, KE)
step15:  }.
step16:  Return (DF) 19
step17:  }
```

11 Dataset Used

The dataset used here for biomass residues in the year between 2002 to 2004 from forest and wasteland [32] with species, areainKilo Hectares (kHa), crop production, biomass generation, surplus in Kiloton per year (kT/Yr), power potential in Megawatts (MWe)and biomass class are described in the table as follows (Table 1).

Another dataset used here for biomass residues in the year between 2002 to 2004 from agricultural land [33] with species, area in Kilo Hectares (kHa), crop production, biomass generation, surplus in Kiloton per year (kT/Yr), power potential in Megawatts (MWe)and biomass class are described in the table as follows (Table 2).

Additionally, the nutrient wise dataset used for biomass residues in the year between 2010 and 2017 [34] with domain, area(geographical location), element (residue) with item in different year, value of units in Kilograms are described in the table as follows (Table 3).

The huge geographical variety of renewable energy resources and energy efficiency potential can be depleted, separating additional energy bases that are concentrated in a small number of countries. Rapid energy security and financial support will be impacted by renewable energy and energy efficiency, as well as the technical growth of energy bases. Thus, the use of this kind of energy is growing each year. A year wise comparison between different renewable sources of energy [35] can be easily described in the table as follows (Table 4).

There is a lot of potential to affect agricultural characteristics in the present land deprived of penetration by making food, feed, fiber or forestry food items. Agricultural crop residues, consisting of stalks and leaves, are abundant, varied and widely spread. Numerous biomass leftovers are created on diverse commodities such as straws from various pulses and cereals, bagasse, rice husk, groundnut shell, stalks, various oil stalks, and so on. They can be measured in Million Tones/Annum as described in following table (Table 5).

12 Exploratory Data Analysis (EDA)

EDA refers to the hazardous methods of implementing preliminary inquiries about data in order to determine decor, see variations, take advantage of instantaneous numbers and graphic symbols with trial theory and patterned conventions. In this section the procedure to carry out the process is checked the null values present in the data itself (Fig. 7).

After dividing the dataset of Tables 1 and 2 into two classes' i.e., forest & wasteland and agricultural land; the algorithm work separately on both. The relation between Biomass Generation, Biomass Surplus, Power Potential & Area

Table 1 Biomass as residues (2002–2004) from forest & wasteland

Species	Biomass	Area (kHa)	Crop production (kT/Yr)	Biomass generation (kT/Yr)	Biomass surplus (kT/Yr)	Power potential (MWe)	Biomass class
Neem	Twigs	0.72	NA	0.002	0.001	NA	Forest & wasteland
Neem	Branches	0.72	NA	0.002	0.001	NA	Forest & wasteland
Neem	Bark	0.72	NA	0.002	0.001	NA	Forest & wasteland
Neem	Leaves	0.72	NA	0.002	0.001	NA	Forest & wasteland
Champak	Bark	0.70	NA	0.002	0.002	NA	Forest & wasteland
Champak	Branches	0.70	NA	0.002	0.002	NA	Forest & wasteland
Champak	Twigs	0.70	NA	0.002	0.002	NA	Forest & wasteland
Champak	Leaves	0.70	NA	0.003	0.002	NA	Forest & wasteland
Abies	Bark	0.70	NA	0.006	0.004	0.001	Forest & wasteland
Abies	Branches	8.00	NA	0.006	0.004	0.001	Forest & wasteland

Table 2 Biomass as residues (2002–2004) from agricultural land

Species	Biomass	Area (kHa)	Crop production (kT/Yr)	Biomass generation (kT/Yr)	Biomass surplus (kT/Yr)	Power potential (MWe)	Biomass class
Areca nut	Husk	262.80	265.40	212.3	74.3	10.4	Agro
Areca nut	Fronds	262.80	265.40	788.5	276	38.6	Agro
Arhar	Husk	2836.90	2048.10	614.4	306.4	36.8	Agro
Arhar	Stalks	2836.90	2048.10	5120.2	822	106.9	Agro
Bajra	Husk	8364.80	6020.00	1805.9	431.3	51.8	Agro
Bajra	Cobs	8364.80	6020.00	1986.5	939.9	122.2	Agro
Bajra	Stalks	8364.80	6020.00	12039.4	1919.5	249.5	Agro
Banana	Residue	106.60	3978.80	11936.5	4176.7	543	Agro
Barley	Stalks	226.70	433.20	563.2	57.5	7.5	Agro
Cashew nut	Stalks	181.50	82.40	148.2	36.1	4.7	Agro

Table 3 Nutrient wise biomass as residues (2010–2017)

Domain	Area	Element	Item	Year	Unit	Value
Crop Residues	India	Residues (Crop residues)	Barley	2010	kg of nutrients	17786899
Crop Residues	India	Residues (Crop residues)	Barley	2011	kg of nutrients	21503473
Crop Residues	India	Residues (Crop residues)	Barley	2012	kg of nutrients	20706873
Crop Residues	India	Residues (Crop residues)	Barley	2013	kg of nutrients	22370731
Crop Residues	India	Residues (Crop residues)	Barley	2014	kg of nutrients	23101922
Crop Residues	India	Residues (Crop residues)	Barley	2015	kg of nutrients	20982772
Crop Residues	India	Residues (Crop residues)	Barley	2016	kg of nutrients	18507027
Crop Residues	India	Residues (Crop residues)	Barley	2017	kg of nutrients	22157346
Crop Residues	India	Residues (Crop residues)	Barley	2010	kg of nutrients	1.07E+08

Table 4 Year wise energy growth for various renewable sources

Source	2014–2015	2015–2016	2016–2017	2017–2018	2018–2019
Large Hydro	129,244	121,377	122,313	126,134	135,040
Small Hydro	8060	8355	7673	5056	8703
Solar	4600	7450	12,086	25,871	39,268
Wind	28,214	28,604	46,011	52,666	62,036
Bio mass	14,944	16,681	14,159	15,252	16,325
Other	414	269	213	358	425
Total	191,025	187,158	204,182	227,973	261,797
Total utility power	1,105,446	1,168,359	1,236,392	1,302,904	1,371,517
% Renewable power	17.28%	16.02%	16.52%	17.50%	19.10%

Table 5 Various biomass residues produced [36]

Type of agricultural residues	Quantity (million tones/annum)
Straws of various pulses & cereals	225.5
Bagasse	31
Rice husk	10
Groundnut shell	11.1
Stalks	2
Various oil stalks	4.5
Others	65.9
Total	350

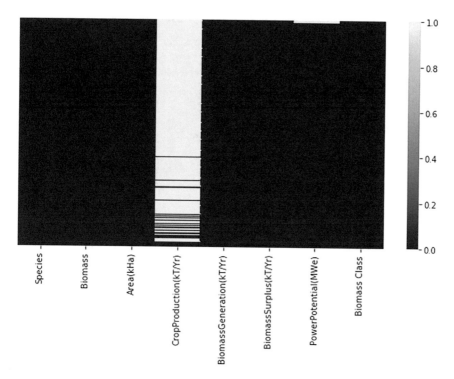

Fig. 7 Heatmap showing the null values present in the raw dataset that needs to be processed

is established within a range of 0.76–1.00. Heat map for correlated value for forest and wasteland dataset is described as (Fig. 8).

Now the correlation table is established, the regular plot of seaborn module is established to check the nature of the graph. Biomass generation and power potentialis plotted as two sides of the coordinates. A curve starting with (0,0) coordinates can be clearly visualized (Fig. 9).

The nature of the graph is linear in nature therefore the linear regression model is applied. It produces the highest accuracy. The type of the model is obtained here. With the help of several types of graphs more outcome scan be gathered. The twigs, branches, bark, leaves and stalk are plotted in horizontal axis and power potential is plotted in the vertical axis, thus the violin plot for power potential of leaves can be shown as maximum (Fig. 10).

The dry mass of all entities in a given land area is the origin of the whole biomass through the biomass and then the zone is found, e.g., biomass of each plot, ecosystem, biomass classroom. In order to be able to be the equivalent of organic matter in different places, the adaptation of organic matter per unit is very important. Biomass generation is directly proportionate with the area covered. The difference between urban, rural, forestry, water body or deserted area is completely different (Fig. 11).

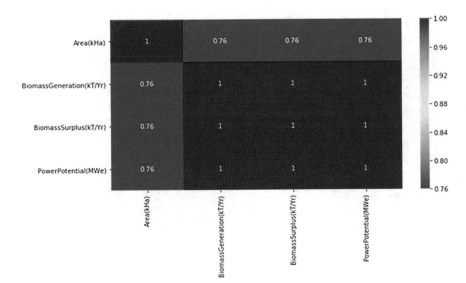

Fig. 8 Heat map for correlated value for forest and wasteland dataset

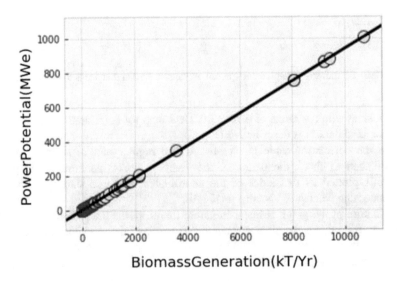

Fig. 9 Regularplot between power potential and biomass generation

This 3D plot describes the insight relation between three important attributes i.e., area of production, biomass generated, and power potential of those biomasses (Fig. 12).

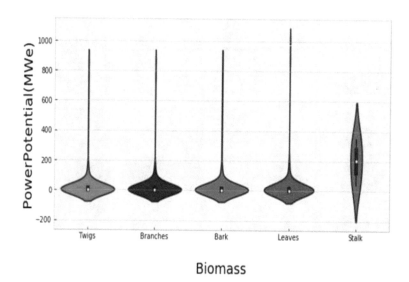

Fig. 10 Violin plot for various biomasses estimating the maximum amount of power potential

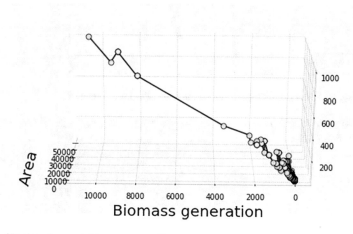

Fig. 11 3D plot of area v/s biomass generation

The pairplot defines the dataset in the form of graphical matrix representation. It is tried to represent the dataset differentiated with various types of biomasses such as twigs, branches, leaves etc.

The insight information of the data is obtained here, now it is time to move towards training the model with the dataset and evaluating. The process continues until it can obtain the highest accuracy. The predicted graph is given below (Fig. 13).

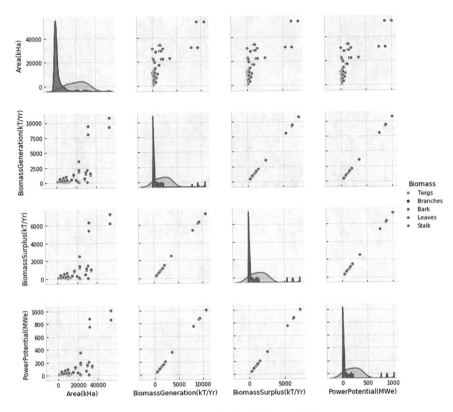

Fig. 12 Pairplot of the dataset segregated on the basis of types of biomasses

Fig. 13 The predicted graph of the forest & wasteland dataset

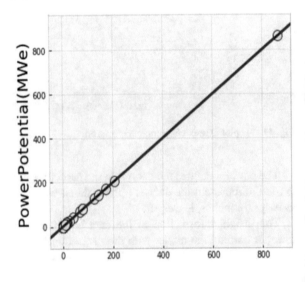

The accuracy of the prediction is 0.9999995507413525 which is similar to 99.99%. Now this is a trained model that can be used to determine the unknown random value that already been tested and is given below (Fig. 14).

This can be clearly realized that the data has been taken by the user and the model predicts the estimated value of power potential with high accuracy. Mean absolute error of the model is 0.008844967090332757 followed by:

Mean squared error:0.0002536417329143844, and
Root mean squared error: 0.015926133646129697

The analysis of the second sub-dataset for agriculture-based biomass done in similar way. In this sub-dataset, crop production is added as an important attribute (Fig. 15).

The biomass generation depends on the quality of the agricultural material. It may have around 50% of water contained in it. After vaporization small pellets (just like condensed piece of same material) can increase the energy shrinkage of the fuel and make it more useful for transport. The power potential relation for agriculture-based biomass is described with biomass generation as shown here (Fig. 16).

The light blue color shows the size of the confidence interval for the regression estimate that is going to apply on the proposed model. Once getting the estimation graph, it is applied the same linear regression model. Consequently, obtained the predicted value with accuracy of 0.996040863715186 which is equal to 99.60%. The errors found are as follows:

Mean absolute error: 18.48907705244445
Mean squared error: 406.8258388146164
Root mean squared error: 20.16992411524189

```
a=int(input("enter area in kHa: "))
b=int(input("enter Biomass generated in kT/yr :  "))
c=int(input("enter the excess biomass produced:  "))

enter area in kHa: 23
enter Biomass generated in kT/yr :   102
enter the excess biomass produced:  12


es=lr.predict([[a,b,c]])
print('The power potential is estimated to be: ',es,'MWe')

The power potential is estimated to be:  [1.68501669] MWe


lr.score(x,y)

0.9999999731951676
```

Fig. 14 Test data for the model to obtain the predicted value

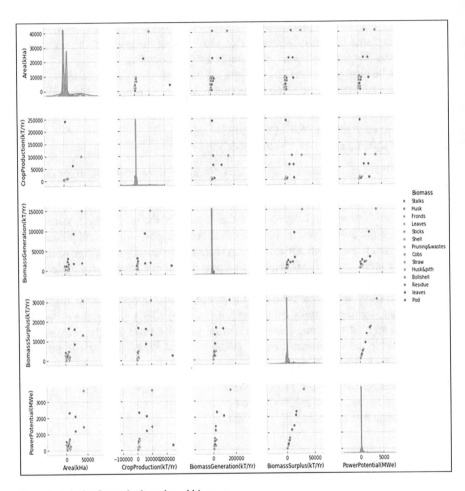

Fig. 15 Pairplot for agriculture-based biomass

The test model is shown below; all the inputs are random here and are according to the users (Fig. 17).

The third dataset contains the information about the total crop residue biomass production during 2010–2017. The large number of residues obtained from rice and paddy followed by wheat, soybeans and maize are realized in graphical representation. The subsequent graph of all types of crop residues is given below (Fig. 18).

For this particular dataset, applied auto regressive model of time series analysis to see whether the production is going up the scale or coming down. Primarily it is checked the autocorrelation of the data using statistical model and then predicted the value using autoregressive model. The detailed predicted graph is shown below (Fig. 19).

Fig. 16 Biomass generation
and power potential relation
for agriculture-based biomass

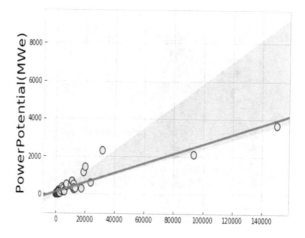

BiomassGeneration(kT/Yr)

---

user input prediction

```
dt.fit(x,y)

LinearRegression(copy_X=True, fit_intercept=True, n_jobs=None, normalize=True)

'Area(kHa)', 'CropProduction(kT/Yr)',
        'BiomassGeneration(kT/Yr)', 'BiomassSurplus(kT/Yr)'

a=int(input("enter species label: "))
b=int(input("enter biomass label "))
c=int(input("enter area in kHa: "))
d=int(input("enter crop production in (kT/y): "))
e=int(input("enter Biomass generated in kT/yr :  "))
f=int(input("enter the excess biomass produced:  "))

enter species label: 2
enter biomass label 3
enter area in kHa: 24
enter crop production in (kT/y): 12
enter Biomass generated in kT/yr :  10
enter the excess biomass produced:  2

es=dt.predict([[a,b,c,d,e,f]])
print('The power potential is estimated to be: ',es,'MWe')

The power potential is estimated to be:  [28.83078949] MWe

dt.score(x,y)

0.996040863715186
```

Fig. 17 Obtaining the predicted value using the test data

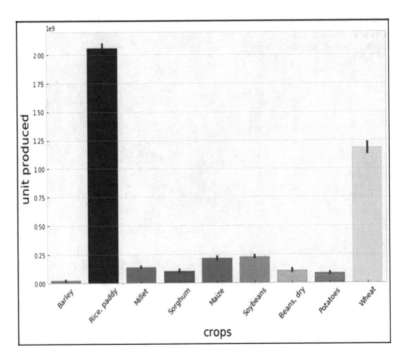

Fig. 18 Crop residue produced per unit

The expected time graph for crop residues created between 2010 and 2017 is described here (Fig. 20).

The KDE plot for expected result is described graphically. The test set value is also used here (Fig. 21).

Highest density is found between 0.4 and 0.6 of the predicted value with respect to 0–0.5 of the test values can be clearly observed. Up to this point it is focused on the core element of the projected work, now moving towards the real time outcome of the power generation from biomass. Dataset-4 is taken here for getting the graphical representation (Figs. 22 and 23).

The above sub graph describes that the biomass energy produced during this tenure has seen growth over deterioration. It can be predicted from the anticipated model that biomass energy will achieve a huge growth in the near future.

13 Advantage

The major advantage of this type of fuel is that they are renewable sources of energy (green energy). Likewise, it provides a backup fuel or secondary fuel for different operations and minimizes the dependencies on traditional fuel. On the other hand,

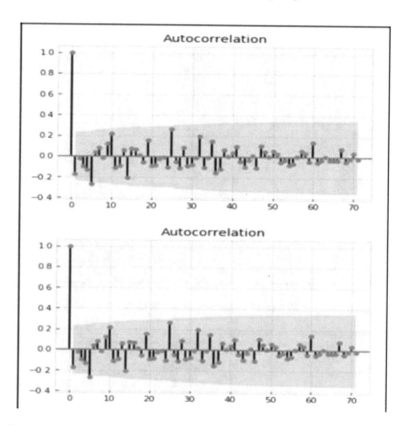

Fig. 19 The autocorrelation graph showing the linearity of the data

it is favorable fuel for any small-scale industry as it can be available anywhere (Village/City). This type of fuel is cheaper as it can be found in end products of crops or garbage's from waste products. They may add a second income source for producers as originates from waste product and less money spends for foreign fuels for the countries like India. The use of Biomass as fuel can reduce landfill operations where contamination of local habitats and destructions of wildlife ecosystems are done on a regular basis. Biomass energy can be converted in other ways as ethanol can be produced from corn.

14 Conclusion

Finally, depending on the needs of consumers, raw data can be exploited in a variety of ways. This information can be accessed from any location and on any system. The end user's desired dataset includes additional information that will be useful in the future. The examined data gives him a clear picture of what he wants. The graph and statistics present a clear picture of biomass synthesis and waste product conversion

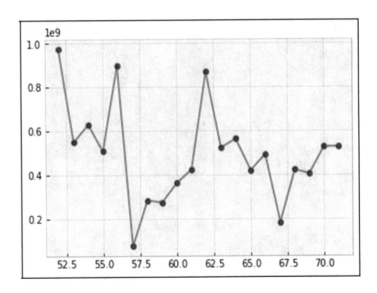

Fig. 20 Predicted time graph for crop residues produced (2010–2017)

Fig. 21 KDEplot for predicted and test set value

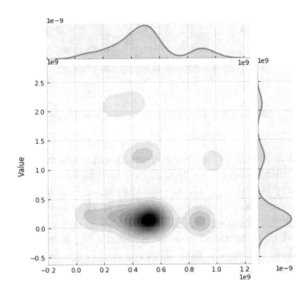

into viable renewable energy sources. Growth and progress in numerous industries currently necessitate a lot of energy without disrupting the natural equilibrium. Data centre power consumption control has resulted in significant energy efficiency gains. The data center's cloud computing infrastructure has been greatly upgraded as a result of this advancement. The expectation is that the perception will save both money and the environment. E-waste disposal is also predicted to put people's

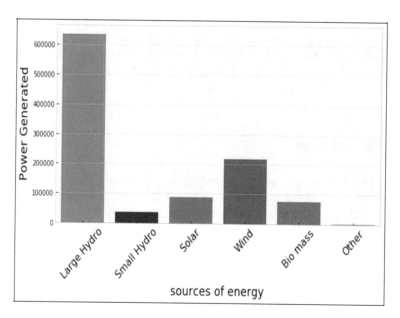

Fig. 22 Power generated from different sources of energy (2014–2019)

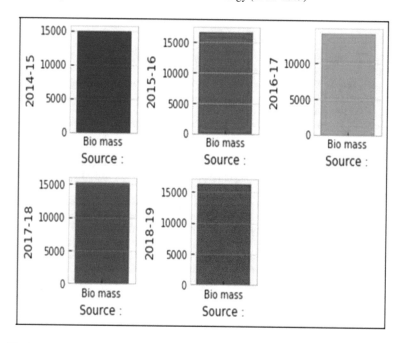

Fig. 23 Comparative study of biomass energy (2014–2019)

lives in jeopardy indefinitely. In order to reduce carbon emissions and provide a functional work environment for official domes, cloud computing and green computing will be organized. Today, time is needed for green cloud computing and environmental sustainability. This renewable energy is the key to the human race's future energy production.

15 Future Scope

It is observed from the preceding analysis that there is a growth in renewable sources of energy from past few years and it has been increasing day by day. Correspondingly, more plants will yield more biomass production and will boost the renewable energy sector. Since working with past data and the prediction from latest data will give more insight of this sector in the near future. In fact, it will help many people to set up the kind of power plant they want to set up to get their desired need of energy. Moreover, it will also help in reducing large amount of trash and converting it into energy.

References

1. National Institute of Standards and Technology Special Publication 500-291 Natl. Inst. Stand. Technol. Spec. Publ. 500–291, 83 pages (2011)
2. Gong, C., Liu, J., Zhang, Q., Chen, H., Gong, Z.: The characteristics of cloud computing. In: 39th International Conference on Parallel Processing Workshops, pp. 275–279 (2010). https://doi.org/10.1109/ICPPW.2010.45
3. Keahey, K., Figueiredo, R., Fortes, J., Freeman, T., Tsugawa, M.: Science clouds: early experiences in cloud computing for scientific applications. Cloud Comput. Appl. **2008**, 825–830 (2008)
4. Kumar, R., Jain, K., Maharwal, H., Jain, N., Dadhich, A.: Apache Cloudstack: open source infrastructure as a service cloud computing platform. Proc. Int. J. Adv. Eng. Technol. Manag. Appl. Sci. **1**(2), 111–116 (2014)
5. Li, W., Shao, H., Wang, S., Zhou, X., Wu, S.: A2CI: a cloud-based, service-oriented geospatial cyberinfrastructure to support atmospheric research. In: Vance, T.C., Merati, N., Yang, C., Yuan, M. (eds.) Cloud Computing in Ocean and Atmospheric Sciences, pp. 137–161 (2016)
6. Liu, Y., Wei, X., Guo, X., Niu, D., Zhang, J., Gong, X., Jiang, Y.: The long-term effects of reforestation on soil microbial biomass carbon in sub-tropic severe red soil degradation areas. For. Ecol. Manag. **285**, 77–84 (2012). https://doi.org/10.1016/j.foreco.2012.08.019
7. Lobell, D.B., Thau, D., Seifert, C., Engle, E., Little, B.: A scalable satellite-based crop yield mapper. Remote Sens. Environ. **164**, 324–333 (2015). https://doi.org/10.1016/j.rse.2015.04.021
8. Ma, Y., Wu, H., Wang, L., Huang, B., Ranjan, R., Zomaya, A., Jie, W.: Remote sensing big data computing: challenges and opportunities. Futur. Gener. Comput. Syst. **51**, 47–60 (2015). https://doi.org/10.1016/j.future.2014.10.029
9. Okoro, S.U., Schickhoff, U., Bohner, J., Schneider, U.A.: A novel approach in monitoring land-cover change in the tropics: oil palm cultivation in the Niger Delta, Nigeria. Erde. **147**, 40–52 (2016)

10. Padarian, J., Minasny, B., McBratney, A.B.: Using Google's cloud-based platform for digital soil mapping. Comput. Geosci. **83**, 80–88 (2015). https://doi.org/10.1016/j.cageo.2015.06.023
11. Patel, N.N., Angiuli, E., Gamba, P., Gaughan, A., Lisini, G., Stevens, F.R., Tatem, A.J., Trianni, G.: Multitemporal settlement and population mapping from Landsat using Google Earth Engine. Int. J. Appl. Earth Obs. Geoinf. **35**, 199–208 (2015). https://doi.org/10.1016/j.jag.2014.09.005
12. Tan, X., Di, L., Deng, M., Fu, J., Shao, G., Gao, M., Sun, Z., Ye, X., Sha, Z., Jin, B.: Building an elastic parallel OGC web processing service on a cloud-based cluster: a case study of remote sensing data processing service. Sustainability. **7**(10), 14245–14258 (2015). https://doi.org/10.3390/su71014245
13. Khurrum, M., Bhutta, S., Omar, A., Yang, X.: Electronic waste: a growing concern in today's environment. Econ. Res. Int. **2011.**, Article ID 474230, 8–20 (2011). https://doi.org/10.1155/2011/474230
14. Perkins, D.N., Drisse, M.-N.B., Nxele, T., Sly, P.D.: E-waste: a global hazard. Ann. Glob. Health. **80**(4), 286–295 (2014). ISSN 2214-9996. https://doi.org/10.1016/j.aogh.2014.10.001
15. Popp, J., Kovács, S., Oláh, J., Divéki, Z., Balázs, E.: Bioeconomy: biomass and biomass-based energy supply and demand. New Biotechnol. **60**, 76–84 (2021). ISSN 1871-6784. https://doi.org/10.1016/j.nbt.2020.10.004
16. Amidon, T.E., Wood, C.D., Shupe, A.M., Wang, Y., Graves, M., Liu, S.: Biorefinery: conversion of woody biomass to chemicals, energy and materials. J. Biobaased Mater. Bioenergy. **2**, 100–120 (2008). https://doi.org/10.1166/jbmb.2008
17. Bartuska, A.: Why Biomass Is Important: The Role of the USDA Forest Service in Managing and Using Biomass for Energy and Other Uses. Speech Given at 25x25 Summit II, Washington, DC (2006). Last Accessed 17 July 2018
18. Chen, Q., McRoberts, R.E., Wang, C., Radtke, P.J.: Forest aboveground biomass mapping and estimation across multiple spatial scales using model-based inference. Remote Sens. Environ. **184**, 350–360 (2016). https://doi.org/10.1016/j.rse.2016.07.023
19. Dong, J., Xiao, X., Menarguez, M.A., Zhang, G., Qin, Y., Thau, D., Biradar, C., Moore, B.: Mapping paddy rice planting area in northeastern Asia with Landsat 8 images, phenology-based algorithm and Google Earth Engine. Remote Sens. Environ. **185**, 142–154 (2016). https://doi.org/10.1016/j.rse.2016.02.016
20. Foody, G.M., Boyd, D.S., Cutler, M.E.J.: Predictive relations of tropical forest biomass from Landsat TM data and their transferability between regions. Remote Sens. Environ. **85**, 463–474 (2003). https://doi.org/10.1016/S0034-4257(03)00039-7
21. Goldblatt, R., You, W., Hanson, G., Khandelwal, A.K.: Detecting the boundaries of urban areas in India: a dataset for pixel-based image classification in Google Earth Engine. Remote Sens. **8**, 634–642 (2016). https://doi.org/10.3390/rs8080634
22. Gorelick, N., Hancher, M., Dixon, M., Ilyushchenko, S., Thau, D., Moore, R.: Google Earth Engine: planetary-scale geospatial analysis for everyone. Remote Sens. Environ. **202**, 18–27 (2017). https://doi.org/10.1016/j.rse.2017.06.031
23. Houghton, R.A.: Aboveground forest biomass and the global carbon balance. Glob. Chang. Biol. **11**(6), 945–958 (2005). https://doi.org/10.1111/j.1365-2486.2005.00955.x
24. Houghton, R.A., Lawrence, K.T., Hackler, J.L., Brown, S.: The spatial distribution of forest biomass in the Brazilian Amazon: a comparison of estimates. Glob. Chang. Biol. **7**, 731–746 (2001). https://doi.org/10.1046/j.1365-2486.2001.00426.x
25. Lu, D., Chen, Q., Wang, G., Liu, L., Li, G., Moran, E.: A survey of remote sensing-based aboveground biomass estimation methods in forest ecosystems. Int. J. Digit. Earth. **9**(1), 63–105 (2016). https://doi.org/10.1080/17538947.2014.990526
26. Sudhakar Reddy, C., Jha, C., Diwakar, P., Dadhwal, V.: Nationwide classification of forest types of India using remote sensing and GIS. Environ. Monit. Assess. **187** (2015). https://doi.org/10.1007/s10661-015-4990-8
27. Nathanson, J. A.: Solid-waste management. Encyclopedia Britannica. https://www.britannica.com/technology/solid-waste-management (2020). Last Accessed 8 Oct 2021

28. New York State's Solid Waste Program. https://www.dec.ny.gov/chemical/8732.html. Last Accessed 8 Oct 2021
29. Yun, Y.: Alcohol Fuels: Current Status and Future Direction, Alcohol Fuels – Current Technologies and Future Prospect. IntechOpen (2020). https://doi.org/10.5772/intechopen.89788. Available on https://www.intechopen.com/books/alcohol-fuels-current-technologies-and-future-prospect/alcohol-fuels-current-status-and-future-direction
30. Williams, C.A., Hasler, N., Gu, H., Zhou, Y.: Forest Carbon Stocks and Fluxes from the NFCMS. Conterminous USA, pp. 1990–2010, ORNL DAAC, Oak Ridge. (2020). https://doi.org/10.3334/ORNLDAAC/1829
31. Schepaschenko, D., Shvidenko, A., Usoltsev, V., et al.: A dataset of forest biomass structure for Eurasia. Sci. Data. **4**, 170070 (2017). https://doi.org/10.1038/sdata.2017.70
32. Basics of Data Preprocessing, Basic Understandings and Techniques of Data Preprocessing. https://medium.com/easyread/basics-of-data-preprocessing-71c314bc7188#:~:text=What%20are%20the%20Techniques%20Provided%20in%20 20Data%20Preprocessing%3F,Transformation%20Constructing%20data %20cube.%20...%20More%20items...%20. Last Accessed 8 Oct 2021
33. Splitting a Dataset into Train and Test Sets. https://www.baeldung.com/cs/train-test-datasets-ratio. Last Accessed 8 Oct 2021
34. Galdi, P., Tagliaferri, R.: Data mining: accuracy and error measures for classification and prediction. In: Encyclopedia of Bioinformatics and Computational Biology, pp. 431–436. Academic (2019). ISBN 9780128114322. https://doi.org/10.1016/B978-0-12-809633-8.20474-3
35. Hiloidhari, M., Das, D., Baruah, D.C.: Bioenergy potential from crop residue biomass in India. Renew. Sust. Energ. Rev. **32**, 504–512 (2014)
36. Berndes, G., Hoogwijk, M., van den Broek, R.: The contribution of biomass in the future global energy supply: a review of 17 studies. Biomass Bioenergy. **25**(1), 1–28 (2003)
37. About Amazon Web Services – Expedite Business Operations and improve agility through Amazon Web Services. https://www.kcsitglobal.com/solution/cloud/amazon-web-services. Last Accessed 23 Jan 2022
38. Mendu, V., Tom, S., Elliott Campbell Jr., J., Stork, J., Jae, J., Crocker, M., Huber, G., DeBolt, S.: Global bioenergy potential from high-lignin agricultural residue. PNAS. **109**(10), 4014–4019 (2012). https://doi.org/10.1073/pnas.1112757109

6G Based Green Mobile Edge Computing for Internet of Things (IoT)

Amartya Mukherjee, Ayan Kumar Panja, Mohammad S. Obaidat, and Debashis De ⓘ

1 Introduction

Fifth generation (5G) and beyond 5G (B5G) mobile communication framework is an emerging framework in today's world. The numerous devices and management systems take part in the development of modern communication as well as computing framework. The introduction of cloud, edge, and fog computing paradigms makes the system more effective for communication and computing systems [1]. The advantage of such a layered form of computing is to optimally utilize the energy and the resources. One of the major concerns in the development of such an efficient system is the optimization of the power consumption of resource-hungry

A. Mukherjee (✉)
Center for Mobile and Cloud Computing, MAKAUT, Kalyani, India

Department of Computer Science, Maulana Abul Kalam Azad University of Technology, Kalyani, India

Department of Computer Science (AIML), Institute of Engineering &Management, Kolkata, India

A. K. Panja
Department of Computer Science (AIML), Institute of Engineering &Management, Kolkata, India
e-mail: ayan.panja@iemcal.com

M. S. Obaidat
Department of Computer Science Engineering, Indian Institute of Technology, Dhanbad, India

King Abdullah II School of Information Technology, University of Jordan, Amman, Jordan

School of Computer and Communication Engineering, University of Science and Technology Beijing, Beijing, China

D. De
Department of Computer Science and Engineering, Centre of Mobile Cloud Computing, Maulana Abul Kalam Azad University of Technology, West Bengal, Nadia, India
e-mail: debashis.de@makautwb.ac.in

devices. The system must be designed in such an optimal way so that they use the minimum amount of power. Most of the mobile computing devices nowadays use complex machines and deep learning algorithms. This needs a huge amount of processing and the memory fetch operation. In a mission-critical scenario, the big challenge is to send a huge amount of mission-critical data to the cloud is sometimes impossible due to poor network connectivity and very limited bandwidth. In such a case the cloud infrastructure might be unavailable for processing. Therefore, we need to plan for an alternative setup for buffering and processing of the data at the edge of the network. Mobile edge computing, dew computing, and fog computing play a major role in this. The fundamental concept of mobile edge computing is the processing of the data at the edge of the network. One of the crucial advantages of this is methodology is optimizing the processing power. Thus, the overall processing requires a very limited amount of energy because most of the edge processors are having very low power circuitry and it may run even in renewable energy resources as well. The green mobile computing technology also can be used in various aspects of disaster management [2]. In a disaster area, the majority of the energy sources are often disrupted. As a result, the devices always depend on alternative energy sources. Therefore, the key things are to develop hardware that consumes minimum power. Besides that, the research on the optimized algorithm is also a core subject of interest. The machine learning algorithm that is running on edge computing devices is generally optimized in the category so that it can run in a low resource and low power machine. Another aspect of the green computing device is the use of a low latency buffer platform, which is often known as the dew layer. The dew computing in this case enables a buffer as a service methodology where we can store the data in a temporary buffer even if the network gateway is not available and the cloud service is not reachable. Ideally, this concept is highly appreciable in the applications like flying ad-hoc networks, aerial sensor networks, among others. The Google loon project, and Facebook Aquila project are some of the concepts where such as edge, dew, and fog computing aspect has been physically developed. The major industrial revolution like industry 4.0 and beyond has ample research scope in this case. The beyond industry 4.0 gives us a glimpse of In-space manufacturing (ISM) where the deployment of the engineering industry in the space to reduce air pollution. In such a case, renewable energy is an utmost necessary thing that ensures optimal delivery of electricity in the production line and the robotic and computation devices.

The rest of the chapter discusses the numerous component and methodologies involved in the development of the Green mobile edge computing system for the Internet of Things.

2   5G and Beyond 5G for Internet of Things

5G and beyond 5G communication is the crucial technological aspect of the Internet of things communication. The primary target of the IoT paradigm is to transfer the data between sensors to the cloud and perform analysis of the same. Moreover, the

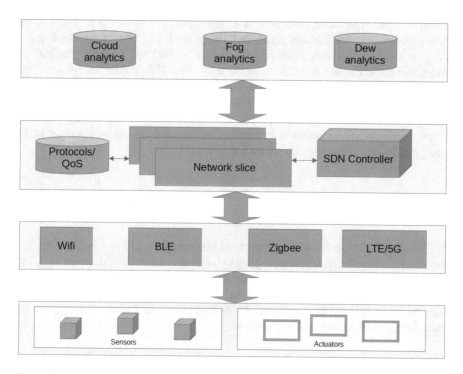

Fig. 1 Complete architecture of the green IoT

decision generated by the analytics systems can be reflected towards the actuator devices which can be able to actuate the system to control various devices and their functionality. The use of lightweight network protocols and proper and optimal networking topology ensures the efficient performance of the IoT ecosystem. The IoT architecture in this context can be visualized as a layered system. The ecosystem here can be conceptualized as 4 layers. In layer 1, the major components are the sensors and actuators. The sensor in this case gathers the physical data from the ambiance. The second layer is the gateway layer. This layer comprises the network gateway. The gateway primarily comprises the heterogeneous network protocols and the communication standard such as Wi-Fi, Bluetooth Low Energy (BLE), Zigbee, and LoRA, [3], among others. The third layer is the network backhaul Layer, in this case, can even be segmented into various other small segments often known as the network slices. These slices are nothing but the virtual environment containing the core and the access network. The function of the slice is to provide a scalable service of network resources. The resources in this case are allocated based on the priority of the user and the services. The protocol and the QoS controllers are also the major part of this layer (Fig. 1).

The fourth layer mainly comprises of analytics engine. The main part of this segment is the cloud, fog, and dew computing infrastructure. This layer may be segregated into 3 typical sub-layers in this case known as cloud layer, fog layer, and dew layer. The cloud layer acts as a data repository in this case. Further, the data processing is done in this layer. To balance the load of the cloud, the fog and the dew level computation come into the picture in this case. In the beginning, the data from the IoT nodes might store in the dew layer. This is often useful when the network latency is extremely high. Also, in some cases, the nodes are outside of the coverage area of the infrastructure network backhaul. In such a case the node may unable to send the message in the cloud. As a result, the information that is gathered in the system might be buffered in a node. The major concern, in this case, is the energy-efficient green communication technology.

2.1 Protocols for Green IoT

IoT protocols can be broadly categorized based on their payload and use of data footprint. Some of the major IoT protocols, in this case, are Message Queuing Telemetry Transport (MQTT), Real-Time Messaging Protocols (RTMP), Real-Time Streaming Protocol (RTSP), and many more. Another very important methodology adopted by Google is Google Remote Procedure Call (GRPC), which is extensively used for green cloud and Micro Services.

2.2 MQTT Protocol

MQTT is the message queuing telemetry transport protocol that ensures a low power and low-cost message delivery. The MQTT protocol is fundamentally based on the publisher and subscriber-based message transfer. A dedicated broker has to be deployed locally or at the cloud level. The job of this broker is to redirect the information from publisher to subscribers. The MQTT messaging primarily performs 2 different types of message transfer QoS levels [4]. The first type of QoS level is known as QoS 0. Here message transfer is not guaranteed. The message might receive by the subscriber or may not be received. In the case of QoS 1, the scenario is different. The system in this case ensures at least one copy of the message received. On the other hand, in QoS 2 the system must ensure exactly 1 message transfer.

In the case of QoS0, MQTT message forwarding has been done at a fast speed. It requires only a single message transfer. It is the most unreliable transfer mode in comparison to all mechanisms. The message is not stored on the sender buffer in this case, and no acknowledgment is received in this case. Therefore, with this QOS 0, there is no possibility of the generation of duplicate messages.

QoS1 on the other hand ensures at least one message is received by the subscriber node. In QoS1 sometimes subscribers may receive more than one message in some cases. This methodology sometimes increases the number of message counts in the whole network. The message in this case must be stored locally at the sender end and redirected to the receiver until it is processed. The message, in this case, is deleted after processing. If the receiver is a broker then it will send the message to subscribers. As the message is received by the subscriber application, the message is sent to the processor device which processes the message. After that, it gets deleted.

In the case of QoS 2, the message gets stored in sender and receiver until and unless it gets processed. This QoS level is having high latency but it is more accurate and safer in terms of transfer of the message. In the first pair of transmissions, the sender transmits the message and acknowledgment received from the receiver that it has stored the message. If the sender does not receive the acknowledgment then it again sends the message with DUP flag set. In this case, the sender has to wait until the acknowledgment is received. In pair 2 of transmissions, the sender tells the receiver that it can complete processing the message. A "PUBREL" is generated in this case and sent to the receiver. If the sender doesn't receive the acknowledgment of "PUBREL" then this message has to be sent again.

In the case of python applications, we can use the MQTT paho package to create an MQTT publish, subscribe application. In this case, we can use paho to create an MQTT client that can publish the message to the broker. In the same way, we can also create the subscriber instance that subscribes to the particular topic and receive the message from the broker. The following code illustrates the MQTT paho publisher and the subscriber instance that is connected to a broker instance. In the case of edge-dew infrastructure, the broker can be deployed in either an edge node or a dew node.

(a) Publisher node

```
importpaho.mqtt.client as paho
client = paho.Client()
data = int(input("Enter data: "))
ifclient.connect('test.mosquitto.org',1883,60)!=0:
print("unable to connect broker !!")
sys.exit(-1)
print('Text message')
client.publish("test1/status",data,0)
print("done!");
client.disconnect()
```

(b) Subscriber node

```
importpaho.mqtt.client as paho
import sys
defonMessage(client, userdata, msg):
print("data coming : ")
print(msg.topic + ": " + msg.payload.decode())
client = paho.Client()
client.on_message = onMessage
ifclient.connect("localhost",1883,60)!=0:
print("unable to connect broker !!")
sys.exit(-1)
```

```
client.subscribe("test1/status")
try:
print("Press CTRL+C to exit...")
client.loop_forever()
except:
print("Broker disconnecting...")
client.disconnect()
```

2.3 gRPC Protocol for Edge, Cloud Microservices

gRPC is a high-performance open-source universal RPC framework [5]. In this framework, the client application directly calls the method on a server application from a different machine in a different location like a local object. On the server-side, the implementation of the interface has been done. On the client-side, the stub has to be run for interacting with the remote method provided on the server-side. Here, gRPC clients and servers run in a heterogeneous environment like the server method may run in a python platform whereas the client method may run in Go, Ruby, Android JAVA, C++, data platforms. Further, gRPC generally uses protocol buffer and various other types of data format like JSON. The initial step to designate a protocol buffer is to create a message block that contains the attributes. This is a small structure message record with a name-value pair field. Once we define the data structure the compiler generates the data access class in our language. The illustration of the gRPC system is mentioned below.

```
message p{
string name = 1;
intid_no = 2;
bool authenticate = 3;
}
The gRPC service with the method parameters has been shown below.
// The service definition.
service G{
  // Sends a greeting message
rpcSayHello (HelloReq) returns (HelloRep) {}
}
// The request message comprises of  user name.
messageHelloReq{
string name = 1;
}
// The response message
messageHelloRep {
string message = 1;
}
```

2.4 IoT Application Development

While the development of the IoT application a major part in the implementation of the hardware and the software components. In an IoT application, the coordination of the software and the hardware component is very much necessary. The fundamental concept of the IoT ecosystem comprises various layers. Layer 1 is the sensor layer that is primarily used for sensing. There are ample scopes to optimize the energy consumption in this layer. The sensors are of various types. Most of the sensors sense an analog data value. It then converts the analog signal to digital data. Further, the data get stored into some temporary buffer. In this context, we can consider various layers where the data can be stored, and buffered.

2.4.1 Edge Level Buffer

In this case, the buffering is done at the edge of the network [6]. The edge computing nodes, which are used for the edge level processing, can do the buffering in this case. The nodes in this case can do the processing of the data as well. This is because the nodes have green processing devices which can do the processing of the data. Moreover, the intermediate data get buffered in the edge buffer temporarily. In most cases, the data preprocessing is done at this level.

2.4.2 Dew Level Buffering

In the next level of hierarchy, the dew computing system has been introduced [7]. In this case, the dew level buffer plays a pivotal role. The dew nodes can be used as data storage. In addition, the nodes are primarily used for computation purposes. To develop a green IoT ecosystem, the Dew nodes play a very crucial role. As we know, the main purpose of dew computing is to ensure support to those areas where the Internet connectivity is poor and there is frequent network disconnectivity. In such a scenario, the data get buffered in a dew node. The network in this case can perform an opportunistic forwarding of the messages to the gateway, which they store in the dew node due to lack of network connectivity. For an MQTT-based IoT system, it is a good idea to place the broker service in the dew node. As a result, the message received by the broker will get redirected to the subscriber node or buffered in the dew node temporarily.

2.5 Green IoT Challenges

The IoT systems primarily comprise numerous sensors and actuator devices. Various researches, therefore, focus on the optimization of the power-hungry resources

Table 1 Comparative study of various research problems in Green IoT based 5G ecosystem

Research title	Research area	Scope	Research direction
A Survey on Green 6G Network: Architecture and Technologies [8]	5G and B5G network communication	Computation storage and buffering	Edge enabled green communication
Towards Green Mobile Edge Computing Offloading Systems with Security Enhancement [9]	Edge-based CPS	Dew level buffering	Dew buffer management in a highly intermittent network scenario
Green UAV communications for 6G: A survey [10]	Energy consumption modeling of the UAV node and the networks	Energy harvesting from on-the-flight UAV node.	Utilization of the harvested energy to drive the low power sensing and the computing equipment
6G CloudNet: Towards a Distributed, Autonomous, and Federated AI-Enabled Cloud and Edge Computing [11]	Multimodal and multi-dimensional network configuration	Edge-dew-cloud network ecosystem design	Hybrid energy-aware load balancing for edge-dew-cloud network architecture.
ECMS: An Edge Intelligent Energy Efficient Model in Mobile Edge Computing [12]	Energy optimization for mobile edge device	Load balancing in mobile edge computing	Load balancing methodology in edge-dew-cloud infrastructure for IoT

like the processor, memory and buffers, storage, and the network. The network protocols must be redesigned and organized so that they can act efficiently in terms of power efficiency and resource utilization. The application layers of such protocols must confirm the effective message transfer in a high battery constrain environment. Table 1 illustrates the various research components of Green IoT and their implementation and scope.

2.6 Network Slicing Under 6G Mobile Edge

The software-defined network is a key methodology that we need to consider to build an efficient and high-performance network ecosystem. The fundamental slice comprises the network function virtualization (NFV). In this concept, we primarily do an emphasis on the access network and the core network. The software-defined access network primarily realizes the hardware components and platforms to enhance the speed of cloud-native environment and leverage the cost-effective IT and network infrastructure. Orchestration, automation, and analytics are the prime component of the access network. The SDN orchestration or SDN policy orchestration implies the coordination of the software actions with the SDN controllers. The controller in this case can produce independent decision-making about the network traffic management, security, fault detection, and many more. The implementation of the slice allocation based on the core and the access network is a primary task in this case. Algorithm 1 in this case signifies the slicing under access and the core network [4, 13]. In this case, the coverage ratio plays a significant role. The algorithm keeps track of the number of active slices and rejected clients. The entire simulation has been carried out in slicesim simulator. In line 5 based on the end of the simulation time, the request has been accessed. In each case, if the AND of access and core network implies the slice index then the corresponding slice goes to the active slice set. The cline is then assigned to the active slice. If the condition is not satisfied then the client goes to reject set. The coverage on the other hand can be computed as the total coverage of the slice based on the network itself. The coverage per user can be derived as the coverage value divided by the number of users. The coverage ratio on the other hand is a ratio between coverage per user to the number of the active slices.

Algorithm 1: Network Slicing Under Access Network and Core Network

1. *Input: user, rad, cent; output : active_slice, α(cov_ratio)*
2. *active_slice $\leftarrow$ {ϕ}*
3. *rej_clinet $\leftarrow$ {ϕ}*
4. *start*
mod1:
5. *for $t = 0$ to sim_time -1*
6. *req $\leftarrow$ get_req(s_i, a_i, c_i)*
7. *for req $= (s_i, a_i, c_i) \in (S, A, C)$*
8. *if index(c_i) $\wedge$ index(a_i)=index(s_i)*
9. *active_slice $\leftarrow$ active_slice $\cup$ req*
10. *else*
11. *req_count $\leftarrow$ req_count+1*
12. *rej_client $\leftarrow$ rej_client $\cup$ req*
mod2:
13. *cov $= \sqrt{\sum_1^{active\_slice} (rad - cent)^2}$*
14. *covpu $=$ cov/user*
15. *$\alpha =$ covpu/active_slice*
16. *return α*
17. *end*

3 Sustainable Green Sensing

With the advent of emerging technologies in the domain of the Internet of Things (IoT) sensors and transducers form the basis upon which whole systems are built. Sensors are deployed to form a network of sensing paradigms connected both in wired and wireless manners. The receptions of signals from the input sensors are converted to digital inputs employing converters for further processing. The digital data if needed are transformed and stored accordingly. The present section gives an overview of wireless sensing and sensor cloud architecture.

3.1 WSNs Application Perspective

WSNs form one of the bases of any remote sensing architecture having their application and use in domains ranging from medical, industrial to military. WSNs are formed with the combined use of heterogeneous or homogeneous sensor nodes. The sensors are deployed with the objective of ambient data gathering in the particular point of interest about different applications. The gathered data is routed efficiently towards the source or sink nodes, which are further routed back to the main server. Energy is one of the most crucial resources in any WSN. Optimizing the network parameters directly impacts the energy utilization of the system. The present section discusses some of the applications of WSN and presents a brief overview and design perspective of the energy-optimized WSN.

Sustainable agriculture is of prime importance in the present smart era. Sustainable agriculture involves minimizing the labor-intensive task, increasing crop yield, and minimizing waste. The very first task lies in selecting the proper soil for the crops. Soil testing involves the estimation of the number of components such as phosphorus, moisture, temperature, nitrogen level, ... etc. Every individual crop requires different levels of such attributes for its proper growth. Paul et al. in [14] proposed a prediction and analysis using machine learning for predicting crop growth. The authors have used the soil testing dataset and have performed analysis using two traditional classification methodologies Naïve Bayes and k-Nearest neighbor. Here, kNN is a distance-based classifier where the nearest neighbor based on the distance is estimated to form the class boundaries. Naïve Bayes is a probabilistic classifier that is based on the Bayes theorem. It can be applied in the following manner as stated in Eq. 1.

$$M(y|x) = \frac{M(y)M(y)}{M(x)} \tag{1}$$

Here, $M(y|x)$ is the probability of class labels occurring such that the given attributes, in this case, are the soil attributes. Here, y is the class label, and x is the soil features. The authors have used three class labels (M) Medium, (H) High, and (L) Low for labeling the quality of the soil. (H) denotes the crop yielding quality is high, while (L) denotes low crop yielding.

Sustainable agriculture requires the development of ambient monitoring of events pertaining to the crops as well as the environment. For any sustainable agriculture development, it is essential to gather the data pertaining to the factors that the crops will require to grow such as rainfall, moisture, other important chemicals and

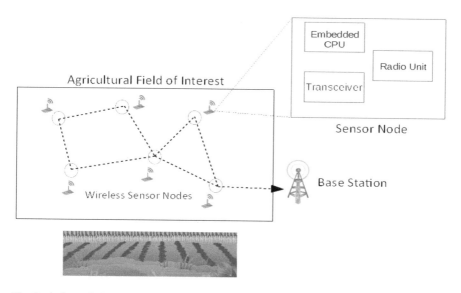

Fig. 2 A Green WSN framework for collecting essential environmental data in the agricultural field

gases, etc. A few of the other factors are the external environmental events that enhance the germination process. Factors such as fungus growth, are insects disrupt and damage the crops. De et al. in [15] proposed a sustainable design of WSN in agriculture. The design of a sustainable agricultural framework is depicted in Fig. 2. The authors have utilized edge-level embedded CPU with each sensor node with memory systems such as flash memory and radio transceivers for transmission. The proposed framework is an ad hoc [16] network platform.

The deployed sensors included various environmental monitoring sensors along with a camera module. The gathered data is routed towards a common sink node or a base station for further analysis and monitoring. Presently with the integration of IoT, the agricultural food industry catered with the use of UAV sprayers, automatic irrigation and fertilizer systems, etc. The use of sensors is also utilized in the harvesting and packaging process. A new term is *"Agrifood 4.0"* proposed by Miranda et al. in [17] denotes the growing technological development in the domain of agriculture. In the present time, the use of agricultural robots, intelligent greenhouses, crop monitoring systems are utilized for better crop management. The application of outdoor sensing is vast. Dyo et al. in [18] proposed a sustainable design for the deployment of sensors in forest areas for wildlife monitoring. The authors proposed a monitoring platform of badgers that had RFID tags and the monitoring was carried out using RFID detection nodes deployed in the forest area. Wireless Personal Area Networks (IEEE 802.15) are used for data transmission. The information is routed in a hop by hop manner towards a sink node which is connected with 3G links. The proposed approach was carried out for figuring the co-location patterns of badgers. Another sustainable sensing design for forests can be found in [19]; the authors have proposed a canopy closure monitoring that estimates the tree shadow on varying solar attitudes. The sensing was done using a photodiode connected with an MSP430 processor and CC240 transceiver. Sustainable deployment of sensors involves increasing the lifetime of the WSN. The authors in [20] have performed an analysis in the deployment of the sensors. Incorrect measurements are another important aspect that is caused due to the sensor calibration. The authors have proposed an efficient place and sensor calibration approach to increase the lifetime.

3.2   Energy Efficient Sensor Networks Integrating 5G & 6G

Beyond 5G (B5G) technologies are in the developmental stage, but are already being integrated into the wireless sensing paradigm. Energy efficiency in WSNs majorly falls mainly into two categories: sustaining the sensor battery and the network lifetime. Beyond 5G technologies use advanced frequency spectrum for efficient routing and transfer mechanism. The data gathering mechanism in a wireless sensor network requires an efficient data aggregation mechanism to increase the lifetime of the network. An efficient edge-level healthcare monitoring system and routing mechanism using 6G technology are presented by Mardini et al. in [21]. An IPv6 based routing protocol for low power and lossy network (RPL) is defined. In the hospital, patient care monitoring requires the use of sensors connected to patients for real-time monitoring. The network system is popularly termed as Wireless Body Area Network(WBAN). The authors have proposed an efficient monitoring system where sensor nodes are deployed throughout the building on multiple floors. An efficient routing framework is proposed pertaining to the criticality of the network packets pertaining to each room. The RPL was developed to be used as a set of methods to perform tasks pertaining to neighbor reachability, getting information on link packets within data packets, and spreading information over the network topology dynamically.

Another work presented by Mukherjee et al. in [22] presents the energy-efficient system model for industrial 6G applications. The sensors nodes as we know are energy-limited nodes, thus the authors have utilized distributed artificial intelligence to cluster the nodes and allocate the resources in energy efficient manner among the nodes. The sensor nodes are clustered and a cluster head is elected among the nodes in the cluster. The framework of the design follows a dynamic management agent (MA), which is responsible for managing all nodes' resources. A Convolution Neural Network (CNN) is used to optimize the data collected by the nodes in the network. The proposed approach balances the power demand of the network and increases the network lifetime.

One of the important aspects of increasing the sensor networks lifetime is to control the network traffic and proposition better packet collision avoidance solutions. Such a solution is proposed by Lv et al. in [23, 24], where the authors have defined software-defined network (SDN) solutions for the 6G platform. The work analyzes the dual-channel architecture of the software-defined sensor node architecture. The results show that the SDN effectively reduces network congestion and increases the quality of service thereby the lifetime of the system.

4 Federated Learning for 6G Mobile Network

Classical machine learning always requires data that must be available in a centralized environment. Human-centric mobile traffic needs distributed machine learning. This is the fundamental backbone for the developed B5G and 6G mobile networks [25]. Nowadays, classical training of the Machine learning model requires the centralization of the training data on a single server. Since a bulk amount of information needs to be uploaded to the cloud data center, transmission latency is very high. User privacy may also be compromised in this case. Low-latency and privacy requirements are crucial in the cutting edge application development paradigm, such as unmanned aerial vehicles, AR-VR applications, driverless vehicles, which leverage a centralized machine learning methodology. Due to limited communication resources, the transmission of the collected data to the data center is crucial. Therefore, it becomes largely significant to process data at edge devices. This results in an emergency of decentralized optimization mechanisms. In the case of decentralized optimization, each site can compute data and send the final intermediate computed value to its nearby or a central node. Decentralized optimization has numerous applications, such as resource allocation optimization, user selection, and trajectory optimization, and distributed intelligent learning design [26]. Leveraging the utility of decentralized optimization and machine learning, FL frameworks are needed to exploit wireless nodes to jointly build, deploy and share ML model with training taking place in local nodes. The emerging Federated Learning (FL) is one of the most challenging distributed learning methodologies in this case [27, 28]. This framework is a prime component in the next-generation Internet of Things (IoT) systems. In FL, Smartphone like devices can cooperatively execute a training and validation task by only uploading local learning models to the ground station (GS) nodes. Figure 3 depicts the distributed learning methodology. Since the data center cannot access the local data sets at the users, FL can protect the data privacy of the users.

4.1 FL Based Mobile Edge Computing in the 6G Era Has the Following Benefits

(i) Personal embedded learning model parameters with small size data set instead of the very large train and test data reduce energy consumption and, effectively reduce transmission latency [29, 30]. FL methodology persists in data security

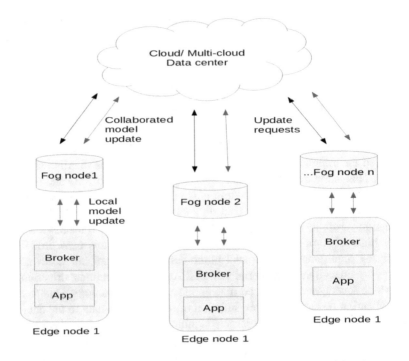

Fig. 3 A collaborative machine learning methodology without centralized training data

as the training data present at each subsystem and the ML model parameter are executed in the local machine. This approach is extremely useful for the development of the Artificial Intelligent of Things applications.

(ii) Often the diversified models with heterogeneous data are used to train several classifiers in a decentralized manner, which increase the chance of achieving considerable good accuracy, especially on a vast domain [31–33]. FL is undoubtedly scalable as the increasing volume of data offers a significant amount of accuracy by increasing the number of computing nodes and edge processing units and providing a unique way-out for huge scalable training and testing where buffer size is the ultimate issue. FL can be used to manipulate extremely precise optimization problems in various domains like network optimization, clustering, user coverage, system management, and many more. Besides, FL enables users to collaboratively train and validate shared classification and regression models for user behavior predictions, user coverage, authentication, and wireless parameter analysis [34–36]. Based on the prediction value obtained, the station can efficiently allocate the network resources for the various devices.

4.2 Artificial Intelligence of Things for Edge Enabled Mobile Computing

The edge cloud orchestration is the primary backbone of Artificial Intelligence of Things (IoT). The fragmentation of the intelligent algorithm in the edge cloud ecosystem is the primary target; in this case, to ensure edge dew fog and cloud level load balancing by logically distributing the intelligent decision [37]. Nowadays most of the IoT devices that are deployed in the perception layer continuously gather a huge amount of data. To achieve maximum performance the AI models get deployed in each layer of the IoT service. The amalgamation of AI and IoT under a single umbrella is majorly considered as AIoT in this case. Various advantages can be considered in this case as explained next.

(a) **Flexibility of the system**: The system is highly flexible as each layer and the device endpoint are equipped with computing and storage modules. The edge servers in this case also may contain simple machine learning modes like feature extractors or classifiers. Various Quality of Service (QoS) has to be guaranteed by the edge devices by numerous delay ranges [38]. Network latency management, in this case, plays a vital role as most of the edge devices are placed in remote places, or sometimes they are part of the vehicular network. The devices that are not intelligent enough can send their data to the cloud for intelligent processing.

(b) **Intelligent decision making**: A large number of edge devices may sense and collect the data. The onboard intelligent predictor can help the whole system to generate a decision. The architecture of the system is deployed in such a way that the large intelligent deep model gets segregated into small components. Typically in the case of neural networks, the input and the second layer can be deployed in an edge device, where the hidden layers may be deployed into the fog and cloud layers [39].

(c) **Knowledge distillation and buffering**: Knowledge distillation signifies a fabrication of a complex AI model in a decentralized manner. Dew computing methodology is extremely useful to achieve this. The deep learning model in this case gets fragmentized and the intermediated data get buffered in a new node. In a mission-critical scenario, the dew-enabled drone network may be used to serve this feature [40–45]. The knowledge distillation method maybe incorporated in the "softmax" output layer to increase efficiency [46, 47]. The hint-based training method is also a popular mechanism that ensures better training accuracy for the AI models in this case.

5   Conclusion

The chapter discusses the various technological aspects of green mobile edge computing for Beyond 5G and 6G aspects. The major challenges in the intermittently connected networks are data gathering and data buffering. We have presented the edge level, fog level, and dew level buffering in this case. The dew level buffering plays a vital role in the intermittently connected network. This ensures the robustness, scalability, and load balancing of the edge-dew-cloud architecture. Moreover, the 6G enabled network slicing mechanism has been highlighted. The allocation of the slice-based on core and access network is also discussed. The state-of-the-art slicing methodologies have been discussed in an algorithmic form. Further, green sensing is another aspect of mobile computing that primarily emphasizes optimized sensing algorithms. The energy-efficient sensing algorithms are extremely useful in such cases. Finally, the federated learning-based with Artificial Intelligent of Things (AIoT) approach has also been addressed in the context of green mobile edge computing for the Internet of Things. The mechanism emphasizes the efficient utilization and fragmentation of the model training aspect by optimizing the available system and network resources.

References

1. Gushev, M.: Dew computing architecture for cyber-physical systems and IoT. Internet of Things. **11**, 100186 (2020)
2. Xu, J., Ota, K., Dong, M.: Big data on the fly: UAV-mounted mobile edge computing for disaster management. IEEE Trans. Netw. Sci. Eng. **7**(4), 2620–2630 (2020)
3. Yao, S., Feng, L., Zhao, J., Zhao, Q., Yang, Q., Jiang, W.: PatternBee: enabling ZigBee-to-BLE direct communication by offset resistant patterns. IEEE Wirel. Commun. (2021)
4. Mukherjee, A., Dey, N., Mondal, A., De, D., Crespo, R.G.: iSocialDrone: QoS aware MQTT middleware for social internet of drone things in 6G-SDN slice. Soft. Comput., 1–17 (2021)
5. de Matos, F.F., Rego, P.A., Trinta, F.A.: Secure computational offloading with gRPC: a performance evaluation in a mobile cloud computing environment. In: Proceedings of the 11th ACM Symposium on Design and Analysis of Intelligent Vehicular Networks and Applications, pp. 45–52 (2021)
6. Qiu, T., Chi, J., Zhou, X., Ning, Z., Atiquzzaman, M., Wu, D.O.: Edge computing in industrial internet of things: architecture, advances and challenges. IEEE Commun. Surv. Tutor. **22**(4), 2462–2488 (2020)
7. Singh, P., Kaur, A., Aujla, G.S., Batth, R.S., Kanhere, S.: Daas: dew computing as a service for intelligent intrusion detection in edge-of-things ecosystem. IEEE Internet Things J. (2020)
8. Goyal, S., Sharma, N., Kaushik, I., Bhushan, B., Kumar, N.: A green 6G network era: architecture and propitious technologies. In: Data Analytics and Management, pp. 59–75. Springer, Singapore (2021)
9. Sun, H., Wang, Q., Ma, X., Xu, Y., Hu, R.Q.: Towards green mobile edge computing offloading systems with security enhancement. In: 2020 Intermountain Engineering, Technology and Computing (IETC), pp. 1–6. IEEE (2020)
10. Jiang, X., Sheng, M., Zhao, N., Xing, C., Weidang, L., Wang, X.: Green UAV communications for 6G: a survey. Chin. J. Aeronaut. (2021)

11. Alimi, I.A., Patel, R.K., Zaouga, A., Muga, N.J., Pinto, A.N., Teixeira, A.L., Monteiro, P.P.: 6G CloudNet: towards a distributed, autonomous, and federated AI-enabled cloud and edge computing. In: 6G Mobile Wireless Networks, pp. 251–283. Springer, Cham (2021)
12. Zhou, Z., Shojafar, M., Abawajy, J., Yin, H., Hongming, L.: ECMS: an edge intelligent energy efficient model in mobile edge computing. IEEE Trans. Green Commun. Netw. (2021)
13. Mukherjee, A., Mukherjee, P., De, D., Dey, N.: QoS-aware 6G-enabled ultra low latency edge-assisted Internet of Drone Things for real-time stride analysis. Comput. Electr. Eng. **95**, 107438 (2021)
14. Paul, M., Vishwakarma, S.K., Verma, A.: Analysis of soil behaviour and prediction of crop yield using data mining approach. In: 2015 International Conference on Computational Intelligence and Communication Networks (CICN), pp. 766–771. IEEE (2015)
15. De La Concepcion, A.R., Stefanelli, R., Trinchero, D.: A wireless sensor network platform optimized for assisted sustainable agriculture. In: IEEE Global Humanitarian Technology Conference (GHTC 2014), pp. 159–165. IEEE (2014)
16. Mohapatra, P., Krishnamurthy, S. (eds.): AD HOC NETWORKS: Technologies and Protocols. Springer (2004)
17. Miranda, J., Ponce, P., Molina, A., Wright, P.: Sensing, smart and sustainable technologies for Agri-Food 4.0. Comput. Ind. **108**, 21–36 (2019)
18. Dyo, V., Ellwood, S.A., Macdonald, D.W., Markham, A., Trigoni, N., Wohlers, R., Mascolo, C., Pásztor, B., Scellato, S., Yousef, K.: WILDSENSING: design and deployment of a sustainable sensor network for wildlife monitoring. ACM Trans. Sens. Netw. (TOSN). **8**(4), 1–33 (2012)
19. Mo, L., He, Y., Liu, Y., Zhao, J., Tang, S.J., Li, X.Y., Dai, G.: Canopy closure estimates with greenorbs: sustainable sensing in the forest. In: Proceedings of the 7th ACM Conference on Embedded Networked Sensor Systems, pp. 99–112 (2009)
20. Mardini, W., Aljawarneh, S., Al-Abdi, A.: Using multiple RPL instances to enhance the performance of new 6G and Internet of Everything (6G/IoE)-based healthcare monitoring systems. Mobile Netw. Appl., 1–17 (2020)
21. Mukherjee, A., Goswami, P., Khan, M.A., Manman, L., Yang, L., Pillai, P.: Energy-efficient resource allocation strategy in massive IoT for industrial 6G applications. IEEE Internet Things J. **8**(7), 5194–5201 (2020)
22. Lv, Z., Kumar, N.: Software defined solutions for sensors in 6G/IoE. Comput. Commun. **153**, 42–47 (2020)
23. Saad, W., Bennis, M., Chen, M.: A vision of 6G wireless systems: applications, trends, technologies, and open research problems. IEEE Netw. **34**(3), 134–142 (2020)
24. Chen, M., Yang, Z., Saad, W., Yin, C., Poor, H.V., Cui, S.: A joint learning and communications framework for federated learning over wireless networks. IEEE Trans. Wirel. Commun. (2020)
25. Konečný, J., McMahan, H.B., Ramage, D., Richtárik, P.: Federated optimization: distributed machine learning for on-device intelligence. arXiv preprint arXiv, 1610.02527 (2016)
26. Zhu, G., Wang, Y., Huang, K.: Broadband analog aggregation for low-latency federated edge learning. IEEE Trans. Wirel. Commun. **19**(1), 491–506 (2019)
27. Zhu, G., Du, Y., Gunduz, D., Huang, K.: One-bit over-the-air aggregation for communication-efficient federated edge learning: design and convergence analysis. arXiv preprint arXiv, 2001.05713 (2020)
28. Zeng, Q., Du, Y., Huang, K., Leung, K.K.: Energy-efficient resource management for federated edge learning with CPU-GPU heterogeneous computing. arXiv preprint arXiv, 2007.07122 (2020)
29. Amiri, M.M., Gündüz, D.: Federated learning over wireless fading channels. IEEE Trans. Wirel. Commun. **19**(5), 3546–3557 (2020)
30. Hosseinalipour, S., Brinton, C.G., Aggarwal, V., Dai, H., Chiang, M.: From federated learning to fog learning: towards large-scale distributed machine learning in heterogeneous wireless networks. arXiv preprint arXiv, 2006.03594 (2020)

31. Hosseinalipour, S., Azam, S.S., Brinton, C.G., Michelusi, N., Aggarwal, V., Love, D.J., Dai, H.: Multi-stage hybrid federated learning over large-scale wireless fog networks. arXiv preprint arXiv, 2007.09511 (2020)
32. Jin, R., He, X., Dai, H.: On the design of communication efficient federated learning over wireless networks. arXiv preprint arXiv, 2004.07351 (2020)
33. Liu, D., Simeone, O.: Privacy for free: wireless federated learning via uncoded transmission with adaptive power control. arXiv preprint arXiv, 2006.05459 (2020)
34. Kassab, R., Simeone, O.: Federated generalized Bayesian learning via distributed stein variational gradient descent. arXiv preprint arXiv, 2009.06419 (2020)
35. Kairouz, P., McMahan, H.B., Avent, B., Bellet, A., Bennis, M., Bhagoji, A.N., Bonawitz, K., Charles, Z., Cormode, G., Cummings, R., et al.: Advances and open problems in federated learning. arXiv preprint arXiv, 1912.04977 (2019)
36. Samarakoon, S., Bennis, M., Saad, W., Debbah, M.: Distributed federated learning for ultra-reliable low-latency vehicular communications. IEEE Trans. Commun. **68**(2), 1146–1159 (2019)
37. Chang, Z., Liu, S., Xiong, X., Cai, Z., Guoqing, T.: A survey of recent advances in edge-computing-powered artificial intelligence of things. IEEE Internet Things J. (2021)
38. Shi, Q., Zhang, Z., Yang, Y., Shan, X., Salam, B., Lee, C.: Artificial Intelligence of Things (AIoT) enabled floor monitoring system for smart home applications. ACS Nano. **15**(11), 18312–18326 (2021)
39. Yu, K., Guo, Z., Yu, S., Wang, W., Lin, J.C.-W., Sato, T.: Secure artificial intelligence of things for implicit group recommendations. IEEE Internet Things J. (2021)
40. Mukherjee, A., De, D., Dey, N.: Dewdrone: dew computing for internet of drone things. IEEE Consum. Electron. Mag. (2021)
41. De, D.: Mobile Cloud Computing: Architectures, Algorithms and Applications. Chapman and Hall/CRC (2019)
42. Mukherjee, A., Gupta, P., De, D.: Mobile cloud computing based energy efficient offloading strategies for femtocell network. In: 2014 Applications and Innovations in Mobile Computing (AIMoC), pp. 28–35. IEEE (2014)
43. Mukherjee, A., De, D., Ghosh, S.K., Buyya, R.: Mobile Edge Computing (2022)
44. Sengupta, A., Gill, S.S., Das, A., De, D.: Mobile edge computing based internet of agricultural things: a systematic review and future directions. Mobile Edge Comput., 415–441 (2021)
45. Pal, S., De, D., Buyya, R.: Artificial Intelligence-Based Internet of Things Systems (2022)
46. Obaidat, M.S., Nicopolitidis, P.: Smart Cities and HomesKey Enabling Technologies. Elsevier (2016)
47. Obaidat, M.S., Anpalagan, A., Woungang, I.: Handbook of Green Information and Communication Systems. Elsevier (2013)

Resource Management for Future Green Mobile Cloud Computing

Mariia Surmenok, Melody Moh, and Teng-Sheng Moh

1 Introduction

Mobile Cloud Computing emerged to fulfill the demand for external processing power for mobile devices. Cell phones, smartwatches, and other wearable devices produce a lot of data and often need to process it. The internal processing power of mobile devices may not satisfy the time-sensitive tasks and may quickly drain the battery. The possibility of uploading the computational tasks from mobile devices to mobile cloud computing allows processing the job faster while saving the mobile device's battery. As the number of mobile devices is constantly growing, the demand for mobile cloud computing increases, requiring the expansion of mobile cloud computing infrastructure.

Cloud infrastructure consumes a lot of energy, which negatively affects the amount of CO_2 emission. Green cloud computing has become an important research topic to address this problem. There is much research concerning the optimization of energy consumption in cloud computing by developing energy-aware resource management modules and effective architectures.

Resource allocation is an essential part of cloud computing. Its main job is to schedule tasks on hosts and supervise running tasks and resources. The resource management goal is to provide the best possible quality of service, which means that tasks should be processed successfully and in a reasonable amount of time. For the best quality of service in mobile cloud computing settings, the resource management module should also consider that mobile devices may change their location over time.

M. Surmenok · M. Moh (✉) · T.-S. Moh
Department of Computer Science, San Jose State University, San Jose, CA, USA
e-mail: melody.moh@sjsu.edu

© The Author(s), under exclusive license to Springer Nature Switzerland AG 2022
D. De et al. (eds.), *Green Mobile Cloud Computing*,
https://doi.org/10.1007/978-3-031-08038-8_14

Another objective of resource management is to increase the resource utilization of underlying cloud computing infrastructure. Thus, it should effectively pack together tasks so that there are a minimum number of idle processing resources but at the same time no overloaded hosts. This is often achieved by an effective initial task placement strategy and, also, by migration tasks during runtime. For example, if all but one task is completed after some time, it may be reasonable to move the last running task to another busier host to turn off the underutilized host. There are many approaches, including evolutionary and machine learning algorithms, predicting the future workload for more effective resource management.

This chapter presents an overview of recent research in resource allocation techniques. It describes virtualization technologies that enable resource allocation in mobile cloud settings and the challenges associated with them. The following sections discuss resource management in a centralized and fog computing environment focusing on energy consumption optimization and quality of service. It then describes on-demand fog formation based on peer-to-peer computing and volunteering devices. Finally, the chapter draws the conclusion and investigates future research opportunities.

2   Architectures and Resource Management Challenges in GMCC

Resource management has different challenges depending on the mobile cloud computing architecture.

The traditional central cloud, depicted in Fig. 1, is characterized by the massive amount of powerful heterogeneous hosts placed in the same location. In order to reduce CO_2 emission, energy-aware resource management is required to optimize the energy consumption in data centers. Thus, the main objective of resource management in traditional data centers is the minimization of the number of underloaded hosts to keep idle hosts shut down. For energy-aware resource management, the challenge is to make an initial placement of tasks on the minimum number of hosts while satisfying the resource requirements and the quality of service. Another challenge is to detect underloaded hosts during the runtime. If the orchestrator is able to find another suitable host to migrate all the tasks from the underloaded host, such an underloaded host can be later shut down to save energy.

The fog computing architecture was proposed by Cisco in 2021. The idea is to place computing resources closer to the users, thus reducing the latency in data transmission. Figure 2 depicts the topology of fog computing. Due to improved latency transmission, fog nodes, placed between mobile devices and a traditional central cloud, can improve energy consumption and provide a better quality of service for time-sensitive applications. The orchestrator for a fog cloud can be centralized or distributed depending on a particular implementation. One of the challenges that resource management in fog architecture faces is making

Fig. 1 Two-layer
architecture where requests
from mobile devices are
processed on traditional
centralized cloud

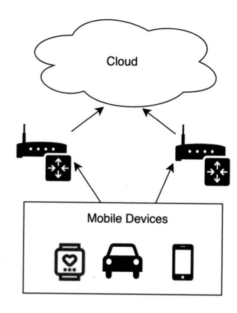

Fig. 2 Three-layer
architecture. Requests from
mobile devices send to the
fog layer for processing. The
fog layer may send requests
to a centralized cloud, for
example, to persist some data.
If fog layer does not have
enough resources to process
request from mobile device,
the request may be directed to
centralized cloud

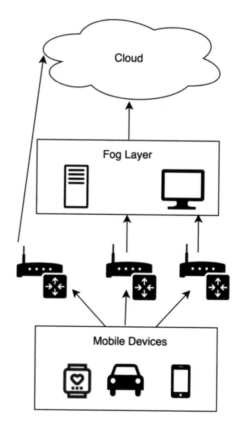

an offloading decision. For each particular task, the resource management module should determine the best place to process the task. Based on the task characteristics, it can be decided to process a task by either mobile device itself, fog node, or send to a traditional central cloud. Another challenge in fog architecture is choosing a suitable fog node for task placement. The resource management service should find the best suitable fog node based on user location and available resources on fog nodes. Also, it may be preferable to place the task on the fog node with access to renewable energy, which can consequently help to reduce CO_2 emissions. Since mobile devices can change their location over time, dynamic resource management may be required. In order to provide the best quality of service and reduce network latency, the task may need to be migrated to another fog node when the mobile device changes its location.

Peer-to-peer technology can be utilized to achieve green mobile cloud computing goals. The idea of peer-to-peer technology is that third-party businesses or individuals share their unutilized processing resources. It will allow forming fog clusters dynamically when there's a demand in a particular location. Peer-to-peer technology can help to improve energy efficiency by using shared devices and can help reduce e-waste. One of the challenges that peer-to-peer technology possesses is that the devices in such a cluster are even more heterogeneous. Another challenge is that the computing power of shared devices can be available for a limited time frame. Thus, in addition to fog computing challenges, resource management should account for time availability when searching for a suitable fog node.

The different architectures have to overcome many challenges to achieve green mobile cloud computing. Some common challenges between traditional cloud and fog architecture are improving resource utilization and reducing the number of running hosts to decrease energy consumption. The introduction of fog computing can improve energy consumption by reducing latency, but schedulers need to be location-aware to leverage this advantage.

3 Virtualization Technologies for Dynamic Resource Allocation for GMCC

There are multiple approaches to host applications on a physical machine. The comparison diagrams of different virtualization approaches are depicted on Fig. 3. Traditionally, virtual machines are used in cloud computing. Virtualization helps to achieve green mobile cloud computing by running multiple tasks on the same physical hosts.

In addition to traditional virtual machines, the recently emerging containerization technology is used to deploy tasks from mobile devices. Mobile cloud computing can use either virtual machines, containers placed on physical hosts, or two-level virtualization where containers are deployed on top of virtual machines. Containers

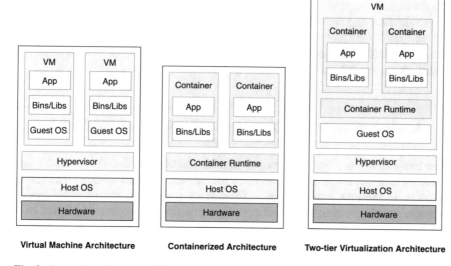

Fig. 3 Comparison between different virtualization technologies. The service can be deployed either inside a VM, a container, or a container placed in a VM

are compact comparing to virtual machines. Therefore, it allows packing more tasks on the same physical host, consequently improving resource utilization and decreasing energy consumption.

If there's a need to migrate a task from one host to another during runtime, the containers have an advantage over virtual machines. Because of its small size, container migration consumes less energy for sending all the information from one host to another.

However, there are still several challenges that need to be solved for containerization technology. Since all the containers placed on the same host share resources, there's a possibility of a security threat. Container security is an active research topic. Some researchers used two-level virtualization to alleviate this problem by placing containers that belong to the same user into a separate virtual machine.

Another challenge that container technology faces is live migration. Live migration is the ability to move a container or virtual machine from one physical host to another without losing the current progress of the task. It is one of the critical components of dynamic resource allocation in order to balance resource utilization and prevent SLA violation during runtime. Live migration is well studied for virtual machines. For containers, live migration is still under development. There is some recent research about live migration for containers, including work around using CRIU. However, such approaches are not widely adopted yet. For example, Kubernetes, one of the most popular container orchestrators, doesn't have live migration.

Both containers and virtual machines can help achieve green mobile cloud computing by improving resource utilization, decreasing the number of running physical hosts, and reducing energy consumption. Virtual machines technology is a well-established tool proved by time. On the other hand, containerization is a promising technology and can help to reduce CO_2 emission even more if some key challenges, such as security and live migration, will be overcome.

4 Analysis of Resource Management in Centralized GMCC

The traditional cloud data centers provide massive computational capabilities and virtually unlimited data storage services for mobile cloud computing. The recent research in resource management is focused on optimizing energy consumption while supporting a high quality of service, particularly in containerized and two-tier virtualized environments. The papers that discuss resource management in a centralized cloud are summarized in Table 1. Some research works also use workload prediction to foresee the nearest future load to improve the decision regarding task placement and tasks migration. The general system model is depicted on Fig. 4.

Zhang et al. [1] proposed an energy-aware framework for two-tier virtualized heterogeneous cloud data centers. In this setting, only the containers belonging to the same job can be placed on the same virtual machine, providing an additional security level. For the problem formulation, the authors used an energy model, including the overhead of creating a virtual machine and the SLA metric. The

Table 1 Summary of Resource Management Methods in Cloud Computing

Publication	Methods used	Objectives		
		Energy	Time	Utilization
Zhang [1]	ARIMA and TSMM	✓	✓	✓
Gholipour [3]	MCDM	✓		✓
HeporCloud [4]	Statistical	✓	✓	
Zhong [5]	BF			✓

ML machine learning, *BF* best fit, *ARIMA* autoregressive integrated moving average, *TSMM* two-sided matching method, *MCDM* multi criteria decision matrix

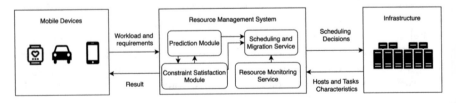

Fig. 4 General system model of resource management in Mobile Cloud Computing

framework had to solve several tasks for the initial placement and dynamic consolidation at runtime, detecting underloaded and overloaded VMs and hosts and making a decision for container migration. To find the best hosts for VMs, Zhang et al. used a many-to-one two-sided matching method where both VMs and hosts calculate the coefficient to find the subset of the desired pair. For underloaded and overloaded host and VMs detection, the authors employed the ARIMA algorithm to predict the resource usage in the nearest future to prevent unnecessary container migration. Their approach outperforms the combination of classical algorithms and state-of-the-art methods in terms of energy consumption by at least 13.8%.

The prediction of future load can help to optimize the energy consumption in mobile cloud computing. Chen et al. [2] used auto-encoder and gated RNN to predict high-dimensional workload for cloud datacenters. The authors used a top-sparse auto-encoder to compress the highly dimensional and highly variable data produced by data centers. This approach helps make an accurate workload prediction for the nearest future. Thus, the resource management module can power up additional hosts in advance to meet future demand. Making hosts available in advance, reduces the time for scaling which consequently improves the quality of service. Also, it helps to minimize energy consumption by powering off unused hosts in response to predicted low demand in the future.

Gholipour et al. [3] proposed a joint VM and container consolidation algorithm for energy-aware resource management in a two-tier virtualized heterogeneous cloud computing data center. The goal is to place containers in the minimum number of virtual machines and place virtual machines on the smallest number of physical servers. Joint VM and container consolidation policy identify whether virtual machine or container should be migrated during runtime. Resource correlation is calculated to find which virtual machine causes the overloading of the server. The multi-criteria decision matrix determines whether the virtual machine or only containers from this virtual machine should be migrated during the runtime. This approach helps to make a more precise decision during runtime and reduce the number of migrations while achieving significant energy reduction compared to other state-of-the-art methods.

Khan et al. [4] considered three types of virtualization technologies plus bare metal at the same time to improve energy usage. They argued that different applications perform better on a particular type. If the best virtualization platform is chosen for a service, it will complete the task faster and help reduce the energy consumption and quality of service. There are four types of platforms in their framework simultaneously, such as bare-metal, containers only, virtual machines only, and containers over a virtual machine. The authors used the ERP metric (energy response time per product) for the problem formulation, which expresses energy consumption and SLA metric. The orchestrator places jobs on a particular platform based on a statistical method finding similar jobs from the past. The migration decision for containers or virtual machines is policy-based and triggered when a specific threshold is reached. The migration is not initiated if the predicted remaining runtime is too small, thus, preventing the migration when it is more beneficial to finish the task on the original host.

Zhong and Buyya [5] considered two main types of jobs, long-running and batch jobs, for cost optimization. They modified the original Kubernetes orchestrator for dynamic resource management of a heterogeneous cloud computing datacenter. To improve the resource utilization of machines, Zhong and Buyya placed the same type of jobs with a similar expected completion time. Thus, the batch jobs will complete at approximately the same time, freeing the whole machine. For dynamic resource management, they employed live task migration via CRIU and task-packing using best fit decreasing. The decision for migration is policy-based and triggered when utilization of the host falls below the 50% threshold. For task scheduling, the authors found out that it may be more practical to place tasks on a single powerful machine than a few less powerful ones since the cost of the more powerful host is less than a couple of slower hosts. Even though the focus of this paper is cost optimization, this paper can be useful for future green mobile cloud computing research. Assuming that the energy consumption of one powerful host is smaller than two less powerful physical machines, a similar approach can be employed to reduce energy consumption in data centers. Thus, moving services from multiple less powerful machines to just a few high-performance hosts can be a part of the energy consumption optimization strategy.

There is much advancement in research for resource management for centralized data centers. However, the speed of resource management modules is still a challenge for time-sensitive mobile cloud computing applications. The resource management modules need to find optimal initial placement for a task quickly, supervise already running tasks and hosts. Furthermore, such a framework needs to detect underloaded and overloaded hosts and make migration decisions to maintain low energy consumption while preventing SLA violations.

5   Analysis of Resource Management in Fog and Edge GMCC

The purpose of fog computing is to provide processing power near edge devices. The workflow example is shown in Fig. 5 where fog nodes process the jobs from mobile devices and use a centralized cloud for permanent data storage. Fog nodes usually are less powerful than the traditional cloud data centers and have different locations along the network. These features bring challenges specific to resource management in fog computing. The papers that discuss resource management in a fog environment are summarized in Table 2.

In their work, Ren et al. [6] proposed a hybrid algorithm to reduce energy consumption in the fog environment. They presented the combination of Genetic (GA) and Ant Colony Optimization (ACO) algorithms for scheduling services into fog nodes. GA and ACO run in parallel and update each other values after each iteration to improve the overall performance and faster convergence. In addition to makespan, energy consumption, and cost, Ren et al. took into account dynamic requirements, where the user requests the decreasing deadline. The authors verified that their approach is scalable to up to 2000 services and 800 physical hosts.

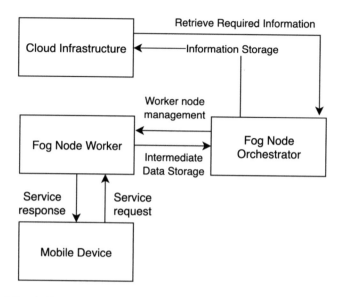

Fig. 5 Workflow in Fog Mobile Cloud Computing

Kauk et al. [7] proposed a Kubernetes-based scheduler for the edge-cloud ecosystem. The objective of their scheduler is to reduce carbon footprint, optimize energy consumption, and improve performance by minimizing the inference among co-located containers. To reduce the interference, Kauk et al. proposed to place similar containers into the same hosts identifying jobs either as CPU or network intensive. The authors wanted to maximize the use of available green energy resources and minimize active hosts. To achieve this, Kauk et al. expressed the problem as an integer linear programming problem and used Mosek solver to find an optimal solution.

Huang et al. [8] used Deep Reinforcement Learning to schedule jobs in Kubernetes clusters. Their Deep Q-Learning model was trained to schedule batch jobs between multiple homogeneous clusters. The goal is to balance the average utilization among clusters and the average utilization of each resource within each cluster, preventing bottlenecks when a particular resource is scarce. Their approach showed better adaptability to changing workloads. However, if the job cannot be scheduled in the current time frame, the scheduler postpones it to some random time in the future, which will not guarantee that it will be scheduled eventually.

Chen et al. [9] also used Deep Reinforcement Learning for dynamic resource management of joint power control and resources for Mobile Edge Computing (MEC). Assuming that mobile devices have limited battery capacity, it is crucial to consider transmission delay over a wireless network and their battery capacity. Chen et al. took into account the importance of minimizing the long-term processing delay. The authors formulated the problem as a Markov decision problem and used Deep Deterministic Policy Gradient (DDPG) to find the optimal offloading scheme.

Table 2 Summary of Resource Management Methods in Fog Computing

Publication	Methods used			Objectives			
	ML	Metaheuristic	Heuristic	Energy	Time	Utilization	Dynamic changes
Ren [6]		GA and ACO		✓		✓	✓
KEIDS [7]			ILP	✓		✓	
RLSK [8]	DQL					✓	
Chen [9]	DDPG			✓	✓		
Tuli [10]	A3C-R2N2				✓		

GA genetic algorithm, *ACO* ant colony optimization, *ILP* integer linear programming, *DQL* Deep-Q-Learning, *DDPG* Deep Deterministic Policy Gradient, *A3C-R2N2* Asynchronous-Advantage-Actor-Critic Residual Recurrent Neural Network

Tuli et al. [10] also used Deep Reinforcement learning for scheduling tasks in a fog environment. Tuli et al. included the mobility factor into their research and accounted for changing resource and bandwidth requirements for the service. They utilize Policy gradient-based Reinforcement learning method (A3C) to accelerate the learning. In their architecture, the authors used multiple actor-agents at the same time. Each agent has its own neural network and is responsible for its own set of fog nodes allowing it to train networks in parallel. The agents update the shared global parameters, which accelerates the exploration of larger state-action space. Using a residual recurrent neural network allowed to approximate function from state to action and find patterns in the data to predict the future workloads.

There are different approaches for scheduling services in mobile fog computing. In addition to efficient energy usage and resource utilization, the resource management module in fog computing needs to consider the changing location of mobile devices to assign the closest fog nodes for computation. Some effort was also put into saving the mobile device's battery and adapting to changing resource and bandwidth requirements for mobile fog computing. The main approaches of recent research in fog resource management are evolutionary algorithms and reinforcement learning. The main challenge of evolutionary algorithms is to converge fast to produce the quick offloading decision. With deep reinforcement learning, the main challenge and future research are defining action and state-space and how to serve the time-sensitive tasks for mobile fog computing effectively.

6 Peer-to-Peer Technology and Resource Management for GMCC

The peer-to-peer architecture allows to find and use resources on nearby devices. This technology can tremendously improve energy consumption due to reduced time for sending the data. Also, Peer-to-peer technology helps to improve the utilization of computational resources that would be otherwise idle or underutilized. Thus, it prevents wasting the energy of running computers nearby and reduces the number of hosts that need to be turned on in data centers, consequently reducing CO_2 emission. In peer-to-peer architecture, the resource management module can be centralized or spread across the network. The papers that discuss resource management in a peer-to-peer environment are summarized in Table 3.

Table 3 Summary of Resource Management Methods in Peer-to-peer environment

Publication	Methods used		Objectives	
	Metaheuristic	Heuristic	Time	Utilization
HYDRA [11]		FF	✓	
Sami [12]	MA		✓	✓

FF first fit, MA memetic algorithm

Jimenez and Schulen [11] proposed a decentralized location-aware orchestrator for the peer-to-peer network. In their peer-to-peer architecture, each node can simultaneously have multiple roles serving as an orchestrator and the worker. Each node has two ids, one to uniquely identify the node and another to identify node location, similarly to IP addresses. For node discovery, the authors employed a distributed hash table and lookup algorithm that iteratively queries nodes to find the closest nodes to a given ID. First-fit decreasing is used for scheduling services. The experiments showed that the proposed architecture successfully scales to at least 20,000 nodes deploying 99.98% of the 30,000 applications submitted and can withstand network partitioning.

Sami and Mourad [12] proposed on-demand fog formation using volunteering devices near the user. They allow individuals or any business to join their list of volunteers. The resource manager on the centralized cloud maintains a database with the recent information about volunteers, including available resources, time availability, and location. When the demand for a service increases, the cloud chooses volunteering devices to create a fog near the user. The orchestrator is created on one of the volunteering devices or, if the job is time-sensitive, the orchestrator is placed in the cloud for faster fog deployment. The container placement problem is solved using a memetic algorithm. The algorithm's objective is to put services on devices with the best time availability and proximity to the user while maintaining the best quality of service. The authors compared the response time for an increasing number of requests and proved that dynamic fog formation outperforms the cloud, static fog, and remote fog. Although the proposed approach showed the best response time and scalability, security is the primary concern in this paper and needs additional research to maintain the security and privacy of mobile services on volunteering devices.

Peer-to-peer architecture is a promising technology to reduce energy consumption and achieve green mobile cloud computing. Some challenges need to be overcome to adopt this approach, including the security and trust issue and node discovery during network partitioning.

7   Conclusion and Future Research Directions for GMCC

This chapter discusses resource allocation in green mobile cloud computing. The main virtualization technologies' overview is presented and their effect on green mobile cloud computing in resource management.

Different cloud architectures were reviewed, including fog and peer-to-peer technology, and the resource allocation challenges associated with them. The state-of-the-art research paper were surveyed highlighting the interesting approaches and techniques.

Possible future research directions in fog mobile cloud computing include:

- solving the challenges of making the offloading decision, such as deciding if the task should be processed on the device itself, fog node, or sent to a centralized cloud.
- task prioritization
- trust issues in a peer-to-peer approach between volunteering devices
- security challenges
- interference and security issues in containerized architecture
- further improvement in resource allocation to achieve efficient and fast scheduling in a heterogeneous cloud with multiple objectives, balancing the energy optimization and quality of service requirements.

References

1. Zhang, C., Wang, Y., Hao, W., Guo, H.: An energy-aware host resource management framework for two-tier virtualized cloud data centers. IEEE Access. **9**, 3526–3544 (2020)
2. Chen, Z., Jia, H., Min, G., Zomaya, A.Y., El-Ghazawi, T.: Towards accurate prediction for high-dimensional and highly-variable cloud workloads with deep learning. IEEE Trans. Parallel Distrib. Syst. **31**(4), 923–934 (2020)
3. Gholipour, N., Arianyan, E., Buyya, R.: A novel energy-aware resource management technique using joint VM and container consolidation approach for green computing in cloud data centers. Simul. Model Pract. Theory. **104**, 102127 (2020)
4. Khan, A.A., Zakarya, M., Rahman, I.U., Khan, R., Buyya, R.: HeporCloud: an energy and performance efficient resource orchestrator for hybrid heterogeneous cloud computing environments. J. Netw. Comput. Appl. **173**, 102869 (2021)
5. Zhong, Z., Buyya, R.: A cost-efficient container orchestration strategy in kubernetes-based cloud computing infrastructures with heterogeneous resources. ACM Trans. Internet Technol. (TOIT). **20**(2), 1–24 (2020)
6. Ren, X., Zhang, Z., Arefzadeh, S.M.: An energy-aware approach for resource managing in the fog-based Internet of Things using a hybrid algorithm. Int. J. Commun. Syst. **34**(1), e4652 (2021)
7. Kaur, K., Garg, S., Kaddoum, G., Ahmed, S.H., Atiquzzaman, M.: KEIDS: Kubernetes based Energy and Interference Driven Scheduler for industrial IoT in edge-cloud ecosystem. IEEE Internet Things J. **7**(5), 4228–4237 (2020)
8. Huang, J., Xiao, C., Weigang, W.: Rlsk: a job scheduler for federated kubernetes clusters based on reinforcement learning. In: 2020 IEEE International Conference on Cloud Engineering (IC2E), pp. 116–123. IEEE (2020)
9. Chen, Y., Liu, Z., Zhang, Y., Yuan, W., Chen, X., Zhao, L.: Deep reinforcement learning-based dynamic resource management for mobile edge computing in industrial internet of things. IEEE Trans. Ind. Inf. **17**(7), 4925–4934 (2020)
10. Tuli, S., Ilager, S., Ramamohanarao, K., Buyya, R.: Dynamic scheduling for stochastic edge-cloud computing environments using a3c learning and residual recurrent neural networks. IEEE Trans. Mob. Comput. **21**(3), 940–954 (2022)
11. Jimenez, L.L., Schelen, O.: HYDRA: decentralized location-aware orchestration of containerized applications. IEEE Trans. Cloud Computing (Early Access). **16** (2020)
12. Sami, H., Mourad, A.: Dynamic on-demand fog formation offering on-the-fly IoT service deployment. IEEE Trans. Netw. Serv. Manag. **17**(2), 1026–1039 (2020)

A Strategy for Advancing Research and Impact in New Computing Paradigms

Rajkumar Buyya, Sukhpal Singh Gill, Satish Narayana Srirama, Rami Bahsoon, and San Murugesan

1 Introduction

Information Technology (IT) is a fertile area for research and new development. It has progressed significantly and gained widespread applications and adoption. Its future potential is vast, and not yet – and never will be – fully known. What new technologies and applications will emerge and which ones will succeed is anybody's guess. Despite its advances, IT still presents several problems and open challenges. Furthermore, several new computing paradigms, technologies and potential high-impact applications scenarios are emerging. These present huge – and yet to be explored – opportunities for researchers and practitioners [1].

R. Buyya (✉)
Cloud Computing and Distributed Systems (CLOUDS) Laboratory, School of Computing and Information Systems, The University of Melbourne, Parkville, VIC, Australia
e-mail: rbuyya@unimelb.edu.au

S. S. Gill
School of Electronic Engineering and Computer Science, Queen Mary University of London, London, UK

S. N. Srirama
School of Computer and Information Sciences, University of Hyderabad, Hyderabad, India

Mobile & Cloud Lab, Institute of Computer Science, University of Tartu, Tartu, Estonia
e-mail: satish.srirama@uohyd.ac.in

R. Bahsoon
School of Computer Science, University of Birmingham, Birmingham, UK
e-mail: r.bahsoon@cs.bham.ac.uk

S. Murugesan
BRITE Professional Services, Perth, Australia
e-mail: san1@internode.net

To capitalize on the full potential of these new opportunities, researchers need to adopt an effective and holistic strategy for advancing their research in new computing paradigms. But many researchers and research groups fail to visualize a big picture and to generate long-term perspectives; instead, they tend to take a narrow approach, which limit their vision and their success. They also tend to lack adequate drive and required skills for impactful community building for new and emerging computing areas and consequently improve their research quality, productivity, visibility, and transnational impacts [2]. Fostering high quality impactful research calls for strong active communities in the respective field. Strong communities often utilize their "collective research intelligence" to sense pathways and streams that are viable, timely and relevant and to identify and address current and potential future research problems of interest.

In this article, we report on our experience in incubating, developing and systematically evaluating research in emerging paradigm, where we consider cloud computing as a representative case. Our reflection extends more than decade and goes back to 2007, where cloud computing was considered as high risk area for academic research. This is because of the various ambiguities revolving around the technology, lack of rigorous literature describing its foundation and fundamentals, lack of realism, and uncertainty about acceptance and the level of adoption. Emerging areas that are considered to be high risk requires careful systematic navigation into the area to roadmap research, formulate fundamentals, and evaluate the potentials of new directions and to uncover new opportunities for applications and adoptions. A holistic strategy is needed to steer continuous development and evaluation of research, to build a community to accelerate impact and level of adoption.

We share our experience on a strategy that we adopted to advance research and build a prosperous community in emerging and new computing research areas of high risk. In retrospect, the strategy has proven to be effective in accelerating research that matters within the cloud computing area, developing and evaluating sound research foundation, and building an international community of researchers, practitioners and adopters of non-trivial scale. Reflecting on our strategy, we propose nine key elements that accelerated research progression and put cloud computing among the well-established computing areas. The key elements, includes the creation of roadmaps, development of simulators and supporting tools, and developing inspiring application demonstrators that prove feasibility and effectiveness of the new research. Systematic reviews, taxonomies, textbooks and industrial experience reports assist in planning. They can be valuable resource for relevant knowledge, incubators for community building, and steer foundational research, addressing research gaps or inspiring futuristic research into open problems in the field [3]. Such material is often the starting point for researchers to formulate new research problems or to revisit existing ones, as it is often the case for many PhD and MSc theses [4]. To extend current research and to formulate new directions, researchers commonly use highly cited scientific articles or look at industrial problems and experiences [5]. Papers reporting on foundational theories and fundamental research often hold material for empirical investigations, evaluation and/or reflection, attracting interest in adoption [6].

In addition, conferences offer a common platform to bring together interested peers to discuss current research, facilitate networking/connections and accelerate the incubation of new research and communities. Moreover, some international grants facilitate international exchange of researchers paving the way for global visibility and impact. Additionally, collaboration also extended toward authored and edited books, which can be used to teach modules within a curriculum in academia or researchers can use them to understand relevant concepts. Several researchers with different skills set can work together to develop simulators, that are versatile and can be used to study a concept or a technique across various fields, before implementing it in a real environment [7]. Ideas validated through simulations can be put in to practice by incorporating them in software systems that support applications and their deployment in practical settings or production infrastructures.

2   Key Strategic Elements for Advancing New Computing Areas

We advocate a holistic, pragmatic research strategy that promotes impactful research and community building in new and emerging areas. It would be of interest to researchers in academic institutions, business and public sectors. The strategy, illustrated in Fig. 1, comprises of nine key elements, which are discussed in conceptually in this section and illustrated them with practical realisation examples from our cloud computing research in next section.

2.1   Identification of Potential Research Area

The first step is to identify one or more promising new areas for research that the researcher or the research group would like to pursue. Sense the potential of a domain either organically through informal discussions and brainstorms or more methodologically. Methodologically, researchers may, for example, find a potential research domain by reviewing technology trends discussed in formal and informal research forums and those outlined by market-research firms such as Gartner (for example, annual Gartner Hype Cycle for Emerging Technologies) and professional societies such as IEEE Computer Society, and visionary scientific publications in broad domains of interest, national scientific strategies, and perspectives on future research directions. Popular promising new research directions can be considered as a base for community formation. Collaboration with industry practitioners would also help in knowing problems areas that requires further research. Good tutorial articles and industrial experience reports would help get the basic knowledge

Fig. 1 Nine key strategic elements for advancing research in new computing areas

about the topic. Collective intelligence and vision are the keys for incubating research streams and building research communities that address timely or futuristic problems.

2.2   *Systematic Reviews with Research Plan*

Next, it is essential to assess current state of development and potential research problems and challenges in the chosen area. In new/emerging computing areas, systematic reviews help identify the state-of-the-art and knowledge gaps, develop taxonomies, create roadmap and identify future directions. This helps learning about seminal work, starting new research or exploring "blue skies" research. Several established scientific journals value and publish such reviews and feature surveys and/or dedicated special sections. Systematic reviews and assessment play a significant role in accelerating impact, formulating new problems, steering research and acting as a benchmark for comparison. Such publications may sometimes have a detrimental role in steering the research into the wrong direction, in the absence of a responsible peer review system and expert input for scrutinizing the compiled material. The use of Systematic Literature Review (SLR) guidelines [8] helps in ensuring comprehensive coverage and limiting bias in selecting material.

2.2.1 Research Plan

Having identified a research area or a topic to pursue, the next crucial and significant activity is to create a research plan and a roadmap. It should include specific areas to be investigated, in the near-term and long-term, timeline, resource requirements and feasibility studies, potential constraints and limitations and anticipated outcomes. Researchers pursue their research work on the chosen area under the guidance of one or more senior researchers and a team leader, closely adhering to the timeline. The research leader takes responsibility to oversee, guide and monitor research progress and research outcomes, which would also include dissemination of research findings to a wider community through publications, seminars, and presentations, and demonstration of application potential of research work and relevance of research. He/she also looks for funding opportunities, formulate specific research proposals and apply for research grants.

2.3 Develop a Simulator

In new/emerging computing areas, researchers are often constrained by the readiness of the technology and availability of required infrastructure to conduct research studies, explore strength and weaknesses, and demonstrate feasibility. In many instances, getting actual physical infrastructure may not be viable due to cost and time constraints and also may not provide all the flexibility that a research study requires. Instead, a simulator is a satisfactory viable option. It can also play a vital role in supporting incubation and growth of research community and to test the proposed methods using lightweight and low-cost environments. Testing new techniques in a real environment is challenging and also costly [14] as one needs invest a lot procure required hardware resources (especially for large-scale experiments) and develop software systems and applications. Researchers use modelling and simulation approach in demonstrating the feasibility of their ideas and carry out experiments to validate their ideas in a controlled environment using simulation tools. Real-world problems can be efficiently tested through simulators as they provide user-friendly environment for exploration and what-if analysis. If off-the-shelf/existing simulator is unable to meet requirements of simulating elements of new computing paradigms, it is advisable to develop a suitable simulator along with graphical user interfaces. A simulator would be immensely helpful to researchers in formulating problems and studying different theoretical models in simulated setups, driving further research and building communities among the respective domain.

2.4 Software Systems

Having evaluated their research, for example, policies/approaches for resource management and application scheduling, through simulation, it is valuable to demonstrate their practical use in real world. This can be achieved by creating appropriate software platforms that would enable potential users in development and testing of real-world applications. These software platforms provide APIs/interfaces for rapid creation of applications and their deployment on a real computing infrastructure. They also support APIs that researchers can use to implement their new resource management and application scheduling polices and evaluate them on real computing systems for real-world applications from domains such as life sciences, health care, and finance.

2.5 Publish Edited Books

As a new research area emerges, several researchers around the world investigate different aspects of it, address challenges associated with that field and publish their findings typically as research papers in conferences or journals. That information, however, remains scattered. To get a quick overview about the emerging area, there is a need for a comprehensive information resource that presents most of the key research work and advances in an integrated manner in a single volume. As no individual researcher will have expertise on all aspects of the emerging field (during its initial days/years), the best option is to edit a new book that brings together contributions from several researchers in the form of individual chapters on different aspects, which are loosely connected. Such edited books serve as initial reference material for researchers, particularly for PhD students and for exploring future directions. Further, edited books will be helpful for academic institutes for introducing relevant modules within their curriculum in degree courses. These books also have been shown to drive interdisciplinary research, by providing case studies, standards and regulations for the respective domains. Edited books also help to bring together researchers in a particular area and create a community that helps in forming collaboration and charting further work. We recommend that senior researchers or the team leader edit a comprehensive book covering many of the related aspects of the research area with contributions from several researchers.

2.6 Organize Conferences and Build a Community

Scientific conferences are very important for dissemination of scientific ideas and act as seeds for high-impact research and building communities. Several studies have shown that physical closeness drives advancements in science and technology and foster research. For example, research on a Paris campus building project [17] showed what occurred when researchers were randomly reassigned to new offices. Researchers began new field-wide partnerships and published groundbreaking articles in high-profile magazines, using a broader selection of keywords relative to prior publications by either partner. Workshops are very common in the research community for qualitative research work embedded within conferences, which provide a platform to learn new techniques, tools and get a chance to participate in brainstorming sessions while solving problems in a group of like-minded people. They also serve as venue for presenting work-in-progress and offer an opportunity for seeking guidance/feedback from research leaders of the area. Further, they can enable industrial and academic collaborations, which can be a foundation for future applied research grants.

Organizations such as IEEE Computer Society and ACM (Association for Computing Machinery) support creation of special interest groups or technical communities that bring together all interested parties to promote new and emerging computing paradigms through establishment of discussion forums, conferences, newsletters, testbeds, guidelines for educational programs, best practices and standards.

2.7 Establish Academic and Industry Collaborations

Academic collaborations drive interdisciplinary research. Additionally, researchers can collaborate with internationally leading researchers especially those who created vision for the field and authored highly cited papers to improve scope and visibility of their research, and to seek opinion and suggestions.

Businesses rely on university researchers for ideas for product developments in new/emerging areas and faculties gain reputation from expanded external research support and collaboration. As much as industry needs new ideas to excel and thrive, scholars require financial and in-kind support from industry to carry out research and maintain professional productivity. These industry collaborations are also becoming mandatory with most of the governmental funding; for example, for Australian Research Council and European Commission research grants research project consortiums are expected to constitute both academic institutions and small and medium-sized enterprises (SMEs). Such collaborations are also needed for facilitating applied research and promoting SMEs and economic growth. Furthermore, industry participation increases the adoptability of the emerging technologies, thus bringing much wider audience/communities onboard.

So, new research teams should try to establish academic and industry collaboration in the chosen area and harness the potential of collaboration.

2.8 Write Text Books

When the field achieves a reasonable maturity, it is timely and critical to develop authored books that present all foundational concepts, technologies, and applications in a consistent and integrated manner. Textbooks provide a good introductory summary or a starting point to a researcher interested to pursue further research. Moreover, they may also provide a consolidated information on previous research about a particular topic as well historical context. Textbooks introduce the new research domains as part of mainstream curriculums thus driving interest in next generation educators and researchers.

2.9 Develop and Offer Educational Programs

It is important to disseminate advances made in a new research and emerging technological developments broadly at Masters and Undergraduate degree programs. This can be achieved by introducing a new subject in existing programs or starting entirely a new program. These programs are also useful to connect someone with the source of information in terms of professional support. For example, a workshop on computational study can provide a chemist an effective platform to learn basic concepts of computational chemistry. Online and offline education programs or workshops can be offered to students and practitioners.

In addition to these strategic elements, researchers need to regularly disseminate their research outcomes broadly using different channels such as trade magazines [13] and social media. By making outcomes of their research work easily accessible to their peers and the broader academic and business communities, they will be able to substantially enhance impact of their work.

3 Adoption of the Strategy in Our Cloud Computing Research

During 2005–2008, Grid computing community begun to influence industrial practices towards creation and delivery of computing services as utilities to support enterprise applications. Companies such as Amazon started to offer rentable computing services via its EC2 (Elastic Compute Cloud) initiative. We (Buyya and team) created a SOA (service-oriented architecture)-based container environment that enables the creation of application platforms (such as Aneka) supporting multiple programming models and deployment of their applications on market-oriented cloud computing environments. We established ourselves as a CLOUDS Lab and proposed a reference architecture for market-oriented cloud computing and created software technologies such as CloudSim and Aneka. Around that time other researchers also started sharing their vision for the field.

In this section, we primarily illustrate effectiveness of the recommended research strategy and guidelines which we adopted in our cloud computing research which made significant impact and globally well recognized.

1. *Initial research:* We, like a few other researchers, drew motivation and inspiration to work on cloud computing from the early seminal publications, our article, "Cloud computing and emerging IT platforms: Vision, hype, and reality for delivering computing as the 5th utility," [11] and "A view of cloud computing" [10] from Berkley researchers. These works inspired many further work and emergence of several commercial offerings in cloud computing area. This is evident from more than 10,000 citations received for these and associated family of papers. Thus, this initial research has contributed in building huge communities around cloud computing and relevant research challenges.

2. *Systematic reviews and taxonomies:* Since the emergence of cloud computing field, many key issues such as energy efficiency were investigated and reviewed along with discussion on taxonomies and future directions [18]. With a decade of progress in the field, cloud computing achieved enormous success in industry and business application and opened up new challenges and research directions. In this context, "A manifesto for future generation cloud computing" [12] has also been prepared, by experts from different subfields of cloud computing, which is driving further the community building in the domain, attracting wide interest from young researchers.

3. *Simulations:* We (Buyya and team) have developed a simulator, called CloudSim, for modelling and simulation of cloud computing environments. It helps researchers in evaluation of their new resource management approaches, algorithms, and policies and application scheduling with specific focus on various performance parameters such as security, time, cost, and energy [16]. This simulator also has shown to bring in much wider audience to the cloud computing domain, as jumping into the domain with these simulators is relatively easy as illustrated by its use in over 5000 research papers published by researchers worldwide.

4. *Software systems:* Researchers are interested to move their work "bench to market" – to transition their work in to a product or a real-world application. Prominent software systems within the cloud computing domain such as Aneka, OpenStack, and Hadoop have driven the research in the respective domains significantly and helped in bringing people from other communities such as data analytics, distributed computing and scientific computing, to the cloud domain. In Cloud computing domain, new resource management and application scheduling algorithms/policies we originally created and evaluated using CloudSim [19]

are demonstrated/implemented for practical deployment by plugging them to real software systems such as Aneka and OpenStack [20].

5. *Edited books:* The prominent researchers within the domain of cloud computing are editing books time to time, which can help researchers to generally understand the concepts. Edited books such as "Cloud Computing: Principles and Paradigms" published in the early days of the field helped researchers to understand the basic concepts and initial research, and are being used as reference material in several courses and curriculums. Later with further advances in the field, books such as "Encyclopedia of Cloud Computing [15]" complemented it.

6. *Conferences and Community:* In its early days several new conferences dedicated to Cloud computing such as IEEE/ACM UCC, CCGrid, IEEE Cloud and ACM SoCC were established. IEEE also established community forums such as the IEEE Technical Committee on Cloud Computing. These provided opportunity to academics, researchers, practitioners to discuss ongoing research and helped new researchers to discuss their ideas with the invited speakers and co-participants to find a chance to collaborate with them.

7. *Academic and Industrial Collaborations:* Educational institutions are collaborating and submitting collaborative research grant proposals both nationally and globally. For instance, European Union has funded a number of collaborative research projects in the cloud computing domain during the past decade [9]. In addition to facilitating research collaboration (both academic and industry), these projects help participating students to visit and work with other research groups which enables them to discuss and improve their work. Moreover, the SMEs and startups resulting from these projects have been the early adapters of cloud computing technology and applications, and drove local economies and Cloud adaption policies at local governments. We collaborated with companies such as CA and Samsung and developed a new framework for ranking of Cloud services, which the Cloud Service Measurement Index Consortium (CSMIC) adopted it.

8. *Text books*: Like few others, we wrote a text book "Mastering Cloud Computing", which introduces foundations, technologies, programming examples, and applications, in a much more unified and consistent manner for broader audience including. It is adopted as a text for Under Graduate (UG) and Post Graduate (PG) courses in several universities worldwide.

9. *Educational programs*: Several educational programs and online courses are offered to deliver the required cloud computing knowledge to the researchers. Various renowned universities are working together to run these education programs to teach basic and advanced and emerging trends. In the University of Melbourne, a dedicated Masters' level program in Distributed Computing was established which now educates close to 500 students each year.

All these demonstrates how the recommended strategic elements have collectively driven our cloud computing research journey from infancy to a well-established one that made tremendous impact in academic and business world.

4 Summary and Conclusions

Drawing on our successful experience, we shared a holistic strategy for advancing research and its impact in new and emerging computing paradigms. We have discussed the role of supporting infrastructure that we developed and used – simulators and software systems, and the role of various types of publications including systematic reviews, taxonomies, research articles and books in supporting community building and accelerating the incubation of research. It is critical to establish community forums and develop educational programs. We illustrated application of our strategy to Cloud computing field from its emerging days (in 2008) to till date. We believe the proposed strategy would serve as a catalyst for new research initiatives to accelerate their research and its impact with confidence.

References

1. Emma, T., Smallman, M., Lock, S., Johnson, C., Austwick, M.: Beyond academia–interrogating research impact in the research excellence framework. PLoS One. **11**(12) (2016)
2. Penfield, T., Baker, M., Scoble, R., Wykes, M.: Assessment, evaluations, and definitions of research impact: a review. Res. Evaluat. **23**(1), 21–32 (2014)
3. Cargill, M., O'Connor, P.: Writing Scientific Research Articles: Strategy and Steps. Wiley (2021)
4. Nayak, M., Narayan, K.: Strengths and weaknesses of online surveys. IOSR J. Human Soc. Sci. **24**(5), 31–38 (2019)
5. Jiao, F., Fang, J., Ci, Y., Tu, W.: Bibliometric analysis based on highly cited papers in computer science. J. Phys. Conf. Ser. **1883**(1), 012053 (2021) IOP Publishing
6. Parker, M., Kingori, P.: Good and bad research collaborations: researchers' views on science and ethics in global health research. PLoS One. **11**(10), e0163579 (2016)
7. Mefteh, W.: Simulation-based design: overview about related works. Math. Comput. Simul. **152**, 81–97 (2018)
8. Torraco, R.J.: Writing integrative reviews of the literature: methods and purposes. Int. J. Adult Vocat. Educ. Technol. (IJAVET). **7**(3), 62–70 (2016)
9. European Commission. EU-funded projects on Software and Cloud Computing. https://ec.europa.eu/digital-single-market/en/programme-and-projects/eu-funded-projects-software-services-cloud-computing
10. Armbrust, M., Fox, A., Griffith, R., Joseph, A.D., Katz, R., Konwinski, A., Lee, G., Patterson, D., Rabkin, A., Stoica, I., Zaharia, M.: A view of cloud computing. Commun. ACM. **53**(4), 50–58 (2010)
11. Buyya, R., Yeo, C.S., Venugopal, S., Broberg, J., Brandic, I.: Cloud computing and emerging IT platforms: vision, hype, and reality for delivering computing as the 5th utility. Futur. Gener. Comput. Syst. **25**(6), 599–616 (2009)
12. Buyya, R., Srirama, S., et al.: A manifesto for future generation cloud computing: research directions for the next decade. ACM Comput. Surv. **51**(5), 1–38 (2018)
13. Buyya, R.:. Seven tips for enhancing your research visibility and impact, technical report, GRIDS-TR-2007-3, CLOUDS Laboratory. The University of Melbourne, Australia, Feb. 8, 2007
14. Brady, C., Orton, K., Weintrop, D., Anton, G., Rodriguez, S., Wilensky, U.: All roads lead to computing: making, participatory simulations, and social computing as pathways to computer science. IEEE Trans. Educ. **60**(1), 59–66 (2016)

15. Murugesan, S., Bojanova, I. (eds.): Encyclopedia of Cloud Computing. Wiley, Hoboken (2016)
16. Calheiros, R.N., Ranjan, R., Beloglazov, A., De Rose, C.A., Buyya, R.: CloudSim: a toolkit for modeling and simulation of cloud computing environments and evaluation of resource provisioning algorithms. Softw Pract Exper. **41**(1), 23–50 (2011)
17. Sohn, E.: The future of the scientific conference. Nature. **64**, S80–S82 (2018)
18. Beloglazov, A., Buyya, R., Lee, Y., Zomaya, Y.: A taxonomy and survey of energy-efficient data centers and cloud computing systems. Adv. Comput. **82**, 47–111 (2011)
19. Beloglazov, A., Buyya, R.: Managing overloaded hosts for dynamic consolidation of virtual machines in cloud data centers under quality of service constraints. IEEE Trans. Parallel Distr. Syst. (TPDS). **24**(7), 1366–1379 (2013)
20. Beloglazov, A., Buyya, R.: OpenStack neat: a framework for dynamic and energy-efficient consolidation of virtual machines in OpenStack clouds. Concurrency Comput. Pract. Exper. **27**(5), 1310–1333 (2015)

New Research Directions for Green Mobile Cloud Computing

Anwesha Mukherjee, Debashis De ⓘ, and Rajkumar Buyya

1 Introduction

Whenever, we integrate more than one technological paradigms, then several issues appear. In mobile cloud computing (MCC), we have discussed issues such as mobility, reliability, security, and network connectivity. As we are focusing green mobile cloud computing (GMCC), meeting the criteria of energy-efficiency is a mandate in this case. This chapter discusses the following topics as future research areas in GMCC:

- Energy harvesting in MCC
- Entropy-based GMCC
- Green Vehicular MCC
- Green Mobile Crowd Sensing
- Green Edge and Fog Computing
- GMCC-based Smart applications
- Geographical Location Aware Mobile Recommender System
- Nature Inspired Optimization Algorithms for GMCC

A. Mukherjee (✉)
Department of Computer Science, Mahishadal Raj College, Mahishadal, Purba Medinipur, West Bengal, India
e-mail: anweshamukherjee@ieee.org

D. De
Department of Computer Science and Engineering, Centre of Mobile Cloud Computing, Maulana Abul Kalam Azad University of Technology, West Bengal, Nadia, India
e-mail: debashis.de@makautwb.ac.in

R. Buyya
Cloud Computing and Distributed Systems (CLOUDS) Laboratory, School of Computing and Information Systems, The University of Melbourne, Parkville, VIC, Australia
e-mail: rbuyya@unimelb.edu.au

© The Author(s), under exclusive license to Springer Nature Switzerland AG 2022
D. De et al. (eds.), *Green Mobile Cloud Computing*,
https://doi.org/10.1007/978-3-031-08038-8_16

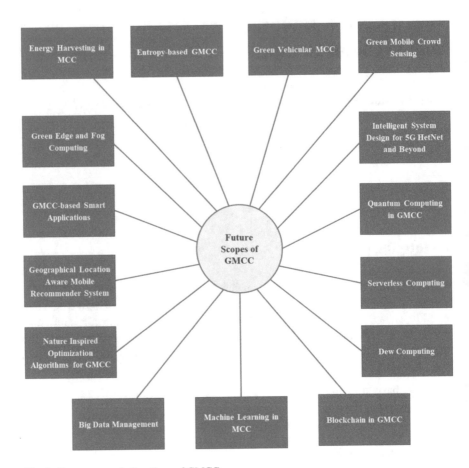

Fig. 1 Future research directions of GMCC

- Big Data Management
- Machine Learning in MCC
- Blockchain in GMCC
- Dew Computing
- Serverless Computing
- Quantum Computing in GMCC
- Intelligent System Design for 5G HetNet and Beyond

A pictorial view of these research directions in GMCC is shown in Fig. 1. We will discuss them in the rest of the chapter.

2   Energy Harvesting in MCC

In energy harvesting, the renewable energy sources such as solar and wind are used as the source of power supply. The work in [1] discussed on the use of solar photovoltaic and biomass resource-based hybrid power supply for the base stations in a cellular network. The renewable sources were used to charge the cloud-enabled small cell base stations in [2]. In [3], its authors integrated MCC with microwave power transfer for computation inside the passive low-complexity devices like sensors, wearable devices etc. In a single-user system, a base station either transfers power or offloads computation from a mobile device to the cloud [3]. The mobile device uses harvested energy for computing given data either locally or by offloading [3]. In [4], its authors considered simultaneous wireless information and power transfer technique to multi-user computation offloading problem in mobile-edge-cloud computing paradigm. Here, energy-limited mobile devices harvest energy from ambient radio-frequency signal [4]. In MCC, the renewable energy sources can be used as a source of power supply to the cloud servers. For the energy-limited mobile devices also energy harvesting can be used [4].

3   Entropy-Based GMCC

The cloud service providers offer three types of services: Software as a Service (SaaS), Platform as a Service (PaaS) and Infrastructure as a Service (IaaS). In a multi-agent network, multiple agents are present within a location. Now a situation may arise when a single agent is unable to solve all the problems. In such situations, intelligent cloud entropy management is required, which is composed of functions, algorithms and methods. Here, fractional entropy and Tsallis entropy can be used [5]. On the other hand, the developers can consider functional and non-functional aspects of quality of service (QoS) while looking for the services fulfilling the requirements like reliability, security, delay, throughput etc. For weightening each aspect entropy was used [6]. Now different users have different requirements, for example, some users require game offloading, some users require web service. As the users' choices vary, the offered services also differ. In most of the situations, users' choices are unpredictable. When huge number of requests of same priority arrive at the same time and they require same resource, then how these all requests will be fulfilled is a challenging research area. Users have to state the level of their QoS requirement and they also consider how much they pay. Now the capacity of the system of the services is required to determine. For this purpose Tsallis entropy can be used [7]. For the user it is tough to decide the QoS requirement level for the requested cloud service. In such a case, fractional entropy based boundary value problem can be used for the multi-agent system [8].

4 Green Vehicular-MCC

While people travel sometimes the vehicles get stuck into the traffic. Accessing Internet service at this time is a popular option for entertainment. In this case, vehicular adhoc network [9, 10], mobile network and cloud computing are integrated to introduce vehicular-MCC. The location of the vehicles are required to update to the cloud for tracking a vehicle when required. This feature can greatly contribute towards efficient rescue operations after any type of accidents or natural disasters. Nowadays most of the users have smart phones which offers a rich sensing platform. The sensing platform contains built-in sensors which detect light, temperature, accelerometers, Global Positioning System (GPS), etc. The vehicular users can monitor the surrounding circumstances, collect information and share it on social networking sites, for example, if an accident has occurred, the vehicular user can inform about it on social network. The other persons then may avoid this route if they are in hurry to reach their destinations.

5 Green Mobile Crowd Sensing

In mobile crowd sensing, a user observes his or her surroundings and collect information, which he or she shares on social domain or with the service providers by using mobile device [11]. Here, a sensing platform is provided with the mobile device to collect data from the surroundings. In mobile crowd sensing, various types, of data are gathered such location information, traffic condition, noise level, etc. The users share these data with others. These data are aggregated inside the cloud and processed for further knowledge extraction and then delivered. Route planning is a popular example of mobile crowd sensing, where based on the GPS information of the mobile device, an optimal route to the destination is determined. Urban sensing [12], participatory sensing [13], corresponding big data management [14], energy-aware crowd sensing [15], use of blockchain in crowd sensing [16], are significant research directions of GMCC.

6 Green Edge and Fog Computing

In mobile edge computing, either the edge server or cloudlets are used to bring resources at the network edge to provide faster service provisioning to the users [17]. Fog computing refers to a distributed computing model that offers a virtualized environment providing computation, storage, and network services between data centers and end devices [18–20]. In fog computing, the intermediate devices between the end node and cloud servers participate in data processing [21]. Fog devices can be used for computation offloading also [22]. Fog computing supports computational resources, protocols for communication, integration with cloud, interface heterogeneity and distributed data analytics to fulfill the necessity of the applications requiring low latency. Power efficiency, security, reliability and resource management are promising research directions of edge and fog computing.

7 GMCC-Based Smart Applications

Smart and low power system design is another promising research direction of MCC. In retail, health care, home monitoring, agriculture, MCC can play an important role. The sensor nodes will be used to collect the object status, and the collected data will be stored and processed inside the cloud. The intended user can access the information using his/her mobile device. The work in [23] proposed a smart retailing system using fog-cloud paradigm. In [24], the fog-cloud paradigm was used for storing and analyzing health data. In [25], edge-fog-cloud paradigm was used in healthcare. In [26], the mobility information of the users was stored and analyzed inside the cloud to guide him/her regarding the nearby the health center or the optimum route to reach the nearby health center when the user is inside a vehicle. The design of MCC-based energy-efficient smart applications is another future research direction of GMCC.

8 Geographical Location Aware Mobile Recommender System

Mobile recommender system refers to the software tools and methods which offer suggestions to the mobile users [27, 28]. Recommender system is one type of information retrieval system that offers recommendations in terms of personalized information. For the non-experienced mobile users, this recommender system helps a lot when a decision has to be taken by the user, for example, appearance of e-commerce websites during the Internet access. The mobile users can access the recommender system anytime anywhere as a mobile application. The georecommendation system can suggest the mobile user regarding various places to visit based on the present geographical location of the user, for example, to suggest the nearby shopping mall, food court, cinema hall, etc. based on the present geographical location of the user.

9   Nature Inspired Algorithms for GMCC

In future generation mobile network, nature inspired algorithms [29] can be used for optimizing energy, throughput, latency, etc. For optimized resource allocation, nature inspired algorithms can be used. In offloading, to select the optimal path towards the device that will execute the application, the nature inspired algorithms can be used. The work in [30] proposed a handoff management strategy based on the bird flocking. In [31] based on the feeding nature of octopus, power-efficient cellular network designing was proposed. The work in [32] proposed an intelligent offloading strategy based on ant colony optimization. The work in [33] used a metaheuristic artificial bee colony optimization method to deal with the workload of the edge server under the limitations of low latency and fast response time. In MCC environment, nature inspired algorithms can also play a significant role for optimizing the energy consumption.

10   Big Data Management

With the explosive increase in the number of mobile subscribers and growing use of the Internet access has resulted in huge volume of data generation. The big data analytics and management [34, 35] is a major research direction of MCC. Integration of Internet of Things (IoT) [36, 37] and MCC has directed towards various research scopes such as energy-efficiency, security, etc. in big data management. Nowadays, the use of blockchain has gained popularity in data analytics and management [38].

11   Machine Learning in MCC

Machine learning has opened a new way to find solutions regarding various problems, such as, scheduling, computation offloading, spammer identification, etc. The work in [39] proposed a distributed computation offloading method using machine learning. The work in [40] proposed a context-sensitive offloading system to get the benefit of machine learning reasoning schemes and robust profiling system for taking offloading decisions with better accuracy. The work in [41] proposed a framework that provides an online training method for the machine learning-based runtime scheduler for dynamically adapting scheduling decisions by observing the previous offloading decisions along with their correctness. The work in [42] considered the execution of machine learning applications to the cloud for improving the energy-efficiency of mobile device and improving the performance by reducing execution time. The work in [43] used a machine learning algorithm to identify spammer in industrial MCC. For cyberattack detection in mobile cloud environment, a deep learning-based framework was proposed in [44]. The use of machine learning for attaining energy-efficiency in MCC is another future research direction.

12   Blockchain in GMCC

For dealing with information security in mobile cloud infrastructure a building information modelling (BIM) system was proposed in [45]. This model facilitates BIM data audit for historical modifications by blockchain in mobile cloud with sharing of big data. The work in [46] proposed a privacy preserving user authentication protocol using blockchain for distributed mobile cloud environment. The work in [47] proposed a cloudlet management scheme using blockchain for multimedia workflow. For blockchain-based authentication of mobile devices a secure authentication management human-centric scheme was proposed in [48]. The work in [49] proposed an electronic health records sharing framework integrating blockchain and decentralized interplanetary file system on a mobile cloud platform. The use of blockchain in GMCC is another future research direction.

13   Dew Computing

Dew computing has opened a new window towards centralized-virtualization-free computation, that allows to scatter multi-typical data into the low-end devices [50]. Dew computing relies on micro-services in vertical, heterogeneous, and distributed way [50]. Dew computing allows data accessibility even when continuous Internet connectivity is unavailable [50]. There are several advantages of dew computing, such as, self-augmentation, self-healing, transparent, self-adaptive, scalability, user-programmability, etc. [50]. Dew computing can perform complex tasks in its vicinity [50]. However, to attain this feature, dew computing requires an advanced modular architecture that can adapt the related features of dew computing-ecosystem [50]. The use of dew computing in IoT was explored in [51–53]. Energy-efficient dew computing is another future research direction of GMCC.

14   Serverless Computing

The term 'serverless computing' has been invented by the industry to refer a programming model and architecture executing small code snippets inside the cloud without control over the resources on which the code is executed [54]. Various cloud service providers, such as, Microsoft, Google, IBM, Amazon, etc. have released serverless computing abilities [54]. In serverless computing the servers are required, however, the developers do not concern regarding the server management [54]. The serverless platform handles the decisions like the number and capacity of servers, and the server capacity is provisioned according to the workload-based requirement [54]. The work in [55] designed a serverless computing platform. It was implemented in .NET deployed in Microsoft Azure, and utilized Windows containers as function execution environments. The design of serverless computing platform for energy-aware MCC is another future research direction.

15 Quantum Computing for GMCC

The integration of quantum computing with cloud is another emerging research direction. The use of quantum computing can provide solutions towards various issues of cloud, such as, security, backup, processing, and vicinity [56]. However, the integration of these two systems is not an easy task [56]. The work in [56] used quantum cryptography and quantum computing to improve the security in cloud computing. The work in [57] discussed on cloud quantum computing. The work in [58] proposed an approach named QuCloud to map quantum programs in cloud environment. The integration of quantum computing with GMCC is another future research direction.

16 Intelligent System Design for 5G HetNet and Beyond

Next generation mobile network will comprise of different categories of base stations like macrocell, microcell, picocell, femtocell, cloud-enabled small cells, Wi-Fi access point, etc. Such a heterogeneous network requires proper deployment strategies in order to achieve energy-efficiency, high data rate, low latency, etc. [59, 60]. Efficient and intelligent resource allocation methods are also required for this heterogeneous mobile network. In next generation mobile network, most of the application processing and data storage will occur inside the cloud. Hence, intelligent big data management and analysis inside the cloud for such heterogeneous networks is a crucial research area. On the other hand, the edge-fog-cloud paradigm is one of the key element of future generation mobile network. Resource allocation, energy-efficiency, security, reliability, etc. are various domains in MCC, which seek significant research contributions.

17 Summary

In this chapter we have highlighted the future research directions of green mobile cloud computing. Energy-efficiency is one of the signficant challenge of MCC to provide an eco-friendly system. Hence, we have considered the energy-efficiency as one of the core aspects in research directions along with mobile crowd sensing, vehicular MCC, edge and fog computing, smart applications, etc. We also covered other research directions of MCC such as mobile recommender system, intelligent system design, use of nature inspired algorithms, big data management, and energy harvesting.

References

1. Hossain, M.S., Jahid, A., Ziaul Islam, K., Rahman, M.F.: Solar PV and biomass resources-based sustainable energy supply for off-grid cellular base stations. IEEE Access. **8**, 53817–53840 (2020)
2. Mukherjee, A., Debashis, D., Ghosh, S.K.: Power-efficient and latency-aware offloading in energy-harvested cloud-enabled small cell network. In: 2020 XXXIIIrd General Assembly and Scientific Symposium of the International Union of Radio Science, pp. 1–4. IEEE, Piscataway, NJ
3. You, C., Huang, K., Chae, H.: Energy efficient mobile cloud computing powered by wireless energy transfer. IEEE J. Sel. Areas Commun. **34**(5), 1757–1771 (2016)
4. Zhang, Y., He, J., Guo, S.: Energy-efficient dynamic task offloading for energy harvesting mobile cloud computing. In: 2018 IEEE International Conference on Networking, Architecture and Storage (NAS), pp. 1–4. IEEE, Piscataway, NJ (2018)
5. Ibrahim, R.W., Jalab, H.A., Gani, A.: Cloud entropy management system involving a fractional power. Entropy. **18**(1), 14 (2016)
6. Wang, Y., Zheng, Z., Lyu, M.R.: Entropy-based service selection with uncertain QoS for mobile cloud computing. In: 2015 IEEE Conference on Collaboration and Internet Computing (CIC), pp. 252–259. IEEE (2015)
7. Ibrahim, R.W., Jalab, H.A., Gani, A.: Entropy solution of fractional dynamic cloud computing system associated with finite boundary condition. Bound. Value Probl. **2016**(1), 1–12 (2016)
8. Ibrahim, R.W., Jalab, H.A., Gani, A.: Perturbation of fractional multi-agent systems in cloud entropy computing. Entropy. **18**(1), 31 (2016)
9. Al-Sultan, S., Al-Doori, M.M., Al-Bayatti, A.H., Zedan, H.: A comprehensive survey on vehicular ad hoc network. J. Netw. Comput. Appl. **37**, 380–392 (2014)
10. Günay, F.B., Öztürk, E., Çavdar, T., Sinan Hanay, Y.: Vehicular ad hoc network (VANET) localization techniques: a survey. Arch. Computat. Meth. Eng. **28**(4), 3001–3033 (2021)
11. Ma, H., Zhao, D., Yuan, P.: Opportunities in mobile crowd sensing. IEEE Commun. Mag. **52**(8), 29–35 (2014)
12. Ghahramani, M., Zhou, M.C., Wang, G.: Urban sensing based on mobile phone data: approaches, applications, and challenges. IEEE/CAA J. Automat. Sin. **7**(3), 627–637 (2020)
13. Xu, Z., Zhang, H., Sugumaran, V., Raymond Choo, K.-K., Mei, L., Zhu, Y.: Participatory sensing-based semantic and spatial analysis of urban emergency events using mobile social media. EURASIP J. Wirel. Commun. Netw. **2016**(1), 1–9 (2016)
14. Karim, A., Siddiqa, A., Safdar, Z., Razzaq, M., Gillani, S.A., Tahir, H., Kiran, S., Ahmed, E., Imran, M.: Big data management in participatory sensing: issues, trends and future directions. Futur. Gener. Comput. Syst. **107**, 942–955 (2020)
15. Sisi, Z., Souri, A.: Blockchain technology for energy-aware mobile crowd sensing approaches in internet of things. Trans. Emerg. Telecommun. Technol., e4217 (2021), published online. https://doi.org/10.1002/ett.4217
16. Huang, J., Kong, L., Dai, H.-N., Ding, W., Cheng, L., Chen, G., Jin, X., Zeng, P.: Blockchain-based mobile crowd sensing in industrial systems. IEEE Trans. Ind. Inf. **16**(10), 6553–6563 (2020)

17. Peng, K., Leung, V., Xu, X., Zheng, L., Wang, J., Huang, Q. A survey on mobile edge computing: focusing on service adoption and provision. Wirel. Commun. Mob. Comput. **2018**, 1–17 (2018)
18. Mahmud, R., Kotagiri, R., Buyya, R.: Fog computing: a taxonomy, survey and future directions. In: Internet of Everything, pp. 103–130. Springer, Singapore (2018)
19. Mukherjee, M., Shu, L., Wang, D.: Survey of fog computing: fundamental, network applications, and research challenges. IEEE Commun. Surv. Tutorials. **20**(3), 1826–1857 (2018)
20. Jalali, F., Hinton, K., Ayre, R., Alpcan, T., Tucker, R.S.: Fog computing may help to save energy in cloud computing. IEEE J. Sel. Areas Commun. **34**(5), 1728–1739 (2016)
21. Mukherjee, A., Deb, P., De, D., Buyya, R.: IoT-F2N: an energy-efficient architectural model for IoT using Femtolet-based fog network. J. Supercomput. **75**(11), 7125–7146 (2019)
22. Mukherjee, A., Deb, P., De, D., Buyya, R.: C2OF2N: a low power cooperative code offloading method for femtolet-based fog network. J. Supercomput. **74**(6), 2412–2448 (2018)
23. Mukherjee, A., De, D., Buyya, R.: E2R-F2N: energy-efficient retailing using a femtolet-based fog network. Softw. Pract. Exp. **49**(3), 498–523 (2019)
24. Mukherjee, A., De, D., Ghosh, S.K.: FogIoHT: a weighted majority game theory based energy-efficient delay-sensitive fog network for internet of health things. Internet Things. **11**, 100181 (2020)
25. Mukherjee, A., Ghosh, S., Behere, A., Ghosh, S.K., Buyya, R.: Internet of health things (IoHT) for personalized health care using integrated edge-fog-cloud network. J. Ambient Intell. Humaniz. Comput. **12**, 943–959 (2021)
26. Ghosh, S., Mukherjee, A., Ghosh, S.K., Buyya, R.: Mobi-iost: mobility-aware cloud-fog-edge-iot collaborative framework for time-critical applications. IEEE Trans. Netw. Sci. Eng. **7**(4), 2271–2285 (2019)
27. Colombo-Mendoza, L.O., Valencia-García, R., Rodríguez-González, A., Alor-Hernández, G., Samper-Zapater, J.J.: RecomMetz: a context-aware knowledge-based mobile recommender system for movie showtimes. Expert Syst. Appl. **42**(3), 1202–1222 (2015)
28. del Carmen Rodríguez-Hernández, M., Ilarri, S.: AI-based mobile context-aware recommender systems from an information management perspective: progress and directions. Knowl.-Based Syst. **215**, 106740 (2021)
29. Mukherjee, A., Deb, P., De, D.: Natural computing in mobile network optimization. In: Handbook of Research on Natural Computing for Optimization Problems, pp. 382–408. IGI Global, Pennsylvania, United States (2016)
30. De, D., Mukherjee, A.: Group handoff management in low power microcell-femtocell network. Digit. Commun. Netw. **3**(1), 55–65 (2017)
31. Mukherjee, A., De, D.: Octopus algorithm for wireless personal communications. Wirel. Pers. Commun. **101**(1), 531–565 (2018)
32. Guo, Y., Zhao, Z., Zhao, R., Lai, S., Dan, Z., Xia, J., Fan, L.: Intelligent offloading strategy design for relaying mobile edge computing networks. IEEE Access. **8**, 35127–35135 (2020)
33. Babar, M., Sohail Khan, M., Din, A., Ali, F., Habib, U., Sup Kwak, K.: Intelligent computation offloading for IoT applications in scalable edge computing using artificial bee colony optimization. Complexity. **2021**, 1–12 (2021)
34. Abro, A., Khuhro, S.A., Pathan, E., Koondhar, I.A., Bhutto, Z.A., Panhwar, M.A.: MCC: integration mobile cloud computing of big data for health-care analytics enhance. Psychol. Educ. J. **58**(2), 3398–3405 (2021)
35. Karimi, Y., Haghi Kashani, M., Akbari, M., Mahdipour, E.: Leveraging big data in smart cities: a systematic review. Concurrency Computat Pract Exper. **33**, e6379 (2021). https://doi.org/10.1002/cpe.6379
36. Singh, S.K., Cha, J., Kim, T.W., Park, J.H.: Machine learning based distributed big data analysis framework for next generation web in IoT. Comput. Sci. Inf. Syst. **00**, 12–12 (2021)
37. Moustafa, Nour. "A systemic IoT–fog–cloud architecture for big-data analytics and cyber security systems: a review of fog computing." In: Secure Edge Computing, pp. 41–50. CRC Press (2021). Publisher Location: Boca Raton, Florida

38. Deepa, N., Pham, Q.-V., Nguyen, D.C., Bhattacharya, S., Prabadevi, B., Gadekallu, T.R., Maddikunta, P.K.R., Fang, F., Pathirana, P.N.: A survey on blockchain for big data: approaches, opportunities, and future directions. arXiv preprint arXiv:2009.00858 (2020)
39. Cao, H., Cai, J.: Distributed multiuser computation offloading for cloudlet-based mobile cloud computing: a game-theoretic machine learning approach. IEEE Trans. Veh. Technol. 67(1), 752–764 (2017)
40. Junior, W., Oliveira, E., Santos, A., Dias, K.: A context-sensitive offloading system using machine-learning classification algorithms for mobile cloud environment. Futur. Gener. Comput. Syst. 90, 503–520 (2019)
41. Eom, H., Figueiredo, R., Cai, H., Zhang, Y., Huang, G.: Malmos: machine learning-based mobile offloading scheduler with online training. In: 2015 3rd IEEE International Conference on Mobile Cloud Computing, Services, and Engineering, pp. 51–60. IEEE, Piscataway, NJ (2015)
42. Sun, K., Chen, Z., Ren, J., Yang, S., Li, J.: M2c: energy efficient mobile cloud system for deep learning. In: 2014 IEEE Conference on Computer Communications Workshops (INFOCOM WKSHPS), pp. 167–168. IEEE, Piscataway, NJ (2014)
43. Qiu, T., Wang, H., Li, K., Ning, H., Sangaiah, A.K., Chen, B.: SIGMM: a novel machine learning algorithm for spammer identification in industrial mobile cloud computing. IEEE Trans. Ind. Inf. 15(4), 2349–2359 (2018)
44. Nguyen, K.K., Hoang, D.T., Niyato, D., Wang, P., Nguyen, D., Dutkiewicz, E.: Cyberattack detection in mobile cloud computing: a deep learning approach. In: 2018 IEEE Wireless Communications and Networking Conference (WCNC), pp. 1–6. IEEE, Piscataway, NJ (2018)
45. Zheng, R., Jiang, J., Hao, X., Ren, W., Xiong, F., Ren, Y.: bcBIM: a blockchain-based big data model for BIM modification audit and provenance in mobile cloud. Math. Probl. Eng. 2019, 1–13 (2019)
46. Vivekanandan, M., Sastry, V.N.: Blockchain based privacy preserving user authentication protocol for distributed Mobile cloud environment. Peer-to-Peer Netw. Appl. 14(3), 1572–1595 (2021)
47. Xu, X., Chen, Y., Yuan, Y., Huang, T., Zhang, X., Qi, L.: Blockchain-based cloudlet management for multimedia workflow in mobile cloud computing. Multimedia Tools and Applications. 79(15), 9819–9844 (2020)
48. Kim, H.-W., Jeong, Y.-S.: Secure authentication-management human-centric scheme for trusting personal resource information on mobile cloud computing with blockchain. HCIS. 8(1), 1–13 (2018)
49. Nguyen, D.C., Pathirana, P.N., Ding, M., Seneviratne, A.: Blockchain for secure ehrs sharing of mobile cloud based e-health systems. IEEE Access. 7(2019), 66792–66806 (2018)
50. Ray, P.P.: An introduction to dew computing: definition, concept and implications. IEEE Access. 6, 723–737 (2017)
51. Gusev, M.: A dew computing solution for IoT streaming devices. In: 2017 40th International Convention on Information and Communication Technology, Electronics and Microelectronics (MIPRO), pp. 387–392. IEEE, Piscataway, NJ (2017)
52. Gushev, M.: Dew computing architecture for cyber-physical systems and IoT. Internet Things. 11, 100186 (2020)
53. Ray, P.P., Dash, D., De, D.: Internet of things-based real-time model study on e-healthcare: device, message service and dew computing. Comput. Netw. 149, 226–239 (2019)
54. Baldini, I., Castro, P., Chang, K., Cheng, P., Fink, S., Ishakian, V., Mitchell, N., et al.: Serverless computing: current trends and open problems. In: Research Advances in Cloud Computing, pp. 1–20. Springer, Singapore (2017)
55. McGrath, G., Brenner, P.R.: Serverless computing: design, implementation, and performance. In: 37th IEEE International Conference on Distributed Computing Systems Workshops (ICDCSW), pp. 405–410. IEEE, Piscataway, NJ (2017)
56. Rahaman, M., Islam, M.M.: A review on progress and problems of quantum computing as a service (QcaaS) in the perspective of cloud computing. Global J. Comput. Sci. Technol. 15(4), 16–18 (2015)

57. Soeparno, H., Perbangsa, A.S.: Cloud quantum computing concept and development: a systematic literature review. Procedia Comput. Sci. **179**, 944–954 (2021)
58. Liu, L., Dou, X.: QuCloud: a new qubit mapping mechanism for multi-programming quantum computing in cloud environment. In: 2021 IEEE International Symposium on High-Performance Computer Architecture (HPCA), pp. 167–178. IEEE, Piscataway, NJ (2021)
59. Deb, P., Mukherjee, A., De, D.: A study of densification management using energy efficient femto-cloud based 5G mobile network. Wirel. Pers. Commun. **101**(4), 2173–2191 (2018)
60. Valenzuela-Valdés, J.F., Palomares, A., González-Macías, J.C., Valenzuela-Valdés, A., Padilla, P., Luna-Valero, F.: On the ultra-dense small cell deployment for 5G networks. In: 2018 IEEE 5G World Forum (5GWF), pp. 369–372. IEEE, Piscataway, NJ (2018)

Printed in the United States
by Baker & Taylor Publisher Services